Rural Modernity in Britain

Rural Modernity in Britain

A Critical Intervention

Edited by Kristin Bluemel and Michael McCluskey

EDINBURGH
University Press

Edinburgh University Press is one of the leading university presses in the UK. We publish academic books and journals in our selected subject areas across the humanities and social sciences, combining cutting-edge scholarship with high editorial and production values to produce academic works of lasting importance. For more information visit our website: edinburghuniversitypress.com

First published in hardback by Edinburgh University Press 2018

Edinburgh University Press Ltd
The Tun – Holyrood Road
12(2f) Jackson's Entry
Edinburgh EH8 8PJ

Typeset in 10.5/13 Adobe Sabon by
Servis Filmsetting Ltd, Stockport, Cheshire

A CIP record for this book is available from the British Library

ISBN 978 1 4744 2095 2 (hardback)
ISBN 978 1 4744 7318 7 (paperback)
ISBN 978 1 4744 2096 9 (webready PDF)
ISBN 978 1 4744 2097 6 (epub)

Contents

List of Illustrations vii
Acknowledgements x

Introduction: Rural Modernity in Britain 1
Kristin Bluemel and Michael McCluskey

Part I: Networks

1. Ringing the Changes: Thomas Hardy's Communication Networks 19
Edward Allen
2. Change in the Village: Filming Rural Britain 33
Michael McCluskey
3. Electricity Comes to the Countryside: Visual Representations of a Connected Countryside in the Early Twentieth Century 50
Rosemary Shirley

Part II: Landscapes

4. Weighing Down the Landscape: The Quarry as a Site of Rural Modernity 69
Samuel Shaw
5. Windmills and Woodblocks: Agnes Miller Parker, Wood Engraving and the Popular Press in Interwar Britain 84
Kristin Bluemel
6. *Hiraeth* and Ambiguous Pastorals: Wales, England and Rural Modernities between the Wars 103
Chris Hopkins

Part III: Communities
7. The 'Uncertainty of Our Climate': Mary Kelly and the Rural Theatre 121
Andrew Walker
8. The Spinster in Eden: Reclaiming Civilisation in Interwar British Rural Fiction 135
Stella Deen
9. Transformative Pastoral: Lewis Grassic Gibbon's *A Scots Quair* 149
Nick Hubble

Part IV: Heritage
10. Borderlands: Visual and Material Culture in the Interwar Anglo-Scottish Borders 167
Ysanne Holt
11. Beyond Portmeirion: The Architecture, Planning and Protests of Clough Williams-Ellis 187
Nigel Harrison and Iain Robertson
12. Celebrating England: 'Heritage' Writing and the Rural Novelist 207
Dominic Head

Part V: Wars
13. Altered Countrysides: Paul Nash, David Jones and Eric Ravilious in Wartime 225
Eluned Summers-Bremner
14. Eden in Sussex: Atheist Moderns and the Berwick Church Murals 239
Hana Leaper and Polly Mills
15. Rural Modernity in a Time of Crisis: Preservation and Reform in the Books of B. T. Batsford 255
Peter Lowe

Notes on Contributors 270
Bibliography 274
Index 294

List of Illustrations

Figure 1.1	Thomas Hardy spies an opportunity.	20
Figure 1.2	Thomas Hardy approaches Guglielmo Marconi (seated front left).	20
Figure 2.1	The village of Chilham, where the church is mentioned in the 'Domesday Book'. Film still from *Chilham: A Kentish Village*, 1934.	38
Figure 2.2	Ye olde village charm in Lenham, Kent. Film still from *Lenham: A Kentish Village*, 1936.	42
Figure 2.3	Rural mobility: a motorised wheelchair in Kent. Film still from *Our Village*, 1935.	43
Figure 2.4	The bus driver is a familiar sight in Hovingham. Film still from *Personalities in Hovingham*, 1930s compilation.	44
Figure 2.5	The village petrol pump in use at Hovingham. Film still from *Personalities in Hovingham*, 1930s compilation.	45
Figure 3.1	Wind turbines and pylons, a view from the train window on a journey through Lincolnshire.	50
Figure 3.2	*Rural Electrification* pamphlet, British Electric Development Agency, 1928.	62
Figure 4.1	Edward Wadsworth, *Granite Quarries, Darby Hill, Oldbury*, 1919.	74
Figure 5.1	Agnes Miller Parker, *Pigsty*, 1926.	87
Figure 5.2	Agnes Miller Parker, selection from title page from *The Fables of Esope*, Gregynog Press, 1931.	90
Figure 5.3	Thomas Bewick, 'Saving the Toll', in *The History of British Birds*, vol. II, 1804.	92
Figure 5.4	Agnes Miller Parker, 'Pike', in *Down the River* by H. E. Bates, Gollancz, 1937.	95

Figure 5.5	Agnes Miller Parker, 'Windmill', in *Down the River* by H. E. Bates, 1937.	96
Figure 5.6	Agnes Miller Parker, 'Roach and Net', in *Down the River* by H. E. Bates, 1937.	97
Figure 5.7	Agnes Miller Parker, 'Hare in Snow', in *Through the Woods* by H. E. Bates, 1936.	97
Figure 5.8	Agnes Miller Parker, 'The Old Girl and Family', in *Down the River* by H. E. Bates, 1937.	98
Figure 9.1	'Map of Kinraddie', endpapers in first Jarrolds of London edition of *Sunset Song*, 1932.	152
Figure 9.2	'Map of Segget', endpapers in first Jarrolds of London edition of *Cloud Howe*, 1933.	153
Figure 9.3	'Map of the Land of *A Scots Quair*', endpapers in first Jarrolds of London edition of *Grey Granite*, 1934.	156
Figure 10.1	Margaret Warwick, *Two Cats by the Fire*, 1923.	171
Figure 10.2	Maurice Grieffenhagen, *Carlisle, the Gateway to Scotland*, 1924.	175
Figure 10.3	*The Sundour Shuttle*, 1937, cover design,	179
Figure 10.4	*Carlisle Art School Prospectus*, 1923–4.	181
Figure 10.5	*Carlisle Art School Prospectus*, 1935–6.	182
Figure 10.6	Decorations for Tullie House Reference Library: *Weaving and Furnishing Fabrics*.	183
Figure 10.7	Decorations for Tullie House Reference Library: *Livestock Sales*.	184
Figure 11.1	The voracious Octopus, on the front cover of Clough Williams-Ellis's preservationist book, *England and the Octopus*, 1928.	191
Figure 11.2	Plan for proposed 'Reilly Green' by Clough Williams-Ellis and Lionel Brett at Bilston, Staffordshire.	193
Figure 11.3	Government House, Portmeirion, 1928–9. Precursor of post-postmodern.	195
Figure 11.4	Laughing Water Restaurant, Cobham, Kent, 1933. Modernist 'roadhouse' in natural surroundings with a nautical theme.	196
Figure 11.5	Williams-Ellis's modern but ambivalent 'functional hut' at Maeshafn.	197
Figure 11.6	Derivative classical/vernacular use of colour and texture at Poundbury, Dorset, c.2005.	198
Figure 11.7	Paganhill Anti-Slavery Arch, Stroud, Gloucestershire, saved from the local council's demolition order.	200

Figure 11.8 Flamboyant 'forced perspective' of the Belltower (or Campanile), Portmeirion. 202
Figure 11.9 Strube's 'Little Man' in the *Daily Express* in the 1930s. 203
Figure 13.1 Paul Nash, *Landscape of the Megaliths*, 1937. 231
Figure 13.2 Eric Ravilious, *Downs in Winter*, 1935. 235
Figure 14.1 Preparatory study for Vanessa Bell, *The Annunciation*, c.1942. 246
Figure 14.2 Duncan Grant, *Christ in Glory*, Berwick Church, 1943. 247
Figure 14.3 Duncan Grant, 'The Bishop's Crook' study, c.1943. 248
Figure 14.4 Duncan Grant, 'Dr Bell Kneeling' study, c.1943. 249
Figure 15.1 Brian Cook, dust jacket design for *The Home Counties* by S. P. B. Mais, Batsford, 1943. 263

The plate section can be found between pages 164 and 165.

Plate 1 *The New Farming Age: Electricity Comes to the Countryside*, British Electric Development Agency, c.1933.
Plate 2 'A Diagrammatic Representation of the Distribution of Electricity in Rural Areas', in *Electricity in the Countryside*, 1939.
Plate 3 William Rothenstein, *The Deserted Quarry*, 1904.
Plate 4 Roger Fry, *Quarry, Bo Peep Farm, Sussex*, 1918.
Plate 5 J. D. Fergusson, *Craigleith Quarry*, 1900.
Plate 6 Paul Nash, *The Menin Road*, 1919.
Plate 7 Paul Nash, *Equivalents for the Megaliths*, 1935.
Plate 8 Eric Ravilious, *Ship's Screw on a Railway Truck*, 1940.
Plate 9 David Jones, *Vexilla Regis*, 1948.
Plate 10 Duncan Grant, *The Victory of Calvary*, Berwick Church, 1944.
Plate 11 Vanessa Bell, *The Nativity*, Berwick Church, c. 1942.
Plate 12 Vanessa Bell, *The Annunciation*, Berwick Church, c. 1942.
Plate 13 Sydney Jones, dust jacket design for *Homes, Towns and Countryside*, edited by Gilbert and Elizabeth McAllister, Batsford, 1945.

Acknowledgements

Rural Modernity in Britain had its beginnings in a 2010 article on documentary films about 'The Postman's Daily Round' that Michael McCluskey published in *The Space Between: Literature and Culture, 1914–1945*, an interdisciplinary journal that Kristin Bluemel was then editing. There Michael referred to his subjects' engagements with rural modernity, a phrase that seemed to capture exactly the kinds of relationships, experiences, materials and processes that Kristin was attempting to describe in her research on the interwar wood engraving revival. While many people and contexts have since furthered their respective scholarly projects, it is to The Space Between Society that both owe their deepest gratitude for years of collegial interest, interaction and inspiration.

The editors would like to thank Monmouth University graduate research assistants John Francis, Michael Sefak and Kendall Turchyn for their valuable bibliographic help. To John McCabe and Deborah Cotler they also extend thanks for technical support preparing the manuscript. The Wayne D. McMurray Chair research funds provided by Monmouth University have supported the rich illustration in the volume, including, most notably, reproduction of its colour plates.

The editors would like to thank the team at Edinburgh University Press that has supported this project in so many ways: to Jackie Jones, Publisher of Literary Studies, for her faith in and support of the book during the acquisition process; to Ersev Ersoy and Adela Ruchova, Assistant Commissioning Editors of Literary Studies, for their attention to all the innumerable details involved in getting the manuscript into production; to James Dale, Managing Desk Editor, for his patience and expertise; and to Ian Davidson, Head of Production, and Rebecca Mackenzie, Project Manager, for their critical guidance regarding the design, illustration and production of this book. We also want to thank the anonymous readers for Edinburgh University Press, who, through their support and challenge, improved the book in important ways.

Edward Allen would like to extend thanks to Alyson and Barry Allen, and Semele Assinder; to Catherine Charlwood; to the National Portrait Gallery for permission to reproduce the photographs; and to Ceri Brough, the Project Archivist at Eton College Library, for hunting down a reference.

Michael McCluskey would like to thank the people and institutions that helped with his research. The British Academy funded his postdoctoral fellowship on amateur film-making in Britain. Megan McCooley and the Yorkshire Film Archive, and Jane King and Stasia Botwright from Screen Archive South East, offered tremendous help in accessing films and providing images. Sir William Worsley kindly granted permission to use the images from his grandfather's films. The British Film Institute, East Anglia Film Archive and National Library of Scotland Moving Image Archive also made films available via their websites. Readers may access some of the films discussed in his chapter online and others by arrangement with these institutions.

Kristin Bluemel extends grateful thanks to all those who assisted with the research and writing of her project, including Peter Quinn, Ian Rogerson, Mimi Ross, and the National Library of Scotland's Sally Harrower and Amy Todman. She would also like to thank Monmouth University for a Grant-in-Aid-of-Creativity that supported travel to Edinburgh and the Agnes Miller Parker Archives. She extends especially warm thanks to Mrs Anne D. Quickenden, Agnes Miller Parker's niece and the executor of her estate, for permission to quote from Agnes Miller Parker's letters and reproduce her copyright wood engravings. Thanks also to the Thomas Bewick Society for permission to reprint Bewick's wood engravings. Kristin hopes both these generous estates will forgive any possible reductions of quality in the reproduced artwork due to digital printing technologies.

Nick Hubble wishes to acknowledge the fact that part of the materials for his chapter was first published by Edinburgh University Press in Nick Hubble, *The Proletarian Answer to the Modernist Question* (2017). He and the editors warmly thank the Mitchell Literary Estate and the Grassic Gibbon Centre for permission to reproduce the endpaper maps from *A Scots Quair*.

Ysanne Holt would like to thank Melanie Gardner from the Tullie House Museum and Stephen White from the Carlisle Library and Archives.

Hana Leaper and Polly Mills acknowledge that in 2014 they were the first of the Angelica Garnett Gift curatorial fellows to have the opportunity to work with the newly arrived archival materials in Vanessa Bell's attic studio at Charleston. The legacy of works attesting to the flourishing of artistic modernity evident at Charleston, Berwick, Rodmell, Farley Farm, Ditchling and numerous other sites has been further augmented by the web of artists' archives and collections now accessible at these locations and at The Keep in Brighton, De La Warr Pavilion in Bexhill, Towner Gallery in Eastbourne, and Jerwood Gallery in Hastings. They would like to thank Dr Darren Clarke and the Estate[s] of Vanessa Bell and Duncan Grant for their generous support throughout this research.

Peter Lowe acknowledges that all his citations from Batsford books and the reproduction of the Batsford jacket cover for *Homes, Towns, and Countryside* are reproduced with kind permission of B. T. Batsford, part of Pavilion Books Company Limited.

Finally, the editors would like to extend personal thanks to the following individuals: Kristin Bluemel would like to thank her husband, George Witte, for supporting her research and writing on Agnes Miller Parker and other British women wood engravers in innumerable ways. Especially meaningful have been his gifts of wood engraved prints by Miller Parker and several of her contemporaries, providing material reminders of the ordinary, everyday pleasures bound up with scholarship on illustration and print and book history. Michael McCluskey would like to thank his parents for introducing him to the appreciation of rural places.

Introduction: Rural Modernity in Britain

Kristin Bluemel and Michael McCluskey

'The last twenty years having witnessed so much change in the village, it is interesting to speculate as to the farther changes that may be looked for in the years to come,' George Sturt writes in *Change in the Village* (1912), his observations on rural social history. In the book's final section, 'The Forward Movement', he sets out his ideas for what he sees as a shift in outlook among the people he observes toward the changing world around them:

> The changes so far observed have been thrust upon the people from the outside – changes in their material or social environment, followed by mere negations on their part, in the abandonment of traditional outlooks and ambitions; and of course in that negative direction the movement must come to an end at last. But when there are no more old habits to be given up, there is still plenty of scope for acquiring new ones, and this is the possibility that has to be considered. What if, quietly and out of sight – so quietly and inconspicuously as to be unnoticed even by the people themselves – their English nature dissatisfied with negations, should have instinctively set to work in a positive direction to discover a new outlook and new ambitions? (pp. 165–6)[1]

Rural Modernity in Britain: A Critical Intervention puts the focus on this new outlook and new ambitions through a study of writers, artists and other agents that investigated and helped to instigate the changes that Sturt saw coming among the rural people he writes about. Quiet and inconspicuous activities are considered in the context of dramatic changes in material and social conditions throughout Britain in order to examine the histories of relations between rural and urban places, economies, classes, identities, images, arts and cultures. The overarching goal of this project is to promote rural people and places as important yet often-ignored subjects for studies of British modernisation, modernism and modernity.

In the early twentieth century, rural areas experienced economic depression, the expansion of transport and communication networks, the rollout of electricity, the loss of land and the erosion of local identities. Who celebrated these changes? Who resisted them? Who documented them? The fifteen chapters of *Rural Modernity in Britain* address these questions through investigations into fiction, non-fiction, film, drama, print and painting, among other genres and media. These essays make the case that the rural means more than the often-studied countryside of southern England and that examination of the cultural production and consumption of rural Britain reveals new stories about British national identity and imagination. Throughout, the book argues that 'rural' and 'modern' should not be seen in opposition but rather as two terms relating to a vital relationship that came under intense pressure during the first half of the twentieth century, particularly during the interwar years. Existing literary studies of interwar Britain examine the rural as a cultural expression of mass market and modernist writers' fixation on 'the countryside', a countryside often narrowed to the scenes of southern England, populated by middle-class artists, and constructed as a site of nostalgic retreat divorced from modernity and modernisation.[2] The modernists' countryside is part of the story of rural modernity in Britain, but a small part. *Rural Modernity in Britain* looks beyond it, assuming that rural regions, communities, classes and figures can originate and sustain histories of and criticism on modernity and the modern.

Rural Modernity in Britain emphasises the great variety of experiences of modernity throughout the different regions that make up rural Britain. Just as there were real differences that marked life in cities and life in rural areas, there were meaningful differences between the rural regions of Britain and differences within rural regions themselves. While it is impossible to address all these differences in a single volume, it is possible to acknowledge that there were diverse responses to modernity and to enrich existing literary, art and cultural histories with studies of rural Britain.[3] To achieve this goal, contributors to this volume pay attention to the distinction between Britain and England; while chapters on English rural places dominate, this is a volume dedicated to recording and exploring evidence of British rural modernity. Critical treatments of literature, art and culture produced in and about the rural areas of Wales and Scotland support the argument of the book.[4] Rural peoples of England, Wales and Scotland, this book argues, faced similar changes to their urban and suburban compatriots, as well as changes particular to their local areas. *Rural Modernity in Britain* complicates existing narratives about national modernisation and British modernism as the isolation, remoteness and peculiar relations to the land that mark rural places made people both receptive to and suspicious of the new social relations and new forms of connectivity brought about by telegraph, telephone, radio and electricity. Traditional rural industries and villages needed to adapt to changes in order to survive.[5] And different models of community and productivity could be fashioned by those who chose to remain in or return to rural places as sites supporting homes, work and dreams. As this book demonstrates, representations of rural life in the interwar period were more than just paeans to a national past. While Stanley Baldwin famously said, in 1924, 'England is the country, and the country is England,'[6] other voices contest his pastoral nationalism and conservative rural nostalgia. Exploring lesser-known figures, regions and genres, the chapters in this volume pry apart those supposedly synonymous terms – rural, country, pastoral, nationalism, nostalgia, conservatism – in order to admit more complex and contradictory data into the critical narrative of modernism and modernity.

Rural, country, rustic, pastoral

There are very good etymological and generic reasons why the rural, as a geographical and especially cultural category, has been treated as antagonistic to modernism and modernity. Modernism, theorised by twentieth-century critics associated with university and metropolitan centres, is a product of cities: Baudelaire's Paris, Wyndham Lewis's London, Kafka's Prague, Alfred Stieglitz's New York.[7] Similarly, modernisms, as they have been theorised by twenty-first-century critics, depend on urban peoples and places to investigate an idea of modernism as a 'paradigmatic shift, a major revolt, beginning in the mid- and late nineteenth century, against the prevalent literary and aesthetic traditions of the Western world'.[8] Shifts, revolts and modern movements: all seem to oppose rural people and places, imagined for better or worse as stolid, static or stagnant. The rural functions as the Other in many of these modernisms and the critical debates surrounding them, even as they are obviously participants in and sources of some component of British modernity.[9] The history of debate about the disciplinary and geographical domains of modern, modernism and modernity means that the rural cannot escape the city or its judgements. This is evident in the first definition accorded to the word 'rural' in the *Oxford English Dictionary*:

> Rural: 1.a. of a person: living in the country as opposed to a town or city; engaged in country occupations; having the appearance or manners of a country person; (in early use also depreciative) lacking in elegance, refinement, or education; boorish.[10]

Contemplating the dominant term in this definition, 'country', Raymond Williams, in *Keywords* (1976), observes that from the thirteenth century it carried the meaning of 'native land', only coming to signify 'of the distinctly rural areas' 300 years later, from the early sixteenth century (p. 81). He explains that the 'widespread use of country as opposed to city began in [the last third of the sixteenth century] . . . with increasing urbanisation and especially the growth of the capital, London' (p. 81). In the seventeenth century, after 100 more years of urbanisation, the terms 'countryfied' and 'country bumpkin' came into use as metropolitan slang (p. 81). Thus the rural life and economies that came, in the nineteenth century, to be referred to with the Scottish term 'countryside' were tainted with negative connotations, also conveyed by the word 'rural' late in the history of the English use of these words and in direct connection to urbanisation and the growth of London's power as a national capital.[11] While judgement of a country person or place as 'more primitive' is more likely nowadays to be attached to the word rustic than rural,[12] in their current usage all these terms – rural, country, rustic – are weighted with the history of urbanisation, development, and the growth of London as a centre of national power. We cannot talk about rural without implying 'town or city'. Nor can we talk about rural without alluding to a history of condescending judgements by urban people about their rural neighbours. This history is rehearsed here in order to acknowledge the paradoxical assumptions sustaining this study of rural modernity: that to identify rural modernity is to set apart as worthy of concentrated and special study a country life and experience while simultaneously assuming that it is inseparable from the history of modernisation more typically associated with cities and urban areas. 'Rural modernity' is a term that embraces the contradictory impulses that characterise so much writing about modernity. It is consistent with Marshall Berman's judgement in *All That Is Solid Melts into Air* that 'To be modern is to live a life of paradox and contradiction' (pp. 13–14).

Rural Modernity in Britain extends scholarly discussion of rural and rustic place addressed many years ago, most often by historians and social scientists. For example, anthropologists Barbara Ching and Gerald W. Creed, in their volume *Knowing Your Place: Rural Identity and Cultural Hierarchy* (1997), describe the aim of their interdisciplinary volume as 'open[ing] a new approach to the subject of rural and urban places in the politics of identity'.[13] In contrast to many theorists of place and space studies, Ching and Creed advocate adoption of 'a theoretical middle ground'

> in which 'place' can be metaphoric yet still refer to a particular physical environment and its associated socio-cultural qualities. In this view, place becomes a *grounded* metaphor. [sic][14]

This approach to place as a *grounded* metaphor that supports discovery and analysis of rural identities as powerful social constructions implicated in other, more studied forms of identity and power also defines the approach of the contributors to this volume. *Rural Modernity in Britain* takes up very different materials and peoples for study, but shares Ching and Creed's determination to make rural place an axis of study for scholars of modernity in the belief that expressions and materials of rural identities are 'a clear attempt on the part of rustic people to assert their value and place in a world dominated by urbane others'.[15] *Rural Modernity in Britain* puts at its centre men and women who set out to know and represent the complicated reality of rural life, who respect its beauties and terrors, who represent its everyday materials, routines and scenes even as they recognise how tedious these things may be. No outsider eye of the urban pastoralist is needed for this vision of an often difficult, threadbare, threatened way of interwar living.

William Empson, in *Some Versions of Pastoral* (1935), describes pastoral as 'a puzzling form which looks proletarian but isn't' (p. 6). Pastoral's elegant, idle, sideways look at working people has deceived many critics, who then confuse it with other forms. For example, the work of rural modernity – verbal, visual, singular or mass-produced – may look pastoral but is not, even when its forms may lead critics to endorse it as more or less experimental, more or less modernist. In contrast to criticism that seeks to categorise rural writing through its aesthetic allegiances with urban arts movements, the defining criteria of rural modernity in this volume, and thus the theory of rural modernity it advances, are not aesthetic or generic but historical, material, social and geographical. These values stand in stark opposition to those endorsed by Clive Bell, one of modernism's 'Men of 1914', in his classic essay of 1914, 'The Aesthetic Hypothesis'. Here, Bell advances both a theory and practice for understanding modern visual art as something apart from and better than representative illustration, documents or descriptive paintings (Clive Bell, p. 6). Art is, in his memorable formulation, 'significant form' (p. 3). This significance is 'unrelated to the significance of life' (p. 10) and, to appreciate art, 'we need bring with us nothing from life . . . we are lifted above the stream of life' (p. 9). This definition of art as pure significant form, apart from the living world, influenced generations of modern art critics. Interestingly, it is consistent with the way pastoral has come to signify in literary critical usage. From pastoral's strictly generic and literary definition, what Renato Poggioli describes as the 'pattern of the bucolic (from *βουκόλος*, guardian of cattle) . . . express[ing] a genuine love of the countryside, as well as the citydweller's yearning for greener pastures', modern pastoral has come to mean and be a place apart, out of the stream of life (Poggioli, p. 4). Poggioli describes pastoral as 'a pause in the process of living', an 'oasis' or 'retirement to the periphery of life' (pp. 9, 11, 11). Paul Fussell agrees, explaining that

> literate ages have used the pastoral genre in large part as a compensatory device, a way of vacationing from actuality. The tradition, all the way from Edmund Spenser in the sixteenth century to Matthew Arnold in the nineteenth, provides a way of realizing conventionally an alternative to the experiential world.[16]

Understood in these terms, pastoral seems to be another version of Bell's modern art, a significant form whose power 'is unrelated to the significance of life'.[17] Bell's modern art, like Fussell's pastoral, depicts that which is outside life, beyond ordinary, everyday experience. Pastoral art, as understood by these mid-century critics, is fundamentally contradictory, its motivation – to express feelings of yearning, longing, often felt as that peculiar feeling of nostalgia or, literally, homesickness – at odds with its function – to provide a thing, a poem, that can satisfy or fulfil those yearnings.[18] Traditional pastoral conjures images of something that is missing from life but that seemingly still exists elsewhere, in another place (the shepherds' fields) or in another time (the Golden Age, childhood). Similarly, modernist pastoral comes to represent something precious that is absent or lost yet is simultaneously received as the very thing that can compensate for such loss.

Studies of modernist pastoral contribute to but do not complete our understanding of interwar British arts and culture, and do not replace the need for studies of rural modernity – the actual, lived, everyday realities of rural people living in and reacting to their modern times and to their experiences of modernisation. The confusion of modernist pastoral with rural modernity is understandable, given critical and institutional hierarchies that elevate modernist aesthetics above the aesthetics of works labelled popular. While it is true that Johanna Drucker could claim, in *Theorizing Modernism* (1994), that in visual arts criticism the urbane, or 'high art modernism', is 'no longer unquestioningly granted a privileged place by virtue of aesthetic concerns' (p. 4), she also had to concede that 'even these rewritings [spearheaded by feminist, deconstructive and cultural theorists] contain critical assumptions that are the legacy of modern art and theory' (p. 4). Aware of the still-powerful effects of what Drucker calls 'the phantoms of received tradition' (p. 4), and writing more than twenty years after Drucker, the scholars contributing to this volume look to other disciplines, other critical traditions, for pathways into debates about British identity, modernity, modernisation and modernism. The 'new modernist studies' have supported this work, demonstrating that even the most elite of modernists can serve as a vehicle for exploring popular literature. [19] For example, in *T. S. Eliot and the Cultural Divide* (2003), 'new modernist' scholar David Chinitz describes Eliot as a writer in whom the forces and figures of elite and popular culture 'perpetually contend', and whose work 'issues from the contest' (p. 7). Those who notice that the urban/rural divide maps more or less directly on to the elite/popular divide might be inclined to borrow Chinitz's metaphor, describing rural modernity as a contest, one conducted in a specific place – rural areas, the country – in which high and low figures and forces perpetually contend.

Constructing rural modernity as cultural contest implies two methodological priorities for the scholars contributing to this volume. First, the chapters of *Rural Modernity in Britain* pursue social and cultural engagements, interconnections and interchanges between rural and urban, popular and elite, owners and workers, traditional and modern, agrarian and industrial, as well as divisions. Second, employing the metaphor of contest encourages scholars to ask about the standards and fields of play. Within modernism and modernity studies, the play of criticism has routinely been conducted on urban and university terrain. In contrast to this history, in the pages of *Rural Modernity in Britain*, people in rural places are central to academic discourse about the history and forms of the modern, modernism and modernity. The literary and cultural works they produce and have an impact on and throw into question the outcome of the contest that is rural modernity, so it cannot be said, with the weary conviction of Ching and Creed, that 'In all of these discourses of place, the urbane has the last word.'[20]

Rural retreat in grim times: critical revaluations

In *The Country and the City* (1973), Raymond Williams famously describes the 'escalator' of nostalgic retrospect that finds 'Old England, settlement, the rural virtues' in the receding pasts of successive generations, demonstrating how the rural counterpoint to the anxieties of urbanisation and industrialisation is reconstituted through each generation of cultural production (p. 12). *Rural Modernity in Britain* argues that the interwar period is a particularly rich resource for studies of the interrelationships between the country, city, modernity and identity as radical developments were met with what Howard Newby describes as a 'welter' of publications about rural life and the revival of traditional arts and crafts (p. 175). More recently, Trevor Wild has argued, in *Village*

England (2004), that 'the appeal of rural idyllism became stronger than ever' amid the threats posed by World War I, economic depression, unemployment and increased mechanisation 'in the turbulent first half of the twentieth century. . . . It was in these grim times that the romanticized virtues of rural England and its timeless villages were elevated to beacons of moral character and a metaphor for national identity' (pp. xv, xvi).

Romantic evocations of rural life appeared in poems, novels and guidebooks published to celebrate the 'quiet beauty' of these seemingly unspoilt bits of Britain.[21] During this period, many writers and artists viewed rural Britain as an escape from an increasingly urbanised world and a retreat to an almost premodern era that 'presented the observer with a view of its past in its present'.[22] Writings and illustrations from the early twentieth century depict rural Britain as 'a retreat and solace from human society and ordinary human consciousness', an impulse that Williams traces back to Virgil.[23] The interwar period consolidated, reproduced and disseminated this image to such effect that it persists in the media of the later decades of the twentieth century and those of today. According to Alex Potts, the 'clichéd stereotypes of chequer-board fields, hedgerows, copses and old buildings nestling in comforting hollows found today in calendars, advertisements, films of "old England" and travel and guide books are in fact largely the creation of the period' (p. 166). In print and on screen, a distinct image of rural Britain was celebrated in the 1920s and 1930s by writers and artists and promoted by media industry professionals as an escape from the crowds, noise, rhythms and responsibilities of modern city life. As John Lowerson argues, 'for many people this was the "real" England and the urge to locate oneself within it was strengthened in the 1930s as never before by a powerful current of "countryside" literature' (p. 260). But it was more than just the literature of the period that created this current. Historians like Jeremy Burchardt and geographers like David Matless have documented popular social movements and civic trends that contributed to the phenomenon of substituting the countryside for England and substituting England for Britain.[24]

In *The Rural Tradition in the English Novel, 1900–1939* (1977), Glen Cavaliero offers a catalogue of writers on 'the rural experience' and distinguishes those that only 'contemplate a static society' from those in which 'we are involved in a changing one' (pp. 16, 31). He acknowledges that many rural writers 'were conscious of the forces of change, and were interested in what was happening around them' yet, unlike the contributors to *Rural Modernity in Britain*, he does not ask how rural areas could be the sites and sources of innovation and experimentation rather than just social tragedy or how the novels that interest him comment on more than just their local, rural concerns but offer instances of the types of changes that were affecting other areas of Britain.[25]

More recent work has looked into treatments of rural Britain and what they can tell us about both British modernity and modernism. Jed Esty's *A Shrinking Island* (2004) offers an influential analysis of the connections between late modernism and a 'renewed interest in native and Anglocentric rituals' amid a crisis of 'metropolitan modernity' (pp. 17, 19). But his shrinking island thesis and the rural subjects he explores to make his point revive the rural-as-retreat rhetoric that dominated much of the interwar writing on the countryside and that persists in much of the current scholarship on writing about rural people and activities. Alexandra Harris's more popular *Romantic Moderns* (2010) argues that activities that revivified English traditions and celebrated local sites were part of a particular interwar strand of English modernism (p. 12). Neal Alexander and James Moran, in *Regional Modernisms* (2013), also puncture perceived oppositions between the rural and the modern. They argue that 'regional modernisms are rarely bound to any one place exclusively, for the particulars of geography and situation may themselves be multiple, shifting, subject to doubt and the contingencies of living' (p. 8). And Sam Wiseman, in *The Reimagining of Place in English Modernism* (2015), builds on Esty's 'foundation' to emphasise 'continuities across representations of urban and rural experience', and to argue that 'these are mutually influential throughout the entire interwar period' (p. 2). The interest in reclaiming regional and rural writers as sources for studies beyond their local concerns is something that extends from Cavaliero's work and aligns the aims of the books discussed above with those of *Rural Modernity in Britain*. Yet the contributors to this volume are just as likely to discover in rural regional texts, crafts and arts particular geographies offered up precisely because they bind readers to one place exclusively. They find that rural regional texts and objects aim to persuade readers that, no matter how deep their investment in distant, perhaps urban, contingencies of national living, representations of particular rural geographies and situations are sufficient to the demands of perception and imagination. This means that, unlike Alexander and Moran, Esty, Wiseman and Harris, the contributors to *Rural Modernity* tend to regard rural writers and artists as living in rural places that are, in their everyday aspects, already sources for studies of modernity. Assuming a modern cultural producer is or may be at home in rural places has an impact not only on what artists, writers, cultural objects and institutions scholars look at, but also on how and why we look at them.

A growing body of work sees rural people not as victims of modernisation projects pushed upon them or as throwbacks to an earlier age but as active agents in transforming the material and cultural conditions in which they lived.[26] *Rural Modernity in Britain* contributes to these and other revisionist studies that seek out the 'rural equivalents' of 'the economic and social forces that produced urban regeneration'.[27] It explores the diverse sites, skills, classes, outlooks and ideologies that the rural includes with chapters on regions like the English-Scottish borders, Yorkshire, Cornwall and Kent, and activities such as wood engraving, weaving, film-making and pageant performances. Examining these sites and activities from the perspectives of those who lived in them, looking 'out' towards the urban and suburban areas of Britain with which they were connected, can help us to understand the impact of modernisation and modernity not just on rural populations but also on the nation.

Those scholars who are most actively promoting this approach to the study of rural places and cultures include Gemma Goodman and Charlotte Mathieson, who make a case in *Gender and Space in Rural Britain, 1840–1920* (2014) for 'expanding the portrayal of rurality away from the myth of a rural idyll to show instead a more diverse and complex picture of rural Britain in the nineteenth and early twentieth century' (p. 1). *Rural Modernity in Britain* contributor Rosemary Shirley's own volume, *Rural Modernity, Everyday Life and Visual Culture* (2015), is largely focused on postwar Britain but its mission is sympathetic to our own. It seeks to extend 'non-urban geographies' beyond the familiar conception of the countryside and to 'reactivat[e] the rural as a site of modernity' (pp. 4, 3). Dominic Head, another contributor to *Rural Modernity in Britain*, argues, in his recently published study *Modernity and the English Rural Novel* (2017), that 'the continuing rural tradition in the English novel [is] a telling response to modernity . . . all the more powerful because of its obliquity'. Head seeks to show how modernity 'is variously defined and constructed' by a range of rural novelists treating 'different manifestations of mechanization, urbanization and social change' (p. 2). Head, Shirley and the contributors to *Gender and Space in Rural Britain* 'present a nuanced portrayal of rural Britain at this time', contributing to the broader project of cracking open the monolithic image of the countryside set out at the opening of this introduction.[28] In what follows, we describe the specific chapters or case studies of *Rural Modernity in Britain* that extend this early work in the field and explain how they not only facilitate interdisciplinary discourse, but also point to critical conversations that will strengthen our theoretical claims on behalf of rural modernity more generally.

The case studies

Part I of the volume, 'Networks', brings together three chapters that examine different ways in which the people in rural Britain were transforming their relations to each other and to people in other areas of the country through new technologies. Edward Allen's chapter, 'Ringing the Changes: Thomas Hardy's Communication Networks', puts an end to a strain of critical grief bemoaning the dissolution of idyllic country habits, including, in particular, the pealing of soundscapes past. Examining 'the sources and channels of rural communication', the chapter finds in Hardy's relation to new sounds a template for rural modernity. In the next chapter, 'Change in the Village: Filming Rural Britain', Michael McCluskey examines amateur films about rural Britain in order to analyse the 'visible evidence' these films provide of the impact of modernisation. He argues that these films show off the traditional activities of local areas, but they also document shifts in rural economies and foreground the technologies and industries that constituted modern village life. Rosemary Shirley's third chapter extends the volume's focus on visible evidence of rural modernity; 'Electricity Comes to the Countryside: Visual Representations of a Connected Countryside in the Early Twentieth Century' examines an extensive range of diagrams, drawings and propaganda from the British Electrical Development Agency (BEDA) that were aimed at rural consumers. Shirley demonstrates that these images promote an understanding of the English countryside and its inhabitants as willing agents in processes that continue to shape our understanding of what it means to be rural.

Part II, 'Landscapes', considers rural romanticism, regional art and archives, national identities, and relations between rural modernity and the pastoral. It begins with Samuel Shaw's 'Weighing Down the Landscape: The Quarry as a Site of Rural Modernity', which considers a wide range of paintings about quarries – many of which are still in rural art galleries – in close relation to the history of rural industries in such regions as Cornwall, West Yorkshire and the Scottish Lowlands. Moving from the visual appeal of the colossal to the miniature, Kristin Bluemel, in 'Windmills and Woodblocks: Agnes Miller Parker, Wood Engraving and the Popular Press in Interwar Britain', examines Agnes Miller Parker's career in order to demonstrate how wood engraving's dependence upon antique craft, modern reproductive print technologies and rural subjects contributes to the paradoxical drama of rural modernity. 'Landscapes' concludes with Chris Hopkins's analysis of interwar Welsh writing in English in his chapter '*Hiraeth* and Ambiguous Pastorals:

Wales, England and Rural Modernities between the Wars'. Explaining that *hiraeth* is a word that is familiar to Welsh speakers and means grief, sadness and longing after the lost or departed and an earnest desire for what might have been, Hopkins explores how a variety of Welsh literary texts in English claimed a distinctive Welsh rural modernity, and describes the implications of these claims for our understanding of the English audiences who consumed these works.

In Part III, 'Communities', three chapters bring together enquiries about performance and voice, gender and community, and regional modernism. Andrew Walker, in 'The "Uncertainty of Our Climate": Mary Kelly and the Rural Theatre', examines the writings of the woman who is best known as the model for Miss La Trobe, the rather eccentric playwright and director in Virginia Woolf's posthumous novel *Between the Acts* (1941). Walker claims that Kelly's own writings, *How to Make a Pageant* (1936) and *Village Theatre* (1939), articulate a vision of the rural theatre as an outgrowth of folk religion and mythology grounded in agricultural and fertility ritual and promoted by modern print culture, helping us understand interwar rural dramatic production in the context of changing class relations. The next chapter, 'The Spinster in Eden: Reclaiming Civilisation in Interwar British Rural Fiction', keeps our focus on women writers and artists in rural areas. Stella Deen traces the actions of middle-aged English spinsters presiding over the rural and urban landscapes of Sylvia Townsend Warner's *Lolly Willowes, or The Loving Huntsman* (1926), E. H. Young's *Miss Mole* (1930) and Winifred Holtby's *South Riding* (1936). Deen discovers in these novels a progression from a libertarian to a communal notion of civilisation, challenging critics' assumptions that rural politics are conservative politics and that rural commitments exclude urban loyalties. This attention to feminist possibilities within rural English communities prepares us for Nick Hubble's 'Transformative Pastoral: Lewis Grassic Gibbon's *A Scots Quair*'. Turning to Gibbon's fictional communities in the Mearns in northeast Scotland, Hubble draws on the work of feminist critics and theories of the pastoral to consider how Gibbon's trilogy relates modern classed subjectivity and intersubjectivity to the 'land' in its broadest conception.

In the past, scholars of rural Britain were quick to interpret interwar interest in British 'heritage' as a powerful sign of the consolidation of a particularly English identity around images and scenes of a rural Britain drenched in conservative politics of class, sex and race. Part IV, 'Heritage', attempts to complicate this critical narrative through examination of craft, art and architecture that take their inspiration from forms or processes associated with rural areas in order to engage with imaginings of a modern Britain. 'Borderlands: Visual and Material Culture in the Interwar Anglo-Scottish Borders', by Ysanne Holt, traces the path of artist Ben Nicholson and his first wife, Winifred Dacre, to a farmhouse in the village of Banks on the edge of the English–Scottish border. Holt finds there, within a rugged terrain often imagined as primitive and romantic, a culture of crafts and especially of textile production that supports a vision of the Borders as fluid, dynamic and avowedly modern, with a distinctive cross-border or 'borderland' aesthetic that merged modernism and modernity and combined national and international sources with local histories and forms of heritage. Also confronting stereotypes of British heritage, Nigel Harrison and Iain Robertson examine the history and politics of Britain's most famous (or infamous) preservationist in 'Beyond Portmeirion: The Architecture, Planning and Protests of Clough Williams-Ellis'. In this chapter, Williams-Ellis, leader of the Campaign to Protect Rural England (CPRE) and the Design and Industries Association, and author of the most famous protest against interwar development, *England and the Octopus* (1928), becomes a figure whose writings and activities yield an interesting tension between his forward-looking, rationalist and modernist ambitions and his desires to protect the places of the English (and occasionally Welsh) countryside from the material manifestations of these ambitions. Concluding the 'Heritage' section is Dominic Head's chapter 'Celebrating England: "Heritage" Writing and the Rural Novelist', which summarises and analyses the heritage writing of novelists Doreen Wallace, H. E. Bates, Adrian Bell, Leo Walmsley and Francis Brett Young. Head argues that the non-fiction genre of heritage writing is ideally suited to the study of rural modernity, with the potential to demonstrate and generate a self-consciousness about nation, class and identity that is inseparable from a pervasive anxiety about modernisation.

Rural Modernity in Britain concludes with Part V, 'Wars', which seeks to understand how writers and artists in rural Britain, in conjunction with urban producers and distributors, integrated that most modern of experiences, world war, into their experiences of rural life and regions. In 'Altered Countrysides: Paul Nash, David Jones and Eric Ravilious in Wartime', Eluned Summers-Bremner considers how three interwar English artists sought comfort from their experiences of World War I in renditions of rural landscape that were also occasions of advance mourning for future international conflict. She argues that in images of the rural by these three men, who were war artists and soldiers, we are looking not at a product of rural nostalgia but at something more prescient. Also examining outsider wartime artists, Hana Leaper and Polly Mills discuss Vanessa Bell's and Duncan Grant's commissioned mural project for Berwick Church, undertaken during the years of World War II. Their chapter, 'Eden in Sussex: Atheist Moderns and the Berwick Church Murals', explores the relationship between dissenting voices in the local community and the support for the mural project from the Church and artistic establishments that overrode these concerns. Rather than dismissing Bell's and Grant's work in Sussex as irrelevant to twentieth-century culture, as do most mainstream historians of art, this chapter demonstrates that the move to the countryside and the privileging of the domestic, local and everyday made Bell and Grant vital interpreters of rural modernity.

The prescient fine art of Nash, Jones and Ravilious, and the atheist church murals of Bell and Grant arguably find their cultural destination in the popular British Heritage and Face of Britain books examined by Peter Lowe in 'Rural Modernity in a Time of Crisis: Preservation and Reform in the Books of B. T. Batsford'. In this final chapter of *Rural Modernity in Britain*, Lowe argues that Batsford's decision to keep volumes from the series in print during wartime enabled the books to play a significant role in the construction of an idea of English and British cultural identity that proved vital to the nation's defence. At the same time, though, wartime events enabled Batsford authors to adopt a more conciliatory tone on the issue of postwar rebuilding and restructuring, contributing to the integration of conflicts over rural modernity into larger debates about exactly which 'Britain' was to emerge from the Second World War and survive into the twenty-first century.

Each chapter in *Rural Modernity in Britain: A Critical Intervention* engages with alternative views and different constructions of distinct rural areas of Britain that were inseparable from those modernising processes and experiences that attended the nation's confrontation with and responses to significant change. The volume section titles on 'Networks', 'Landscapes', 'Communities', 'Heritage' and 'Wars' draw attention to dominant themes that organise these alternative views and different constructions. However, since each chapter also provides detailed studies of artefacts and ideas that appear in chapters in other sections, we have included 'In dialogue with' editorial notes at the end of each chapter, directing readers to alternate sections of the book. These suggestions for continued interdisciplinary conversation reinforce the rhetorical and structural commitments of the volume to diverse methodological approaches for the study of rural modernity. They also represent our intention that this volume function as a classroom text, inspiring students of twentieth-century literature, arts and culture to engage with new materials in the interdisciplinary study of modernity. Together, the chapters seek to persuade readers that rural areas cannot be viewed only as retreats from modernity but must also be seen as modern spaces inviting us to consider the diverse effects of new ways of moving, communicating, producing and perceiving. Writers, artists and designers who granted rural people subjectivity and represented rural places and activities as central to the nation's experience of modernity offer more than mere depictions of objects arranged in a seemingly disappearing landscape. Their work provides examples of the ways in which local communities were responding to the opportunities made available to them. Moreover, many of these writers, artists and designers offered up their treatments of rural subjects for contemplation and consumption by rural peoples themselves. This is not to suggest that the project of discovering and theorising rural modernity should be limited to examination of rural or regional objects, images and audiences, but rather that these things can teach us about active cultural agents in the processes of national modernisation. The scholars contributing to this volume hope to extend their study and conversation about the rural, the modern and the nation to twenty-first-century readers who may recognise, in the history of interwar rural Britain, sources for understanding their own engagements with modernity.

Notes

The editors are indebted to many people for help with this Introduction and volume. We particularly wish to thank Ben Child of Colgate University, who shared with us selected chapters from his excellent and at that time unpublished manuscript *Uneven Ground: Figurations of the Rural Modern in the U.S. South, 1890–1940*, which meaningfully influenced our theorising of British rural modernity. The annual conference of The Space Between: Literature and Culture, 1914–1945 has been a constant source of intellectual development for both editors, and many of its regular members provided encouragement and enthusiasm over the course of this volume's development.

1. George Bourne was the pseudonym of George Sturt.
2. See, for example, Lowerson, Chase, Burchardt, Newby, Howkins or Wild for accounts of this tradition in popular culture. For a classic account of the literal and literary escapes of interwar literary elites to 'pastoralia' – both English and European – see Cunningham, 'Somewhere the Good Place?' For a more recent account, see Alexandra Harris.
3. For literary studies of American rural modernity see Casey, Farland and Child. See Brooker and Thacker for essays that construct a spatial history of modernisms in relation to the geographies of postmodernism, globalisation and postcolonialism, and Gaonkar for essays that advance site-based readings of modernities from transnational and transcultural perspectives.

4. This study does not address rural modernity in Northern Ireland, even though it was, after 1922, a British nation or region equal in political status to Scotland and Wales. Irish rural modernity deserves full treatment by scholars with expertise in the Irish nations' separate experiences of and creative reactions to modernisation. For a study that addresses several of these concerns, see Frawley, *Irish Pastoral*.
5. See for example Brassley, Burchardt and Sayer's study *Transforming the Countryside* for comparative study of electrification, rurality, and modernity in England, Wales, and Scotland.
6. 'England', pp. 6–7.
7. See, for example, Bradbury and McFarlane's classic study, *Modernism*.
8. Eysteinsson, p. 2.
9. See, for example, Bradshaw and Dettmar's *Companion to Modernist Literature and Culture*, whose last section, 'Other Modernisms', fails even here, at the end, to find room among chapters on 'Modernism and Gender', 'Modernism Queered' and 'Global Modernisms' for examination of modernism's relation to rural experiences, culture and sites.
10. 'Rural', in *Oxford English Dictionary*.
11. Williams, *Keywords*, p. 81.
12. 'Rural', in *Online Etymological Dictionary*.
13. Preface, p. vii.
14. 'Recognizing Rusticity', p. 7.
15. Ching and Creed, 'Recognizing Rusticity', p. 28.
16. 'Persistence of Pastoral', pp. 181–2.
17. Clive Bell, p. 10.
18. Poggioli, p. 40.
19. See Walkowitz and Mao's introduction to *Bad Modernisms* for a useful definition and brief history of new modernist studies.
20. 'Recognizing Rusticity', p. 22.
21. Rouse, 'South Country', p. 71.
22. Blunden, *The Face of England*, p. 120.
23. *The Country and the City*, p. 129.
24. See Matless, *Landscape and Englishness*, and Burchardt, *Paradise Lost*. For a sense of the history of the 'Englishness' thesis to which these studies respond, see Wiener's landmark *English Culture and the Decline of the Industrial Spirit* and period studies by Colls and Dodd, *Englishness*; Boyes, *The Imagined Village*; and Giles and Middleton, *Writing Englishness*. See Mandler, 'Against "Englishness"', for a compelling refutation of the Englishness thesis.
25. Cavaliero, p. 100.
26. See, for example, Brassley, Burchardt and Thompson, *English Countryside*; Outka, *Consuming Traditions*; and Clewell's *Modernism and Nostalgia*.
27. Brassley, Burchardt and Thompson, *English Countryside*, p. 6.
28. Goodman and Mathieson, p. 2.

Part I

Networks

Chapter 1

Ringing the Changes: Thomas Hardy's Communication Networks

Edward Allen

One morning during the hot summer of 1908, Thomas Hardy looked in on his club, the Athenaeum, to check his post and to pen a grievance. 'I *am* getting tired of London, & think of returning Monday, or perhaps Tuesday – Monday if I can,' he advised his bed-ridden wife, dithering and perhaps a little depressed to realise that some things get worse before they get better: 'I have to lunch at the House of Commons to-morrow, which is my last "function" I think.'[1] No written evidence survives to tell us anything juicy about his attendance at this 'function' – the inverted commas probably say it all – so for Hardy we may assume that lunch went down without a hiccup, an unremarkable end to a summer spent railing between Dorset and the capital. Yet we can *picture* that function. Filed away in the House of Commons Library for the best part of seventy years until gifted to the National Portrait Gallery in 1974, a sequence of photographs remains a testament to life on parliament's river terrace, and shows Thomas Hardy at his function.[2] It is easy to spot him: he is the only one who has refused to dispense with his hat, and in the first properly choreographed picture he appears to be glancing out of shot, against the grain of the composition (Figure 1.1). The glance, as it turns out, is an expression of movement, because in the next picture he is to be seen nearing the end of the back row, having followed his nose and flouted the instructions of the camera-eye (Figure 1.2). We will never know the cause of this disruptive behaviour – impatience, whimsy, a call of nature – but it is quite possible that the restive writer had spied a kindred spirit at the edge of the gathered party. For there, positioned at the end of the front row, can be seen a figure no more used to standing still than Thomas Hardy, and one who may also have deemed himself an outsider in this political company: the inventor, engineer and entrepreneur Guglielmo Marconi, whose contribution to 'wireless telegraphy' had already made waves in the British press.

This chapter aims to think imaginatively about the sources and

Figure 1.1 Thomas Hardy spies an opportunity. National Portrait Gallery.

Figure 1.2 Thomas Hardy approaches Guglielmo Marconi (seated front left). National Portrait Gallery.

channels of rural communication at the *fin de siècle*, and it begins with the thought that these apparently innocuous photographs – fusty and monochrome – may provide a more than usually colourful insight into the development of Hardy's modernity. At the time, his brush with Marconi may have looked to most bystanders the stuff of incongruity; today, we would call it a networking opportunity. And if, in bringing that familiar phrase to bear on Thomas Hardy, we detect the crackle of anachronism, it is a comfort to know that he may in fact have considered his encounter with Bologna's media giant well overdue. As to whether Marconi had figured yet on his radar, Hardy had teased the journalist William Archer some years before, in conversation, by seeming to confuse electromagnetism with the stuff of 'rural superstitions'; Hardy had not been drawn on the matter of 'thought-transference' but had nonetheless welcomed the chance to assure Archer and the readers of the *Pall Mall Magazine* that he knew who Marconi and Tesla were, and that 'the genuineness of wireless telegraphy' had by no means stretched him beyond belief.[3] True, he would continue to indulge a deep-seated conviction in 'the supernatural' – and a love of ghost stories in particular – but it does not follow that Hardy refused to acknowledge in later years the real-life magic of mass media, as biographers have sometimes implied, and the ways in which such media promised to render his home on the outskirts of Dorchester newly open to the interference of distant voices.

That promise of domestic polyphony has more often been characterised as a threat from Hardy's perspective, and the modernisation of his country house, Max Gate, a necessary evil: in the final years of his life, for instance, the house was furnished with a telephone connection and a wireless set, and although Florence Hardy 'was right to do this', Claire Tomalin concedes, it seems 'the master was too old to change his ways'.[4] Maybe it *is* too much to suppose that his sudden acquisition of a telephone code (Dorchester 43) altered the writer's attitude to discursive practices in and around his beloved Dorset, but as for wireless technology, there is good reason to believe that Marconi's equipment came to occupy a charmed place in the social fabric of Max Gate. That Hardy later claimed to have been 'inveigled' into buying the equipment must be considered a last-ditch attempt to play the country bumpkin, for we know that he soon found cause not only to value but also to upgrade his wireless, on account of its calming influence on the household (including his dog), and the manner in which it had sensitised him to the desires and capacity of a new kind of audience.[5] Whilst doubtful of the 'effect' broadcasting would have on the novel – a form he had forsaken, in any case, some years before – Hardy was alive to the idea that poems might fare rather well on the airwaves; 'it would in fact advertise them', he advised his publisher George Macmillan in March 1924, always keen to boost his work's circulation, and very possibly encouraged by the reception of his verse drama, *The Famous Tragedy of the Queen of Cornwall*, just the previous year.[6] Scholars have noticed before that Macmillan had been glad, on the author's behalf, to accept the BBC's plan to broadcast the play on its opening night in Dorchester, and it has always been understood that this plan had been scuttled at the eleventh hour by a decision to treat listeners instead to Mendelssohn's take on *A Midsummer Night's Dream*.[7] This may not be the whole story, as this clipping from the *Dorset Daily Echo*, dated 29 November 1923, makes plain:

> Transmission of his New Tragedy
> Through the courtesy of the Marconi Wireless Telegraph Company, a special receiving set was installed at Max Gate, the residence of Mr. Hardy, by Captain R. M. Dawes (the company's district agent). By this means the author 'listened-in' to the play, and expressed his great appreciation of the perfect reception. The transmission of the tragedy from the Bournemouth Station was very well received in all parts of Dorset. The transmission was made by means of a land wire from Dorchester to Bournemouth, and the play was then transmitted by wireless.
>
> Two microphones had been arranged in the hall, one suspended in front of the stage and another at the side.[8]

The dramatist not only listened in, according to this forgotten source, but listened in *appreciatively* to the efforts of the Hardy Players, for whom the production would remain a highlight, as well as a compelling instance of their bid to establish a voice for the company that would sound beyond the borders of Wessex.[9] In this case, Bournemouth was the limit. Yet how suggestive it is to imagine Hardy sitting there in Max Gate at the grand old age of eighty-three, impressed by 'the perfect reception', and perhaps minded to acknowledge how far his provider had come since that 'function' on parliament's river terrace, back in 1908. No longer perched at the end of a row, trying to get into shot, Marconi had become a household name.

It is not at all surprising that this sound event has eluded critical attention, nor that its presumed cancellation has done little to encourage scholars to think of Hardy as a media darling. The wireless outfit in Bournemouth (station 6BM) had been operational for only a matter of weeks in November 1923, and the BBC itself – a company, and not yet a corporation – was still fumbling its way towards a robust policy on matters of commissioning and repurposing content; so much of the company's early history must seem, even by today's standards, improvised and beleaguered, troubled at every turn by the conflicting interests of politicians, the Post Office, licence holders and a whole host of private schemes.[10] Verifying the company's day-to-day activities at this time poses numerous difficulties, and such difficulties are naturally compounded by the fact of the material conditions that pertain to a medium where, quite literally, anything goes: in the manner of its close relative, telephony, wireless broadcasting is at heart an ephemeral mode of communication, which was never really intended to operate in connection with any kind of storage facility. It is difficult to know what Thomas Hardy would have made of a device that streams and stores as a matter of course, though one suspects he would have greeted it in much the same mood as the farming folk greet the latest technological attempt to improve upon the 'broadcast' method in *The Mayor of Casterbridge* (1886): 'Its arrival created about as much sensation in the corn-market as a flying machine would create at Charing Cross.'[11]

The object of fascination in *The Mayor of Casterbridge* is not a radio, of course, but a seed drill, though it is striking that one witness to the contraption's appearance, the newcomer Lucetta Templeman, assumes the narrator's perspective in likening it to 'a musical instrument': '"Why, it is a sort of agricultural piano," she said' (p. 238). Hers is a lone voice amidst the general hubbub of speculation, and Donald Farfrae is swift to scotch her suggestion that the '"wonderful new drill . . . is a stupid thing"' (p. 240). It is a small but telling exchange, not least because it forces into relation precisely the matters of moneyed innovation and shifting cultural standards that lie at the centre of Hardy's troubled pastoral vision. Farfrae is by no means an unmusical soul, yet he is deaf to all but the machine's practical relevance, and the air of fancy that characterises Templeman's assessment is easily dispelled as he makes the case for the ways in which the seed drill has already '"revolutionize[d]"' agrarian procedure in other regions of England, to the east and north (pp. 240–1). For him, as for other green-fingered grafters in Hardy's fiction – Gabriel Oak, Angel Clare – the wish to master his craft does not amount so much to a rejection of labour-saving technology as to its elegiac embrace, a sort of heart-rending desire to meet the demands of an industry in transition and to toughen others to the idea that their prospects are bound up with the future of the machine: '"Ay: ay . . . It must be so!"'[12] By urging the residents of Casterbridge to modernise, Farfrae not only recognises the lie of the land, but also – it may be unconsciously – comes that little bit closer to apprehending the technology in question as a mode of communication. If, as Jonathan Sterne reminds us, the root of technology is '*techné*' – a practical art, and a progenitor of technique, which sits somewhere between craft and creation – then it is important to acknowledge that even a technology that threatens to efface '"the romance of the sower"' requires a loving touch, the performance of 'embodied knowledge', and 'the unfolding of a sensibility' that has the affective potential to move and inspire others.[13] Farfrae's sensibility is not yet 'cultured', in Sterne's terms, in the sense that the local community in which he intends to operate has no feeling for the practical necessity of the seed drill, nor for the ways in which it may improve numerous labourers' quality of life. As it is, Farfrae's commitment to his profession is wilfully mistaken by Templeman, who considers his 'mercantile' devotion to the machine a hindrance to further interaction. '"Well, don't forsake the machine for us,"' she teases, and with that, she and Elizabeth-Jane Newson vanish from the scene (p. 241). Of the seed drill, needless to say, we hear no more.

This interest in farming technology – it may seem a deviation – was prompted by an attempt to characterise the mode of attention that applies so often in Hardy's fiction to the sound of progress in rural places. Although, technically speaking, it lies a country mile from Marconi's wireless set, the seed drill has the curious effect of unearthing a knot of attitudes that would resurface in debates about network-building at the turn of the century. Some of these attitudes are deep-rooted, pertaining as they do to the manner in which agricultural communities are bound together, and the ways in which such communities expect to commune with the land, cultivating a sustainable relationship with it by resisting efforts to streamline the means of production. Other sorts of attitudes are not so easily defined, and have to do rather with a lingering, contrary suspicion of technologies that appear to do their work without leaving a trace. In this respect, the seed drill and wireless are alike; but in this respect, too, they depart in material effect from the technology that has come to absorb recent critics – electric telegraphy – and which seems to have absorbed Hardy in his lifelong struggle to articulate the nature of urban–rural connection. This is a technology that has sparked, once again, a debate among readers of Victorian fiction, in large part because so many novels of the period attest to its startling tangibility. In the opening pages of Hardy's eighth published novel, *A Laodicean* (1880–1), the architect and hero of the piece, George Somerset, hears 'a single wire of telegraph' before he sees it, and upon following it into deepest darkest Wessex is prompted to interpret its humming incursion of the neighbourhood as a symptom of modernity: 'the presence of this mark of civilization seemed to signify that [Sleeping-Green's] inhabitants were not quite so far in the rear of their age as might be imagined' (p. 16). From the very first, Somerset senses that this 'friendly wire' is carrying something more than mere information, for it tingles with a kind of lyrical energy too, which naturally resists casual decryption, and therefore serves to entice him even further off the beaten path. 'The wire sang on overhead with dying falls and melodious rises that invited him to follow,' and that is exactly what Somerset does – '[p]lunging with it across the down' until he reaches Stancy Castle – little knowing that the mass of 'musical threads' will enable him to form an attachment with the Gothic pile that will seem at times a queer domestic harmony (pp. 16–17).[14]

Far, indeed, from engendering 'the intellectual and moral kinship of all mankind', for which the narrator believes the telegraph has become a symbol, the wire connecting Stancy Castle with outlying settlements only appears to make a mess of social relations in the neighbourhood.[15] There are, in several senses, no clean lines when it comes to electric telegraphy: most of the characters like to tell themselves that 'speed and easy frequency' number among its new-fangled virtues, but rather than rendering far-flung interaction more efficient, the technology breeds a sort of time-consuming materiality that has a way of corrupting, as well as collapsing, the distance between hamlet and town, feudal England and *le gai Paris* (p. 241). Its chief correlative, of course, is the clandestine telegram, the like of which is increasingly felt to clog up and preoccupy the household of Hardy's dexterous heroine, Paula Power. Just as some of us struggle today to ignore the ping of mobile phones, alerting us to new messages and notifications, the castle's mistress feels obliged to tend the 'telegraph instrument' whenever it shows 'signs of life', and the haptic aspect of the telegrapher's devotion – coaxing code into papery message – is everywhere felt in a novel in which criminal ingenuity knows no bounds, least of all those of the country and the city (p. 214). It stands to reason that if it is possible to 'concoct' a telegram, as one character dares to boast, then it is quite easy to 'forge' one too (pp. 276, 324). In doing so, the harbingers of modernism who intrude upon the territory of Sleeping-Green encourage the locals not to consider connecting with the wider world, but to think ever more carefully about what is at stake when you know that 'intercepting' has become the latest pastime (p. 255).[16]

It will be clear that the ubiquitous telegram provides a particularly rich illustration of the condition to which J. Hillis Miller once gestured when he wrote of the 'distance and desire' that give shape to Hardy's fiction.[17] As we have seen, there is only so much we can say and surmise about the novelist's broadcasting – of sound or seed – but so long as we remain sensitive to the subtle operation of radio's prototype, telegraphy, there will always be ways for us to gauge Hardy's warmth for the kind of romance that belongs in a media ecology. His novels have long provided an optic through which one might survey 'the difference between burgh and champaign', of course; but the effect of recuperating his telegraphic impulses, in recent criticism, has been to expose the lesser-known regions of Hardy country, and so to do what Raymond Williams advised shortly after Miller, which is to think of Hardy as a 'border' case, caught 'between love of place and an experience of change'.[18] The hinterland of Sleeping-Green in *A Laodicean*, the 'strange town' of Hardy's ninth novel, *Two on a Tower* (1882), a coastal railway terminus in *The Well-Beloved* (1897), which was to be the last stop on his journey with the novel form – these and other neglected locations have begun to come to light, have begun to seem *legible* to us, because telegraphy has shown us the way.[19] To explore the locations of these late, peculiar novels might be to apprehend a truth about Hardy's unhurried approach to registering media innovation, yet it is worth noting that he had always had his finger on the pulse when it comes to circulating telegrams. In March 1871, not six months after the government's move to extend the Telegraph Acts of 1868–9, Hardy had published his first novel, *Desperate Remedies*, a capersome book, long in the making, and one that bears all the traces of a lately nationalised telegraph network.[20] There are many odd things about the style and diction of *Desperate Remedies*, as reviewers had been quick to notice, but one utterance that could not be termed an oddity – for it comes and goes like any other idiom – is use of the verb *to telegraph* towards the end of Volume II. Indeed, whatever its crimes of characterisation or design, *Desperate Remedies* is remarkable for the mood of sheer normality in which its conspirators and informants go about their business. '"I'll go and telegraph,"' Edward Springrove declares, and no one so much as turns a hair (p. 265).

It would not be an exaggeration to say that some of the most fruitful work on Hardy in recent years has taken telegraphy as its subject, freely mixing matters of narrative intrigue with the machinations of his late lyric poetics.[21] Where the previous generation proved unresponsive to the 'multitudinous series of raps' that momentarily lends a rhythm to the plotting of *Desperate Remedies*,[22] this one has been careful to pick up on such signals, and to detect in Hardy's later fiction 'the spectral affiliation of a disembodied modern culture'.[23] Yet it may be that the risk for scholars now has to do with mistaking this instantiation of modernism for a sort of proxy arrangement, whereby Hardy is implicitly understood to have found his region wanting – unstructured, technophobic, barren to all but home-grown talents – and so to have gone in search of metropolitan solutions. That he did so quite literally by decamping to London provides the story of *Thomas Hardy: Half a Londoner* (2016), in which Mark Ford reminds us that Hardy's journey to the capital in April 1862 as an apprentice architect gave rise to a five-year sojourn that would equip him in ways he can scarcely have foreseen on the platform of Dorchester station. '[H]ad he not launched himself into a London life,'

Ford contends, 'it is hard to see how he could have gained, for all his intellectual precocity, the kinds of perspective on Dorset that would eventually enable him to transform it into Wessex' (p. 13). According to this timely and compelling intervention in the author's biography, one would be hard pressed 'in even his most regionally circumscribed novels' to overlook 'the spectral presence of the city';[24] and you can see what Ford means when you think back to something as frivolous as the provenance of Tess's 'morning costume', which to her seems nothing less than heaven-sent: '"How thoughtful you've been!"' she coos to her guardian Angel. '"No, no, Tess; just an order to a tradeswoman in London – nothing more."'[25]

Nothing will come of nothing, of course, and for Hardy the city was always something. To put it another way, as David Trotter has, London remained a crucial coordinate for the architect-turned-writer because in London 'he had invested in networking'.[26] There are good reasons to pursue this line of thought, and so to wonder, for instance, 'about the London Hardy's returning natives bring with them on their return to Wessex'.[27] With a view to transposing that thought, we might attend by way of conclusion to the connection implied in this book's title, *Rural Modernity in Britain*, and to one instance of networking that Hardy's natives do not have to leave Wessex to understand, not because the city has not got it but because the country has known this network all along:

> As they came out of church the ringers swung the bells off their rests, and a limited peal of three notes broke forth – the power of expressing joy in such a small parish ranging no further. Passing by the tower with her husband on the path to the gate she could feel the vibrant air humming round them from the louvred belfry in the circle of sound, and it matched the highly-charged mental atmosphere in which she was living.[28]

Dressed in her morning costume, Tess exits the church with Angel and a spring in her step. She has already assumed the habit of a metropolitan – a native gone rogue – for she believes that her marriage certificate will in fact fulfil the function of a one-way ticket. '"We shall go away, a very long distance,"' Tess thinks to herself earlier in Chapter 33, '"hundreds of miles from these parts, and such as this can never happen again, and no ghost of the past reach there"' (p. 208). Just for a moment, however, as Tess floats through the churchyard on her wedding day, all thoughts of escape seem to evaporate in the wake of the pealing bells. It is not the first time we have witnessed Tess tuning into the ecclesiastical soundscape: in Chapter 23, in the early days of their courtship, Tess allows Angel to whisk her across a flooded lane in a flurry of sport and muscular piety ('they could hear the church-bell calling – as yet nearly a mile off') (p. 142). So we know that a peal, however 'limited', commands a particular power, and a particular kind of attention, in this sorry tale, such that it is difficult not to hear the bells of Chapter 33 as a belated wake-up call. For once the church bells have 'died away', Tess has nowhere to turn but her wedding carriage, whose associations are not lost on one who believes she has seen the vehicle before, and which consequently prompts her to worry that she is to figure in the next chapter of '"the legend of the D'Urberville coach"' (p. 213). Rather than transporting her to pastures new, the carriage in fact signals the next leg of a long, spiritual journey that will end as any crime of passion must in this period – with the striking of the hour and with proof of her execution (p. 397).

Tess's nuptial scene reverberates beyond its immediate occasion, yet one could be forgiven for not feeling especially rapt by this 'circle of sound' that envelops the heroine. 'The rural peals of the nineteenth century, which have become for us the sound of another time,' laments Alain Corbin, 'were *listened to*, and evaluated according to a system of affects that is now lost to us':

> They bear witness to a different relation to the world and to the sacred as well as to a different way of being inscribed in time and space, and of experiencing time and space. The reading of the auditory environment would then constitute one of the procedures involved in the construction of identities, both of individuals and of communities. Bell ringing constituted a language and founded a system of communication that has gradually broken down.[29]

The beauty of Corbin's writing on campanology consists in an elegiac quality that we hear played out time and again in the pealing of the nineteenth-century novel. '[T]he vibrant air humming round them' amounts in *Tess of the D'Urbervilles* to a medium that is rich in semiotic possibility, and yet it speaks to the newly-wed in a language that is not easily parsed. For most listeners, of course, such spectacles of sound do not require much interpretative labour, but the burden of meaning frequently exceeds the basic stream of data in Hardy's fiction. In *The Return of the Native* (1878), the marriage of her son, Clym, reaches the ear of Mrs Yeobright on the crest of a breeze – 'the notes of distant bells, gaily starting off in a peal' – and as so often in this novel, the intrusion signals a plot twist: '"Then it is over," she murmured. "Well, well! and life too will be over soon"' (p. 214). There is some truth in this rumination, as it transpires, though the stirring of intuition is likely to seem less uncanny when you realise that it is the product of 'the ringers at East Egdon', whose opening *round* – 'one, two, three, four, five' – will soon break out into a new sequence. In campanological circles this is called *change ringing*; for Mrs Yeobright, it is the beginning of the end.

Hardy knew what bells can do. His stories and poems are full of them:

wedding peals, death knells, 'dumb' bells, bells to dampen the 'buzz of groggy conversation', bells and tolls and sirens.[30] We hear this last kind of distress signal in the middle of *Desperate Remedies*, as the villagers clump around the fire, struggling to articulate a state of emergency:

> Several seemed paralysed at first, and stood transfixed, their rigid faces looking like red-hot iron in the glaring light. In the confusion a woman cried, 'Ring the bells backwards!' and three or four of the old and superstitious entered the belfry and jangled them indescribably. (p. 179)

The remedy, you might say, is desperate, and it is an act that must sound all the more wretched if you catch between these lines the sobbing of Shakespeare's Ophelia, whose own sense of alarm sadly falls on deaf ears ('And I . . ./Now see what noble and most sovereign reason/Like sweet bells jangled out of time and harsh').[31] Whatever literary undertones his writing seems to have absorbed, Thomas Hardy's affection and respect for bells stem in large part from a life lived on local terms, where the threat of changing circumstances – or mutability – is rarely more momentous than the threat of being muted altogether. In *Far from the Madding Crowd* (1874), we hear this apprehension shiver into recognisable form in the snowstorm of Chapter 11, as a bell 'los[es] its voice' amidst the 'chaotic sky-full of crowding flakes' (p. 75), and we see the anxiety creep once again into Hardy's thoughts on the occasion of editing his first wife's memoir, *Some Recollections*, upon her death in 1912:

> It was a very poor parish and the church had been a long while out of repair for want of funds [. . .]. The tower went on cracking from year to year and the bells remained in {the} little North Transept {to which they had been removed for safety} their mouths open upward. (p. 48)[32]

Some Recollections bears the tell-tale traces of a grieving husband. His annotations and emendations bespeak a twofold horror – the horror of his having got it all so dreadfully wrong, and a milder kind that has to do with Emma's faltering memory. In these lines, which recall Hardy's fateful secondment to St Juliot Church in March 1870, we see Emma returning to the site of her first sustained interaction with her husband-to-be; but we also see Hardy himself attempting to curate the scene, as though polishing up a memory that now requires, as the church once did, a bit of restoration. After all these years, the sentimental architect is still determined to do right by those neglected bells, whose 'safety' appears (in two ways) to be firmly in his hands.

In fiction as in fact, Hardy would remain alert to the art of bell ringing, partly because he could discern its network potential. Among the few theorists to think along these lines, John Durham Peters has lately recognised its affinity with the telegraph, which was harnessed for similar reasons in the 1850s, not only to spread the news, but also 'to spread the news of when exactly 1:00pm was' (p. 223). The delineation of time zones has a curiously resonant history, yet the special thing about bell ringing, in Hardy's tolling and telling, resides in its capacity to stall the otherwise harassed commuter, and so to heighten one's attention to other kinds of temporal configuration that have taken root in the Wessex soil:

> The wind, indeed, seemed made for the scene, as the scene seemed made for the hour. Part of its tone was quite special; what was heard there could be heard nowhere else. Gusts in innumerable series followed each other from the north-west, and when each one of them raced past the sound of its progress resolved into three. Treble, tenor, and bass notes were to be found therein. The general ricochet of the whole over pits and prominences had the gravest pitch of the chime. Next there could be heard the baritone buzz of a holly tree. Below these in force, above them in pitch, a dwindled voice strove hard at a husky tune, which was the peculiar local sound alluded to. Thinner and less immediately traceable than the other two, it was far more impressive than either. In it lay what may be called the linguistic peculiarity of the heath; and being audible nowhere on earth off a heath, it afforded a shadow of reason for the woman's tenseness, which continued as unbroken as ever.[33]

This is our first glimpse of Eustacia Vye, 'a closely wrapped female figure', whose relationship with Egdon Heath is beyond even the narrator's ken. Even so, the mystery of this 'scene' rather seems to arise from the interpretative challenges posed by the land beneath her feet and from the 'linguistic peculiarity' of a terrain that operates precisely as a sounding board. Stranger still, perhaps, is Hardy's suggestion that the tonal quality of the heath is consistent with a chime effect. Eustacia turns in due course from this musical drama, apparently unmoved by 'the tune still played on the dead heath-bells'; for the moment, however, she and time stand still, together, in a pleasing state of 'tenseness', as though prompted to do so by the 'dwindled voice' that struggles to rise above the strong northwesterly (p. 58). Hardy would return to Egdon Heath, and to the problems of mapping it, but rarely with the same feeling for the tonal intersection that gives Eustacia pause for thought before she proceeds to broaden her horizons. Hers is a 'desponding reverie', yet there is some comfort in her knowing the reverie has a 'local' source.[34]

The aim of this chapter has been to sound out the limits of Thomas Hardy's modernity. It is a complicated brew. The temptation to perpetuate the orthodoxies of media history are strong in his case, especially given the recent turn in Hardy studies, which might encourage one to characterise his sometimes vicious enthusiasm for infrastructure as a hangover from his London days. In the spirit of remaining sensitive and open to the possibilities of a modernity that found ways to operate and make sense of itself on its own terms, in its own time, it behoves us to loosen our hold on the idea that all things modern originated amidst the termini and switchboards of urban life. To do so is sometimes easier said than done, and Hardy certainly struggled on occasion to resist the idea that London had become the purveyor of time itself, as when he tuned in on 31 December 1925 to hear 'Big Ben striking twelve'.[35] Yet nothing – not even a midnight broadcast – could mitigate his feeling in these years of upheaval that the country had somehow been nudged out of sync:

> Speaking of bells, I should like to ask cursorily why the old sets of chimes have been removed from nearly all our country churches. The midnight wayfarer, in passing along the sleeping village or town, was cheered by the outburst of a stumbling tune, which possessed the added charm of being probably heeded by no ear but his own. Or, when lying awake in sickness, the denizen would catch the same notes, persuading him that all was right with the world. But one may go half across England and hear no chimes at midnight now.[36]

Chiming and charming in equal measure, Hardy's dwindling vision of rural modernity may still give us the odd sleepless night.

In dialogue with: Chapter 6, '*Hiraeth* and Ambiguous Pastorals' (II: Landscapes) [rural fiction; regional pastoral]; Chapter 14, 'Eden in Sussex' (V: Wars) [modernist artists outside modernism; country churches].

Notes

1. Thomas Hardy to Emma Lavinia Hardy, [16 July 1908], p. 325.
2. The pictures in question are catalogued at the National Portrait Gallery in the 'remainder' collection: NPG x135567 – NPG x135569. They are doubly attributed to Roland Parker Stone and to his father, Sir John Benjamin Stone, the Member of Parliament for East Birmingham (1895–1910) and a distinguished photographer. The luncheon in question appears to have been thrown for the diplomat and Japanese Minister for Foreign Affairs, Jutaro Komura.
3. 'Real Conversations', p. 57.
4. Tomalin, p. 352. Writing of Hardy's mood at the turn of the century, Paul Turner similarly maintains that 'past–present contrasts in his own life meant more to Hardy then than new technology', p. 168.
5. Hardy to J. C. Squire, 3 June 1924, pp. 252–3. Hardy mentions in this letter that Squire's broadcast, 'An Appreciation of the Life and Work of Thomas Hardy', had been 'beautifully delivered'. Florence had written earlier the same year to John Drinkwater, announcing their wireless upgrade and intimating that the new set would 'amuse' her husband: Florence Hardy to John Drinkwater.
6. Hardy to George Macmillan, 8 March 1924, p. 240.

7. See, for instance, Paul Turner, *The Life*, p. 247; and Keith Wilson, *Thomas Hardy on Stage*, pp. 130–1.
8. [Anon.], 'Mr. Thomas Hardy "Listens In"', p. 1.
9. For more on the history of the Hardy Players, see Michael Millgate's biography, Chapter 28.
10. See Asa Briggs.
11. Hardy, *Mayor*, pp. 240, 238.
12. Hardy, *Mayor*, p. 240.
13. Hardy, *Mayor*, p. 240; Sterne, 'Communication as Techné', p. 92.
14. For more on the 'queer effects of communication machines' in *A Laodicean*, see Kate Thomas, *Postal Pleasures*, p. 128.
15. Hardy, *A Laodicean*, p. 18.
16. It is worth acknowledging, as John Schad has, that Hardy added this instance of interception when he came to revise the serial novel for single-volume publication in 1881 (see 'Notes', p. 409). The addition has the twofold effect of emphasising Captain De Stancy's villainy and of pointing up the way in which Hardy had come, in the process of writing and rereading the novel, to relish the possibility of foul play in the arena of telecommunications.
17. Miller, *Thomas Hardy: Distance and Desire.*
18. Hardy, *Mayor*, p. 95; Williams, *The Country and the City*, p. 284.
19. *Two on a Tower: A Romance*, p. 233; *The Pursuit of the Well-Beloved* and *The Well-Beloved*, p. 197.
20. The Telegraph Acts of 1868–9, and their extension in 1870, brought the telegraph network under the auspices of the General Post Office (GPO), rendering the service at once affordable and accessible to people across the British Isles. For two quite different accounts, see Ken Beauchamp, *History of Telegraphy*, pp. 51–93; and Roland Wenzlhuemer, *Connecting the Nineteenth-Century World*, pp. 163–210.
21. See, for instance, Karin Koehler, *Thomas Hardy and Victorian Communication*; and Julian Wolfreys, *Thomas Hardy*, esp. Chapters 3–4.
22. *Desperate Remedies*, p. 266.
23. Wolfreys, *Dickens to Hardy*, p. 213.
24. Ford, p. 11.
25. Hardy, *Tess of the D'Urbervilles*, p. 206.
26. Trotter, review of Mark Ford, *Thomas Hardy: Half a Londoner*, p. 127.
27. Trotter, p. 129.
28. *Tess*, p. 213.
29. Corbin, p. xix.
30. 'No Bell-Ringing: A Ballad of Durnover', pp. 911–12; *A Laodicean*, p. 369.
31. *Hamlet*, pp. 292–3.
32. Emma Hardy, *Some Recollections*, p. 48. Thomas Hardy's revisions appear here in curly brackets.
33. *The Return of the Native*, p. 56.
34. *The Return of the Native*, p. 59.
35. Hardy, *Personal Notebooks*, p. 92.
36. Hardy, 'Memories of Church Restoration', p. 212.

Chapter 2

Change in the Village: Filming Rural Britain

Michael McCluskey

The village has served as a longstanding model for British national identity. Changes to the village are ways of discussing the broader changes that shape the nation, and – in the interwar period – the seeming stability of traditional village life served as a counter-narrative to the disruptions brought about by modernity. In their critique of contemporary life in Britain, *Culture and Environment: A Training in Critical Awareness* (1933), F. R. Leavis and Denys Thompson turned to the work of George Bourne (a pseudonym of George Sturt), a writer who documented the changes he saw in village life a generation earlier in his books *Change in the Village* (1912) and *The Wheelwright's Shop* (1923). Leavis and Thompson bring in these examples as evidence of the social changes they want to emphasise, but Bourne's work is more nuanced than they let on. As the Introduction to *Rural Modernity in Britain* demonstrates, Bourne was one of many commentators that saw village populations neither as completely resistant to (or even ignorant of) the opportunities brought about by modernity nor as receptacles for the ideas espoused by mostly urban-based commentators uncomfortable with the changes they saw around them. This chapter brings amateur film-makers to these discussions and considers what moving images of rural Britain from the 1920s and 1930s can tell us about the changes faced by these communities and the ways in which film featured as a response to them. It focuses on films that depict village life in different parts of Britain, made by men and women who used the technology of cinema to take stock of the activities occurring around them. They document the 'change in the village' that Bourne and others describe and capture the rituals that continued – or were revitalised – during a period that saw shifts in village economies, infrastructure and social interactions. These films overlap with interwar fiction and non-fiction, but they also offer access to places and exchanges otherwise absent from these familiar depictions. As social documents they present a complex portrait of rural life and provide rich material for studies of social history, interwar literature and amateur cinema, a growing field in film, media and cultural studies.

Amateur film-making increased in popularity in this period as cameras became more portable and less expensive. Film-makers participated in the broader documentary activities of the interwar years, activities that included the explosion of publications about the English countryside. Films made by the rural residents themselves challenge the image of the rural idyll presented in these celebrations of country life and provide visible evidence of what Patricia Zimmermann describes as 'an historical process of social control over representation' (p. xv). As Christopher Bailey contends, 'rural communities have been participants in, rather than victims of, processes of social and economic restructuring',[1] and this chapter considers how rural film-making provided a means of participation. The films featured here assert a modern rural identity that at times sits at odds with widespread representations of the countryside from the period and that lingers in more recent studies of interwar Britain. They also challenge the contentions of Leavis, Thompson and other interwar commentators that new technologies were disrupting traditional forms of community. These films not only document community activities and the close-knit relationships that undergird them but also are instantiations themselves of the new forms of community that emerged as a result of technologies including cinema.

Documenting village modernity

Writing in 1936, Sydney Jones presented modernity as a crucial part of village revitalisation:

> Meanwhile the villages are alive again with gramophones and the wireless, telephones, the Grid system, movement on the roads, mechanized agriculture, National Park production, the canning industry, and Government quotas [. . .]. Reading the signs of the times, the energetic parsons strive to keep spiritual and social balance among the villagers. Motor 'bus services connect almost everywhere, gaily painted petrol devices have displaced the old parish pumps, roadside inns and tea-gardens are busy, village stocks now make resting-places for tired hikers and white lines on the roads point to an outer world beyond. The villagers have risen to present opportunities. Good luck to them. (p. 36)

This endorsement of rural modernity and the successful integration of the old and the new were the subjects of state-sponsored films that encouraged the adoption of these new practices through their own anatomies of the modern village. *To-Day We Live* (1937) uses an elderly woman as the spokesperson for change. She explains the shifting patterns of behaviour in village life as the rural bus service provides access to jobs and entertainments in nearby towns. While this opened up opportunities, it reduced the role of the village as social centre and, as F. G. Thomas claimed, could lead to the 'disintegration of rural life'.[2] This trend could be countered, the film contends, through the construction of a village hall to host activities that might bring rural residents back together. The village hall was an interwar intervention in rural community life, a response to the social disintegration that many writers described. The film promotes the construction of such a hall, partially paid for by a grant from the film's funder, the National Council of Social Service.

The film *Around the Village Green* (1937) begins with the announcement '[t]he old order is changing'. As its title suggests, the film uses an unnamed village to catalogue the changes that have come to rural communities in recent years and to explain how these changes have improved the economic and social lives of rural residents. 'There's hardly a thatched cottage that hasn't got its radio, and old as well as new cottages are wired for electricity,' the film's narrator tells us alongside images of an idyllic village similar to those seen in the many books about rural Britain published in the 1930s. These images and the film's commentary offer examples of the ways in which new technologies have been integrated into the everyday lives of interwar villagers. 'Modern transport', such as 'the development of a countrywide system of buses', has enlarged 'the scope of village life' without spoiling its charm, and 'community halls are also being built to attract social activities back to the village'.

These documentary films and publications such as those by Jones and Thomas use the village to intervene in wider debates about land use, modernisation and the state of the nation. The documentary films in particular were made expressly to inform audiences about the opportunities available to rural communities and to show that modern services need not disrupt traditional ways of life. As a contemporary review of *Around the Village Green* stated, the film 'presents a well-balanced picture of tradition and innovation in an English village, which is not sentimental nor exaggerated'.[3] Indeed, the underlying argument of both films is that, for village life to continue, residents must adopt the practices put on screen and successfully balance tradition and innovation. The aims of amateur films about rural villages are not as explicit, and many of them might have been made with no express aim in mind other than entertainment. Nevertheless, the images they construct – and the act of filming itself – can help us to understand how new forms of transport, commerce and community-building were integrated into existing ways of life.

Village biographies

One of the most popular genres of interwar amateur film was the 'village biography', a term used here for the first time to identify this genre. Village biographies are brief films that introduce viewers to the people, places, activities and history of a particular village. These films have their parallel in the fictional and non-fictional literary portraits of village life that also proliferated in this period. William Beach Thomas's *The Happy Village* (1928), Francis Brett Young's *Portrait of a Village* (1937), Adrian Bell's *Men and the Fields* (1939) and even the more fantastical stories about the village of Mortmere written by Christopher Isherwood and Edward Upward in the late 1920s all share an approach similar to the cinematic village biographies made by amateur film-makers. Rather than having a structured plot, they present brief sketches of village life in this period of transition, a period in which the seeming 'standardization of people' was wiping away local and regional identities, and new forms of transport and communication were eroding the rural community.[4] As a particular genre of rural amateur film, village biographies challenge both these claims. They provide evidence of the persistence of local traditions and social interactions, and they show how the modern machinery of film-making introduced a new form of community building.

Our Village (1935) opens with a shot of the local church, the traditional heart of village life, then moves on to the pub and the local manor house, and ends with a public celebration to mark the 1935 Jubilee. The film maps out different village meeting places and becomes one itself as the recording and editing of moving images bring together people and places in Speldhurst, Kent. The title *Our Village* indicates that this is meant to be an insular production: that is, intended to be screened for the people of the village. Intertitles provide information that is meant to prompt viewers with a knowledge of Speldhurst rather than explain sequences to an outsider. The two men who appear on screen after the opening shot of the church are not identified; an intertitle that follows states 'Funds? No difficulty at all – only a matter of another gala week!' The presumed joke is that this is the local vicar thinking of ideas to raise money for the church. While the scene becomes legible to the outsider with the juxtaposition of church, men and intertitle, it is a sequence constructed for those with insider knowledge of all the figures involved.

In the Yorkshire village of Fenwick, the local vicar, Reverend George Allan, filmed scenes of everyday life in the interwar period. His compilations, *Fenwick Events of 1931*, *Fenwick Events of 1933* and *Fenwick Events of 1934*, present portraits of the village community during his residency. *Fenwick Events of 1931* follows a format similar to that of *Our Village* and other village biographies made by residents themselves. The film presents a series of portraits of people and places with intertitles that knowingly wink to a presumed local audience, yet which are not indecipherable to those unfamiliar with Fenwick. The 'Fenwick youngster' introduced by intertitle, for example, is in fact an elderly man almost Victorian in appearance, working in a garden. Other people include the local teacher, the postman, the blacksmith: figures that appear in many village biographies. (The introduction of this cast of characters is one of the features of this genre of amateur film and an indicator that most, if not all, of these were intended to be screened for these people and the villagers that know them.)

In *Linthwaite* (1938), the local teacher, Lucy Fairbank, is the film-maker and presents individual portraits of residents framed in doorways, as well as a large community gathering to celebrate the anniversary of the village church. *Personalities in Hovingham Village* (1930s compilation) and other films of this Yorkshire village were made by Colonel Sir William Worsley, the owner of the estate that included the village itself. This compilation shows construction scenes around the village such as digging a drain, framing a new building, masonry work and surveying, as well as the personalities familiar to village residents such as the local policeman.

The cinematic village biographies described above (as well as many others) were made by local residents, seemingly for local residents. However, village biographies were also a touristic mode of cinema, one in which the camera is made complicit in the act of consuming rural areas as beauty spots and heritage sites. The Barnes brothers were twin film-makers who made several films in the 1930s, including *Chilham: A Kentish Village* (1934) and *Lenham: A Kentish Village* (1936). *Chilham* opens with an explanatory intertitle establishing the history of the village and linking it to Julius Caesar and Roman Britain; a later intertitle notes that the church is mentioned in the 'Domesday Book'. The film pans across the Tudor buildings of the village square (Figure 2.1), and successive shots show the local pub, churchyard and Chilham Mill. *Lenham* follows a similar pattern. The opening intertitle connects the village to British history by noting the charter granted to it by Henry III, and later ones pick out the dates of historic buildings. The details read like information prepared for a school project and, in fact, the Barnes brothers (born in 1920) were schoolboys when they made their 1930s films. These schoolboy productions, however, are self-consciously packaged as professional films with detailed credits at the beginning about the role each brother played. While the brothers made fiction films as well, these village biographies suggest that they

Figure 2.1 The village of Chilham, where the church is mentioned in the Domesday Book. Film still from *Chilham: A Kentish Village*, 1934, John and William Barnes, courtesy of Screen Archive South East.

believed such films of rural life were also marketable and could help them to make their name: another indication of the popularity of village images at this time.

These films document what appear to be thriving villages and celebrate community activities and local traditions. Village biographies offer scenes of annual fetes, local interpretations of national events, and traditional village jobs such as blacksmith and joiner. While they might be read as a sign of resistance to claims that village life was disintegrating, they could also be seen as direct responses to change in the village, a way of creating a lasting record before such scenes and people disappeared for good. Village biographies, then, are also interventions in the broader process of cultural cataloguing of the period and contribute to the inventory of activities, identities and industries disappearing amid national modernisation.

Village industries

The interwar period saw the decline of some village industries, the emergence of new ones, and – for many – the transition to a service economy that provided tourists with 'a view of its past in its present'.[5] In his fictionalised *Portrait of a Village*, Francis Brett Young notes the appeal of 'a village of unindustrialized England perpetually preserved' (p. 13) but goes on to show that no such interwar village exists. His portrait includes examples of the opportunities and disappointments brought on by village modernity:

> the petrol age, which has carried George Mason up in the world from a state of mere dabbler in the elementary mechanics of bicycles to that of a garage proprietor, a 'stockist' of tyres and spare parts, and the owner of the brown bus, has reduced poor Mr. Webber, a craftsman without a job, to the condition of retailer of dog leads and muzzles. (p. 23)

In addition, the village shop has suffered, as customers are able to get to larger towns more easily and visit 'Woolworth's buzzing counters' (p. 19). Adrian Bell also describes the impact of modernity on village economies in *Men and the Fields* and notes the decline of small village mills, as larger producers could supply packaged flour and grains more cheaply and easily.

Interwar amateur films document these shifts and present moving images of a diverse range of village industries. A 1923 film shows the work of the Deanston Mill in rural Perthshire; another from 1935 presents the Glenboig Clayworks. Jenny Brown made several films about rural life in Scotland in the 1930s and after, including crofting and fishing, and her work was recognised by John Grierson, who included one of her films in the library of the GPO Film Unit, the training ground for the first generation of British documentary film-makers. Lucy Fairbank's film of Linthwaite presents a long-distance shot of the Mallinson and Sons wool textile mill, and a successive shot shows workers returning to the village. Farming, of course, features in interwar amateur films, and while many capture the horse-drawn plough, others, such as Sussex's *Elsted Manor Farms* (1932–48), document the mechanisation of agriculture. In addition to farming, one of the frequent images is rural craft work. The loss of traditional craft industries was of particular concern to interwar commentators, and this attention made those that still pursued such craft work objects of fascination. Publications positioned village craftsmen and women as heritage sites in themselves, something for tourists to seek out on excursions into rural Britain. Dying craft industries were tied to a thriving tourist industry: traditional labour linked to economic modernity.

Interwar amateur films offer additional evidence of this sustained interest in craft workers, the seemingly 'living relics' of an older way of life that could render any village a living museum – albeit a museum with modern services, as these films also demonstrate.[6] The film *Chair Bodging and Chair Making in the Chiltern Hills* (1934–5) ostensibly documents 'the last of the bodgers' and their 'ancient craft', as the opening intertitle indicates. While the men that appear on screen are old, evidence that these are indeed the 'last of' their breed is not forthcoming and thus the film opens with the sort of sly suggestion that publications used to create an air of urgency; the film and the workers seem more important if the work is almost extinct. H. J. Massingham even included the bodger as one of the *Country Relics* he documents in his 1939 study. A bodger makes the rounded legs and stretchers of Windsor chairs (and other models) from local beechwoods. The film's opening sequence shows three bodgers working on location in the woods, where, traditionally, they also set up their temporary homes. As John Seymour explains, these workers 'would purchase a stand of trees, clear a space to set up their temporary living quarters and go about the business of selecting just the right trees from which to make the chair legs and stretchers' (p. 33). The film documents how bodging connects landscape with local industry; we see the source of the wood that will be made into chairs, and the workers for whom the land is both their (temporary) home and source of income. The film also demonstrates that this source of income was not exactly dying out for this 'village of woodworkers'. Another intertitle helps to explain that a '[m]ore mechanized' form of production has brought the industry more up to date but 'it still has use for craftsmen'. The film ends with scenes of a 'countryside factory' with much younger workers, an example of how an ancient industry could be adapted to a modern rural economy.

Another craft industry is shown in the 1930s compilation film *Country Magazine*: the making of traditional 'trug' baskets in the Sussex village of Herstmonceux. As in the film about bodging – and in the many films of rural craft making from this period – the emphasis is on the hands-on labour of a small-scale production process. The trugs are made by an unnamed craftsman, who begins by splitting pieces of wood into thin slats and then assembles a basket with other components. The sequence ends with a shot of completed baskets stacked together on the workshop floor and the name of the company, H. Reed and Son, clearly displayed on a sign above them. This final shot suggests the film might have been made as some sort of advertisement for the firm – a firm that still exists on the same site (though under the name The Truggery) where Ruben Reed starting making them in 1899.

These films about bodging and basket making are just two examples of documents that challenge the idea that 'the old ways of work' have died.[7] Leavis and Thompson turned to the wheelwright to make their argument that machines were killing off traditional forms of rural labour. Amateur films from this same period, however, show workers like the joiner and blacksmith as part of contemporary village life and demonstrate the sustained interest in rural craft work as both means of production and object of historic, touristic interest. As the bodgers are filmed (by local history enthusiast Eustace Alliott), they occasionally acknowledge the camera; one even waits for instructions, nods, then begins his handiwork. The act of filming renders these workers rural performers staging a sequence for an outsider in addition to going on with what the films suggests is their normal workday. Performing rurality was part of the tourist trade for many villages, and these films provide a glimpse of the encounter between the old world and the modern world promised by interwar writers on rural Britain. Modernisation put the village in 'fancy dress', Massingham complained, and the films provide many examples.[8]

Interwar amateur films show that the past not only could be 'resurrected' to appeal to modern consumers, as John Lowerson claims (p. 260), but also could be constructed on site through architectures that offer the 'commodified authentic' that Elizabeth Outka sees as part of 'the growing commercial possibilities of a nostalgic version' of rural England (p. 6). The film *Thatchers Old World Tea House* (1934) presents a model of such architecture and serves as a metaphor for the broader process of rural redevelopment. The camera captures the clearing of land, men using hand tools working with bricks and beams, a steamroller flattening out the car park, and a thatcher working on the roof of what would become a roadside tea house that catered mostly to passing motorists. Additional sequences show the business in operation and bunches of flowers sold near the entrance. The film captures the blend of old and new, tradition and modernity, that marked the interwar village's adaptations to modern life; the 'old world' could be resurrected for the modern consumer through the construction of a modern facility that catered to visitors.

The Barnes brothers' film *Lenham* points out the services the village offers in addition to its historic buildings. While, as noted above, this film follows a similar format to their earlier village biography of *Chilham*, it is much more interested in the village as potential tourist site. Cars and lorries are parked all around Lenham's village square, an indication of the village's accessibility and popularity. A close-up shot captures Ye Olde Checquers Tea Rooms (Figure 2.2), a place for refreshment and lodging named for what an earlier intertitle identifies as 'the old Market House, known as "the Chequers"', also in the village square. The two lingering shots of the tea rooms are included in the film's montage of village modernity. Shots of cars and lorries amid 'the picturesque half-timbered houses' cut to a shot of the village garage with

Figure 2.2 Ye olde village charm in Lenham, Kent. Film still from *Lenham: A Kentish Village*, 1936, John and William Barnes, courtesy of Screen Archive South East.

its sign 'Automobile Engineers'. This cuts to the tea rooms and finally a shot of a car moving through the square in front of the Dog and Bear, a historic site but also a 'commercial hotel', as the sign states. An intertitle notes that Queen Mary and Queen Elizabeth both stayed here, and the film sequence indicates that modern travellers are now welcome.

Films of interwar villages situate them solidly in 'the petrol age' that Brett Young describes in *Portrait of a Village* (p. 23), and document responses to the 'changing market conditions' faced by rural populations.[9] Services such as tea rooms appealed to the tourist market while other services such as rural buses and electricity created opportunities for the villagers themselves.

Village technologies

Through the technology of cinema, film-makers captured the technologies that connected rural villagers to the rest of Britain. While radio and telephone services greatly reduced the isolation of many villages, films from the 1920s and 1930s for the most part do not record the use of these devices, as lighting concerns made indoor filming a

Figure 2.3 Rural mobility: a motorized wheel chair in Kent. Film still from *Our Village*, 1935, E. R. Wood, courtesy of Screen Archive South East.

rare occurrence. Rather, interwar amateur films look outward at the forms of mobility and sources of energy that allowed for a 'Rural Awakening'.[10]

In his study of *The Changing Village* (1939), F. G. Thomas argues that the younger generation of rural residents was 'infatuated by mobility' (p. 20), but films suggest all ages took advantage of the bus services and delivery vans that moved into and out of the village. The film *Our Village* offers a direct challenge to Thomas's view that it was only the young who were interested in motorised forms of transport. Amid shots of people moving through the village, the film-maker includes an elderly woman in a motorised wheelchair (Figure 2.3). Most rural residents, however, relied on other forms of transport, particularly the bus service that linked rural areas to each other and to the greater variety of services offered in nearby market towns and cities.

As a 1933 article in *The Times* described, rural buses, 'with their constant windings backwards and forwards, are like shuttles weaving together the threads of rural life so that each strand becomes part of a pattern'.[11] The article links this modern service to rural craft to communicate the connecting thread that such transport offers otherwise isolated populations. Films weave the bus into the everyday activities they document and present the bus driver as a regular figure around the

Figure 2.4 The bus driver is a familiar sight in Hovingham. Film still from *Personalities in Hovingham*, 1930s compilation, Col. Sir William Worsley, courtesy of Sir William Worsley and Yorkshire Film Archive.

village. In *Personalities in Hovingham Village*, Worsley announces the appearance of the bus with the intertitle 'Any more for Malton?'. The line suggests an announcement made by the bus driver, who appears in the next sequence. Worsley films the bus starting off after a village stop and heading toward the camera, where it stops again. The next shot presents the driver next to his bus, just one of the familiar village personalities that Worsley documents (Figure 2.4). A similar shot of the driver posed next to his bus appears in *Our Village*.

Fairbanks begins her film of *Linthwaite* with a shot of the local church, a frequent opening shot in many village biographies. The scene is then interrupted by the arrival of the bus, which stops and allows several passengers to exit. The juxtaposition of the church and rural bus communicates tradition and modernity, and the way in which the rural bus service has been successfully integrated into the life of the village. The film *Fernhurst Village Bus* (c. 1936) makes this service the main feature and shows children and adults boarding a bus and waving out of the window. While some interwar writers like Thomas and Brett Young saw 'the top-heavy brown bus' as a threat to village life, others demonstrate its indispensability – even its ordinariness – in the lives of rural

Figure 2.5 The village petrol pump in use at Hovingham. Film still from *Personalities in Hovingham*, 1930s compilation, Col. Sir William Worsley, courtesy of Sir William Worsley and Yorkshire Film Archive.

populations. Amateur films present the village bus service as a sight as familiar as the local church, shop and school.

Films also suggest the pride villagers had in the energy sources that fuelled these activities. While the petrol pump was an object of scorn for many interwar commentators, film-makers feature it as another familiar, friendly part of the village. Petrol pumps 'were a particular target for moral outrage' in the interwar period,[12] and critics such as C. E. M. Joad linked them to the 'tentacles' of urban modernity that were disrupting rural ways of life.[13] In her novel *The Village Doctor* (1929), Sheila Kaye-Smith nostalgically looks back to a rural England 'unspoilt by the builder or the market-gardener, by the petrol-pump or the motor-car' (p. 1), but Elizabeth Stucley, in her guide *The Village Organizer* (1935), presents a more familiar scene: 'I climbed the hill and looked down on the village. It was the English village of history and fiction; grey stone church, thatched and whitewashed cottages; only the petrol pumps outside the garage struck a modern note' (p. xi). This modern note is picked out as a significant part of Hovingham. Worsley includes as one of the village personalities 'Walter Skelton of the Spa Garage' and presents a tightly framed shot of Skelton next to his Shell pump and then filling a motorcycle (Figure 2.5).

'The Petrol Pump' gets its own intertitle in *Fenwick*. Film-maker Rev. Allan shows an unnamed worker manning the pump and then pans right to situate them in the village landscape. The sequence of 'The Busy Corner' in this film also shows petrol pumps in the background, another example of a village business providing a service for the petrol age. In 'The Garage in Drover's Hollow' (1924–5), one of the Upward and Isherwood Mortmere stories, Isherwood makes the rural garage a valuable source of income for itself and other village businesses because of its unscrupulous practices aimed at outsiders. Amateur films of petrol pumps and garages also present them as valuable – and respectable – resources for the village.

While motor services were needed only by certain village residents and visitors, electricity could affect the entire community. In *Transforming the Countryside: The Electrification of Rural Britain* (2017), Paul Brassley, Jeremy Burchardt and Karen Sayer look into the perhaps 'naïve myth' that 'the countryside was "less modern" than the city and therefore less receptive to electrification' (p. 8). The chapters they bring together in this collection consider the 'cultural/human aspects of adoption – the ways in which mains electricity was presented to consumers by its enthusiasts, politicians and so forth, and the negotiations involved in its adoption' (p. 8).

Worsley's *Hovingham Compilation* (1930–48) shows the electrification of the village in a section titled '1932 Electricity'. The camera presents a tightly framed, low-angle shot of a man on a pole tending to a wire. The camera pans right to show another pole and a cottage, a possible indication of a village house now electrified. The camera then comes down to street level and pans around to show the cottage in the wider setting of the village, along with the slender poles that bring electricity. The sequence suggests that the poles, wires and electricity service itself will not disturb the peace and beauty of the village. Worsley, the film-maker and village landlord, endorses the electrification of Hovingham and uses film to record what he presents as a smooth transition. G. F. Baker captures a scene that details the labour of electrification more closely. As Baker was the owner of an electrical shop in the Yorkshire village of Stillington, he was most likely interested in the technical process and keen to promote it. A 1936 sequence from the compilation *Stillington, York, and Easingwold* (1931–42) shows workers erecting an electricity pole on a clearly windy day. A truck carries wires across a field to a more distant pole, and close-up shots show workers around the site, while not providing any detail about where this rural setting sits in relation to the villages it will supply. This could be any rural installation, the film suggests, while also avoiding details of what these poles and wires might do to village houses, buildings and views.

In 1928, William Beach Thomas noted the positive impact that electrification could have on rural residents:

> Cottage owners are beginning to put electric light into cottages, and it will dissipate the days of darkness very quickly. Few influences have more depressed the dweller in country cottages than mere physical darkness. Reading has been and, for the moment still is, a physical discomfort. Vital life has ceased daily with the arrival of night. But the day dawns, the poorest can read and listen, and in the sphere of listening, come in touch with the best the world has to give.[14]

Beach Thomas focuses on the positive effects of electricity on individual householders, yet village electrification also provided new ways of bringing residents together. The electrification of rural areas coincided with the 'nationwide enthusiasm for constructing village or parish halls'.[15] The village hall provided a new communal space for residents, and electricity increased the number of activities that could be held in the hall. Film screenings, for example, became a new form of village entertainment. F. G. Thomas describes how '[s]tragglers, too, visit the village as they have done from time immemorial, though transport has increased their number and kind. The wandering entertainer, offering a programme of conjuring and films, arrives in his car.'[16] F. G. Thomas, however, was also one of the leading proponents of film as part of rural education programmes and promoted 'experiment in film-making' among villagers themselves.[17] As he argues in 'The New Learning', his 1932 essay on cinema and rural education:

> the cinema has penetrated the rural areas: its influence is evident in the manners and costume of the young village boy and girl. Film societies, village clubs, adult study groups, schools, home cinemas, television and the myriad social groups within our society are the future medium for the film, in ways and means which we cannot at the moment perhaps visualize. (p. 56)

Thomas makes it clear that cinema is a significant source of influence on his conception of the changing village. His work in rural Devon brought him first-hand accounts of these changes but also showed how cinema could be part of a community-building, empowering practice. Amateur cinema could allow villagers not just to be taught by outsiders (through programmes such as the Workers' Educational Association) but also to teach themselves and others about the changes they were observing. The changes observed by Worsley, Allan, Fairbank, the Barnes brothers, Baker and others reflect their personal interests and perspectives and provide evidence of the modern elements of village life.

Conclusion: Conservative cameras

The cine camera is not just a recorder of exchanges, but an instigator, a prompt for interaction among camera, camera subject and camera operator. Amateur films not only captured examples of rural modernity, but also they were examples themselves of interwar rural Britain's integration of modern machines and modes of exchange. These films reflect the power of moving images to shape our perceptions of people and places at particular moments in time. They contribute to an archive of source material that the work here hopefully encourages others to mine in their own explorations of interwar rural Britain, ideas of community and the history of technology, as well as other studies. This chapter has only touched on a small number of films, and even then, has focused on examples of a rural and modern identity being articulated by the film-maker with the aid of the camera and (in most cases) knowledge of aspects of village life we see on screen. Yet – for all their expressions of rural modernity and the examples they themselves provide as instantiations of the rural/modern exchange – they present a particularly conservative image of interwar rurality. These are not radical films that challenge our thinking about the social and economic structure of interwar villages in the 1920s and 1930s, and the relationships that sustain community development. The film-makers are familiar sources of influence (the vicar, squire, school teacher, shop owner) and emphasise the maintenance of the status quo, not the upset of traditional values or overturn of power structures. While they provide evidence of the 'vivid factors of immediate experience' that F. G. Thomas finds useful in film,[18] they stress the familiarity of such experiences and conserve the cohesive image of the village ideal.

In dialogue with: Chapter 5 'Windmills and Woodblocks' (II: Landscapes) [visual culture; everyday technologies]; Chapter 7 'The "Uncertainty of Our Climate"' (III: Communities) [village arts; rural actors and directors].

Notes

1. 'Making and Meaning in the English Countryside', p. 137.
2. *The Changing Village*, p. 16.
3. Farr, p. 201.

4. Leavis and Thompson, p. 32.
5. Blunden, *The Face of England*, p. 120.
6. Bailey, 'Rural Industries and the Image of the Countryside', p. 136.
7. Leavis and Thompson, p. 68.
8. Wild, p. 136.
9. Brassley, 'The Wheelwright', p. 219.
10. 'Rural Awakening', p. 15.
11. 'Rural Awakening', p. 15.
12. Moran, p. 81.
13. Joad, 'The People's Claim', p. 81.
14. *The Happy Village*, p. 9.
15. Wild, p. 123.
16. *The Changing Village*, p. 22.
17. 'The New Learning', p. 56.
18. 'The New Learning', p. 57.

Chapter 3

Electricity Comes to the Countryside: Visual Representations of a Connected Countryside in the Early Twentieth Century

Rosemary Shirley

Figure 3.1 Wind turbines and pylons, a view from the train window on a journey through Lincolnshire.

From the train window: a plantation of wind turbines (Figure 3.1). These are the flat lands of Lincolnshire, made more relentlessly horizontal by these huge verticals. Smooth and white, their needle-sharp sails slowly furrow the air. Spaced at regular intervals, they punctuate this farmland–fenland mathematical grid. Trees mark the forgotten field boundaries and absent hedges – grubbed up to create giant super-fields. In the presence of these new structures, the chestnuts and oaks, in place for 200 years or more, look like the tiny trees used by architects to adorn their models. Amongst these pale giants stand the still-functioning relics of another form of power supply; as testament to the grand plan of the last generation, the pylon's latticework stands out black against the grey sky. Lines of wire add more horizontals to this expansive landscape, like a musical score sheet. In the foreground a string of modest wooden poles and wire carries electricity to the local population.

Rural places have always supported the grand infrastructural projects of modernity. A system of canals, then later the rail network and later still motorways, promised connection and transport of goods and people. Acts of destruction and creation, each one in turn added a layer of patterned ground to the landscape. The passage of the Electricity Supply Act in 1926 and the construction in the years following of the national grid with its ambitious system of transmission towers and wires contributed a new stratum to this palimpsest, and with it a new iteration of rural modernity.[1]

This chapter examines reactions to the introduction of the physical infrastructure of the national grid into the British countryside. It maps the often angry and polemic responses from sections of the public, together with those from commentators concerned with the aesthetic appearance of rural places and their preservation. It argues, however, that a significant contrast can be made between these anxious responses to technological interventions in the landscape and a set of films and pamphlets created by the British Electrical Development Agency (BEDA). These materials were designed to promote rural electrification and offer a surprisingly different vision of rural modernity. They were created in order to communicate ideas about the countryside to rural residents, rather than tourists or city dwellers, and with this change in perspective we find the countryside reimagined as a forward-looking, active site of modernity, rather than a passive landscape set to be exploited and despoiled by the installation of pylons and wires.

Ever since electricity became available for a domestic market, it has been aligned with the idea of modernity. In his social history of design, *Objects of Desire* (1986), Adrian Forty recounts that, in the early years of electrical supply during the late nineteenth and early twentieth centuries, the general public regarded the power source with fear and superstition. It was seen as an invisible killer, with old ladies keeping plugs in every socket in their household in order to keep the electricity from seeping out (p. 189). Fear was often based on a misunderstanding of the properties of this new technology and on users subscribing to electricity the attributes of gas – the power source to which they had become used. An example of this is noted by Wolfgang Schivelbusch in his study of the affective histories of the industrialisation of light, in which he includes an extract from a French scientific magazine recounting a conversation between a woman and her husband on looking at an electric light chandelier in a theatre:

> If one were to break a wire, would the electricity leak out into the auditorium? Wouldn't that be dangerous for the audience?
>
> My dear wife, one can breathe electricity without the least danger. And in any case, it would rise and collect under the ceiling at once, so we would have nothing to fear. (p. 78)

It was felt by the producers and promoters of electricity that many of these anxieties were based on superstition and irrationality, and that the most effective way to counter these fears was to superimpose a more powerful narrative on to electricity: namely, that it was a fuel of the future, a truly modern power source. A wide range of propaganda methods was utilised to spread this millenarian view of electricity, including films, advertising posters, pamphlets, exhibitions and showrooms displaying the latest electrical consumer products.

Electricity was regularly represented at world fairs and expositions as an exciting technological and social development that signified the birth of the modern age. For the 1937 International Exhibition in Paris, the Fauvist painter Raoul Dufy was commissioned to create a monumental mural 10 metres high and 60 metres long for the exhibition's Pavilion of Light and Electricity. His brief was 'to promote the role of electricity in national life'.[2] Dufy's mural, called *La Fée Électricité* (*The Electricity Fairy*), shows the development of electricity, its applications, and by association the march of civilisation in a sequence that surrounds the viewer.[3] Notably, the mural begins by depicting a premodern past that is dominated by green fields. As the images move forward in time and also in terms of human progress, the colour palette changes towards blues and purples, and the imagery becomes denser and increasingly urban. The final panels show neon lights, factories, a power station, an orchestra and choir, and a structure that could be the Eiffel Tower but also looks a little like a pylon. The formal qualities of this composition draw on the familiar idea of the rural as being situated in the past, far away from the era of modernity in terms of time and geography. The implication here is that electricity and, by extension, modernity belong to the city rather than the country.

This is a familiar discourse: the countryside defined in contrast to the city by its opposition to modernity. In *The Country and the City*, Raymond Williams asserts that 'The common image of the country is now an image of the past' (p. 297), a statement that is echoed in popular representations of the countryside both in the early years of the twentieth century and today. Many television programmes, advertising campaigns and tourism campaigns derive their power from presenting rural communities and locations as alternatives to the tensions, pressures and ugliness of modern everyday life.[4]

This formulation can be seen in David Lefebvre Lowenthal's four constructed narratives that, he argues, characterise how the countryside is thought of and spoken about: *insularity*, *artifice*, *stability* and *order*. These persistent rhetorical devices can be seen to contribute to the idea that the countryside, or its place in the national imaginary, stands in opposition to some of the major characteristics associated with modernity. The countryside's insularity is a refusal of cosmopolitanism or border crossing; its artifice is used to extinguish difference and maintain a contrived permanence; an emphasis on stability becomes denial of change; and the importance of order is an attempt to reproduce rigid social and geographical structures.[5] This ideology contributed to rural places being embedded in the national imagination as outside of modernity, and as a result, once the countryside became appropriated (or regarded) as the ground of national electrification, particularly in terms of the siting of pylons, transmission poles and wires, anxieties about development and preservation increased. We can conclude from this that one of the primary effects of the Electrical Supply Act was to trouble the boundaries between the country and the city.

The wirescape and rural modernity

Today the presence of pylons in the landscape is hardly remarked upon. The eight or so decades since their first appearance have rendered them a taken-for-granted feature. However, our contemporary experience of encountering the colossal turbines of a wind farm can remind us of how disturbing and/or exhilarating the installation of the first pylons must have been. The presence of these structures in the landscape prompts an evaluation of the felt experience of modernity in rural places. In the early twentieth century, chroniclers of the affective nature of urban modernity such as Walter Benjamin and Georg Simmel centre on an overwhelming feeling of fragmentation and confusion that characterises the experience of the modern city.[6] However, the countryside presents a different register and, as a counterpoint to the urban experience, rural modernity could usefully be thought about as being experienced as moments of profound contrast rather than as a constant onslaught of minor shocks.[7] Pylons contrast completely with the landscape that surrounds them. They are much taller than the tallest trees and far higher than church steeples, the structures habitually used to measure scale in rural places.

The great scale of these structures in terms of their height but also their reach across the countryside is a feature of Stephen Spender's poem *The Pylons*, written in the 1930s in response to the installation of the first wave of national grid transmission towers. The other element is the noise; the electric fizz that accompanies power lines feels tangible in the air. While one could not breathe electricity, as was once feared, there is something chemical here that permeates the atmosphere, making it feel radically different from the windblown open air of pylon-free spaces. In addition, the hard steel structures and angular design contrast strongly with the organic material of the fields and hillsides they traverse.

It is the contrast in scale, their material properties – for example, the use of industrially produced steel – and the perceived modernity of the design of the towers that made the installation of pylons during the 1920s and 1930s so controversial. During this period, a stream of letters to *The Times* protested against planned lines of transmission towers, especially through areas identified as landscape amenity, like the Lake District and the South Downs.[8] One letter writer picks out the installation of overhead electricity cables in the Lake District as evidence of the 'defacements of "progress"' that they were being forced to suffer.[9] Forms of localised protest also took place, and the government held a public inquiry into plans to situate pylons across the South Downs, though to little effect.[10] One of the strongest voices of protest came from Clough Williams-Ellis, architect and chair of the Campaign to Protect Rural England. In his book *England and the Octopus* (1928), he outlines his position on pylons and the associated transmission wires in a section he calls the 'Devil's Dictionary', which includes other evils such as golf courses, bungalows and petrol pumps. Williams-Ellis acknowledges the need for the national grid project but argues that it will come at the cost of amenity. He laments that nothing can be done to disguise the electricity transmission lines, 'even when these traverse the loveliest little valleys of Merioneth, destroying their scale and importing a sense of sophistication and "Progress" of which they were until now so soothingly innocent'.[11] His descriptions speak of the contrasts present in visual and felt experiences of rural modernity. They highlight in particular the contrast in scale between the pylons and the surrounding landscape. They also repeat the ingrained notion that the rural should not play host to or be an active participant in modernity, that it should remain 'soothingly innocent' of such developments.[12]

Williams-Ellis's views could be critiqued as a metropolitan perspective, or at least one of privilege. His objections are based on the way the countryside looks. It is treated as 'a view': something experienced from a distance rather than necessarily lived in.[13] The countryside is characterised as a victim of modernity in need of protection. Local residents themselves were not necessarily opposed to the installation of transmission towers and wires; pylons signified the potential for an electricity supply in rural areas, radically transforming and perhaps improving lived experience in the countryside.[14] However, taken as whole, Williams-Ellis's treatise is not against modern developments altogether but argues for their sensitive, design-led implementation, rather than hasty application driven by profit motive.

Other commentators adopted a different view on pylons in the landscape. The architect John Leslie Martin, writing in *Circle*, a publication he edited with the St Ives-based avant-garde artists Ben Nicholson and Naum Gabo, asserted that pylons were part of the 'new aesthetics' found in technological design that would inform a new generation of designers and artists. He wrote that

> The new aesthetic exists in the motor car and the aeroplane, in the steel bridge and the line of electricity pylons. Its values, precision, economy, exact finish, are not merely the result of technical limitation. They are the product of artistic selection. (p. 216)

While the new aesthetics of precision, economy and exact finish, typified by the steel frameworks of pylons, might make a considerable contrast with the surrounding landscape, Martin sees these insertions as exciting visions of the future.[15] Interestingly, all the elements listed by Martin in this quotation are agents of connectivity themselves. These networks are, for Martin, at the very heart of the new modern age, and the rural landscape is playing a central role in this.

Similarly enthusiastic, the *Architectural Review* in 1929 made its position clear on the infrastructure necessary for the transmission of electricity. It paired two photographs, one titled *Electrification I. How it should not be done* and the other *Electrification II. How it should be done.* The former showed a set of wooden poles and wires stretching across a series of fields, while the latter showed a run of steel pylons, their scale dwarfing the surround trees, the sun glinting off their metallic surfaces. This is perhaps a surprising position; the wooden poles are made of natural materials and are in keeping with the scale of the trees they pass by. The *Architectural Review*, however, was one of the key promoters of modernist design in the interwar period and thus favours the sleek addition to the landscape and even encourages the CPRE to do the same: 'the great height of the beautiful lattice towers required for main transmission lines, and the majestic sweep of the catenary formed by the suspended wires, produces an effect of size, rhythm and magnificence which could hardly be surpassed by a Roman aqueduct'.[16]

In reality, such a comparison is spurious, as the two systems perform different roles. The high-tension wires strung between pylons carry high-voltage electricity over long distances, whereas the system of wooden poles and wires carries lower-voltage electricity from substations for use in homes, farms and other industries. The *Architectural Review* seems unconcerned with how rural areas might tap into this national system and focuses more on the grand architectures of transmission rather than the specifics of rural connectivity. This demonstrates a common way of imagining rural areas as empty spaces in between cities; the landscape is host to the dramatic new pylons but seemingly in no need of electricity itself. The new system of pylons carried electricity from large, efficient power stations situated close to natural reserves of coal and water, often in rural places, to the cities that needed it. This arrangement draws on more ancient notions of the countryside feeding the city and sets up an interdependent hierarchy between these locations, which casts the country as servant of the city.[17]

The national grid connected the rural and urban both conceptually and physically, something of which Williams-Ellis and the CPRE were particularly wary. The 1920s saw heavy industry move from the centre of cities to the outskirts, particularly in London, increasing the footprint of urban development on rural land. At the same time, commuter suburbs were growing in size and the use of personal motor transport was increasing.[18] One of the central anxieties so well expressed by Williams-Ellis in *England and the Octopus* was that differences between the country and the city were being eroded by careless development:

> We are modifying both town and country, removing the worst reproaches from the one and much of its essential charms from the other. We plant trees in the town and bungalows in the country, thus averaging England out into a dull uneventfulness whereby one place becomes the same as any other. (p. 21)

Later, this problem with geographical conformity was taken up by architect Ian Nairn in his publication *Outrage* (1955), which identified what he called the 'wirescape' as an agent in the creep of subtopia – a state caused by ill-designed and unchecked development which erases the differences between town and country (p. 373).

> Wire obliterates the pattern of the countryside just as surely as though it were a blanket of semi-detached housing. The view becomes wire and pylon first and site second. In some cases it becomes wire and pylon everywhere and site nowhere. (p. 379)

Nairn compares electricity wires with semi-detached housing, a form of development that was directly associated with the spread of town and village footprints. Here wire is an agent in the connection of the town and the countryside, and generates anxieties about the preservation of the distinctiveness of rural places. The wires seem to be collapsing distance and pulling countrysides closer to the city.

The all-electric countryside

In a special 1933 electricity-themed supplement to the *Architectural Review*, the BEDA described itself as

> the central educational and propaganda organisation for British Electricity Supply Undertakings. By means of national advertising, editorial articles in the press, lectures and exhibitions, the Association is constantly endeavouring to bring to the attention of all classes of consumer the advantages of electrification.[19]

In the 1920s, the BEDA turned its focus on to the British countryside. Up until the development of the national grid in 1926, the BEDA had been primarily concerned with encouraging urban and suburban households to increase their electricity use through marketing electric consumer goods such as electric cookers, washing machines, irons, toasters and water heaters. This was done through magazine advertisements, films, and the electricity showrooms that were opening in almost every town and city.

In order for the electrification of rural places to be economically viable, it was important for as many households, farms and other industries in a given area to subscribe to the service, as installing a substation and a line of poles and wires practically cost as much for one house as it did for a whole village. It was also important to the BEDA that customers used as much electricity as possible. They saw their job as building demand. Due to economies of scale, the price per unit dropped as the amount used increased, a fact that was repeatedly emphasised in all the BEDA rural electrification material. This meant customers were encouraged to expand electricity use beyond lighting, as was the case for many farmers, to almost all household, agricultural and industrial tasks. A BEDA leaflet called *Electricity on the Farm* emphasised the link between electricity and prosperity, and advocated that customers use a myriad of electrical gadgets, including such luxuries as an electric horse-grooming kit (p. 10). The possibility for electricity to transform every aspect of country life on the farm and in the farmhouse was demonstrated to full effect at the Royal Agricultural Show in 1936, which was rebranded by the BEDA as the All-Electric Royal Show. The large-scale outdoor exhibition area featured electric flood lights, electric cafeteria, electric pumping station, electric dairy, electric hot water and electric heating.[20]

After the creation of the national grid, rural electrification increased significantly. In 1920, only 7 per cent of rural areas was connected, with 21 per cent of the rural population benefiting. By 1928, the figure had increased to 42 per cent of rural areas connected and 67 per cent of the population served. This rose again by 1936, when 90 per cent of rural areas was connected, reaching 85 per cent of the rural population.[21] However, it is important to note that many of these rural farms and households may have been using electricity only for lighting.[22] The heady days of all-electric horse grooming were beyond the economic resources of many rural families. In her essay on electricity use in rural homes, Karen Sayer nuances this statistical picture of rural electrification, pointing out that limited availability, high cost and questionable reliability continued to affect the process until the 1960s (p. 117). In addition, Sayer usefully reminds us that the promotional materials generated by electricity companies and agencies like the BEDA can play only a limited role in telling us about the engagement with or take-up of rural electrification in the UK, so it is important not to treat this material as if it is revealing new attitudes to rural electrification amongst rural populations.[23] However, the range of propaganda material created by the BEDA between the wars is fascinating because it remains a relatively rare example of material designed to communicate ideas about the countryside and rural modernity, not to tourists or metropolitan audiences, but to the people who lived and worked in rural places. When we perform a visual reading of these documents they reveal a vision of rural modernity that offers an interesting alternative to those ideas circulated by commentators such as the CPRE or the *Architectural Review*. In these images we see rural modernity made an attractive and almost utopian possibility. Rural people and places are depicted as active participants in processes of modernity rather than as victims.

New visions of rural modernity

An example of these new visions of rural modernity can be seen in the cover artwork for a booklet produced by the BEDA in the early 1930s (Plate 1). In this image the sky is orange, indicating a sunrise; a new day is dawning and so is *The New Farming Age*, the booklet's title. The words arc across the sky and are flanked by lines as if the phrase itself is the sun coming up over the horizon. Promotional materials produced by the BEDA tell their readers so often that electricity will bring heat and light that it makes sense to align rural electrification with the sun. This metaphor was taken literally in BEDA's materials relating to poultry farming, one agricultural activity where electricity could be seen to increase productivity directly. In one of the publications on the subject, a farm is depicted at night with dark buildings silhouetted against an inky blue sky. The moon is out but inside the chicken sheds it is daylight. The hens are warmed by electric light and fooled into thinking it is day instead of night and summer instead of winter, prolonging the egg-laying season into the darker months. James Purdon notes that part of what we now think of as the affective nature of the national grid was its ability to collapse time and space with the promise of instantaneous connection to electricity across great distances (p. 47). We can see from this poultry-farming example that rural electrification also had the potential to change perceptions of time in other ways. Extending daylight hours and suppressing seasonal change in the countryside meant more than just the potential for longer working hours and more comfortable winters. Here electricity fundamentally changes the seasons and the effects they have on livestock. This could also be seen in electrical consumer goods such as chest freezers, which were initially marketed as tools that would allow rural consumers to 'Beat the Seasons' and enjoy home-grown soft fruit in January.[24]

Another element to note in the *New Farming Age* image is that the electricity transmission wires and poles take centre-stage, cutting a dynamic line across the centre of the picture. Following the wires, the viewer's eye is taken across a landscape of green fields, hedges and a stile towards a farm in the distance. As discussed above, the CPRE was highly sensitive to the presence of transmission wires in the landscape, and the *Architectural Review* used an image of wooden poles and lines as an example of how rural electrification 'should not be done'. Here, however, the BEDA uses the visual imagery of connection to herald a bright new future for the countryside, making the wires and poles a prominent feature of the design. The lines representing electricity wires extend beyond the limits of the page on the left of the image, indicating that they continue infinitely elsewhere and connect the apparently isolated farm with the rest of the network, the rest of the country and the future.

Another BEDA booklet from the same period, also intended for rural readers, similarly highlights the presence of wires in the countryside. *Electricity in the Countryside* features a drawing of a village, which includes a church, manor house, cottages, outlying farms and other industries (Plate 2). It is intended to explain to the rural customer why the installation of electric power in the countryside is more expensive than in towns. Here electricity cables are depicted as red lines of progress. They stretch across the page to the very edge, again giving the impression that they carry on beyond the drawing, connecting the village with the rest of the country. The next page even goes on to make a virtue of the amount of wire that is being used in this grand project. It shows a drawing of Planet Earth, flanked by two enormous wooden poles from which emanate more red wires that link to an outline of Britain and then go on to wrap themselves around the world. The accompanying commentary reads: '40,000 Miles of Distribution Line – The Total length of high and low voltage distribution line used in the British countryside would go nearly twice round the earth.'[25] Rather than Nairn's vision of a wirescape destroying the distinctions between the city and the country and, crucially, the aesthetics of the view, these documents present rural Britain and its residents as active, central players in a significant and extensive project of modernity. It is also interesting to note that in the distribution diagram the countryside is seen as more than a heritage site or landscape amenity to be preserved. Instead it is portrayed as a complex site of production and industry. As well as a traditional-looking village, the drawing also includes an industrial sand and gravel pit. The accompanying text makes it clear that it is because of the economic benefits of supplying this business with electricity that it becomes worthwhile to run poles and wires through this area, granting village residents access to an electrical supply.

It is productive to compare BEDA images that imagine a future where rural places fully embrace aspects of modernity represented by the national grid with the imagery that appears in the film *The Face of Britain*. This film, made in 1935 by director Paul Rotha, was sponsored by the Central Electricity Board, although this is not stated in the film's credits. It begins with a harvest scene showing horse-drawn machinery and stooks of corn being stacked by hand. The sequence is presented by Rotha as the past, but this was the way that much of agriculture still looked in 1935. Rotha's approach aligns with the image of rural Britain as outside of modernity, which Williams and Lowenthal critique, and supports David Matless's assertion that, for many commentators, the idea of travelling into the countryside is to travel back in time.[26] The film speaks of the imagined isolation of the rural community, presenting it as something we all desire: 'Most of us have longed for a return to that epoch when in those villages men lived and died with little thought outside the life of their self-contained community.' It shows a panorama of the countryside with no visible traces of modernity, no pylons or electricity wires, no traffic, roads or visible industry other than farming. Rotha then goes on to portray the smoke age or industrial revolution, which, the film argues, continues to despoil the landscape and impose ruinous living conditions on the workers. The third section of the film introduces electricity as the solution that will move society on from the dirt and grime of the smoke age. Rotha sidesteps the issue of electricity produced by the smoky process of burning coal and focuses instead on the perceived purity of hydroelectric power. Here the countryside is acknowledged as both a host for pylons and a group of potential consumers: 'Pylons carry their living load over mountains, fields and rivers, never checking in their stride as they carry the new power to the waiting cities and the eager countryside.'[27] The film concludes with a section called 'The New Age'. We are told there will be more time for leisure, in which the countryside will play another important role 'for getting away from the sphere of work into the open countryside'.[28] The film ends with a shot of a couple looking out over a landscape curiously free from pylons or indeed any sign of modernity. The shot seems to indicate that this is what we are aiming for. Perhaps, as in William Morris's *News from Nowhere*, the future is rosy because it looks more like the past.

At the beginning of its rural electrification marketing scheme in 1928, the BEDA also made a film to promote the benefits of electricity to residents of rural areas. With a running time of over two hours, it is very different from Rotha's film. It portrays in detail the benefits of electrification using twenty-six different farms and locations around Chester. The contents of the film are described in some detail in a *Rural Electrification* publicity leaflet, designed to entice local groups like the Women's Institute to show it at one of their meetings and encourage their members to subscribe to the electrification scheme (Figure 3.2). Like the BEDA sources discussed above, the film represents rural Britain as a complex network of homes, farms and other industries, including a maker of horse boxes, a quarry, saw mill, butcher's, milk plant, bread-making factory, brick works, plant nursery and grain warehouse. It too confronts head-on the controversial issue of transmission lines and poles, stating:

> Whatever the method of generation the first essential for economic supply in rural areas is low cost of transmission: this can only be secured by the use of overhead lines on account of the additional cost involved in laying underground cables.

The text then notes that in the film these words will be accompanied by an 'Out-door view of overhead transmission, high pressure and low tension lines showing that these do not really spoil the landscape'.[29]

The difference between the image of rural electrification presented in this film and its accompanying leaflet and that put forward by preservationists such as the CPRE can be seen if we compare the covers of this leaflet with the cover of Williams-Ellis's *England and the Octopus*

Figure 3.2 *Rural Electrification* Pamphlet, British Electric Development Agency, 1928. Courtesy of the Science and Society Picture Library.

(Figure 11.1), published in the same year. Williams-Ellis's book sees rural England being grasped in the haphazard tentacles of a greedy purple beast representing modern development. The BEDA image almost inverts this scenario. Rather than the tentacles of development ranging down the page and engulfing the village, beams of orange light radiate upwards. Similar buildings and views feature in each image; however, Williams-Ellis presents them as choked by urban tentacles, whereas the BEDA leaflet shows farms and villages illuminated by useful, modern, electric beams.

Conclusion: A counter-narrative for the countryside

It is important for rural places not to be habitually characterised as being outside of modernity or as being its passive victim. Time passes in rural places as it does in urban locations, and the countryside has experienced and continues to experience the impact of modernisation. It often looks and feels different from the urban modernity that is more usually discussed, but it is nonetheless a powerful factor in the lives of rural residents. We continue, however, to be surrounded by images and other cultural productions that situate the rural in an imaginary premodern past. This is a seductive proposition and one that gains potency from its long history. It makes elements such as pylons, which we associate with modernity, seem out of place in the countryside. Because of this, they become the target of anxieties about change, environmental pollution and – because the landscape is so connected to it – national identity. This is evident in the commentary on pylons from the CPRE and letters to *The Times* and in some aspects of the *Architectural Review* articles discussed above.

Imagery produced by the BEDA to promote rural electrification offers a different and much less familiar picture of the countryside. Here rural transmission lines are depicted as an exciting step towards the future – which will literally connect formerly isolated rural locations with the rest of the country – rather than as an aberration spoiling the view. While we need to be mindful that these materials were produced as propaganda and do not necessarily represent how rural communities felt about electrification or individuals' abilities to engage with the scheme, they nevertheless provide visual representations of an imagined form of rural modernity in the early decades of the twentieth century. They create a compelling counter-narrative to dominant stories of modernity and may indeed be unique in the history of British visual culture.

In dialogue with: Chapter 10 'Borderlands' (IV: Heritage) [visual and material culture; regional art and archives]; Chapter 12 'Celebrating England' (IV: Heritage) [popular print culture; Englishness].

Notes

1. The national grid aimed to rationalise this system, focusing on the connection of large and efficient power stations into a network that enabled the power they generated to be carried to the areas that needed it most. The aim was to make it possible for more people in both rural and urban locations to be connected to a supply of relatively affordable electricity. The network of high-tension wires and transmission towers that stretched across the country made it economically possible to supply, for the first time, wide expanses of rural areas with electricity. For a detailed account of this landmark legislation, see Hannah.
2. Contensou, p.4.
3. Aligning new technology with benevolent supernatural figures was a recognisable trope in propaganda of this time. Forty describes an Electrical Development Association (EDA) poster from 1927, in which electricity is personified as a 'genie-like spirit [who] promised to carry out all the unconditional tasks of the world'. The EDA went on to develop a sprite character, who announced 'I'm all electric' at every opportunity throughout the 1930s, and in the promotion of another revolutionary form of connective technology in 1936 the GPO created a film featuring the *Fairy of the Phone* to educate users about telephone etiquette.
4. For a more detailed account of representations in popular culture, see Shirley, *Rural Modernity*, p. 7.
5. Lefebvre Lowenthal, 'European Landscapes', pp. 15–38.
6. See Benjamin, *Illuminations*; and Simmel, 'The Metropolis and Mental Life'.
7. For a more detailed account of this conceptualisation of rural modernity, see Shirley, *Rural Modernity*, p. 110.
8. See, for example, Scholes, p. 9, and Spenoe, p. 8.
9. Spenoe, p. 8.
10. Weightman, p. 154.
11. Weightman, p. 144.
12. This is a long-established cultural trope and is outlined in Williams, *The Country and the City*, p. 9.
13. Although Williams-Ellis did live in a rural location, in a country house that he inherited in what is now the Snowdonia National Park, his experience of living in the landscape was through choice and privilege.
14. See Luckin.
15. It should also be noted that the design values of economy, precision and exact finish are already present in the countryside through forms of vernacular architecture like dry-stone walls. These obviously look very different to the modernity of pylon design but are generated through a similar set of principles.

16. 'Concrete Bridges and Transmission Poles', p. 248.
17. See Steel, *Hungry City*.
18. Williams-Ellis, *Octopus*, p. 5.
19. 'Electrical Development', p. li.
20. See *The Triumph of Electricity at the Royal Show.*
21. Ditt, p. 29.
22. Ditt, p. 30.
23. Ditt, p. 118.
24. Shirley, 'Pylons and Frozen Peas', p. 148.
25. *Electricity in the Countryside*, p. 4.
26. Shirley, *Rural Modernity*, p. 52; Matless, *Landscape*, p. 64.
27. *Face of Britain*.
28. *Face of Britain*.
29. *Rural Electrification*, p. 3.

Part II

Landscapes

Chapter 4

Weighing Down the Landscape: The Quarry as a Site of Rural Modernity

Samuel Shaw

In 1932, the critic, artist and museum administrator D. S. MacColl reviewed the second volume of memoirs penned by his friend and contemporary, the artist William Rothenstein (1872–1945). The review provided an excuse to look back over the past thirty or forty years of art and to reflect upon Rothenstein's position within it. MacColl paints a swift but familiar picture of modern art, one in which 'representation has been having a poor time' and 'design has decided to set up for itself' (p. 76). In 'preaching a fuller immersion in the subject, and development of design from within it, instead of a clamp from without', Rothenstein appears to fall into what was, by 1932, something of an aesthetic hinterland – not abstract enough to be fully 'modern', yet clearly speaking the language of what, in response to Roger Fry's 1910 exhibition, we now call Post-Impressionism.[1] The obvious touchstone here, as MacColl realises, is Paul Cézanne, for whom Rothenstein had equivocal admiration. MacColl and Rothenstein clearly differ in their estimation of the French artist; nonetheless, MacColl recognises in this review that Rothenstein's critical doctrine was built on similar foundations, even if the results looked a little different.[2]

The review celebrates few specific examples of Rothenstein's work, but mentions in passing a painting to which MacColl refers, intriguingly, as having been 'born too soon' (p. 77). This painting, titled *The Deserted Quarry* (Plate 3) and completed in 1904, may seem a somewhat surprising work to be plucked out of the artist's œuvre and be remarked upon for its innovation. *The Deserted Quarry* had hitherto, and has since, attracted much less critical attention than other works by Rothenstein; the more obviously modern subject matter of urban scenes has tended to suit popular narratives of early twentieth-century British art. This is not a surprise: the painting is distinctly gloomy and brooding, even romantic, and seems at first sight to have been born in the nineteenth century. Despite the Impressionistic handling and what one critic described as its 'curiously original' design, exemplified by the high horizon and bold placing of the diagonal derrick that cuts across the top third of the canvas, the subject is not what most would expect from a modern painting.[3] The geological theme seems better suited to looking back than forward, to the consideration of origins rather than futures. The scene depicted – an abandoned quarry in Hawksworth, West Yorkshire – appears to be a rural rather than an urban subject, and even when one considers that the quarrying industry was not only flourishing in 1904, but also undergoing increasing modernisation, Rothenstein's representation appears unwilling to engage with these features.[4] This is, as one alternative title for the painting reminds us, an 'old quarry' or, as yet another title had it (locating the scene securely in the nineteenth century), 'A Deserted Quarry in Bronté country' [sic].[5] Nostalgia appears to be the keynote here. As the artist recalled in his memoirs, in reference to another quarry in the region: 'there hung about it that haunted atmosphere peculiar to places where men have once been quick and busy, but which, long deserted, are slowly readopted by the old earth'.[6] Read in the light of such comments, this painting feels like a disavowal, or at least a diffident apprehension, of modernity.

So why did MacColl alight on this painting in 1932 and make the claim that it was somehow ahead of its time? On what grounds *might* a representation of a quarry suit certain narratives of modern art? This chapter argues that these questions are worth asking, not merely as a means of understanding the art of William Rothenstein, but also as a means of understanding much wider concerns regarding the relationship between rurality and modernity, universality and regionality, modern form and subject matter.

The quarry and Cubism

Although the link is not made explicit, it is very possible that, in his reference to *The Deserted Quarry*'s innovation, MacColl was thinking again of Cézanne, whose paintings of the abandoned sandstone quarries of Bibémus in Aix-en-Provence (created in the 1890s–1900s), though relatively unknown to British audiences in 1904, had by the 1930s come to be seen as foundational works in the development of modern art. He is, thus, entering Rothenstein's name into a genealogy of modern quarry painting that begins with Cézanne (and, possibly, Van Gogh, who also painted quarries in the 1880s) and leads directly to the formal innovations of artists such as Pablo Picasso and Georges Braque, who, though they may not have represented quarries directly, mined a similar subject matter in search of the particular formal characteristics that would come to be associated with Cubism.[7] As Gertrude Stein once suggested, Cubism could be read not merely as an analytical mode imposed on subject matter the artist chose, but also as a language drawn from patterns found, most frequently, in rocks, stone buildings, mountains and quarries.[8] The modern, formalist aesthetic was, in this sense, not created but found. Cézanne's so-called 'desire to give sculptural weight and volume to the instantaneity of vision achieved by the Impressionists' drew him, quite naturally, to the stones that gave literal weight and structure to the rural landscape.[9] Indeed, Rothenstein's son, the critic and museum director John Rothenstein, pointed to Cézanne's obsession with the 'rocky or bony framework of things', hinting that the artist's approach was somehow akin to that of a quarryman, chipping away at the details to reveal the inner core.[10] The fact that Post-Impressionist art is often referred to as 'sculptural' extends this analogy: it is painting that aspires to being rock or stone, especially when the subject of that painting is, in fact, rock or stone.

Rothenstein, as suggested by MacColl and by this chapter, was attracted to his deserted quarry for many of the reasons that Cézanne was drawn to the abandoned quarries of Bibémus. Although Rothenstein's paintings have rarely been considered in the same breath as those of Cézanne, let alone Picasso and Braque, the critical language he was using around the turn of the century, as already noted, does suggest a nascent formalism, albeit one in which (as MacColl noted) 'design' was sought not simply on its own terms, but as a means of revealing the 'hidden forces' of existence.[11] Only a few years before painting *The Deserted Quarry*, Rothenstein had written the first English monograph on Goya (1900), in which he praised the Spanish artist for having 'brought back to painting the old architectural sense, and squareness of proportion and design, which the artists of the last century had allowed to dwindle into the vignette'.[12] A quarry was, arguably, a shortcut to a well-designed painting. You did not need to impose 'the old architectural sense' on a quarry: it was already there, in the heaviness and squareness of the stone. It was Cubism simply waiting to happen (given a slight push over the precipice of style). This is surely why, in MacColl's words, Rothenstein's painting was 'born too soon to deserve the praises given after 1910 to less solid and cubical inspiration' (pp. 76–7).[13]

MacColl's comment may have been somewhat tongue in cheek; however, it opens up an interesting line of enquiry: namely, the idea that the subject of the quarry, if appropriately framed, may, on account of certain formal qualities and regardless of wider social meaning, have been innately modern or have become so by virtue of its visual similarities with the language of Cubism. The specificity of this landscape, or the quarrying industry in general, does not concern MacColl, although the basic subject (the quarry) does, as this seems to carry with it the promise of a new approach to form, as yet unappreciated in 1904, though well understood by 1932. Rothenstein is being praised not so much for creating an innovative painting but for finding the right landscape from which to extract it. Subject is important only so far as it yields itself willingly to a particular set of formal characteristics, typified (to use words MacColl employed to describe another painting by Rothenstein) by 'weightiness of pose, and a certain gravity'.[14] In this sense, the quarry emerges as a site of modernity *despite* its typical rural setting. It offers weight and solidity to a subject sometimes regarded as soft and yielding.

This argument is an important and hitherto unheeded one, which goes some way to explain the presence of quarries among subjects regularly chosen by European artists in the early twentieth century. Despite the relative neglect of the subject in critical discourse, modern artists owed a lot to quarries. Many modern sculptures, of course, were literally born of quarries, especially in the years directly before the First World War when direct carving was in the ascendency among modern sculptors. However, painters also regularly turned to quarries for inspiration. Representations of quarries can be found in the work of a wide range of painters working in Britain in the early twentieth century, from John Singer Sargent to Paul Nash, and Roger Fry to Philip Wilson Steer.[15] Yet, these artists did not seek or find the same things in their subject matter. Just as there are many types of quarry – from limestone and slate to gravel and sand – let alone methods of extraction, uses and associations, so there have been many different ways of representing them, from the gleaming and industrious quarry scenes of Sargent, to the dour and silent quarry depicted by William Rothenstein. For some artists, quarries were seen as romantic spaces presenting wide-open vistas; for others, they represented a disordered, claustrophobic environment. For all the quarries that are represented teeming with activity, there are an equal number that are, like Rothenstein's, completely deserted and that could easily be confused (as Rothenstein liked to confuse them) with cliffs by the sea, especially in cases when the quarries had been filled.[16] When workers are depicted, it is again with great variety. In most paintings, men appear dotted about like ants, but in a few cases, such as those by Alfred Palmer (1877–1941), they take centre-stage.[17] As with images of the urban industrial scene produced during the same period, there appears to be great uncertainty as to how to position the worker within the landscape, an uncertainty to which most artists responded by not including them at all. Palmer is rare in facing up to the realities of the Dorset quarrymen; however, while he highlights the physicality of their trade, he also slips into a heroic mode in which the shirtless workers lose their individuality and become just another regional variant on the rural everyman. Ultimately, the complexities of a working quarry seem to have resisted easy assimilation through art, which may explain why, despite its widespread popularity, few artists beyond Cézanne returned to it repeatedly.

Unearthing rural modernity

Two further examples establish connections between British artists and the European modernist tradition. For the purposes of this argument, they offer a pathway for artists of the next generation seeking to tackle rural subjects and, to paraphrase Paul Nash's famous 1932 article, 'go modern'.[18] These examples are taken from the work of artists who are seen as central figures in competing narratives of modern art in Britain, in which modern form and subject matter bear significant but sometimes unequal weight.

The first is a drawing by the artist Edward Wadsworth (1889–1949), who shared William Rothenstein's West Yorkshire upbringing and who, from about 1910 onwards, pursued a self-consciously avant-garde approach to form that brought him into the orbit of Wyndham Lewis. Wadsworth's experiments in form, mostly produced between 1910 and 1920, revolved around a tight selection of subjects: cityscapes, harbours, aerial views and sites of industry, including quarries.[19] Wadsworth's drawing *Granite Quarries, Darby Hill, Oldbury* (1919) (Figure 4.1), has been described as 'regular forms reduced to simple planes', and it is evident that what we see is a distillation of what Wadsworth saw in a particular West Midlands landscape. Nonetheless, an element of abstraction was obviously innate in the man-made landscape itself: a form of land art, arguably, before such a term existed. This is a sculpted landscape, albeit one that has been formed not with aesthetics in mind, or by a single hand, but from collective industrial need. It is a landscape formed by men and by machinery, and yet dominated still by the raw materials of nature. There is enough nature visible, it could be argued, for it to be read, still, as a landscape.

Unlike Rothenstein's image, however, Wadsworth's *Granite Quarries* is not easy to read as a *rural* landscape. The granite quarries of Oldbury, located just outside West Bromwich, near Birmingham, covered an extensive site and, though no city is visible on the horizon of Wadsworth's drawing, this can hardly be categorised as countryside

Figure 4.1 Edward Wadsworth (1889–1949), *Granite Quarries, Darby Hill, Oldbury*, 1919, ink on paper. © Tate, London 2017.

either. In contrast to Wadsworth's ambiguously urban quarry painting, Roger Fry's almost-contemporary 1918 painting, *Quarry, Bo Peep Farm* (Plate 4), represents a small quarry located in a securely rural setting in the South Downs of Sussex.

Here the rocks are obscured by vegetation and topped with mossy green grass. However, it seems highly likely that Fry chose the subject for reasons similar to Wadsworth's. In fact, in Fry's case, it is probably fair to assume that this is a direct homage to Cézanne's quarry paintings. This is countryside, clearly, and yet it is also a man-made landscape in the sense of it representing both a wall of stone mined by human hands and an abstracted likeness of that stone formed by Fry, in which even the leaves of the trees take on the angular, hefty qualities of stone.[20] The painting is especially remarkable when seen in the context of an earlier representation of a quarry by the same artist: Fry's 1903 watercolour, *Betchworth Limeworks*, a distinctly picturesque landscape in which the far-off limestone quarries are not immediately recognisable as a site of rural industry.[21] The motive for this earlier image, it could be claimed, lay not in the formal characteristics of the stone, but in its pleasing whiteness: a quality that clearly attracted John Singer Sargent to the marble quarries of Carrara, where it is the reflectiveness rather than the weight of the marble that the artist values.[22] Sargent's approach, arguably, typifies that of the artist preoccupied with an Impressionist approach to light, with passing effects rather than essential qualities.

By 1918, however, a shift had occurred, and thereafter most artists were much more interested in structure than surface and much more receptive in general to the aesthetics of the industrial. This shift is neatly expressed in a passage in Andy Friend's group biography *Ravilious & Co*, in which Virginia Woolf complains in 1932 (the same year that MacColl drew fresh attention to Rothenstein's 1904 quarry painting) of the appearance of '3 incredibly vast galvanised sheds at the foot of Asheham' in Sussex, part of a local quarry and cement works. She goes on: 'the entire marsh is commanded by these glaring monstrosities and all my walks that side, not only the downs, ruined'.[23] At the same time that Woolf was writing these words, locally based artists of the younger generation, such as Eric Ravilious and Peggy Angus, were setting up their canvases directly in front of the very same galvanised sheds. It was, surely, works such as Wadsworth's *Granite Quarries* and Fry's *Bo Peep Farm*, which took the examples of Cézanne and Rothenstein and ran with them, that made this shift possible, encouraging artists to see what one person considered an unwelcome intrusion into the rural landscape as something that not only belonged there but also was worthy of being pictured. The question remains as to whether Ravilious and Angus were drawn entirely by the form and colour of the cement works, which in Angus's resulting painting, *Cement Works* (1934), assume a distinctly Cubist assemblage, or whether they were also driven by a desire to record aspects of local industry.[24]

Celebration and ambivalence

The so-called 'extractive industries' of quarrying and mining were central to the industrial revolution.[25] Many of the key quarrying sites in Britain had already existed for centuries; nonetheless, their output radically increased in the late nineteenth and first half of the twentieth centuries as the expansion of cities, road and rail networks, harbours and related industries demanded larger and larger amounts of stone.[26] The history of the quarrying industry has proved difficult to tell, however. There was some uncertainty, well into the twentieth century, as to what even constituted a quarry, an issue that bedevilled those trying to compile national statistics. Nevertheless, it is clear that it was an industry that had an impact on thousands of people across the country. Inevitably, some regions contained more quarries than others; however, with an estimated 88,753 people employed in quarries in 1901, quarrying was evidently crucial to the nation's modern identity at the turn of the century.[27] Indeed, during a period in which many industries went into decline, the quarrying industry continued to grow into the 1950s. Modernisation, best seen through the process of mergers and mechanisation, ensured that production expanded even while the number of firms, personnel and working quarries stood still or declined.[28] In light of this, though modern artists may have been attracted initially to the formal qualities of the quarry, they cannot have been entirely unaware of the site's significance within the wider national story.

Given this history, it is especially important to register the fact that images seeking to engage directly with the quarrying industry – as opposed to images in which quarries simply appear – remain rare. There is, for instance, no obvious twentieth-century equivalent to Henry Hawkins's dramatic painting *The Penrhyn Slate Quarry* (1832), painted on the cusp of the Victorian age and at the heart of the industrial revolution. This grand painting depicts the huge slate quarry in Bethesda, Wales, being worked over by hundreds of men. It is a triumphant, perhaps unintentionally intimidating record of a thriving industry, which takes particular pleasure in the epic, shadowy sweep of the hollowed location swarming with life. As Annie Ravenhill-Johnson has noted, 'In this painting, nature is being conquered'; modernity is reshaping the rural (p. 37). Hawkins's painting celebrates a modern industrial spirit ignored in later works: not too surprising, perhaps, as the painting was commissioned by the quarry's owner, Lord Penrhyn. Even Wadsworth, whose work is perhaps closest in spirit to this brooding canvas, tended to depopulate his quarries, following a general trend noted above, in which quarries are represented as being tended by a small collection of relatively calm-looking men usually seen from a distance and rarely involved in active industry. Once the image is populated, it reads less as a landscape in which the quarry could still be mistaken for a mountain, and more obviously as a social document. The process of modernisation is evident, and the possibility of the rural and the modern co-existing seems less likely. De-population of the industrial space, regardless of whether or not it reflects a social reality, offers the viewer a kinder vision of rural modernity. This is not to say, however, that the social history of the quarrying industry cannot be recovered through modern paintings of quarries: simply that it is obscured, as further examples will reveal.

Following his early explorations of the industrial Midlands, Edward Wadsworth would return to the quarry theme much later in his career in his 1942 painting *A Limestone Quarry*.[29] As before, the artist derives obvious pleasure from the sharp lines of the man-made quarry, contrasting here with the soft curves of the landscape that surrounds it. However, unlike *Granite Quarries, Darby Hill, Oldbury*, this quarry is situated in an uneasy relationship to the landscape around it, creating an image that, like much of Wadsworth's later work, bears the mark of Surrealism. Here the artist appears to be thinking about the quarry as a subject with its own claims to modernity, beyond a sculptural quality that happened to meet the demands of artists searching for some ballast against the broken brushstrokes of Impressionism. This painting engages with the strangeness of quarries, their liminality as sites that tend to exist in rural settings or in semi-rural suburbs, but which take on qualities associated with the urban. *A Limestone Quarry* is said to represent Topley Pike quarry, located outside Buxton and within the boundaries of the Peak District National Park. This is a site of industry carved into the rolling hills of a national park, blowing black smoke across the Derbyshire landscape. The lack of any human figures adds, seemingly, to the quiet menace of the image. The quarry is not contained within the hills but is inflicted upon the landscape like a wound. As so often in Wadsworth's work, modern industry, even in the depths of the Derbyshire landscape, carries with it echoes of modern warfare. This painting does not welcome modernity, though it does seem to enjoy the incongruity it offers the rural.

If Wadsworth's 1942 quarry is a dreamlike battlefield, Walter Bell's *Derbyshire Quarry* of 1937 strikes a completely different note. Bell's industrial buildings are clad in the same colours of the landscape and nestle neatly within the surroundings. The smoke that rises from the chimneys, on the far left of the canvas, is pale chalky brown rather than a choking black. Modernity has not been inflicted upon the rural landscape but lives naturally within it. This is as calm an image of a working quarry as you might expect to see: a measured celebration of rural modernity, perhaps, that nonetheless keeps its distance from the site itself. Bell's image is rare, among modern paintings at least, in making the quarry seem like a natural part of the landscape. It is reminiscent, indeed, of images made prior to the industrial expansion of the mid-nineteenth century, in which a quarry might exist as a background feature of a picturesque rural landscape – see, for example, *Landscape with a Woman in a Quarry* by William James Müller, c.1830 (National Trust). Such representations give us industrial sites bearing little sign of actual industry. You might be forgiven, looking at Bell's image, for still believing that the quarrying industry of Britain remained a contained, small-scale affair.

The liminal quarry

Ambivalence over the significance of the modern quarrying industry is the keynote of most modern representations, with many such images anticipating the post-industrial landscape long before it became a widespread reality. A set of images related to a particular site, that of Craigleith in Edinburgh, a large sandstone quarry that flourished in the nineteenth century, provides rich illustration of this quality. Stone from Craigleith was exported to Europe and the United States, as well as providing the raw material for many of Edinburgh's buildings.[30] The relationship between the city and the quarry, indeed, appears to be the subject of John Bell's painting of this site, *Edinburgh from Craigleith Quarry* (c.1860, City of Edinburgh Council), in which the sunken quarry dominates the foreground with the city rising up in the distance. Sunlight breaks through the clouds and bathes the sandstone in a warm protective glow. Though the chasm that has been opened up by several decades of quarrying is substantial and could be read as a vast and violent scar on the landscape, it does not seem as though Bell is encouraging such a reading. The painting seems instead to take great pleasure in the quarry as a geological wonder, nestled within a bucolic landscape only partially disfigured by the apparatus of industry. Water lies at the bottom of the pit – the quarry was subject to regular flooding – and trees bend lovingly over it, creating the sense that industry is simply passing through this landscape as opposed to irrecoverably altering it. Modernity, industry and rurality are allowed to co-exist so long as the first two are tucked away.

In the early twentieth century, several artists, including J. D. Fergusson (*Craigleith Quarry*, 1900) (Plate 5) and James Paterson (*Edinburgh from Craigleith Quarry*, undated, c.1900), returned to Craigleith, now coming towards the end of its long life as a site of industry.[31] Armed with a very different approach to laying paint on canvas and dealing with a different industrial reality, these two painters nevertheless shared Bell's basic vision. Craigleith, now more of a lake than a working quarry, allows Fergusson and Paterson to engage with the industrial landscape at one remove. The post- or inter-industrial site offers a landscape that is, or was, modern, but which is also arguably still rural enough to qualify as a landscape.[32] There is anxiety in these images: the anxiety of the post-industrial suburbs, where once busy quarries lie waterlogged and tall derricks stand abandoned. There is recognition here that a modern landscape necessitates some sort of engagement with the conditions and apparatus of modernity, even if industry has moved on and that apparatus is rendered in loose, hazy brushstrokes. However, the painting's style ensures that the heavy machinery used to lift rocks from the quarry in Fergusson's painting, despite or because of its centrality, could nonetheless be mistaken for a tree or the spire of a church – just as Paterson's quarry can equally easily be misidentified as a reservoir or lake. The creamy rock carries no weight here and there are no straight lines to be found. Geometric rocks and hard stone buildings would go on to feature heavily in Fergusson's art, confirming his place as a major force in Scottish Post-Impressionist painting. Here, however, even in the face of a quarry, design dissolves and the landscape remains fluid. If the painting engages with the history of Craigleith, it does so by drawing attention to its liminality: the quarry is an uncertain presence in the picture, glimpsed but not fully comprehended, central but fragmented.

The quarry and modernism/s

The suburban quarry is also explored in James Dickson Innes's 1906 painting *View of Llanelli from the Furnace Quarry*, in which the city is, again, seen from the viewpoint of the quarry, the source of materials for many of its buildings. Innes's painting, like those of Paterson, Fergusson and Bell, is clearly fascinated by the unusual space of the quarry, which rises like a mountain in the foreground, blocking off the sun. It is a site of industry posing as a natural wonder. Like Rothenstein, it would seem, Innes is also attracted by the weight and solidity of the rocks, finding in them something that is both romantic and challenging in a purely formal sense. And yet there is, of course, a third meaning here, which lies – like so many of these images – in the title of the work: its regional specificity.

Until recently, discussion of the local has rarely featured in narratives of modernism. If Rothenstein's *The Deserted Quarry* is to be understood as a formal exercise, does it matter where that quarry is? Rothenstein's changes of title (only in one of the three does he specify the exact location of the quarry) suggest that he himself was unsure, and it is rare to find critics paying any attention to such details, typically writing to a national, largely metropolitan audience. After all, if Rothenstein is to form part of a wider narrative of European modernism – and gain wider popular recognition – it is probably going to be on the grounds of the formal qualities that were central to his artistic vision and not any preoccupation he may have had with the particularities of the quarrying industry in West Yorkshire around 1900. However, if we are serious about expanding our understanding of modernity, as we should be, beyond the usual artistic suspects, sites and centres, we should still pursue the latter reading, not just in this case but in all images representing quarries created during this period, almost all of which wear their locality on their sleeve. While a comparison of representations of quarries, as offered above, reveals key unifying themes, it should be underlined that there is no universal quarry image, as material (along with the means of extracting it) varies from region to region, bringing a host of local associations that will not be immediately apparent to all viewers. Slate from Wales, granite from Scotland, sandstone from Yorkshire, chalk from Sussex – all carry their own meanings.

To return once more to Rothenstein's image, there is no doubt that this quarry had personal connections for the artist; he recalled playing in local quarries as a child and remained deeply attached to the colours and textures of West Yorkshire stone.[33] In 1897, Yorkshire produced 746,517 tons of sandstone – more than any other county – ensuring that quarries were a crucial contributor to the local and national economy.[34] The contemporary urban landscape of Bradford, a city whose population expanded from around 13,000 to 200,000 during the nineteenth century, was constructed from stone carved out of quarries like this, with the quality and colour of quarried stone a key source of regional pride. The year 1904, when this image was painted, was an important year for the city of Bradford, owing to the Exhibition of Art and Industry held at Lister Park from May to September, which showcased the city's notable contribution to the textile industry (the industry in which Rothenstein's own father had thrived since his emigration from Germany in the 1860s). The year 1904 also marked the inaugural exhibition of a magnificent new art gallery, the Cartwright Hall, named after the industrialist Edmund Cartwright, inventor of the power loom. Rothenstein helped organise this show and many of his works featured in it. The gallery, designed by J. W. Simpson and E. J. Milner Allen, was built in local sandstone, sourced from over twenty quarries.[35] It is possible that the Hawksworth quarry pictured by Rothenstein was one of these. G. A. T. Middleton's 1905 *Building Materials: Their Nature, Properties and Manufacture*, one of the best contemporary guides to quarried stone in Britain, describes Hawksworth sandstone as especially appropriate for building: 'varies from light yellow to dark grey [. . .] good weathering stone, becomes harder with exposure; close-grained' (p. 89). Though it seems a little strange that Rothenstein should have chosen, in the summer of 1904, to ignore the festivities in Lister Park or the tall mills of the city centre and set his canvas up beside a deserted quarry outside of the city boundaries, it can nevertheless be argued that he still had the city in his sights. Paradoxically, the notable expansion of the quarrying industry through the 1900s, belied as it is by the post-industrial sites pictured by Fergusson and Paterson, was not stalled by quarry closures such as this one, but stimulated by them. At the root of the expansion was the increased number of conglomerates, encouraging a lesser number of larger quarries over a larger number of small ones. It seems improbable that Rothenstein was consciously drawing attention to this peculiarity by picturing a deserted quarry or that he saw in the quarry's abandonment a metaphor for the subsequent demise of Bradford's industrial prowess post-1904. Nevertheless, he was obviously interested and invested in the particular character and popularity of Yorkshire sandstone, reminding us that this is not just any old quarry, but a specific place, captured at a very particular moment. It is a quarry that lies at the intersection between at least three possible narratives of modernity: a pan-European narrative of formal innovation, a national narrative of industrial modernity and the narrative of modernity in West Yorkshire.

The local associations here drawn out of Rothenstein's 1904 painting can be found in many other representations of quarries, to such an extent that a single chapter could not possibly promise to extract them all. The benefits of embarking upon a wider study of such images should, however, be clear, as other studies also suggest. An especially challenging model can be found in one of the only previous examinations of the quarrying industry in relationship to rural modernity, James Wilkes's remarkable study of Purbeck in Dorset, which devotes a whole chapter to quarrying. Wilkes's close attention to a single, small region speaks to wider concerns over the narrow, exclusive narrative of modernity in which local variations, non-urban subject matter and cultural products that fall outside of a very specific style are given short shrift. Aside from the close study of Rothenstein's painting, the boundaries of this chapter have been slightly looser in an effort to accommodate as many readings as possible and to cover a wider (though far from comprehensive) range of images. It argues both for the importance of local readings and for an understanding of the wider social history of quarries while drawing attention to a disciplinary narrative in which such meanings have been flattened in favour of a more universal, formalist account, albeit one in which subject matter remains strangely fundamental. The relationship between a representation of a quarry, a rural landscape and a modern landscape has proven hard to define: therein lies the significance of images that challenge the secure boundaries scholars have traditionally used to categorise twentieth-century art.

In dialogue with: Chapter 1 'Ringing the Changes' (I: Networks) [representing rural technologies]; Chapter 11 'Beyond Portmeirion' (IV: Heritage) [rural romanticism; design and the material environment].

Notes

1. MacColl, p. 76.
2. For Rothenstein's opinion of Cézanne, see his memoirs: William Rothenstein, *Men and Memories, Vols I and II* and *Since Fifty*.
3. Symons, p. 23.
4. The quarry in the painting is probably the one located off Odda Lane in Hawksworth, since reopened. For the most recent and comprehensive history of the modern quarrying industry in Britain, see Spires.
5. The painting has also been catalogued as *An Old Quarry, Hawksworth*. The title referencing the Brontës was used for an exhibition held at the Art Institute of Chicago in 1912.
6. William Rothenstein, *Men and Memories, Vol. I*, p. 14.
7. See, for instance, Van Gogh's *Entrance to a Quarry*, 1889 (Van Gogh Museum, Amsterdam). Picasso painted a quarry in 1896, well before his Cubist period.
8. John Rothenstein recalls Stein saying of Picasso's early Cubist landscapes, '"it was the sheer austere *squareness* of buildings like *that* which set him off along the road to Cubism rather than any ideas about form"'. See *Brave Day*, p. 25.
9. See Spector.
10. John Rothenstein, *Modern English Painters*, p. 21.
11. William Rothenstein, *Men and Memories, Vol. II*, p. 226. 'Form is the discipline imposed on the universe by the hidden God,' he wrote in *Men and Memories, Vol. I*, p. 326.
12. William Rothenstein, *Goya*, p. 27.
13. The reference here is clearly to Roger Fry's 1910 Post-Impressionist exhibition.
14. MacColl, p. 77. He is quoting an earlier review here, written – he claims – in 1900.
15. Examples of works by all of these artists, and many others mentioned later in this essay, can be found in the catalogue of paintings in public ownership in the UK: see the website 'Art UK'.
16. Rothenstein noted, in recollection of quarries in the Bradford area, 'To climb among the ledges of these old quarries . . . was like climbing among cliffs and rocks by the sea.' See William Rothenstein, *Men and Memories, Vol. I*, p. 14. Shortly after he painted *The Deserted Quarry*, he embarked upon a series of paintings of actual cliffs by the sea, such as *Nature's Ramparts* (1908) and *White Cliffs, Vaucottes* (1908).
17. See, for example, Palmer's *Purbeck Cliffside Quarrymen* (1920s) and *Dorset Quarrymen, Three Workers* (1940s).
18. Nash, '"Going Modern" and "Being British"'. Nash contributed to the history of quarry painting in the form of a mural design overseen by William Rothenstein. The mural was never completed but the design is owned by Leeds Art Gallery.
19. For a recent discussion of Wadsworth's early work, see Black, pp. 89–101.
20. Margaret Morris's *The Quarry, Wrenfaur, Harlech* (c.1920) appears to share Fry's debt to Cézanne.

21. For illustration of this watercolour and further discussion of Fry's art, see Spalding, *Roger Fry*.
22. For recent discussion and reproduction of Sargent's Carrara paintings, see Hirshler and Carbone.
23. Friend, *Ravilious & Co*, p. 150.
24. Ravilious's friend and fellow artist Helen Binyon describes the cement works primarily in terms of the challenge they set the artist in terms of colour and mood; though she notes that the 'cement gets everywhere', this is not seen as an inconvenience for the workers so much as a point of interest for the artist. Friend, p. 152.
25. Burt, pp. 417–50.
26. Spires, p. 10.
27. Spires, p. 167. If these numbers are correct, roughly 1 in every 200 employed people worked in a quarry at that time.
28. Spires, pp. 178–83.
29. The painting is now in a private collection. For a recent auction record, see 'Paintings – Lot 203' at the website 'Wooley and Wallis'.
30. See Arkley, Browne and Hyslop.
31. Though it did not close until 1942, the quarry was inactive for large periods after 1900; in the 1920s, for instance, only twelve men were employed. The site was covered over after the Second World War and is now occupied by a Sainsbury's supermarket. See Arkley, Browne and Hyslop.
32. The use of the term inter-industrial alludes to the fact that quarries frequently open and close according to demand; an abandoned quarry has not necessarily come to the end of its industrial life.
33. William Rothenstein, *Men and Memories, Vol. I*, p. 14.
34. Spires, p. 200.
35. Bishop, 'Cartwright Memorial Hall', pp. 26–38.

Chapter 5

Windmills and Woodblocks: Agnes Miller Parker, Wood Engraving and the Popular Press in Interwar Britain

Kristin Bluemel

Agnes Miller Parker's wood-engraved illustrations and the books that were built around them bring together materials, personalities, geographies and technologies that seem to challenge conventional understandings of modern artists' relationships to the forces of modernity. Her 1936 *Through the Woods* and its 1937 sequel, *Down the River*, with texts by the popular regional novelist and *Country Life* journalist H. E. Bates, were best-sellers, confirming in the public imagination the associations of the black-and-white forms of wood engraving with rustic landscapes and natural subjects even as they were seen to 'elevate' into art the mass-marketed books in which they appeared. The success of these books represents the symbolic consolidation of Miller Parker's reputation as one of the best wood engravers of her generation, as well as validation of claims by art historians that the years between 1919 and 1945 'will be remembered above all as the great period of autographic wood engraving'.[1] This chapter is an investigation into this generally unknown history that lies between modern art and British book illustration. It seeks to understand the curiously shifting cultural status of wood engraving as a symptom of and inspiration to the cult of the countryside that so preoccupied interwar readers, revealing how circulations between historic 'craft', modern reproductive print technologies and rural subjects place Parker and her art at the centre of the drama of modernity even as she tried to conduct a quiet life on Britain's rural peripheries.

This chapter builds its argument about Agnes Miller Parker's participation in and witness to rural modernity in large part out of the research and critical readings of art and print historians. Such an approach raises several questions about the everyday practices of artists and the people who write about them. Where do illustrators fit in the hierarchies and judgements of literary critics and cultural taste makers, both in the 1930s and today? How do we gauge the value and meaning of texts that ask us to read them as verbal and visual objects? Miller Parker's prints, illustrations and blocks – the material objects testifying to her years of specialised art practice – suggest answers to these questions, but they also redirect us to the materials of her life. It makes a difference to our understanding of the role of books and illustration in literary history that Miller Parker left the urban centres of Glasgow and London for rural communities quite remote from the galleries, printers and publishing houses on which her livelihood depended. This difference, a difference of geography, is so significant that it demands we understand the art and artist not only in relation to forces of modernity, but also in relation to forces of rural modernity, as they were felt both by Miller Parker and those who helped produce her books, and by Miller Parker's audience, those who purchased and consumed her art. Not only must we consider activity at the sites of production, and the ways in which an interwar woman artist experiences the world and represents scenes of rural Britain in her modern texts, but also we should consider activity at sites of consumption, the ways in which Miller Parker's texts construct rural modernity through their published encounters with specific readers.

Rural modernity and the pastoral

Genre theory supports the analysis of relations between works of pastoral modernism and works of rural modernity, even or especially when they are the same works. Paul Fussell reminds us, in 'On the Persistence of Pastoral', that all genres have psychological origins and defining motivations. Pastoral, motivated by an 'urge to escape the actual to lodge in something closer to the ideal', was one of the ten original literary genres, and it opposes or balances the genre of the epic, which is motivated by a 'need to contemplate heroes'.[2] To cite Renato Poggioli's more fanciful explanation, 'The shepherd of poetry finds his emblem not in the wise and prudent ant of the fable, who works all year round to be ready to face the challenge of winter, but in the carefree grasshopper, who spends all summer in song and dance.'[3] Poggioli's metaphor and Fussell's history of pastoral imply that forms of writing as diverse as those produced by Bloomsbury experimentalists or World War I veterans can represent the 'modern urban imagination' in its full engagement with the pastoral project. All are tourists dreaming an ideal world and their literature is 'recognizable as a displacement of the former image of the longed-for, the traditional pastoral scene of quiet inland waters, shade trees, sheep-filled meadows, and silence broken only by the songs of shepherds or birds'.[4] This description evokes Miller Parker's black-and-white reproductions of inland scenes, shade trees, birds, and if not shepherds, then ramblers, fishermen and game wardens. Her wood engravings of natural scenes function as modern (if not modernist) pastoral.

But what about those images of shepherds, sheep or their modern displacements that are not dreams of elsewhere, but rather representations of a contemporary reality, an immediate present? If one is part of a community of fishermen, smelling the smells of the fish and seaweed and oil and tar, how long can images of boats remain an ideal? When does the rural life become a precondition for cultures and arts of modernity that, in Fussell's terms, are more epic or heroic than pastoral in their impulses?

Formal analysis and close reading of texts, the approaches of the critics who inherited the purist ideologies of a pastoral modernism, will not readily reveal the possibility of a heroic stance, let alone an *anti*-pastoral motive, in arts representing traditionally pastoral themes. Yet it is just this motive that this chapter ascribes to the engravings of Agnes Miller Parker. It also contends that Miller Parker will come alive for critics of twentieth-century literature and culture once we join analysis of word and image to historical research on the methods, technologies and market conditions – to say nothing of studio and home life conditions – that governed the making of her books and their distribution and sale to the British public.[5] Only then will we discover Miller Parker's engagement with the project of modernity, in all its complex relation to the rural places she called home.

Gregynog, Montgomeryshire

Edward Hodnett, in his landmark *Five Centuries of English Book Illustration*, writes that 'Few engravers on wood have been the equal of Agnes Miller Parker', who was 'at the top of her form in the 1930s . . . when illustrating books of essays dealing with nature' (p. 273). Her 'use of white lines, arbitrary whites, and patterned shading' made her renderings of animals and natural scenes in the 1931 Gregynog *Fables of Esope* 'one of the cornerstones of the new school of autographic wood engraving' (p. 273). William McCance was integral to the success of *Esope*. He was Miller Parker's collaborator and also her husband; like her, he was a talented Scottish painter trained at the Glasgow School of Art. They had married in 1918 despite the objections of Miller Parker's family, and both worked as instructors at their alma mater before

Figure 5.1 Agnes Miller Parker, *Pigsty*, 1926, 3 x 4 1/16 inches.

moving to London in 1920. They painted and exhibited in London, earning attention in a 1925 *Daily Chronicle* article titled 'The Chiswick Group' for being '"the clever couple from Scotland who believe in Cubist methods"'.[6] Although Miller Parker had never studied wood engraving formally, she was, by 1926, producing wood-engraved prints of rural subjects (for example, *Pigsty*, *Stevedores* and *Blacksmith's Shop*) that, despite their debts to Cubism, especially William Roberts's English Vorticism, show her characteristic management of composition through use of light rather than line (Figure 5.1).[7]

Cubist or realist, pigs or ploughs, wood-engraved prints rarely sell, and as Miller Parker's most astute critic, Ian Rogerson, points out, Miller Parker had to learn the old lesson that 'the only way in which the wood engraver's art could become widely known was through the medium of book illustration'.[8] Miller Parker's correspondence in the National Art Library archives presents evidence of the vital support book illustration provided throughout her working life. She writes in a

13 December 1934 letter to Philip Gibbons, her 'champion', advisor and most actively supportive reader, 'If I could only get a book to illustrate I'd be glad. Small freelance jobs don't really pay.'[9]

In 1930, she and McCance had been offered residencies at Gregynog Hall, a mansion in Montgomeryshire, Wales, bought in 1920 by the wealthy and philanthropic Davies sisters for purposes of founding an arts and crafts centre.[10] Roderick Cave in *The Private Press* includes Gregynog in the 'triumvirate' of great private presses established in the wake of World War I, but suggests that the source of both the founder sisters' philanthropic aim and the conflicts that characterised their relations with resident artists was 'considerable unease at the source of their wealth (derived from the South Wales coalfields)' (p. 173).[11] We have virtually no record from Miller Parker about her time at Gregynog, but it seems that she and McCance were persuaded to move to Wales by their married friends, the wood engravers Blair Hughes-Stanton and his wife, Gertrude Hermes, who were already at Gregynog. McCance served as Gregynog controller while Hughes-Stanton, Miller Parker and Hermes served as illustrators, the women being paid £100 retaining fees as advances towards their work.[12]

Moving to Gregynog was a bold decision that meant departing the city with its communities of artists, art producers and art consumers for relative isolation in mid-Wales. Miller Parker and McCance had before them the example of the previous Gregynog team, artists Horace Walter Bray and Robert Ashwin Maynard, who had left for London when 'the isolation of Montgomeryshire had taken its toll on them'.[13] Yet rural Wales not only supported Miller Parker's and McCance's commitment to rural living, but also inspired some of their most critically acclaimed work. Gregynog in the early 1930s was earning a reputation for publishing 'provocative and exciting' books, despite the conservatism of the Davies sisters.[14] These qualities – experimentation, provocation, excitement – are usually associated with modernist literature and modernist art, not fine art books, and let alone fine art books about traditional subjects. Yet with publication of that very limited, very luxurious leather-bound edition of *Esope* in 1931, the Gregynog Press became the toast and envy of all fine presses throughout Britain. In the words of print historian and wood engraving expert Joanna Selborne, 'The book is universally recognized as one of the corner-stones of fine bookmaking and was largely responsible for establishing the [Gregynog] press's reputation' (p. 383). It certainly seemed to assure Miller Parker's future as a professional artist, supported by the investments in her work by a group of wealthy collectors who comprised most of her very limited readership.

Art and book historians agree that Miller Parker's wood-engraved illustrations in *The Fables of Esope* are a triumph of the form, an achievement rarely surpassed by any other wood engraver in her generation. Rogerson comments that despite sluggish Depression-era sales, '*Esope* was ultimately to become one of the most sought-after private press books' (p. 27). He reports that Francis Meynell, the director of the Nonesuch Press and an authoritative critic on book design, was so impressed by the Gregynog *Esope* that he vowed to get the book reviewed in the literary pages of *The Observer*. In the midst of preparing a radio programme on design, Meynell selected a page from *Esope* for reproduction in *The Listener*, the print vehicle of the BBC.[15] In another popular literary review, the *London Mercury*, the printer and critic Bernard Newdigate described Miller Parker's illustrations for *Esope* as 'brilliantly executed'.[16] These efforts on *Esope*'s behalf demonstrate that it was a book that commanded attention from readerships associated initially with a fine print audience, which eagerly promoted it to a more popular audience. While Rogerson reports that the first issue of 250 copies of *Esope* was priced at either 5 or 12 guineas for wealthy collectors and libraries, he gives Meynell credit for bringing Miller Parker's wood-engraved illustrations 'before the general public for the first time' (p. 26).

The title page of *Esope* attracts the most attention from art and book historians, who invariably cite McCance's skills of page design and lettering and Miller Parker's skills as the illustrator whose grasshopper seems so alert, so real that he threatens to hop off the page (Figure 5.2). However, upon examination with a magnifying glass, Miller Parker's grasshopper is mere abstraction, minute white lines on a black background that assumes meaning against the paper page. The curvilinear white geometric stage or spot light against which Miller Parker's antennaed central figure appears is perhaps her most easily recognised design feature, the printed effect of her physical work carving out large areas on the block. On the title page of *Esope*, for example, it is this white space that draws our eyes to the tiny wolves, buck and crows restlessly positioned beyond her grasshopper, contributing drama and movement to what might otherwise seem a static scene in an eternal mythical moment.

Wood engraving is a form of relief printing, which means that each engraved line or speck left by the artist's tool on the block appears white once run through a press. The black of Miller Parker's grasshopper is the inky reminder of the original raised wood surface of her block; it is the meaning that emerges from the surface she has not engraved. This technique of leaving white lines on a black ink background requires the

Figure 5.2 Agnes Miller Parker, selection from title page of *The Fables of Esope*, Gregynog Press, 1931.

artist to visualise her subject in terms of lights rather than darks; it is the inverse approach of intaglio printing, which requires the artist to anticipate a black line wherever her hand has carved the copper. Like Impressionist painting, which is also known for its experiments with representing outdoor light, wood engraving lent itself to outdoor subjects. During the interwar wood engraving revival in Britain, there were enough practitioners pursuing the representation of outdoor scenes in this medium that wood engraving itself became associated with nature, with animals, and with the rural spaces of the nation and the national imaginary.

Miller Parker's letters record her pleasure working outdoors, her delight in the countryside and her distaste for the city. For example, she describes in an 8 February 1937 letter written from her Buckinghamshire home all the 'excitement' in her garden: 'wild plum blossom . . . snowdrops & primroses popping up all over the place'. She also exclaims over the sprouting bulbs she had planted and delights in the hazel catkins that 'make a grand display by our gate'.[17] This joy in both the cultivated and the wild plants of her rural home contrasts with her feelings about a trip to London in April 1937 to see her publisher, Victor Gollancz, an Artists

International Association (AIA) exhibition, specimens at the zoo and Natural History Museum, and to attend an AIA meeting and a gallery show. 'I do like this countryside of ours and thought London a horrible mess with all its coronation stands and turn up.'[18]

Comparing Miller Parker's wood engravings to those of her colleague and friend at Gregynog, Gertrude Hermes, Rogerson praises Miller Parker's work for its close contact 'with the natural expression of feeling' and its ability to 'express native colour and an affinity with the modern English landscape with spontaneous enjoyment' (p. 29). For those unfamiliar with the techniques and terminology of printing, these words may not make much sense. What could it mean to describe a black-and-white wood engraving as expressing 'colour' or find in the lines of Miller Parker's geometric designs an 'affinity with the modern English landscape'? Rogerson is here describing Miller Parker's illustrations for Rhys Davies's *Daisy Matthews and Three Other Tales* (1932), undertaken for Robert Gibbings, owner of the Golden Cockerel Press and himself a celebrated wood engraver. Miller Parker's subjects in this private press book, published contemporaneously with her Gregynog books, feature more erotic scenes in indoor spaces, although the qualities of landscape arguably parallel those of *Esope* in their stylised forms. As for descriptions of 'colour' in wood engravings, what Rogerson and other experts mean is that Miller Parker could, with her tools and blocks, black ink and white paper, produce unusually vibrant and varied illusions of grey tones. Rogerson marvels, for example, at her 'use of the fleck on top of beautifully laid cross-hatching [which] created a coruscation of light not seen before and introduced a distinct new element into the vocabulary of the wood engraver' (p. 24). Selborne mentions Parker's new methods, primarily her use of a very fine tint tool, which produced her uniquely delicate images (p. 384). These critics recognise that Miller Parker's techniques advanced what print historian Richard Benson describes in *The Printed Picture* as one of the central problems in 'the technological development of printing: how do you describe gray when your ink is black?' (p. 10). The solution, discovered centuries ago by intaglio engravers like Albrecht Dürer, is to create groups of closely arranged black lines. If these are viewed from a short distance away, 'the eye blends the lines and spaces to read variable tone'.[19] While other interwar wood engravers such as Paul Nash, Eric Ravilious, Gwen Raverat, Joan Hassall, Hermes and Hughes-Stanton were also skilled at creating illusions of variations of tone, arguably none did so with as much effect on popular imaginings of the animals and environments of rural Britain as Agnes Miller Parker.

Figure 5.3 Thomas Bewick, 'Saving the Toll' in *The History of British Birds*, vol. II, 1804, p. 173, 3 3/8 x 1 ¾ inches.

Cherryburn, Northumberland

Aesop's fables have been a popular subject for generations of wood engravers. Thomas Bewick, the man whom Edward Hodnett describes as 'the main influence in the revival of autographic white-line wood engraving in the 1920s', began his career as an illustrator with *Select Fables* (1776) (p. 93). His illustrations imitated those of the first English white-line engraver Elisha Kirkall, [20] whose edition of Samuel Croxall's *Fables of Aesop and Others* (1722) he admired; Bewick's biographer Jenny Uglow notes that he kept his crumpled copy of Croxall from childhood to the end of his life (p. 14). Apprenticed and then employed in Ralph Beilby's steel engravers' shop in Newcastle upon Tyne, Bewick began experimenting with steel engraving tools on the end rather than cross-grain of a boxwood plank.[21] He eventually discovered that he could create with this method not only imitations of others' work, but miniature worlds of his own, primarily scenes remembered from his youth wandering the countryside around Newcastle or working on his father's farm, Cherryburn. Hodnett describes Bewick's original vignettes, which appeared as tailpieces in his mature work *General History of Quadrupeds* (1790) and the volumes of his *History of British Birds* (1797, 1804) as 'in themselves rural essays, close to the preoccupations of countrypeople' (p. 93) (Figure 5.3).

Just as important for print culture as Bewick's association of natural and country scenes with the medium of wood engraving was the fact that his tiny blocks were capable of withstanding the enormous pressure of a conventional printing press, and could be locked up in a chase with metal type, making it possible to imprint a page with both pictures and words at a single pass. If the print scholar William Ivins is correct that 'all civilization grew out of written language pointing to a picture',[22] the influence of Bewick on English culture cannot be overestimated. Benson argues that in the history of print and language such humble artefacts as Bewick's *Aesop* are more important even than fine collectable books like Miller Parker's *Esope* 'because their social function has been enormously more influential'.[23] That influence rests upon the printer's capacity to multiply pictures. Once image and type could be transferred simultaneously to paper, they could move and, 'Like language itself, . . . spread throughout human culture' (p. 8). Although book historians and literary scholars have no good way to cite illustrators in bibliographic entries, the pictures in the books they read are, in Benson's estimation, 'as important as language' (p. 3). Together, pictures and language 'form the glue that holds society together' (p. 3).

From this perspective, any scholarly account attending only to the forms of a picture – their subjects and designs – without considering the picture's methods of production and reproduction and its relation to language cannot fully say what the picture means. In Benson's words, 'the making dictates the form, and whatever meaning there might be flows from those steps and from the cultural context in which the picture is viewed' (p. 2). This means that while the subjects of Miller Parker's *Esope* may be ancient and her methods of engraving wood blocks indebted to eighteenth-century practices, the prints and illustrations produced from those blocks are 'second generation pictures', artefacts that transcend their static condition by virtue of the modern technologies that moved them from block to paper to market to reader.[24] Miller Parker's pastoral subjects do not preclude or negate the modernity of her art because her art depends on the most sophisticated print and communication technologies of the period for its reproduction in books, its identity as illustration inviting consumption by quite ordinary people, in quite ordinary ways. Nor does it preclude or negate what Fussell would recognise as the anti-pastoral, heroic motives of Miller's practice. Miller Parker, working in wilful exile from urban art centres, can best be allied with the wise and prudent ant of the fable, or better yet the ant's wife, who labours all year round to be ready to face the challenge of winter with little opportunity for pastoral escape.

Albrighton, Shropshire, and Pheasant's Hill, Buckinghamshire

No one in 1931, the year *Esope* was published, could have anticipated that Miller Parker's real triumph would come several years later after she moved, along with her husband, cats, and spitstickers, burins and tint tools, into an abandoned windmill in Albrighton, Shropshire.[25] While there, contending with resident doves, lack of heat and a wandering husband, Miller Parker earned what was in retrospect to serve as her most important commission. In 1935, the mass-market publisher Victor Gollancz asked if she would be interested in creating wood engravings for a book of natural history that would be part of his series of countryside books illustrated with black-and-white wood engravings.[26] The first book in the series, Clare Leighton's *Four Hedges: A Gardener's Chronicle* (1935), had been extremely popular, both its texts and its images appealing to a reading public that seemed to have an insatiable appetite for books on country living and scenes of rural life. Due to its high-quality commercial printing and relatively low sales price, Miller Parker's first book for Gollancz, *Through the Woods: The English Woodland – April to April*, with a commissioned text by H. E. Bates, was just as successful as Leighton's. Hodnett notes approvingly that *Through the Woods* 'did much to create a public awareness of the pleasures of wood-engraved illustrations' (p. 273).

Miller Parker and Bates had first worked together as illustrator and author of *The House with the Apricot*, one of the texts published by Robert Gibbings in his 'Guinea' series of limited editions for the Golden Cockerel Press.[27] By the mid-1930s, Bates was publishing popular novels of rural Northamptonshire life, including *The Fallow Land* (1932) and *The Poacher* (1935), put out by Jonathan Cape, in addition to volumes of short stories and a regular column for *Country Life*.[28] Miller Parker had also worked for Jonathan Cape, providing wood-engraved illustrations for Hugh Edward's novel, *Helen between Cupids* and Adrien Le Corbeau's *The Forest Giant*, both published in 1935. Her experience with Cape led her to complain to Gibbons in a letter of that year that 'after Gregynog's printing I find it difficult to get reconciled to the slap dash style of mass production',[29] but she nonetheless accepted Gollancz's commission due to the pressing need for income.

Correspondence in the National Art Library archives shows that Gollancz consulted Miller Parker about virtually every aspect of the project, although he rejected her suggestion that McCance write the text to accompany her illustrations. When the project was completed, Miller Parker and Bates were mutually impressed by each other's work,

Figure 5.4 Agnes Miller Parker, 'Pike', in *Down the River* by H. E. Bates, Gollancz, 1937, p. 94, 4 ¾ x 2 ½ inches.

with Miller Parker describing her collaborator as 'a fine chap' and Bates describing her work as 'masterly'.[30] McCance was also enthusiastic, exclaiming in a July 1936 letter to Gibbons that 'Gollancz is a gem to work for' and that 'This book of Agens [sic] is going to be *the* book of the year – or many years as far as popular unlimited editions are concerned: published at 10/6.'[31] McCance's comment about the book's price is important, as it points to the moment that new printing technologies and methods transformed Miller Parker from an exclusive to a popular artist.

McCance's admiration for *Through the Woods* was not universally shared by reviewers. Miller Parker confided to Gibbons in a letter of 22 October 1936, 'When I get depressed reading Tory Press on the book I turn back to your congratulatory telegram and am cheered again. How the reviewers are twisting poor Bate's [sic] text!'[32] After publication of *Down the River*, her second collaboration with Bates, she was more optimistic. In an 18 October 1937 letter to Gibbons, we find one of Miller Parker's most complete aesthetic statements about the meaning and purpose of her illustrations in a defence of her collaboration with Bates and of illustrated books more generally. She begins, 'I'm so glad you like Bates' writing so much too. He didn't get his fair share of appreciation last year but I think he will walk off with the laurels this year.' She scolds reviewers for not bothering to 'read the text before they criticize a block', defending her wood engraving of a pike that she thinks has been unfairly characterised as 'stuffed' (Figure 5.4). Her pike is still because it is a response to these words of Bates:

> [T]here is no stillness like the stillness of a sunning pike. He lies as stiff and immobile as a rod of yellowish steel. No bird, and I believe no animal, attains that same perfection of rigidity. It is at once dynamic and sinister [. . .]. [I] t looks, at first sight, a sleepy and gentle pose, almost feline, the mere silky shadow of a great leaf drowning dimly in the sun-clear water. (pp. 92–3)

Miller Parker's faith in Bates's words seems justified by this passage, which aims for no dramatic narrative effects but can represent the complex, multi-modal conversation that emerges in *Down the River* when his words are put in dialogue with Miller Parker's wood engravings.

It is this conversation Miller Parker defends in her letter to Gibbons with the exasperated cry, 'And why should not a good piece of writing have some decorations!' She ends by consoling herself and Gibbons with the idea that even for a popular unlimited edition, it is the ideal readers, the specialists and art patrons, who matter: 'As long as some folks like yourself, like the book as a complete whole as you do I am happy.'[33] Miller Parker's defence of *Down the River* resists the implication of the book's reviewers that 'decoration' – by which she means, in self-effacing fashion, her wood engravings – is a sign of diminished aesthetic significance, an easily interpreted sign of low literary aspiration on the part of artist and reader. More importantly, she rejects the idea that the components of illustrated books can be judged separately. Rather, she insists that the books she has illustrated with wood engravings must be assessed as 'a complete whole'.

For the Gollancz books, Miller Parker produced a total of 156 wood-engraved illustrations, all of which adopt a realistic style that shows off her scientist's eye for detail (Figures 5.5, 5.6, 5.7, 5.8).

Figure 5.5 Agnes Miller Parker, 'Windmill' in *Down the River* by H. E. Bates, 1937, p. 115, 1 9/16 x 2 inches.

Figure 5.6 Agnes Miller Parker, 'Roach and Net', in *Down the River* by H. E. Bates, 1937, p. 45, 1 9/16 w x 2 1/16 inches.

Figure 5.7 Agnes Miller Parker, 'Hare in Snow', in *Through the Woods* by H. E. Bates, 1936, p. 124, 4 1/16 x 4 1/8 inches.

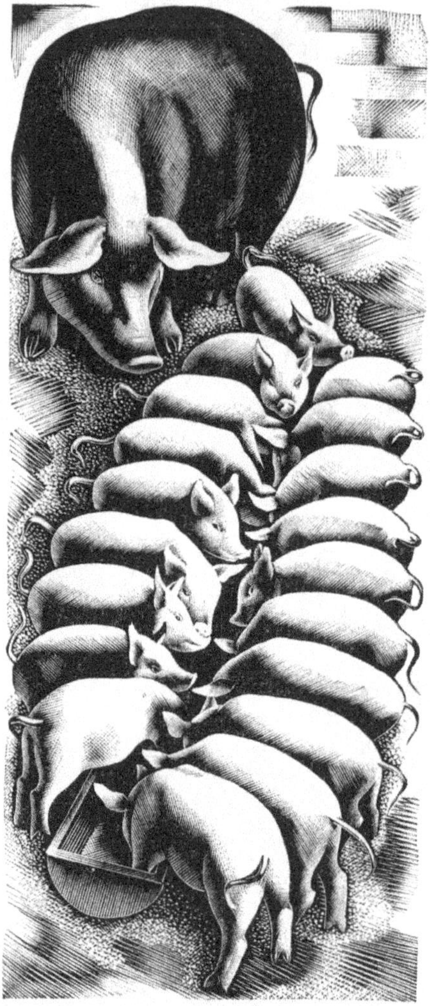

Figure 5.8 Agnes Miller Parker, 'The Old Girl and Family' in *Down the River* by H. E. Bates, 1937, p. 37, 2 5/16" x 5 5/16 inches.

Her animals are still caught within white spotlights, as were her animals in *Esope*, but the white backgrounds are liberated from the Vorticist geometry of her Gregynog illustrations. In Selborne's words, 'Even though these are naturalistic depictions, they are also highly personal and original compositions, no longer confined within frames but alive with movement and rhythmic shape' (p. 388).

'Movement and rhythmic shape': these words have described many a modernist composition, but here they refer to naturalistic renderings of woodland and riverside scenes. This is a case where a modern artist becomes more innovative as she departs from abstraction. Whether or not this innovation can or should be called modernist, it is important to note the historical conditions that grant Miller Parker's wood engravings a place in the study of rural modernity. Produced through the artist's direct observation of natural subjects in rural locations around Albrighton and, after the summer of 1936, Pheasant's Hill, Hambleden, the wood engravings in *Through the Woods* and *Down the River* were commissioned by a London trade publisher who had found, in the tail end of the Depression, a mass market for illustrated wood-engraved books for adults about rural life.[34] Using the most technologically advanced reproductive methods available to him, he was able to successfully publish mass market books that were illustrated with the kind of art associated until that point with collectors' volumes produced by private and fine presses like Gregynog and Golden Cockerel. While the rural themes of each illustration in *Through the Woods* and *Down the River* are obvious to even a casual reader, the modernity of these same illustrations is most evident in the books themselves, produced by modern trade-printing technologies and publishing methods. Hidden modernity is still real modernity, however, and it is the argument of this chapter that scholars of interwar British literary and print culture need to engage with the less respected 'middlebrow' genres and virtually unknown techniques of book illustration in order to understand the significance of the collaboration between Agnes Miller Parker, H. E. Bates and Victor Gollancz, and also to understand the possibility and significance of rural modernity in Britain.[35]

Isle of Arran, Firth of Clyde

In 1955, after almost forty years of marriage, Agnes Miller Parker left William McCance and moved to Glasgow to live with her brothers. We have a record of McCance's reaction to this rupture in his letter to Philip Gibbons of 25 August 1955, but we do not have any direct record of Miller Parker's feelings about this crisis.[36] It is in the letters of her friends, such as William and Dorothy Bell, Jessica Knish, Lavinia Derwent, Bernard Chambers, Peggy Grieves and Celandine Kennington, that we can begin to see beyond the catkins, snowdrops and primroses, and imagine the tense domestic climate in which Miller Parker engraved her quiet images of rural and wild outdoor life. These letters from her ageing friends exert a pressure, an imprint, upon any scholarly study of Miller Parker's art, career and life yet, to date, no scholar has told that partial story. Where does it fit in studies of the artist and her art? It seems ugly and irrelevant beside the record of beauty and purpose in her prints and books. Yet this chapter argues that Miller Parker's wood engravings and rural modernity more generally cannot be discovered unless we understand the materials and processes that led to the creation and consumption of the books, words, type and pictures that fascinate us. Cultural objects like Miller Parker's limited Gregynog books or unlimited Gollancz books might appear 'mere' pastoral, guilty of inspiring nostalgia, sentiment and idealisation of a timeless nature or, worse yet, an idealised nation. But this reading falters against the reality of the conditions of production of her wood-engraved books and collapses altogether against the archival record of domestic suffering. Then the cooing doves in the windmill, the idyllic views of wooded hills may seem a defence against or, conversely, components of the spousal violence and emotional manipulation that Miller Parker's friends describe in their letters.

While Miller Parker sought a house on the Isle of Arran, her closest friends begged her to stay on the mainland, interpreting her departure from Glasgow as a regrettable 'hideout' or 'burial' in a distant countryside. Miller Parker's move to Arran might very well have been a retreat, but we are reminded by the archive she left behind that retreat to the countryside is sometimes necessary and not at all romantic or nostalgic. This archive also preserves materials suggesting that what looks like retreat may, in fact, be the inverse. A brief article of 19 September 1958 in the newspaper *The Bulletin* introduces readers to 'Scots artist, Agnes Millar [sic] Parker' in her 'quiet, sunny house in Riddrie', quoting Miller Parker as saying 'Now I'm looking for a house in the country, or by the sea. . . . I'd like to live on an island best of all – I love fishing, and sailing, and swimming.'[37] These are not the words of a defeated woman escaping from the modern world but rather those of someone independently, even heroically, advancing her art and income as she freely pursues her dreams.

The letters shared between artist and friends – one of whom described her flight from her husband as 'the best thing' she had ever done and another of whom declared her past 'a waste' – point to another hidden aspect of Miller Parker's engagement with modernity. While spousal jealousy and abuse drive many an old tale, the story of a woman taking her professional reputation and her engraver's tools to start life over again at the age of sixty is uniquely modern. It confirms that remote and rural areas of Britain could serve as a source of modern art, artistic identity and a newly possible kind of female independence.

In dialogue with: Chapter 10 'Borderlands' (IV: Heritage) [Scotland; art versus craft]; Chapter 13 'Altered Countrysides' (V: Wars) [visual culture; rural landscapes].

Notes

1. Hodnett, p. 239. Autographic wood engravers are not copyists, but artists who design and engrave their own images.
2. Fussell, p. 183.
3. Poggioli, p. 5.
4. Fussell, p. 201.
5. See Bluemel, 'Rural Modernity and the Wood Engraving Revival' and 'The Saltire Chapbooks'. See also Leaper, '"Old-fashioned modern"', on the related form of lino-cuts.
6. Quoted in Rogerson, pp. 12–13.
7. Selborne, p. 383; Rogerson, pp. 16–17.
8. Rogerson, pp. 13–14.
9. National Art Library (hereafter referred to as NAL), London, Victoria and Albert Museum, Agnes Miller Parker Correspondence, Box MS L26 1983, letter from Agnes Miller Parker to Philip Gibbons, 28 November 1935.
10. Rogerson, p. 18.
11. The other two worthies are the Golden Cockerel Press and Francis Meynell's Nonesuch Press.
12. Rogerson, p. 28.
13. Cave, p. 175.
14. Rogerson, p. 21.
15. Rogerson, pp. 26–7.
16. Quoted in Rogerson, p. 26.
17. NAL, Box MS L26 1983, letter from AMP to Philip Gibbons, 8 February 1937.
18. NAL, Box MS L26 1983, AMP to Philip Gibbons, 25 April 1937.
19. Benson, p. 10.
20. Hodnett, p. 93.
21. See Uglow, pp. 45–52.
22. Quoted in Benson, p. 22.
23. Lowry and Galassi, describing Benson's 'essential subject', p. 1.
24. Benson, p. 2.
25. Rogerson, p. 33, dates the move to October 1933. Miller Parker and McCance remained there for over two years.
26. Selborne, p. 387.
27. Rogerson, p. 29.
28. Dean Baldwin, pp. 124–5.
29. NAL, Box MS L26 1983, AMP to Philip Gibbons, 28 November 1935. Quoted in Selborne, p. 387.
30. Selborne, p. 388.
31. NAL, Box MS L26 1983, William McCance to Philip Gibbons, July 1936.
32. NAL, Box MS L26 1983, AMP to Philip Gibbons, 22 October 1936.

33. NAL, Box MS L26 1983, AMP to Philip Gibbons, 18 October 1937.
34. See NAL, Box MS L26 1983, William McCance letter to Philip Gibbons, July 1936, for a description of the rural environment that surrounded their new home in Pheasant's Hill.
35. See Macdonald, Grover, and Brown and Grover.
36. See NAL, Box MS L26 1983.
37. National Library of Scotland, Agnes Miller Parker Archive, File 2.

Chapter 6

Hiraeth and Ambiguous Pastorals: Wales, England and Rural Modernities between the Wars

Chris Hopkins

In a 1937 review of Rhys Davies's novel *A Time to Laugh*, the Welsh writer Glyn Jones found occasion to criticise the book thus:

> underlying the individually interesting characters and incidents I could discover no urgent unifying principle (love, hate, *hiraeth*, the pride of life), no tension forcing a design upon them as the discharge of an electric current will galvanise inert filings into a pattern.[1]

Hiraeth is a word that is very familiar to Welsh speakers and describes what might be seen as an abidingly pastoral aspect of Welsh culture. *Geiriadur Prifysgol Cymru* (The University of Wales Dictionary, 1979) defines the word as meaning 'grief or sadness after the lost or departed, longing, yearning, nostalgia, wistfulness, homesickness, earnest desire *for what might have been*'.[2] To an extent, the word points back to ancient histories, to the sense that Wales is one of the remaining outposts of what was once the wholly Celtic realm of Britain, but it also points towards the more recent Welsh experience of rapid industrialisation in the nineteenth and twentieth centuries during which coal, iron, steel, slate and railways made their marks on a culture that nevertheless often maintained that it remained essentially an organic and rural community – and, for those very reasons, superior to English culture and society. This chapter will trace some of the ways in which the relationship between past and present, rural and urban, arises in quite specific (if often awkward) forms in Welsh culture and history, and is then (re)presented to English (and indeed other Anglophone) readers and audiences as an ambiguous, pastoral narrative about how the supplanting of the rural by the modern might offer stories of both loss and consolation.

The chapter will first explore the Welsh rural modernity constructed by Welsh writers in English and contrast its sense of community with that produced and consumed by metropolitan, modern England. The texts examined here will be the periodical *Wales* and the novel *Rhondda*

Roundabout (1934) by Jack Jones. The chapter then examines the appeal of *hiraeth,* despite its specifically Welsh roots, among English readers and audiences during the interwar period and their fascination with popular texts that presented Wales's strong associations with both the rural past and the industrial modern. This section looks at Emlyn Williams's play *The Corn is Green* (1938) and Richard Llewellyn's novel *How Green was My Valley* (1939), which both maintained hit status in the years just prior to and immediately after the outbreak of war. Both of these works reached even wider audiences through film versions; *How Green was My Valley* was made into a film in 1941 by the director John Ford and was a success in both England and Wales, while *The Corn is Green* also had a successful film adaption in 1945. Despite their wide impact, these two texts and their adaptations remain under-studied. While their relative authenticity is arguable, all of these narratives represent to their audiences the simultaneous differences and identifications between Welshness and Englishness. All explore complex oppositions in the interwar period between rural and modern, organic community and culture and urban alienation, the lost past, the uncertain present and the potentiality of the future.

Wales and Welshness

The myths and imaginings do have some factual roots, for there was something unusual in the ways in which industry and pastoral, urban and village, tradition and modernity were interwoven in Wales. Welsh writing in English and English writing about Wales during the 1930s often used pastoral modes in their representations of the Welsh experience of industrialisation, but equally they also drew on the fact that in many ways the industrialisation of Wales did not mean a displacement from a village-like sense of community into a more anonymous urban modernity.[3] Pit towns and villages were often close communities with a relatively shallow class hierarchy. As Gwyn A. Williams points out, 'Not only in village and small town Wales, but in whole areas of industrial society, the concept of the *gwerin* [the people; democracy] seemed capable of infinite extension' (p. 238). Partly from this actual social and economic basis, there arose a strong Welsh sense that Wales and Welshness were in essence rural entities, threatened but not destroyed by an alien, imported and exploitative English industrial modern culture – a culture sometimes seen as bringing some benefits once adapted by the Welsh. These oppositions are shown in the violent response to a Welsh writer who was an exception in his hostility to the construction of Wales as rural nation. Caradoc Evans became notorious as the 'best-hated man in Wales' after the publication of his linked short story collection, *My People*, in 1915. At the core of every one of these short stories was a profound critique of the cherished idea that Welsh identity was rooted in the twin pillars of rural life and Nonconformist belief. As John Harris explains in the Introduction to his 1987 edition of *My People*:

> the liberal-non-conformist leadership . . . encouraged the view of *y werin* (the common people) as an unblemished repository of God-given talent, wisdom and right feeling. The rural Welsh had been spared the moral stains that so marked their urban brothers, recently translated to the industrial south and there exposed to English contamination. (p. 39)

Evans attacked this underpinning narrative unmercifully, and it was this that made many of his Welsh readers feel insulted, doubly so because the stories were written in English and thus exposed Wales to a quite unmerited English superiority. Thus the *Carmarthen Journal* complained bitterly that Evans had betrayed his people to the Englishman 'who over his pint of beer in his squalid dirty gin-shops treats his neighbours with a lengthy dissertation upon the barbarians who live somewhere on the other side of the Severn'.[4] Though Evans generally worked through satire in his fiction, a rare non-fiction commentary about his vision of Wales suggests that he too saw the possibility of a future and better Wales that did combine industry, the rural and modernity in one organic community: 'We are not dead. We have intellect: it is in the coal-pits, in the universities, and in the fields . . . they and those who come after them will create a new Wales – a Wales for the Welsh.'[5] The vision of Wales centred on the Welsh-speaking rural regions of west Wales that *My People* ridiculed is here notably replaced by an industrial–rural democratic and egalitarian modernity centred on South Wales, an area that was indeed then less purely Welsh-speaking, since the coal-fields and iron-work of the nineteenth century had attracted migrants from southern and western England and from Ireland.[6]

Much of the creative and critical writing in the two important Welsh literary magazines of the 1930s, *Wales* and *Welsh Review*, continued to assert that Wales was different from England in the way it kept the industrial and the rural in contact, even though industry was still seen as a colonial blot.[7] Indeed, it is notable that Caradoc Evans was a supporter of *Wales*, writing of the first number that 'I like its note and courage. It is easily the best thing that has come out of Wales. It is nice to look at a list of contributors without a *Parch* [Nonconformist minister].'[8] The second issue equally had paid Caradoc the tribute of making him the subject of the first of their series of 'Bibliographies of

Modern Welsh Authors', suggesting that he was a founding figure in the genealogy of Welsh writing in English.[9] The magazine often argued for a modern, democratic, egalitarian Wales of the kind Caradoc outlined. The manifesto-esque invitation to subscribe to the magazine in issue No. 1 (back cover) was presumably by the editor, Keidrych Rhys, and contrasted the alienated society and culture of England with the organic unity of Wales:

> British culture is a fact but the English contribution to it is very small . . . there is actually no such thing as 'English' culture; a few individuals may be highly cultured, but the people as a whole are crass.
> Welsh literature is carried on, not by a clique of moneyed dilettantes, but by the small shopkeepers, the blacksmiths, the non-conformist ministers, by the miners, quarrymen, and the railwaymen.
> [. . .]
> We publish this journal in English so that it may spread far beyond the frontiers of Wales, and because we realise the beauty of the English language better than the English themselves, who have so shamefully misused it.
> [. . .]
> Though we write in English, we are rooted in Wales.

The inclusion of Nonconformist ministers might not have pleased Caradoc Evans but there are notable exclusions too: the farmer and farm-labourer are sadly missing, and most women are also implicitly ruled out by this occupational list. However, the blacksmith may serve to represent the rural contribution to a culture that is seen as wholly masculine. The mission of Wales to reintroduce the lost beauty of the English language to the English may indeed, as we shall see, map on to a fantasy English version of *hiraeth,* as well as asserting the superiority of Welsh culture over that of its apparent colonial overlord. The final metaphor of the passage is, of course, a pastoral and organic one: 'we are rooted in Wales'. Similarly, the Faber & Faber advert for *Welsh Short Stories* (1937) in No. 3 (unpaginated end-pages) uses landscape and occupation to suggest a social and cultural unity of industrial and rural experience as representative of Wales: '[the stories] have a wide range of subject . . . there are tales of the mountains, the valleys, and the Border country, tales of farming, mining, war, of preachers, poachers, quarrymen, and tramps'. Though the advert is not, of course, necessarily the work of a *Wales* writer, the collection did include a number of regular contributors, among whom were Glyn Jones himself, Rhys Davies and Caradoc Evans.

Curiously, this Faber publication was itself the topic for a highly critical poem by Mair Evans, published in *Wales* issue No. 4 (March 1938). 'Tradition and The Faber Stories' worries away at the question of how representative the stories are of Welshness:

> It's no
> book of which a countryman may well be proud
> rather would one leave than live with most of the characters
> for all 'the world is too little with us'
> peasant life is too poor a thing
> its song seems sadly lacking. (ll. 11–16)

The poem is perhaps overly anxious to stake its claim to a modernist style through avoiding the direct statement and obvious coherence, but seems to deal with Welshness by invoking the oppositions of city and country and finding both awkward, neither alone explaining Wales. It is largely a poem of negation, but nevertheless the terms that it feels the varied Faber stories provide give it no choice but to see Wales as both modern and rural, though neither quite fits fully.

This awkward rural modernity is an almost constant topic in *Wales*, as two more examples can show. Meurig Walter's 'Rhondda Poems', printed immediately after 'Tradition and the Faber Stories', gives a sense of this mixture, which is again critical but also slightly fonder:

> Below, Ferndale squats in a gash of cwm,
> its trellised streets spat from a tube of road
> that crashes through: streets huddling fire from cliques,
> coloned by chapels and commaed by pubs
> and cinemas, inoculating soul –
> silicosed men against the hate-red cough
> of discontent and breathless war for food. (ll. 1–7)[10]

The town is in a natural setting, a *cwm* being the Welsh word for a valley, but it also offers urban amenities, the streets, the plural chapels and pubs that give some shelter or distraction from industrial ills. Indeed, the poem sees the benefits and ills of the modern as intertwined, as the commonest lung disease of the miners is made into a metaphor for discontent against which these social institutions are partly medicinal. The enfolding mountains are not conventionally aestheticised but they are still part of the scene: 'Flanked by moon-greased eggs of mountain sprawled tense/to chest a sore back of sky' (ll. 8–9). The town's houses are poor – 'gummed together like a toy', 'glum and squint' – but their 'rows converge':

> Upon the Strand, where hill is wall-steep dam
> against the overflow of valley streets,
> and but a thread of road drawn taut, drawn down
> from Little Moscow up beyond the hills. (ll. 17–20)

The language here suggests some contention between country and city as the hill stops the streets from spreading any further. The hills are the essential setting for these urban settlements, despite their contacts with modern world politics; Little Moscow was the name first given to the Rhondda town of Maerdy in 1930 after its militant communist miners left the more moderate socialist National South Wales Miners' Federation. Indeed, both Maerdy and Ferndale (Glynrhedynog) are neighbouring towns that epitomised the rapid nineteenth-century industrialisation of South Wales. In the poem they are self-contained yet connected urban communities within sight of their still visible and palpable pre-industrial origins.

There is a similar sense of the intertwined nature of South Welsh life (and death) in Vernon Watkins's poem, 'The Collier':[11]

> When I was born on Amman hill
> A dark bird crossed the sun.
> Sharp on the floor the shadow fell;
> I was the youngest son. (ll. 1–4)

Though the first stanza looks at first sight to have a purely natural setting, suitable to birth and beginnings, it is also full of ominous signs (the 'dark bird crossing the sun', the 'shadow') that establish the poem's set of simultaneous oppositions and links between sky–light–sun–outdoors–above-ground–colour–gold and dark–shadow–indoors–black–pit–night–stain–darkness. This is a fated place where death is in life from the beginning and where natural and industrial seep into each other. Even at school the first-person speaker's language is infected by premonitions of underground:

> And when I went to the County School
> I worked in a shaft of light.
> In the wood of the desk I cut my name:
> Dai for Dynamite. (ll. 5–8)

Is the school a place of freedom and light, or do the words 'worked in a shaft' suggest it as the first step in industrial servitude? Does his nickname suggest his explosive vitality or rather that he is slated for destruction?

The third stanza envisages his brothers as organic with the landscape but perhaps also as part of the coal-pits, admonitory figures who have either finished learning or finished teaching. They seem to see what should be a welcome escape from school as running into worse danger:

> The tall black hills my brothers stood;
> Their lessons were done.
> From the door of the school when I ran out
> They frowned to watch me run. (ll. 9–12)

There is just one stanza (5) that sees speaker and nature as mutually supporting (the egg-stealing probably intended to be seen as innocent at the time):

> I learnt the valley flowers' names
> And the rough bark knew my knees
> I brought home trout from the river
> And spotted eggs from the trees. (ll. 17–20)

This is presumably the gap between school and work, but 'Soon as I went from the County School/I worked in a shaft' Said Jim/'You will get your chain of gold . . ./but not for a likely time' (stanza 7). In this stanza and the two that follow, three characters (perhaps the speakers' brothers) suggest or perhaps suffer increasingly ominous fates, and where earlier in the poem light was crossed by dark, light is now extinguished and attempts at human expression or communication take place in the dark. In the final stanza the speaker recalls these exchanges:

> They changed words there in darkness
> And still through my head they run,
> And white on my limbs is the linen sheet
> And gold on my neck the sun. (ll. 41–4)

The speaker has achieved his gold chain and a pure light, but only in death, and even then he is haunted by conversations in the dark. Watkins's poem sustains complex patterns of opposition: contrast and interchange between rural and industrial, a life-cycle drawing on the industrial age and allusions to primitive and/or biblical stories.

Ideas about complex connections and oppositions in Welsh experience between modern and rural are picked up repeatedly in creative and editorial pieces in the magazine. The pugnacious editorial in issue No. 2 continued the theme: 'The present-day problems of the real Welsh writer are many, varying tremendously from those of others writing across our frontier [. . .] we are not a "literary" clique; once more we stress that we are with the People' (pp. 35–7). The editorial goes on to ridicule the alleged ways in which readers have tried to classify *Wales* through deploying clichés of national identity: 'We've been accused of trying to be "European": I've read your magazine and I'm just like the man in Acts viii 30 31.' Acts VIII, verses 30 and 31 are about the difficulties of reading without guidance:

> **30** And Philip ran thither to *him*, and heard him read the prophet Esaias, and said, Understandest thou what thou readest?
> **31** And he said, How can I, except some man should guide me? And he desired Philip that he would come up and sit with him. (King James Bible)

The 'European' reference presumably suggest that *Wales* is an avant-garde, modernist publication understandable only by disciples, though the unexplained biblical reference also suggests the ready frame of reference provided by non-conformism in Wales. A scathing attack on BBC radio's failure to understand contemporary Welsh writing in English reasserts the sharp contrast between the possibility of an authentic Welsh culture and the fragmented urban, hierarchical and commercial 'culture' of English modernity. The editors write:

> If we are given a reasonable chance we hope to print work by our younger writers – an opportunity denied them in the English Literary Map of log-rolling, cocktail parties, book clubs, knighthoods, O.M.s and superannuated effeminacy in Bloomsbury editorial chairs. (p. 37)

English literature is, from *Wales*'s point of view, an old boy network, while more popular culture is differently but equally devoid of engagement with the real. While the contemporary writers of *Wales* are of the 'People', the English people are offered ready-made goods: 'a potted and standardised individuality – Priestley's jolly, beer-drinking workingman' or the cinema that caters to their highly generic preferences, a false relationship indicated here by the adoption of the format of the customer survey: 'The women preferred: (1) Society Drama, (2) Thriller Adventure, (3) Musical Comedy, (4) Love-Romance, (5) Comedy, (6) Historical, (7) War.' Similarly sharp commentaries by Keidrych Rhys in the guise of his twenty-one 'Notes for a New Editor' in issue 8/9 of August 1939 partly mock rural Wales yet also assert the wholeness of Welsh culture when compared to English:

> 9. The Welsh – they are after all predominantly hard-hit farmers and smallholders – too poor to buy books, even if they had the leisure. But Foyles' 2d. libraries will soon reach every hamlet.
> [. . .]
> 11. When a tablet was unveiled at a farm outside my village, to the late Llewellyn Williams, a popular politician, novelist and historian, quite a gathering of local bards took part in the broadcast ceremony: that couldn't possibly occur in an English village, I feel. (p. 247)

Note 9 at least makes up for the absence of farmers from the subscription notice in Issue 1, but appears to see rural literary culture as unlikely, or as possible only in the equally unlikely event that modern English mass marketing eventually reaches all parts of Wales. However, (and despite the magazine's generally critical response to the BBC), note 11 is more positive in seeing a unified Welsh culture that is distinctive, and part of a modern nation in which mass communications and village culture are part of a cultural continuum.

Welsh community: *Rhondda Roundabout*

There is a related sense of a unified rural yet also urbanised South Welsh culture in Jack Jones's novel *Rhondda Roundabout*, very famous in the 1930s and 1940s, and set in exactly the kind of Rhondda town also portrayed in Meurig Walter's 'Rhondda Poems'. The novel was well regarded in Wales but also very well received in England, and so forms a bridge between more authentically Welsh texts of rural modernity and those that are perhaps partly re-presenting the resulting sense of *hiraeth* for English readers. *Wales* might not necessarily have approved of the novel, given its tendency to be suspicious of anything that might be seen as stereotyping Welsh identities. Indeed, *Wales* makes what looks like a satirical link between the last three texts discussed here in a paragraph on a talk by the Welsh-speaking Welsh Nationalist writer Saunders Lewis. Titled 'Is There an Anglo-Welsh Literature?', it slyly notes, 'however soon night-must-fall, the corn remains green as ever, and that stockinged visionary Mr Roundabout keeps the best elements of Welsh metropolitan culture before the English eye'.[12] The first two references are to Emlyn Williams's two successful plays, which premiered in London, while the third is presumably about *Rhondda Roundabout*, seeing it as an over-optimistic window into South Wales communities.

Nevertheless, Jones's novel was praised within Wales. Notably, Lloyd George is quoted on the dust-wrapper as declaring it 'a gripping story which deserves to be widely read', while the Swansea-based *Western Mail* said that the novel was 'a miracle of realism. It is the Rhondda Valley speaking.'[13] A review in the *Times Literary Supplement* emphasised the novel's focus on an ensemble cast of characters rather than a few individuals, and its depiction of the place and its community: 'all the life of the district goes its way, finding its expression in chapel gatherings and political meetings, in singing festivals and boxing shows, in drama weeks and in betting'.[14] These do seem key features in the novel and the successful 1939 play adaptation that followed, stressing the maintenance of community despite the appalling unemployment in the Rhondda in the 1930s.

As in Meurig Walter's poem, the geographical location of an urban environment within walking distance of the mountains is constantly stressed in *Rhondda Roundabout*. It is an intensely specific, local environment that is also conscious of its contact with world-historical events. The novel opens with a bravura paragraph that celebrates the complex material deprivation and cultural richness of the fictional town of Beulah: 'Revolutionary and riotous; religious and musical; sporting and artistic, coal bearing Rhondda. The starting point of hunger marches, religious revivals, and communist miners' delegations to Russia' (p. 7). The town is both silent and full of activity, industrial and pastoral:

> . . . and in the Rhondda's twenty townships 'the faithful few' were on their way to morning service at one or other of the Rhondda's hundred chapels and score of churches as the gambling schools on the mountain-sides were settling down to ha'penny nap and banker. Right on top of the mountain men could be seen exercising greyhounds in readiness for 'The Dogs', the new industry of Britain's distressed areas; and Bandy Bowen, the Rhondda contender for the Welsh lightweight championship, uses the top of the mountain to do the road-work which is an essential preparation for his eliminating contest with Harry Morgan of Llanelli. (p. 8)

Religious observance and gambling, national and local, work and leisure, city and country are all brought together in Beulah and in this opening paragraph. It is not coincidental that the novel's central figure is a pastor, the new young minister of Beulah, the Reverend Dan Price, BA. While Caradoc Evans and (often) *Wales* were sceptical about non-conformity, in this novel the minister is a central and unifying figure in a community that has the benefits of urban culture combined with the closeness of a village. Dan decides to get to know not just the Nonconformist elite, but also all the people of the town and its surrounding valleys:

> Once he had made a tour on the lumbering, clanking, slow double-decker trams. From the top deck he noted the beginning and end of towns and villages, and those in between places, neither towns nor villages . . . After his tram-tour was completed, he climbed the high mountains and viewed the Rhondda panoramically from different points. Then he started another tour on foot, spending a whole day investigating conditions in each of the places, conversing with different people, having a 'close-up' view of things industrial and social. (p. 73)

His mission is notably both traditionally pastoral and contemporarily documentary, just as the terrain is halfway between town and village. Looking down from the high mountains may suggest biblical echoes, while the tram tour, the 'investigation of conditions' and the 'close-up' camera shot all suggest his combination of tradition and modern sociological methodology.

Dan's reflections on his brief preaching tour to London also pick up through comparison some of the assertions of organic community that we have met already in *Wales*, though without the defensive satire. The visit confirms his sense of the strengths of Beulah as compared to the modern Babylon:

> But what struck me on the Saturday night when I arrived was the spirit of indifference . . . no warmth of feeling such as one finds here in the Rhondda

> ... By now at least two out of every three people I meet know me as the Pastor of Beulah ... but in that huge place people look through me ... Rushing, roaring screaming, scrambling. Crowds rushing down and being shot up again. I stood a long time looking at a sign which said: 'The centre of the world' ... 'Centre of which world?' I asked myself. (p. 172)

Beulah is both urban and a community, and is full of a culture that is both home-produced and accessible to all. First of all there are the sermons, a genre much appreciated and eagerly praised or criticised by chapel-goers, and the art in which Dan is seen as a leader – not, in his case, just for his rhetorical skills, but also for his authentic exploration of contemporary ethical dilemmas. During the course of the novel, various of the chapels and other societies also produce plays, put on drama competitions (in both English and Welsh languages), and host large concerts and operettas in which the citizens of Beulah perform, each according to his or her talents, while Old Evans the draper lends Dan a copy of Burton's *The Anatomy of Melancholy*, which he has been reading. Plays produced include *Candida*, *The Doll's House*, *Man and Superman*, *Outward Bound*, *Twelfth Night*, *The Importance of Being Earnest*, *The Farmer's Wife* and *The Second Mrs Tanqueray*. None of these is a very contemporary piece and could fairly be said to satisfy a 'broadbrow' audience, but it is mainly a list of thoughtful drama rather than 'escapist' pieces. As with drama, music and religion, so too Beulah has an active political life with frequent well-attended political performances by the Labour, Liberal and Communist parties, who have much to oppose and propose, given the novel's setting in the years around 1931 and the financial and political crises of that period. This is the cultural life of Beulah, which involves everyone in one or more of its aspects (and which might indeed be seen, as *Wales* suggests, as somewhat idealised, particularly in the lack of real conflict).

Welsh education: *The Corn is Green* and *How Green was My Valley*

These patterns of seeing Wales as simultaneously rural and industrialised are reproduced in works that have often been seen as less authentic versions of Wales packaged for export. Emlyn Williams's *The Corn is Green* and Richard Llewellyn's *How Green was My Valley* were both hugely successful. Written in English, they were in fact representations of the experiences of Welsh-speaking communities. Though there are studies of each of these two texts, they have rarely been discussed together in great detail despite their interesting similarities and their closeness in date. Emlyn Williams's play deals with the establishment of a voluntary school at the end of the nineteenth century in 'a small village in a remote Welsh countryside'.[15] The Welsh-speaking villagers are at best only partial citizens of a modern literate culture. The post-mistress complains that 'Nobody but me can write, and no good *me* writin', because nobody but me can read.'[16] Yet unlike the Anglophone gentry of the village (such as the squire, who thinks only 'a funny kind of chap' would own 'all these books'), the villagers do possess a 'culture', expressed through singing and oral poetry. Into this oddly asymmetrical cultural hierarchy comes Miss Moffatt, MA, who is English, progressive and a champion of literate (and we wonder if therefore English) culture for all. The play concerns her establishment of a school in the village and in particular her relationship with the young miner Morgan Evans, who eventually wins a scholarship to Oxford. At the opening of the play Morgan does not know the English word 'taught' ('tott?', he asks), but can write in his first English essay:

> The mine is dark . . . If a light come in the mine . . . the rivers in the mine will run fast with the voice of many women; the walls will fall in, and it will be the end of the world . . . But when I walk through the . . . shaft in the dark, I can touch with my hands the leaves on the trees, and underneath . . . where the corn is green.[17]

At the end of the play he sets off for Oxford, saying 'I shall – always remember.' Though the play has a sense of the gains of education and the advantages of the modern language of England, there is also a strong sense of loss and cultural dislocation.

This feeling of loss is predominant in Richard Llewellyn's *How Green was My Valley*, where the central character, Huw Morgan is, like Morgan Evans, a boy with an aptitude for learning. However, his experience of the National School (a kind of school established by the Anglican Church in Wales in the nineteenth century that was consciously intended as a missionary venture) is a largely negative one, outside what the novel represents as the nurturing if often austere culture of true Welshness. Set (probably) in the period before 1914, the novel tells of the education of Huw Morgan at home, at chapel and at school. The first two places of learning are undoubtedly valued above the formal learning of the National School, where Huw is persecuted by the English and Anglicised masters for speaking Welsh. Curiously, the narrative is retrospective, told from an unspecified point at which Huw as an adult is forced to leave the family home that is, like the rest of the valley, about to be destroyed by a collapsing slag heap. His family are all dead and the valley is deserted; there is no history of Wales after this point, and the narrator's only identity is that given to him by the past; he has no future. Where Morgan Evans is partly the hero of a progressive narrative, Huw Morgan is the hero of a nostalgic lament for the loss of a culture. His education only enables him to describe how green his valley was and how total its destruction has been. The National School is, on the whole, aligned with the forces of Anglicisation and destruction, though Huw's learning of English there may be seen to have a value in allowing him to tell (or write) this narrative of loss.

Both texts are interested in clashes between the two languages and cultures, between modernity and tradition, and in complex definitions of English and Welsh cultures and identities and their working out in the individual. These concerns are focused particularly through the institution of the school, a modernising institution that can be seen partly to promise realisation of individual and national aspirations and partly to suppress and destroy them. The texts not only represent some Welsh views of these issues, but also, in their success in England, can be seen to have important meanings for English audiences, perhaps providing them also with valuable narratives of nostalgia and possibility.[18] Both texts, and their contexts, are undoubtedly underpinned by a set of fundamental and potent oppositions: England/Wales, English/Welsh, articulacy/inarticulacy, education/ignorance, enlightenment/barbarity, modernity/the primitive, industry/pastoral. The nineteenth-century setting is not incidental; both works are focused on education and on a period of transition, when the modern and something that may be imagined as its contrary meet in a place where industry and the rural are co-located. Doubtless, what audiences saw in these narratives was complex and variable. Two possibilities that both texts contain in tension are forward-pointing narratives of development and nostalgic narratives of a belonging that has now been utterly lost. It is almost as if, for English audiences, these two texts can give them a sense for their own use of that reputedly fundamental Welsh feeling of *hiraeth* ('a longing for home').

Gwyneth Roberts, in her book about nineteenth-century English interventions in Welsh education, *The Language of the Blue Books*, summarises John Berger's ideas about 'cultures of progress' and 'cultures of survival':

> Cultures of progress . . . see their present as much better than their past and their future as brighter still; they are forward-looking because the future offers them the prospect of even greater expansion and the hope of even greater success. Cultures of survival, on the other hand, see their present as less glorious than their past, and their future as doubtful and full of anxiety; their only prospect of maintaining even their present precarious position lies in the repetition of acts which keep their traditions alive, in a struggle against

> heavy odds in which victory lies not in defeating their enemies but in resisting their enemies' domination. (p. 236)

How Green was My Valley is surely written mainly from a culture of survival perspective, though with an ambiguous counterpoint of educational development, while *The Corn is Green* is given its energy by the tension between the culture of progress and the culture of survival. These viewpoints undoubtedly do come partly from a certain sense of the real national situation of Wales in the 1930s, but they also represent two major responses to modernity. It is perhaps no surprise, then, to detect at least elements of literary modernism in these two 'middlebrow' or 'broadbrow' texts, since high modernism was equally responding to the contradictory narrative of modernity, with its promise of the realisation of identity and its fearful potential for the dissolution of identity. Just as Woolf and Lawrence cling to 'the culture of survival' in their attempts to save the inner life from industrialism, but embrace the 'culture of progress' in their quest for modern techniques that will bring enlightenment, so too these humbler stories about schooling treat some of the complexities of modern life in ways that were widely accessible in a culture that was, at least, one of mass literacy. The best-seller or 'runaway' success status of both texts and of their film versions in England in the late 1930s and early 1940s tells us something of their appeal.

Though this space permits treatment of these patterns only in one literary periodical, two novels and one play, the simultaneous sense of a particular culture that has become modern without losing contact with aspects of the rural is a recurring motif in the 1930s in Welsh writing in English and in what some might call Welsh writing for the English. Sometimes the rural and the modern are reconciled, but more often they are in uncomfortable but productive tension.

In dialogue with: Chapter 7 'The "Uncertainty of Our Climate"' (III: Communities) [cultural inheritance and national identity; rural drama]; Chapter 9 'Transformative Pastoral' (III: Communities) [pastoral; narratives of labour and working-class culture].

Notes

1. p. 30.
2. See Durey, p. 8, footnote 2.
3. See Hopkins, 'Depressed Pastorals?'
4. Quoted in John Harris, 'Introduction', p. 45.

5. Quoted in John Harris, 'Introduction', p. 40, p. 46.
6. See Gwyn A. Williams, p. 245.
7. See a comparison of the two periodicals in my essay '*Wales* and *Welsh Review*'.
8. *Wales*, 3 (Autumn 1937), inside cover.
9. *Wales*, 2 (Summer 1937), p. 78.
10. *Wales*, 4 (March 1938), p. 150.
11. *Wales*, 6/7 (March 1939), pp. 205–6.
12. *Wales*, 10 (October 1939), p. 283.
13. Both quoted in a Faber & Faber advertisement in the *Times Literary Supplement*, 7 June 1934, p. 405. All references to the novel are to the 1949 edition.
14. West, 7 June 1934, p. 406.
15. I, i, opening stage direction.
16. I, i.
17. I, ii. The play makes considerable use of ellipses. In all quotations from the play, ellipses are original unless given in square brackets.
18. Harding, p. 104.

Part III

Communities

Chapter 7

The 'Uncertainty of Our Climate': Mary Kelly and the Rural Theatre

Andrew Walker

'We must be an optimistic people, for, in spite of the notorious uncertainty of our climate, we continue to produce pageants and outdoor plays.'
Mary Kelly, *How to Make a Pageant* (1941)[1]

Mary Kelly's proclamation of optimism in the face of uncertainty arises out of the complex background of political turmoil and social upheaval in England that she found concentrated in the rural hamlet of Kelly that she called home. Indeed, her description of the place as one marked by a mere 'uncertainty' might stand as a moderating revision, given the evidence of precipitous decline discovered in the history of rural England from the 1870s to the interwar years.[2] Kelly's contrasting optimism – even writing under the looming threat of a second world war – is situated in a rural arts context she finds filled with potential. Conceived out of such confidence, Kelly's development of the rural arts theatre 'was perceived and practised as a privileged means to regenerate village life', going beyond the duty to service inherited from her family's class and church background to incorporate the legacy of increasing democratisation after the Great War.[3] Since the Victorian era, rural life had been increasingly shaped by literacy education, the development of widely available print culture and the encroachment of the industrialised city, all of which would threaten existent rural mores.[4] At the same time, many working people – urban, suburban and rural – enjoyed increased leisure time and responded to a national political discourse urging them to seek out more social autonomy. Some did so by pursuing new cultural activities and altering traditions of performance. Although the entrenched class privileges of a previous age allowed Kelly's rural arts scheme to take flight, it was ultimately the interwar developments of increased education and independence of the working classes that allowed it to flourish. However much Kelly understood her climate as one of disruption and uncertainty, her work demonstrates a confidence that the changes wrought by modernity brought increased opportunities for rural performance.

Where scholars of literature make mention of Kelly, it is usually as a purported model for the character of Miss La Trobe, the rather eccentric playwright and director in Virginia Woolf's posthumous novel *Between the Acts* (1941), or as a collaborator with better-known figures like Vita Sackville-West and E. M. Forster. Yet her work began in 1919 with the formation of the Kelly Players and their performance of her religious drama, *Joseph*, at her family's estate in Devon. Developing and producing her own plays on a near-yearly basis, Kelly eventually founded the Village Drama Society, marking the revitalisation of a rural tradition of playmaking worthy of study in its own right. Throughout the 1920s and 1930s, Kelly's model of village productions, which required original scripts based on local history and used as actors and stagehands tenant farmers and labourers from the surrounding area, exploded in number and in popularity. This success led her to pen two particularly influential books on rural arts: one was a handbook largely comprised of practical advice for village dramatists, entitled *How to Make a Pageant* (1936), the other a theoretical treatise and history of the interwar dramatic movement entitled *Village Theatre* (1939). In these two volumes, Kelly elucidates the dramatic impulse of rural communities and the rituals that undergird them, displaying a vision for the rural arts that would result in the flourishing of village theatre in England during the interwar period. Although the pageants and plays that so fascinated Kelly are genres often perceived as more educational than aesthetically affecting, amateurish productions more than vital developments in historical and literary form, her work demands reappraisal in any account of modernity's relation to rural arts performance and community.[5]

Accounts of village theatre commonly describe the village drama movement as an expression of agrarian nostalgia and portray Kelly's commitment to local development and performance as a continuance of class patronage or an imposition of an idealised past.[6] However, Kelly's founding of the local Women's Institute and her organisation of the Kelly Players might also be seen as an embrace of the democratic change wrought by the industrialisation of agrarian life and the increasing education of the labouring classes. Rather than being a commodified performance of rural idyll or nationalistic fervour, Kelly's vision is one grounded in her desire to create platforms that give expression to rural labourers.[7] Such a vision is surely less nostalgic than one 'informed by progressivist cultural innovation'.[8] The possibilities of rural production under modernising conditions fascinated Kelly, and she advocated public performances and group dynamics emerging from and dependent on the particular conditions of the large, rural spaces where her plays and pageants were performed. This chapter argues that the rural settings of Kelly's work inspired her engagement with the themes of historicity, community and agrarian life, and supported her efforts to advance village drama through the large networks of Women's Institutes and drama societies, which performed and expanded the dramatic productions of the era.[9] By utilising rural networks developed in the aftermath of the Great War, highlighting the dissolution and renegotiation of certain class boundaries during the interwar period, and reimagining rural notions and experiences of history, Kelly's dramatic work exemplifies the development of rural modernity in England. Rather than reaffirming a simplified picture of an eccentric enthusiast like La Trobe, Kelly's contributions to interwar rural communities demonstrate a rural arts context highly attuned to the challenges and uncertainties of the age and help us to gain a clearer understanding of both rural modernity at its site of practice and one of its little-understood figures.

Rural drama, rural networks

Describing rural life in *Village Theatre*, Kelly notes that it was only after the Great War that 'the countryside as a whole awakened and set about remaking its life' (p. 142) in response to economic, social and technological changes.[10] This process of remaking the rural included the development of an artistic consciousness and cultivation of cosmopolitan interest among its people, particularly those who had been abroad during the war and, as she explains in *Village Theatre*, 'mixed with other men of all sorts, had heard about all kinds of different lives, and they had also, for the first time in their lives, made the acquaintance of the theatre' (p. 142). This cosmopolitan exposure had its direct counterpart in the isolation of the rural women, for whom the war had meant the solitude of agrarian life and its attendant forms of labour. In the aftermath of the war, rural women welcomed the development of social societies and programmes to counter such seclusion, turning to a Canadian invention, the Women's Institute, for an early model.[11] Begun in 1915 in Britain, the Women's Institute movement was intended to

> improve and develop conditions of rural life and to advance the education of countrywomen in citizenship, in public questions both national and international, in music, drama and other cultural subjects, also to secure instruction and training in all branches of agriculture, handicrafts, domestic science and social welfare.[12]

Taking as one of their main objectives the instruction of women in villages perceived to have a 'rural character', chapters of local Women's Institutes developed quickly, cropping up across the country by the hundreds in mere months.[13] Each of the rural institutes 'insist[ed] on social equality within its borders', ensuring that 'the lady of the manor has learnt as much as the labourer's wife'.[14] For a local institute to take part in the larger organisation, it had to adopt a rather strict standard of democratic processes, such as secret balloting, in an attempt to dampen inclinations toward class privilege. For Kelly, the central cultural arena in which this move towards democratisation was able to be realised was in the drama, a form whose large central casts relied on the class mixing and educational enterprises that the Women's Institutes were able to facilitate.

As a result, Kelly's early development of the Village Drama Society, combined with the organisational process provided by the Women's Institutes, provided a structure to 'develop drama particularly in the villages'.[15] At a time of advances in rural travel, the Women's Institutes were key way-points that served as instructional centres and provided dramatic settings.[16] The nature of Kelly's first visits was almost uniformly educational, as Kelly reports in *Village Theatre* that she 'had always to explain the word drama. The large majority of the villages had never seen a play at all' (p. 145). By relying on the Women's Institutes' infrastructure and modernising sympathies, Kelly was able to increase the exposure of rural audiences to drama rapidly while advancing the Institutes' mission to develop rural arts. Such a reliance on the Women's Institutes as a network for theatrical development also had its drawbacks. However much the Women's Institutes made a point of including men in the dramatic endeavour of putting on a play, the endeavour remained stubbornly gendered.[17] In describing the kinds of visits that she would make, Kelly noted that while men were invited to the open meetings, 'only the parson and the schoolmaster dared to set foot inside', with the other rural men coming to 'consider the drama as a pastime "only fit for women and children"'.[18] Kelly regrets, to some extent, the limitations of such gendered exclusivity: 'village drama might have been established everywhere as community drama if the Women's Institutes had followed their first policy, and worked in this for the whole village rather than for a section of it'.[19] According to Kelly, many of the women who made up the leadership of the Women's Institutes were clearly aware of the problem of a single-sexed organisation. Kelly herself acknowledges that 'men do distrust petticoat government, and will never flock to join a drama group under the name of the W. I.', but she insists that the inclusion of the rural men was essential, 'for the only loyalty which can inspire [the drama] must be to the village itself'.[20]

The most successful attempt at integration among these dramatic networks was ultimately realised in the unification in 1932 of the Village Drama Society with the British Drama League, previously founded by Geoffrey Whitworth in 1919. While the British Drama League 'included the village in its general work for the drama',[21] the merging of the two allowed for the specific inclusion of village drama into the structures of the more broadly focused British Drama League. The British Drama League library had, by the early 1930s, become a central source for village dramas, including pieces with localised diction and set for a large cast. Kelly would acknowledge that the library built by Whitworth, touching on every element of stagecraft, 'provides the daily bread of amateur players and repertory theatres', and 'makes it possible for every producer to gain a real knowledge of his art, so that the blind need no longer lead the blind, and no one need fall into any ditch'.[22] Holding conferences and dispatching consultants to far-flung hamlets, the League would organise schools to assist in the development of both actors and producers, and build an 'information bureau' to solve everyday issues. Additionally, the League was responsible for the development of the National Community Theatre Festival – first developed by the Women's Institutes and an outgrowth of the National Festival of the League – which helped develop and legitimise works written by amateur, first-time playwrights. Yet, at the time of the merger with the British Drama League, Kelly believed the supply of plays appropriate for rural life to be severely limited. The plays that made up the British Drama League's largely traditional repository were mostly drawing-room comedies and Shakespearean reproductions that necessitated an acting style and development unknown to villagers and beyond their skills and interests. In response to this shortcoming, the merging of the institutions allowed the Village Drama Society to seek out and perform pieces found suitable for rural environments: farces and outdoor plays, pantomimes and religious plays, various historical dramas written by amateur local historians and country parsons. Most notably, Kelly would invite members of the Women's Institutes and the British Drama League to craft local plays themselves. The League, of which Kelly served as Village Drama Secretary after the organisations' combination, helped over 600 societies to form, all of which would produce original rural theatre by 1939.[23]

With the assistance of both the National Council of Social Service and the Rural Community Councils, the whole network that enabled the production of rural theatre had the effect of taking dramatic depictions of rural life away from urban centres and placing them in the hands of the rural inhabitants themselves. Despite these highly developed networks often being headquartered in towns and led by individuals with professional backgrounds in cities, their structure and task remained highly decentralised, leading Kelly to declare that village theatre 'must be treated on a county basis'.[24] While the explosion of village theatre in England coincided with a much larger international movement toward local performance and regionalised understandings of drama,[25] Kelly's unique development of the rural theatre in England highlights the ways that rural networks and localised guilds and societies were responsible for its shaping. Though only briefly described here, the institutes and councils developed in the aftermath of the Great War were, for Kelly and for the rural theatre of England more broadly, key catalysts for rural autonomy and theatrical development.

Theatrical latency, modern potency

A historical account and a theoretical treatise, *Village Theatre* both catalogues and envisions the development of a dramatic production that would energise what Kelly recognises as the latent potential of rural inhabitants to work as actors and producers, and not merely to serve as passive audiences. As Kelly herself states, the networks that had enabled the development of village theatre were primarily about the enrichment of rural life:

> all these societies, committees, minutes, memoranda, and reports are nothing but a means to an end, and that end is the freeing of the artist in the soul of the ordinary man and woman. Not our old friend, the Man-in-the-street, but the Man-in-the-field.[26]

The series of questions that Kelly asks of these rural figures – 'do they need a drama of their own? Have they anything to express which has not been expressed for them many times? Have they anything to contribute to the universal art of the drama, and if they have, what form is it likely to take?' (p. 156) – all demonstrate the anxiety over the position of the rural inhabitant within the conditions of modernity. Although the chief distinction made in Kelly's book – that between the 'Man-in-the-street' and the 'Man-in-the-field' – undoubtedly hazards stereotypes of the urban and rural, it highlights Kelly's interest in giving voice to agricultural workers and recognising their potential as artists.

Rural villages' agricultural heritage and character were, for Kelly, constitutive of an unbroken tradition that contained within it a unique theatrical sensibility. Drawing out her distinction between the urban and the rural, Kelly argues in *Village Theatre* that the villager 'knows without instruction that the fulfilment of one life depends on the sacrifice of another, and he knows his own place in the great wheel of Nature', while the city dweller

> is only familiar with the finished product of science: the corn spirit can mean nothing to the woman who buys self-rising flour in a paper bag, and to the Cockney child milk is something produced from a bottle which comes first from the dairy shop. (p. 158)

The rural environment is, in Kelly's terms, one in which the 'people do not *live in* a place, they *belong to* it' (p. 158). For Kelly, this sense of belonging is developed in the immediacy and totality of the farm labourer's work. Unlike the office or factory worker, the rural dweller's labour necessarily involves 'so much technique, and so many skilled crafts' (p. 160). The forces of nature shape the drama of rural living, as the rural inhabitant

> has everywhere great and powerful enemies who are ready at any time to destroy him, in the winds, rains, snows, frosts, and droughts – great protagonists in the drama of Nature, and antagonists in the drama of his own life. These things, only known to the townsman as bad weather, have a vital reality for the countryman, and the long conflict with the natural powers makes up his life.[27]

Kelly's climatic awareness recognises natural corollaries to the looming threats of the Second World War and rapid industrial change, yet is capable of placing them in an unbroken rhythm of dramatic change.

Although Kelly believed that increasing industrialisation might result in the 'stifling out of existence the countryman's more spiritual side', she believed the drama was able to expose a 'sense of beauty lying beneath the surface'.[28] Kelly's vision of rural sensitivity – of the land-worker 'pitted against mighty powers of evil' on the one hand, and 'the still unconquerable spirit of life' on the other – characterises theatre as having been an outgrowth of folk religion and mythology grounded in agricultural and fertility ritual. Like T. S. Eliot and many of those associated with the Religious Drama Society, formed in 1928, Kelly believed that religious communities provided the lifeblood of rural dramatic works, grounded, as they are, in the rhythms of both the ecumenical calendar and the natural progression of the seasons. Kelly argued that this ritualistic sense of natural rhythms and contact with nature would form the extraordinary capability of rural dramatic performers and producers. In describing the 'survival' of the village theatre, Kelly remarks that it is common faith that served as catalyst:

> It was not made from an artistic, nor from an archaeological motive, but from faith, a faith shared by the playwright, producer, and people alike; and

so, because it contained that quality without which the drama cannot exist, it has taken root and lived.[29]

Without a religious community, the continuity of the rural theatre would be in jeopardy and the life of the rural inhabitant suppressed. For Kelly, the natural and supernatural symbols that marked rural drama remained grounded in the agricultural and religious habits of its practitioners, granting them an inherent authenticity at once under threat but also newly expressible under modern conditions.

Central to Kelly's vision of rural theatre was a belief that rural productions were common to the whole of the community. Complete with choruses, large casts and orchestras, and with a significant percentage of the population taking part in its production, Kelly repeatedly emphasises that 'Village Theatre must be a thing of the community if it is to mean anything' (p. 178). Although Kelly's works betray a now-quaint kind of generalisation among rural inhabitants, an amateur sort of anthropology that now reads as overly simplified if not occasionally condescending, she nonetheless remained highly aware of the diversity of rural experience:

> All this is generalization, a dangerous occupation, but one that is, to some extent, necessary if one is to see the problems of village theatre as a whole. Country people are, of course, as individual as any other set of people; any given village is like the world in miniature, so diverse are the characters that inhabit it. (p. 166)[30]

Though the rural environment was often pictured as remote and villagers as dominated by a monoculture, Kelly insists upon its roundedness and diversity as a wellspring of dramatic potential, features recognisable in her encouraging of the consideration of local dialect, the appropriate use of local materials in costuming, and reliance on the local landscape for character types. Despite her occasional inclinations to essentialist, romantic theorising, Kelly nonetheless remains an important figure for studies of rural modernity, in part because she recognises and promotes the unique diversity of the rural village to act as a salve on the more egregious by-products of industrialisation and urban-centred visions of modernity. However much the educational tools created from the Women's Institutes and the Rural Councils might be of advantage, Kelly argues,

> the real value of all this is in putting into the hands of the countryman those tools by which he will be able one day to create for himself a theatre which will give a true expression to all that he has learnt from the great teacher, Nature, to all that he has suffered, to his philosophy, to his humour. (p. 187)

Once this vision is achieved, Kelly believes the rural dramatist will have again made an original contribution to the history of the drama.

Modern history, modern pageantry

In Jed Esty's *A Shrinking Island*, interwar British pageantry is seen in relation to 'late modernism' and its move toward a shrinking national consciousness, a repatriation of cultural creation and historical awareness.[31] In Esty's schema, the historically inflected pageantry advocated by Kelly in *How to Make a Pageant* might mark a kind of historical stasis, yet the distinctly rural and hyperlocalised vision of Kelly seems to move beyond such simplifying claims. As her collaborator Charles Henderson would contend in the introduction to Kelly's 1929 pageant *Bradstone*, hers was a vision for rural performance in which '[t]he history of any English parish is the history of England in miniature'.[32] Although the clear majority of Kelly's book is devoted to the details of pageantry production – including sections on stagecraft, organisation, crowd control and business management – Kelly's handbook also lovingly crafts a vision for pageantry that goes beyond the reactionary milieu in which it seems so grounded. Rather than the vitalising, historical enactment of the 'growing pains of humanity', which Kelly would advocate in light of the climate of modernity that surrounded them,[33] much of the contemporaneous pageantry relied on an easy, nostalgic sense of national or regional pride, minimising or ignoring any distinctly modernising impulses. For example, in the work of Louis Napoleon Parker, whose large pageants at the beginning of the twentieth century were largely responsible for the resurgence of the form, the desire for a new 'National Drama' was a reaction against 'the modernizing spirit, which destroys all loveliness and has no loveliness to put in its place . . . [and] is just precisely the kind of spirit which a properly organized and properly conducted pageant is designed to kill'.[34] Yet, as Ben Harker has shown, the later pageants of the 1930s became much more highly contested forms for projecting political and cultural ideologies, conveying historical consciousness as a space for negotiation of values (p. 437). In part, this is a change wrought by Kelly and the Village Theatre movement.

In Kelly's estimation, little had changed in postwar pageantry since Parker's revival. Despite the increasing popularity of the form, pageants were typically used as fundraisers for local hospitals and charities, drawing large sums of money from wealthy benefactors and tourists seeking out large-scale spectacle. At least one reason for their appeal was their generic conformity. Kelly spells out the formula, beginning with 'the Spirit of the Ages, or Father Time, or some such personage, who "narrates" . . . between the episodes, to explain what they are about'.[35] Kelly goes on to describe the varying 'Episodes', including Roman occupation and the founding of an abbey, ending with 'a grand round-up of Spirits – of Peace, of Harmony, of the District Nursing Association, of the Women's Institutes and the British Legion, of Victory of the Empire – all singing "Land of Hope and Glory"' (p. 5). To enliven these formulaic structures, each of the pageants would make use of 'unconnected episodes, real crowds, mass movement and colour, processions and horses, music and dancing, on a beautiful outdoor stage: first of all an appeal to the eye, and then an attempt to reproduce history in a romantic light' (p. 4). By utilising amateur players – individuals 'drawn in from the tennis-courts, the barracks, the stables, the highways and the hedges' (p. 4) – the pageant allows for an involvement of crowds that would be impossible on the professional stage. Yet, where she describes the audiences who currently seek out pageantry of the Parker kind, she does so with disdain, calling them 'uncontrolled, and ignorant', claiming that they were only there to 'pick out [their] friends in unfamiliar clothes, to admire them or laugh at them, and to enjoy to the full incongruity – not to experience any emotion or to make any effort of understanding or imagination' (p. 4).

Unlike Parker's call for a pageantry that would resist modernity, content with its status as an act of charity, Kelly envisioned a vibrant avant-garde form capable of embodying the dramatic potential of the village people necessary to sustain it. With the development of such a pageant, the nature of both the players and the audience would change. As Kelly argues,

> the pageant will no longer be merely a social affair, but a tremendous effort of imagination and presentation. The audience will no longer sit as apathetically as is possible on a wooden seat without a back, but will form part of the play as an audience should, and will be made to experience something that is thoroughly disturbing.[36]

This final line, Kelly's insistence on the 'thoroughly disturbing', is one of her clearest affirmations of modern methods, disrupting an all-too-familiar experience and demonstrating a much deeper resolve and more progressive vision. In order to take advantage of such progressive potential, Kelly argues for a pageant that induces mass emotion. Indeed, she theorises that the 'value of the pageant to dramatist and to producer is that it can give mass emotion to a greater degree than any other form of play' (p. 6). Only by harnessing the communal nature of rural villagers and by utilising the rural landscape as its grounding will the modern pageant–play find sure footing in the era. Yet such mass emotion is, as Kelly recognised, both 'its opportunity and its problem', given the mass movements shaping the political climate. In a telling interlude in *Village Theatre*, Kelly highlights a key theatrical memory. While observing a 'processional pageant' in Hamburg in 1936, Kelly is struck by the town being 'filled with the arrogant, brutal, overgrown children who form the S. S. and the Storm Troopers of Nazi Germany; their faces set in one mould, their minds obviously carrying one idea'. Yet, so too did the procession include – in 'marked contrast' with the Nazi marchers –

> the calm quiet faces of the peasants, who had no real part or lot in all this Nazi nonsense, but who performed, as their fathers had done, and with the same grave precision and concentration as the English Morris-dancers, intricate dances and movements with banners and long wagoners' whips.[37]

This observation at once betrays a seemingly nostalgic, oversimplified view of the 'peasant' that Kelly occasionally succumbs to, yet it also demonstrates Kelly's belief in the deep history of performance found in the traditions of the rural dweller.

In *The Book of the Kellys*, a family history begun by Mary and completed after her death by her stepsister Margaret, history and its relation to the rural landscape are pictured in idealised, pastoral terms. In this reading, the Kelly countryside 'stands well away from the troubled tide of history', with the rural landscape providing a kind of idyll, one in which history's 'waves never broke over it to destroy the essential peace of this green isle'.[38] Such a naïve sentiment was certainly seen in the contemporaneous pageantry of the age, for

> If any definite idea lurks behind them [the pageants], it is that of continuity, a vague desire to remember the days that are past . . . and to preserve, even if only for a little while longer, that bond which ties us to our country by an intimate love of some corner of it.[39]

But such pageants must, argues Kelly, give way to pageants attuned to a more dialectical engagement with history, ones capable of demonstrating

> the real drama of history; the conflict between the individual and the mass, the force of strong ideas driving men forward, the reaction from them that pulls them back, the dominance or the defeat of character and intellect, the growing-pains of humanity. (pp. 8–9)

For the producers of British pageantry in the interwar years, the threat of a second world war and a creeping climate of totalitarianism led to a pageant that is anything but an anti-modern act of nostalgia. The pageant described by Kelly is one attuned to the trouble of constructing a communal endeavour capable of letting the landscape speak, allowing such localised history and geography to form the basis for playwriting. It is a vision for the pageant that offers 'a sense of continuity and of depth',[40] one that allows the deep sense of history embedded in rural traditions to be performed and revitalised.

Optimism and uncertainty

Kelly's grand project of recapturing the dramatic potential of rural villages was ultimately the result of several contemporary factors: the after-effects of the Great War, declining gentry power and increasing democratisation, and the ground-breaking efforts to advance rural education and community through local organisations like the Women's Institutes and drama guilds. Although her dramatic vision remained based in a drama that predated the modern moment, it nonetheless stakes out a progressive possibility of a *théâtre de milieu*, of the shared and common life that might constitute a village theatre prepared for modernity's uncertainties. For Kelly, rural life was able to maintain a kind of coherence that was less common in the modern city; agricultural labourers were, 'above all others', able 'to have in common a special experience of life'.[41] While Kelly acknowledged that 'the wireless has broken down the barriers of distance . . . the countryside is now linked up by buses', the dramatic potential of the rural inhabitant would remain so long as the natural life that sustains it persists. Like the rural Germans she had seen performing their part in the processional pageant, the natural drama of agricultural work 'will continue to create a people who will remain a little apart, not merged in the mass, not tossed here and there with every vain blast of political doctrine, but going quietly on their way'.[42] Though she traces the contours of the movement to the date of publication of *Village Theatre*, her book ultimately relies on a prophetic note more than a historical claim, saying only that she 'can see no reason why [the villager] should not one day speak for himself' (p. 187). Kelly's work suggests that one of rural modernity's chief features is its response to the uncertain climate of the interwar period, and it demands reconsideration in this light. Although Kelly ends her book just at the outbreak of war, as village theatre and pageantry began to falter, she nevertheless maintains a faith in rural arts and people that even the prospect of the impending war could not dampen. It was, for Kelly, only a 'temporary darkening' (p. vii).

In dialogue with: Chapter 1 'Ringing the Changes' (I: Networks) [performance and voice]; Chapter 14 'Eden in Sussex' (V: Wars) [Christianity in community; villages].

Notes

1. p. 1.
2. Brassley, Burchardt and Thompson, 'Introduction', p. 1.
3. Wallis, 'Drama in the Villages', p. 102.
4. Wallis, 'Drama in the Villages', p. 103.
5. As Nicoll puts it, 'all that can be said is that these various individual efforts . . . deserve praise for their meritorious aims, but cannot, with the best will in the world, be deemed of any significant dramatic value' (p. 246).
6. This view is typified in the simplistic historical oppositions posed in an economic context, like that by Wiener (p. 6), and in the associations with the earlier development of pageantry by Parker.
7. See Outka's discussions of 'nostalgic nationalism' and 'originary authenticity', *Consuming Traditions*, pp. 4–8. Kelly presents a rurally located response to the city-driven commodification identified by Outka.
8. Wallis, 'Unlocking the Secret Soul', p. 348. See also Maggie B. Gale: 'Inter-war theatre has traditionally been seen as conservative and as somehow failing to reflect the cultural upheavals which surrounded it' ('Introduction', p. 1).
9. For a look at the parallel use of rural village halls, see Jeremy Burchardt's '"A New Rural Civilization": Village Halls, Community and Citizenship in the 1920s'.
10. Burchardt, *Paradise Lost*, p. 148.
11. *Village Theatre*, p. 142.
12. Quoted in Perriton, p. 83.
13. As Wallis notes, 'In her play-list booklet *Drama in the Village* (c. 1937), Kelly distinguishes between purely rural villages, which have their own distinct personalities . . . and those which now include an urban population, "where it is hard to say what a 'village audience' really is"' (qtd in 'Unlocking the Secret Soul', p. 356). The Women's Institutes were especially prominent in those distinctly rural environs.
14. *Village Theatre*, p. 143.
15. *Village Theatre*, pp. 143–4.
16. Wild, *Village England*, p. 114.
17. The gendered nature of the Women's Institutes has been widely documented, most notably by Courtney, p. 44.
18. *Village Theatre*, p. 146. The Women's Institutes came to be known as the 'acceptable face of feminism', Andrews, p. 7. See also Gale's 'Errant Nymphs'.
19. *Village Theatre*, p. 147.
20. *Village Theatre*, p. 147.
21. *Village Theatre*, p. 44.
22. *Village Theatre*, p. 148.

23. Wallis, 'Unlocking the Secret Soul', p. 350.
24. *Village Theatre*, p. 149.
25. Nicoll argues that the achievements of the village drama movement ought to be more expansively examined within the wider frame of the 'regional drama', including work like that of W. B. Yeats in his establishment of the Abbey Theatre. See Nicoll, pp. 248–50.
26. *Village Theatre*, p. 156.
27. *Village Theatre*, p. 159.
28. *Village Theatre*, p. 144.
29. *Village Theatre*, p. 118.
30. Kelly's book, though highly localised in its concerns, is very much attuned to international senses of the rural. See especially Chapter 15 of *Village Theatre*: 'Village Theatre in Other Lands'.
31. See Esty, Chapter 2.
32. 'Preface', p. 7.
33. *How to Make a Pageant*, p. 9.
34. Quoted in Wallis, 'Delving the Levels of Memory', p. 196.
35. *How to Make a Pageant*, pp. 4–5.
36. *How to Make a Pageant*, p. 6.
37. *Village Theatre*, p. 157.
38. Quoted in Wallis, 'Unlocking the Secret Soul', p. 347.
39. *How to Make a Pageant*, p. 8.
40. Wallis, 'Delving the Levels of Memory', p. 199. Central to Kelly's work was her deep sense of place history, something she located in the English garden. See *How to Make a Pageant*, pp. 2–4.
41. *Village Theatre*, p. 157.
42. *Village Theatre*, p. 167.

Chapter 8

The Spinster in Eden: Reclaiming Civilisation in Interwar British Rural Fiction

Stella Deen

Studies of rural modernity are enriched when works about women, written by women, are considered in terms of each other and, in their numbers and popularity, as distinctive expressions of women's social and political position in post-World War I modernity. In three such works, Sylvia Townsend Warner's *Lolly Willowes, or The Loving Huntsman* (1926), E. H. Young's *Miss Mole* (1930) and Winifred Holtby's *South Riding* (1936), a middle-aged spinster presides over rural and urban landscapes. Each novel surveys a community's recovery from the war and ties its resiliency to continuity between urban and rural England, a continuity that is inscribed by the spinster's historically recent and exuberant mobility. Each protagonist is well served by her love for a rural place that she has been obliged to leave, a love that later redounds to her in the form of enriched apprehension of a landscape and an expertise that can be applied to the reconstruction of the postwar community.

These interwar spinster novels claim that the formerly pitiable spinster has been energised and empowered by her new citizenship and by her war experience, and that her insights and gifts uniquely suit her to regenerate postwar civilisation. 'Ecstasy, power and devotion have enriched them; they have served a cause greater than their own personal advantage,' says Winifred Holtby about twentieth-century spinsters in *Women and a Changing Civilization* (1935; p. 129). All human beings, she adds, feel pleasure in creation: 'We are made sufficiently like the image of the God of Genesis that we require to build a world for our satisfaction, to rest on the seventh day and know that it is good' (p. 126). For the first time in her history, the spinster is poised to build this world, and this happy coincidence of her talents and her opportunities places her in an English Eden. Her rural heritage is the source of the spinster's Eden – the vision that propels her to match new citizens' gifts or needs with opportunity. The spinster in Eden's free movement and versatility are her key signature. She moves between city and country, drawing on expertise in both environments. Indeed, the facility with which the spinster in Eden travels between urban and rural environments reflects the new porousness of the rural village. The Great War saw an acceleration of changes that would impose new economic, agricultural and demographic patterns on rural areas. Notably, daily commuters to rural villages, especially male and female white-collar workers, introduced 'new skills, different traditions and expectations, and even ways of life'.[1] The three novels under discussion both emphasise the modernity of their protagonists' mobility and envision its distinct advantages. As a benefit of her dual experience as a city dweller and a countrywoman, each protagonist touts an education supplemented by life experience that leads her to seek adventure and that endows her with an ability to shift her point of view. In *Miss Mole* and *South Riding*, moreover, the spinster's full experience, including her sexual experience and her working life, is central to her ability to rebuild the postwar community.

This implication in her community sets the spinster in Eden apart from the urban *flâneuse*. To be sure, freedom of movement characterises both the metropolitan and the rural woman, but while the *flâneuse* 'rejoices in [her] incognito', exhilarated, like Baudelaire's *flâneur*, by the 'ebb and flow of movement' and feeling no obligation to the human beings who constitute it,[2] the spinster in Eden is empowered by the human encounters made possible by rural spaces and traditions. Still, the visibility of her movement is initially read by others as disturbance, a troublesome ambiguity, and an unwillingness to be fixed within established gender and class roles.[3] For example, Hannah Mole, the titular character of E. H. Young's novel, is a disconcertingly double figure: a farmer's daughter who inserts enigmatic literary allusions into the dinner table conversation, a housekeeper who owns a cottage on a Somerset farm, a woman whose 'double masquerade of housekeeper and lady' inspires mistrust and resentment in her employer, Robert Corder.[4] Moreover, the mobile spinster is representative of disruption and continued instability following the war. Although non-combatants, each of the three protagonists has been shaken and scarred by the war, and each shares the suffering of others in the rural village who bear similar unhealed wounds.

The spinster's mobility, then, is two-sided: an index of her open wounds and misfitting place, but also a sign of her nimbleness vis-à-vis more static members of the community. The spinster-in-Eden novels may invoke or even concede to the courtship plot (*Miss Mole* and *South Riding*), or may be read as *Bildungsroman* (*Lolly Willowes*), but these plots are subordinated to the development and resolution of conflicts in heterogeneous postwar communities. The novels, whose publication dates span ten years, each imagine this heterogeneity differently, but all three explore the ramifications of these demographic trends through represented clashes between rural and urban folk, men and women, conservatism and progress.

Each novel also imagines community as a process of recognising those who are on the margins, not in order to assimilate them into a mainstream, but so as to set in motion an exchange of perspectives that results in the mutual humanisation of citizens. None of the novels imagines that this process leads to consensus about the myriad politically fraught concerns that postwar citizens face.[5] Instead, they focus on the *process* of mutual humanisation. Having stood on the margins of prewar society, the spinster has already cultivated the skill of seeing herself with the eyes of others. Hannah Mole, for example, is half-pleased to be nicknamed 'Miss Fitt' by an elderly neighbour. 'See the joke? That's what you are and if you don't know it you'll soon find out,' he warns (p. 112). With its former hierarchy dismantled, no longer headed by a large landowner and a vicar, the modern rural village in these novels can be viewed as a collection of misfits. New residents, driven from the city under economic duress or seeking refuge from the militarism and commercialism of the city, either readily make themselves at home, like Mr Saunter in *Lolly Willowes*, or feel themselves in exile, like Mr Mitchell in *South Riding*.

As she begins to cultivate affiliations, the spinster in Eden engages in a process of revision or of retelling that results in what could be called 'the mutual humanisation of misfits'. The product of human encounters in modern rural spaces and structures, such humanisation highlights the contrast between urban anonymity and rural knowableness. *South Riding* offers a simple example of such humanisation. Fred Mitchell, an insurance salesman fallen on hard times, must testify before the Public Assistance Committee, to which he has applied for outdoor relief. He experiences the hearing as an acute humiliation. As Mitchell struggles for speech, the big-estate farmer Robert Carne perceives Mitchell's distress and tells an anecdote about 'a chap I met last week', in reality himself, who endured a similar humiliation when he set out to borrow money from his brother. The anecdote finishes with an irony that makes Mitchell and the committee members laugh, as Carne's brother taps him first, and Carne 'went home and sold some furniture an' lent it' (p. 288). For Mitchell, 'the crisis was passed. He was a man among men, a human being – a pariah no longer' (p. 288). The story is representative of other human exchanges in the rural South Riding. They do not efface strong disagreements but they do bring 'misfits' into the mainstream, cutting across the lines of politics, social class, gender and occupation. Ultimately, Holtby represents such exchanges as enlarging human sympathy and capacity for effective activism.

In the spinster-in-Eden novels, mutual humanisation makes purposeful the accidental co-existence of individuals in the postwar rural village, affiliating them in mutual recognition and obligation, and transforming a rural place into a community. Such a community would not efface differences, for, as Holtby says when she calls for 'greater elasticity' in political, economic and domestic arrangements, it is desirable not to 'reduce all men and women to the same dull pattern' but, rather, to 'release their richness of variety'.[6] Nonetheless, in their plot structures and narrative techniques – Holtby's panoramic inclusion, Warner's elicitation of Socratically derived truths, Young's foregrounding of problem-solving within a family, congregation and neighbourhood – the novels shift their emphasis from the realisation of the protagonist's individual happiness to the identification and achievement of a principled rural community. Warner, for example, chooses not to end *Lolly Willowes* with protagonist Laura's recognition of her vocation as a witch, but with her articulation of a new creed, which melds with a feminist manifesto spoken on behalf of women 'all over England, all over Europe . . . growing old' (p. 239). Similarly, Hannah fears and bemoans her own future at the outset of *Miss Mole*, but realising that her own history is bound up with the health and freedom of women in a younger generation, works to modernise archaic notions coupling female ignorance and female chastity. I argue that the project of each novel is to parlay the disruption and uncertainty of the postwar era into an opportunity to shape rural communities on new principles following the war, and that the spinster – energised, enfranchised, professionally and often sexually experienced – comes into her own for the first time in her history to preside over this coalescing of a community.

Miss Mole

Hannah Mole attains this enfranchisement via zigzagging movements. At the outset of the novel, her mobility signifies economic instability rather than autonomy. But Hannah's rural heritage, shaping her way of seeing the land and undergirding her confidence, prompts her again and again to translate that instability into serendipity.

Raised on a farm in Somerset, Hannah has recently been displaced to Upper Radstowe, a prosperous district across the river from Hannah's 'own country' (p. 30). (Young set most of her eleven novels in this fictionalised version of Clifton, where the Brunel suspension bridge links Somerset to the city of Bristol.) The country permeates Upper Radstowe, where, in Hannah's eyes, the autumn leaves nourish the earth and the expanse of the Downs confirms her liberty to roam. Moreover, the country supplements and provides a corrective to Hannah's personal experiences of fortune or misfortune. When she walks on the Downs, 'she could feel that while her own affairs were in a sad condition, those of the earth were doing well and beautifully' (p. 23). This fundamental faith will be the rural source of Hannah's creation of an Eden, the surprising result of her embroiling herself in and resolving her fellow residents' problems. Identifying with a country whose complexity seems to double her own, Hannah forms her principles of integrity on the strength of this affiliation. Growing up on a farm, for example, Hannah acquired 'an intimate, frank knowledge of sexual processes' (p. 69), never imbued with the disgust that afflicts the city-bred Corder family attitude toward sex. Although 'her own peculiar kind of integrity' (p. 235) will be severely tested in the novel, Hannah turns to her subjective and internalised construction of the country for an authority independent of bourgeois mores.

Nonetheless, the opening chapters of *Miss Mole* impress us with the tenuous economic position of the unmarried woman. Homeless and impoverished, Hannah Mole reflects the modern predicament of Upper Radstowe, where the shock of the war's losses has not yet been fully absorbed even as new residents seek recognition and a chance to rebuild the community on modern terms. A middle-aged spinster, Hannah arouses and fuels the expression of prejudices about unmarried women. When he calls her 'Miss Fitt', Hannah tells her elderly neighbour that 'My name is Mole' (p. 111). Confident and adventuresome, Hannah is, however, under cover, a spy who has made her way inside the house of Radstowe's Nonconformist minister, entrusted to guide his daughters into adulthood – and a woman with 'a past'. Quietly observing the dramas of the family, she keeps much of her own story concealed.

Hannah is indeed a 'Miss Fitt', secretly rebelling against the officiousness and codes of respectability of the dominant class. As is true for Warner's Laura Willowes and Holtby's Sarah Burton, Hannah's position at the margin has fostered her critique of patriarchal dominance. She has no investment in maintaining prewar structures of power. Hannah also fails to 'fit' in the sense that her life history inscribes a path of displacement. Upon the death of her parents, she has had to sell the family farm in Somerset, although she has retained a cottage on it. Rent payment from its tenant – a lover who betrayed her – is theoretical only. She has a record of paid work, as well as a record of regular dismissal from it, she hints. She has undertaken war service, perhaps in the Bradford munitions factory, and nursed a wounded soldier, and yet her current prospects drastically contract this heroic activity, sweeping her back to the days of 'superfluous' women. Thus as she sets out to assume her new post as housekeeper to the Corder family, she sees herself as 'a detachment of an army of women like herself who went from house to house . . . a sad multitude of women with carefully pleasant faces, hiding their ailments, lowering their ages and thankfully accepting less than they earned' (p. 51).

In the midst of evident displacement and instability, Hannah's 'Eden' grows out of her conviction of her own ineradicable connection to an integral, enduring nature. At the same time, seeing below the surface of the landscape, Hannah sanctions her own experience, sorting out its confusion as signs of complexity rather than duplicity. Like her fellow 'spinsters in Eden', the diverse roles Hannah has played in both rural and urban settings furnish her with a practical expertise and a significant knowledge of human affairs. Above all, Hannah's sense of an integrity based in the enduring earth and informing her own life prompts her to take risks and find the common ground between proponents of tradition and advocates for modernity in the postwar community.

Not all the risks she takes turn out well for Hannah personally, but each of them contributes directly or indirectly to the rebuilding of a community in the neighbourhood of Upper Radstowe. The trajectory of Hannah's movement early in the novel illustrates this pattern. Just before the action of the novel begins, Hannah has escaped, under the pretence of needing black mending thread, from the overheated and 'crowded little sitting-room' (p. 8) where she works as a companion to the elderly Mrs Widdows. This transgression leads to her discovery and rescue of the young Mr Ridding from an attempted suicide and to her friendship with his landlady, then to her dismissal from her situation with Mrs Widdows, to her temporary homelessness, to her search for employment and to her new position as housekeeper to the Corders. Her risky behaviour crucially engages a chain of human interactions sparked by compassion and supporting the rural principles of dignity and integrity. This embryonic community challenges the old guards of tradition and respectability.

Lolly Willowes

Laura Willowes, useful in her brother's household for most of her adult life, decides to quit London for a rural village in the Chilterns, Great Mop, unknown to everyone in her family. Great Mop enjoys a stock of eccentric rural characters, but they generate no conflict in the present time of the novel. Instead, its rural features are conducive to Laura's peace and security, including dry ditches into which she may drop for a nap, cowslips that recall her country childhood, and hilltops that provide lessons in perspective.

Although for years Laura has puzzled over the signs of her subconscious dissatisfaction with her urban and passive life, the First World War and its aftermath awaken her. She notices a gap between her own and her brother and sister-in-law's resumption of life after the war. Henry and Caroline take a 'demure, Willowes-like satisfaction in the family tree that had endured the gale with an unflinching green heart' (p. 72) and talk of better days to come, which then 'proved to be modelled as closely as possible on the days that were past' (p. 73). But Laura is disturbed by the naturalisation of war detritus: 'The sandbags had rotted and burst and the barbed-wire had been absorbed into the farmer's fences' (p. 74). The family, too, is a 'landscape' that has been altered by the war, and if one would not wish to naturalise the sudden disappearance of husbands and children, none of war's phenomena can be accepted with complacency. Laura's insight is a turning point in her ultimate decision to break from her family and leave London. Declining to rally around 'old and honourable' patriotic symbols, Laura henceforth rejects authorised meanings in favour of first-hand experience and original interpretation. If Laura's decisive break represents a return to the first impulses of Protestantism – her awakening will involve her first-hand reading of Scripture – it also reflects the modernist belief that all vision is subjective and there can be no authorised interpretations. Laura's individual happiness and her realisation of a community in Great Mop depend on her seeing rural England differently.

Seeing authentically in *Lolly Willowes* has nothing to do with capturing a static, pastoral beauty. Laura's vision of the Chilterns begins with a yearning for an anti-pastoral, unstaid rural environment, including the unsheltered hills, 'unchastened gusts' of wind and 'riotous gurgling' of rain (p. 109). To see authentically in *Lolly Willowes* is to integrate the history of its residents into the rural environment so as to particularise, animate and dignify both the inhabitants and the place.[7] Laura learns to see past the geography of Great Mop to understand its social and cultural scape; to see metaphorically, using physical geography to gain a new perspective on power; and to see into theological history to discover its ideological uses. Laura's election to witchhood makes it natural for her to adopt Satan's ethos of turning an 'undesiring and unjudging gaze' on others (p. 252).

At the end of *Lolly Willowes*, Laura famously announces that one becomes a witch 'to have a life of one's own' (p. 243). Yet the self-realisation of Laura's *Bildungsroman* only partially captures the novel's telos. *Lolly Willowes* also shares much with fables, those stories of everywoman, and in its conclusion, with manifestos, those statements of feminist principle written on behalf of an entire gender. The passive, middle-aged Laura not only is characteristic of 'decayed gentlewomen' all over England who need an escape from dullness (p. 238), but also she is an exemplary misfit in a village of misfits. In the course of her education at Great Mop, Laura comes to recognise that she can affiliate herself with like-minded others.[8] Those who were overlooked, on the margin of prewar and urban society – perhaps having fled, like Laura – are now at the centre of, or entirely populate, postwar rural society.

What will motivate these refugees, dissidents and misfits to affiliate themselves? For Laura, affiliation begins with stories of herself in relation to others. When Laura was a child, her mother filled this role, including Laura in ritual visits to the family graveyard and telling the tales of ancestors buried therein. In Great Mop, Laura's landlady, Mrs Leak, performs this function. Delineating the history of the villagers, Mrs Leak models a female narrative authority as old as the Witch of Endor and initiates Laura into the community. Mrs Leak is a storyteller as described by Walter Benjamin, a figure who knits together the members of a community by recounting the lore of faraway places or distant times. The storyteller 'takes what he tells from experience – his own or that reported by others. And he, in turn, makes it the experience of those who are listening to his tale.'[9] This is a humanising function that Benjamin believes counters the erosion of community under forces of modernity. The changes in the material and social conditions of daily life have so accelerated, Benjamin finds, or (for example, in the case of war) are so at odds with individual experience, that a chasm opens up between material reality and experience, exposing the 'tiny, fragile human body' (p. 84). Although Benjamin locates the storyteller in the past, in a valorised premodernity, he makes it clear that such storytelling helps members of the community to regain their human stature. Through Mrs Leak, Laura hears of Great Mop's colourful and strong-willed inhabitants, who do not conform to any notion of rural serenity.

If Mrs Leak re-envisions eccentricity as the very essence of life in Great Mop, it is left to Laura to articulate the communal principles that dignify the village residents. Laura humanises each 'misfit' by reinterpreting common stories of origins, identity, vocation and belonging: folk tales, biblical stories and patriotic narratives. Initiated by Mrs Leak, Laura takes up her vocation as storyteller. Having understood her right to original interpretation, Laura is liberated from the mind-forged manacles in whose bonds she had accepted without question the God of the Anglican Church, the wisdom of Henry's financial investments, and the duty of the unmarried woman to be useful to her family. Others are liberated too, as Laura views them not through these patriarchal lenses but through her reimagined origins for them.[10]

Lessons in perspective help to liberate Laura's vision, generating reversals of moral truths in the tradition of William Blake and presenting ways of being alternative to the 'bondage' dictated by 'custom, public opinion, law, church, and state'.[11] As she learns to use the topography of the Chiltern hills to manipulate her perspective, Laura experiments with enlarging or diminishing the importance of others. She practises on her friend, Mr Saunter: 'No doubt but he was like Adam. And she, watching him from above – for the field sloped down from the gate to the pens – was like God' (p. 143). Laura's exercise both empowers herself and humanises Mr Saunter. Like Laura, Mr Saunter is a misfit, a refugee in Great Mop who has been changed by the war. But to Laura, watching the soldier-turned-henkeeper, Mr Saunter takes on the proportions of a first and supremely dignified human being, so integral that he has no need for an Eve but is 'intact, with all his ribs about him' (p. 134). Laura's musing also leads her to develop her recent comparison of herself to God, a God who did not require Adam's obedience, but used him 'as an intermediate step' before 'settling down to the peace of a heaven unpeopled of contradiction' (p. 143). Laura's reconception of Genesis helps her create a modern rural community in which members recognise one another's inviolable integrity and turn on one another an unproprietary gaze.

Telling a new story of herself in relation to others, Laura achieves more than a release from her family's psychological hold on her. She also revises the story of women in Western civilisation, beginning with the foundational stories of Adam and Eve, God and Satan. Thus creating a new Eden, Laura dismantles the authority of received wisdom and tells a new, feminist story of her place in British civilisation and the cosmos. Rural places and rural alliances have made this story possible.

South Riding

South Riding's realism captures the complex and diverse social scape of a Yorkshire rural community between the two world wars. The town of Kiplington includes ex-servicemen, families on public assistance, preachers, labour activists, schoolgirls, sufferers from mental illness and struggling farmers. Holtby's panoramic treatment assures that no one is left out and that the rural can afford a vision of the whole without sacrificing particularity. It implicitly asserts that the full range of the region's population must be seen, accounted for and taken care of.[12] *South Riding*'s representation of this diversity, Lisa Regan argues, 'challenges homogenizing discourses of nationhood even as it summons them' (p. 139).[13]

Holtby's commitment to representing unassimilated diversity is manifested in narrative techniques such as the juxtaposition of opposing viewpoints and the brief spotlighting of individual characters' plights or contributions. Yet the challenge to building a community – faced by county government, labour unions and professional leaders – is how to reconcile diverse experiences, needs and viewpoints. Holtby self-consciously shows this process to be incomplete at the end of the novel. The decisive elements of positive change in the community are not democratic consensus and legislation (despite the novel's focus on the activity of the county council) but individuals' subjection to another point of view – especially under the influence of an ally or an opponent in the emerging community – and the enlarged perspective that ensues.

Accommodating a new diversity requires attention to each person's individuality. But counterbalancing that effort is the ability of community leaders to shift from a personal to an impersonal perspective. Throughout *South Riding*, to arrive at that impersonal perspective, Sarah draws on the specialised skills and perspective of the unmarried middle-aged woman: education, worldly experience and a spirit of adventure. The thirty-nine-year-old has 'an inexhaustible curiosity about the contemporary world and its inhabitants' (p. 48). She views teaching as an occasion to 'inoculate' the spirits of her pupils 'with some of her own courage, optimism and unstaled delight' (p. 48). To this enthusiasm will be added Sarah's exposure to antipathetic points of view and their often uncomfortable influence on her.

A Yorkshire native, Sarah has been educated in Leeds and Oxford, and has worked as a teacher in South Africa and London. Like Hannah Mole, her life experience inscribes continuity between rural and urban, and even cosmopolitan, environments. While at first she hesitates to return to Yorkshire, concerned that she will 'grow slack and stagnant' (p. 46), as she travels by bus from the city of Kingsport to Kiplington, she expresses her appreciation both for the rural landscape and for the warehouses, stores, offices and docks of Kingsport. 'Ships, journeys, adventures were glorious to Sarah' (p. 46). In *South Riding*, the spinster's expertise in both rural and urban environments enables her to forge alliances across lines of difference. For example, Sarah's facility motivates her crucial assistance, late one night, to her political opponent Robert Carne, during a cow's difficult calving. Although her 'years of urban experience had prevented her from recognising the sounds' of the labouring cow (p. 163), that same urban experience grounds her creed of self-determination and individual responsibility (associated specifically with a London feminist network), so that instead of driving on from the sounds of distress, she plunges into the night to determine who needs help. Looking in the window of the shed, she sizes up the situation quickly, but could still pass on from the scene, unnoticed. Instead, she reasons, on this eve of Easter, that 'birth and death were matters of common interest' (p. 163) and turns decisively into the shed. Once inside, Sarah's rural experience and 'inherited instinct' (p. 163) take over, enabling her to lend indispensable intellectual and physical aid.

Holtby additionally envisions more far-reaching benefits of the spinster's ability to link rural and urban milieux. Sarah brings her pupils in rural Kiplington into a metropolitan feminist intellectual community when she imparts to them the creed of 'Take what you want . . . and pay for it.' Lady Rhondda, who quotes this 'old Spanish proverb' (p. 163) in her autobiography, is the source of this inspiration. Sarah's work as a teacher thus provides for her rural female pupils a link to the reading, conversations and collective work of metropolitan women activists. In this initial formulation of the motto, which will be revised under the influence of her new community, Sarah instils in her pupils a code of self-determination and individual responsibility. She reasons that, in turn, the training 'not to fear, not to hate' will give us 'some hope for society' (p. 161).

Near the conclusion of *South Riding*, Holtby fully develops her vision of mutual humanising, showing its potential benefits to a rural community in the form of individual citizens' renewed encouragement, fresh insight and reawakened activism. Sarah Burton and Councilwoman Emma Beddows meet, following Sarah's discouragement in the wake of her thwarted love affair with Robert Carne and his recent death. In a recurring motif, one woman passes a baton to another to advance a common good. In this fully developed example of that pattern, Sarah's conversation with the older Mrs Beddows forces her to confront and share her humiliation in love; then it clears the way for her renewed goals of teaching girls and spreading her own 'gospel of resolution and independence' (p. 118). Yet Sarah's capacity to create a community is not complete until a final scene at Maythorpe, the farm of the late Carne, in which she experiences a spiritual enlargement that frees her to pursue the principled goals that Carne had opposed. Holtby outlines a programme for change that, however initially spurred by individual autonomy, evolves into an individual's transcendent, enlarged and impersonal set of goals.

In the conversation between Mrs Beddows and Sarah, the two women collaborate to resolve questions about Carne and the circumstances of his death. Early in the conversation, they expose and demonstrate their capacity for love and their vulnerability to the humiliation that may attend it. On the basis of this mutual assurance of the other's humanity, further collaborations ensue: each woman can relieve a doubt nagging the other woman. As Holtby develops the motif of the relayed baton, the teacher is taught by the older woman, preparing the teacher to arrive at an important insight and revision of her earlier motto and expanding her teaching abilities. Sarah subsequently revises the simple transactional model of 'Take what you want and pay for it,' her conversation with Mrs Beddows helping her to understand the unevenness, and even the intangibility, of need and ability in the community: 'She knew now that the costliest things are not the ones for which those who take can pay' (p. 475). The younger woman moves from a sense of herself as an individual agent working under the guidance of her own values to a recognition of her dependence on others to achieve her goals.

Immediately following her interview with Emma Beddows, Sarah drives alone to Maythorpe, destined now for the site of a much-needed nursing home. In a soliloquy to the dead man whom she loved, Sarah feels a spiritual enlargement and a mutual exchange. 'She had become part of him and he of her, because she loved him. He had entered into her as part of the composition of her nature, so that they no longer stood in hostile camps' (p. 476). Holtby supplies for her unmarried protagonist a platonic alternative to the marriage plot that paves the way for Sarah's gifts to be realised in teaching.[14] Before this moment, Sarah had found herself at an impasse. Loving Carne and suffering after his sudden death, how could she work against the conservative, old-world values that he stood for? And how could she work for what he believed in, not sharing these beliefs? Sarah's epiphany clears the way for her to pursue the civic goals that she believes will strengthen the community; her enlarged nature is given an appropriate outlet and the promise of real impact on a generation of schoolgirls.[15]

Sarah's spiritual encounter with Carne underscores Holtby's vision that communal welfare advances as individuals realise their interdependence. 'Her rational, decisive, rather crude personality seemed to enlarge itself, with desperate travail of the imagination, until it could comprehend also his slow rectitude, his courage in resignation, his simplicity of belief' (p. 476). Holtby describes as a compassionate enlargement of Sarah's nature what this chapter calls the mutual humanisation of misfits: 'It was as though, each of them having known love so intensely even though not for each other, they had entered into some element greater than themselves' (p. 476).

Both in fictional and in non-fictional fora, Holtby explored the idea of individual perfection and its dependence on a strong community based on equality of opportunity. Ten years before the publication of *South Riding*, Holtby had argued that the 'unity of creation, revealed by science, tells us' that no human being 'can attain to full perfection until his brethren share his opportunities'.[16] In *South Riding*, then, Sarah realises that 'we are members one of another. We cannot escape this partnership. This is what it means – to belong to a community' (pp. 490–1). And it is in modern rural Yorkshire that Sarah both discovers and creates the conditions for that community.

Mutual recognition in the postwar rural community

The spinster-in-Eden novels, whose pattern is replicated in novels such as Virginia Woolf's *Between the Acts* (1941) and Lettice Cooper's *National Provincial* (1938), reflect an optimism that the unmarried, experienced and newly enfranchised woman is poised to play a leading role in the rebuilding of postwar English rural life. Both her exemption from the marriage bar in the professions and her freedom from the responsibilities of marriage and childcare lead her to realise her talents outside the domestic realm, among her neighbours and in the civic sphere.

The spinster's expertise in rural matters is crucial to her success in rebuilding communities confronting unprecedented change in the wake of the Great War. Yet this rural knowledge does not lend itself to the preservation of a threatened rural heritage. Strikingly, in each novel, the spinster translates that rural expertise into improvement of human social conditions. In each novel, the spinster enjoys a botanical or agricultural expertise that helps her to become an insider in a new village. Often, her way of seeing a rural place leads to the amelioration of decaying social and economic conditions in rural communities. Thus the spinster-in-Eden novels envision a role for human beings in the country that transcends that of spectator, visitor or urban exile.

Documenting the plight of new and misfitting residents of postwar rural communities, the three novels discussed in this chapter maintain their focus on social and economic forces. The previously suspicious mobility of the New Woman is now an asset. Released from domesticity, the unmarried woman gets bruised in the decidedly unpastoral humanscapes in which she roams. Yet that bruising only equips her more definitively for the task of articulating the principles by which misfits become integral and respected citizens, laying the groundwork for her cultivation of a new Eden.

In dialogue with: Chapter 2 'Change in the Village' (I: Networks) [recording rural change; 'seeing differently']; Chapter 6 '*Hiraeth* or Ambiguous Pastorals' (II: Landscapes) [popular fiction; representations of rural renewal].

Notes

1. Howkins, p. 101.
2. Baudelaire, 'The Painter', p. 9.
3. On ambivalence about the spinster's mobility, see especially Katz.
4. E. H. Young, p. 200.
5. In surveying and developing the idea of community in this period, both Jessica Berman and Lisa Regan applaud models that resist the goal of political consensus so as to protect a plurality of voices. Both also see this protection as a means of resisting totalitarian nationalism.
6. *Women*, p. 192.
7. By contrasting particularised and reflective with superficial, commercialised and imperialistic modes of seeing England, *Lolly Willlowes* anticipates much of the interwar campaign urging Britons to visit distinct regions, to apprehend them as aspects of British heritage and to preserve them.
8. Said makes a useful distinction between a critic's 'filiation', determined by his birthplace or nationality, and his 'affiliation', chosen, among other factors, 'by social and political conviction' (p. 25).
9. Benjamin, 'The Storyteller', p. 87.
10. *Lolly Willowes* has enjoyed a distinguished feminist reception, beginning with Jane Marcus's '"A Wilderness of One's Own"'.
11. Warner, p. 223.
12. Phyllis Bentley's early monograph on the English regional novel foregrounds its representation of both diversity and particularity, which Bentley links to what Raymond Williams calls a 'knowable community'. In regional novels, characters appear 'strongly individual, because well known to all in that district; in their own home town or village persons never become anonymous "masses", but remain individual men' (Bentley, p. 45).
13. Regan offers a comprehensive and compelling study of Holtby's evolving vision of community.
14. Feminist critics have expressed strong interest in Holtby's treatment of the marriage plot. Diana Wallace, Gan and Regan each find that Carne's death removes the element of Sarah's active choice. In contrast, this chapter's focus on *South Riding*'s representation of an unmarried woman's reconstruction of a postwar community leads to the conclusion that unfulfilled love contributes to the valuable diversity of Sarah's life experiences without shaping the novel into a failed marriage plot.
15. In essays such as 'Is Family Life a Handicap?', Holtby similarly posits that the experience of private life may enhance capacity for civic action.
16. 'Bring Up Your Rears', p. 200.

Chapter 9

Transformative Pastoral: Lewis Grassic Gibbon's *A Scots Quair*

Nick Hubble

Lewis Grassic Gibbon described himself as 'a revolutionary writer',[1] and his most famous work, the trilogy *A Scots Quair*, appears to be a story of the movement away from the hardship and isolation of a rural peasant life, which hindered collective action, towards urban modernity and the possibilities for organisation offered by the industrial city.[2] However, the trilogy does not end with the young communist, Ewan Tavendale, leading a hunger march on London but with his mother, now Chris Ogilvie, returning to Cairndhu, the rural croft where she was born. The closing sentences of the third volume, *Grey Granite* (1934), are often taken to imply that Chris dies while sitting on the hillside above Cairndhu as night falls:

> Lights had sprung up far in the hills, in little touns for a sunset minute while the folk tired and went off to their beds, miles away, thin peeks in the summer dark.
>
> Time she went home herself.
>
> But she still sat on as one by one the lights went out and the rain came beating the stones about her, and falling all that night while she still sat there, presently feeling no longer the touch of the rain or hearing the sound of the lapwings going by. (p. 496)

On this reading, the novel ends with a symbolic return to the land, which seems antithetical to Gibbon's self-proclaimed revolutionary intent. Left-wing critics, including Gibbon's writer peers James Barke and Hugh MacDiarmid, have persistently complained about what Ian A. Bell describes as the 'lack of engagement with urban working-class lives' in *Grey Granite*: 'the collective experience of the workplace remains drastically under-recorded by the author, and the narrative concludes with an elegiac return to a rural environment'.[3]

This chapter proposes a radically different reading of the text, which not only relates it to the complex concept of rural modernity identified by Kristin Bluemel as concerned simultaneously with both alienated and organic relationships to nature,[4] but also considers it as belonging to at least three other genres besides socialist realism: modernism, pastoral and fantasy. The last of these is signalled from the outset in the opening sentence of the first volume of the trilogy, *Sunset Song* (1932):

> Kinraddie lands had been won by a Norman childe, Cospatric de Gondeshil, in the days of William the Lyon, when gryphons and suchlike beasts still roamed the Scots countryside and folk would waken in their beds to hear the children screaming, with a great wolf-beast, come through the hide window, tearing at their throats. (p. 15)

The critic John Clute has argued that most of the great fantasy writers of the twentieth century, such as J. R. R. Tolkien, were shaped by the traumatic experience of the First World War, which caused them 'to turn away from the world to shame it' by adopting a narrative structure with the four phases of 'wrongness', 'thinning', 'recognition' and 'return'.[5] *A Scots Quair* follows this model: *Sunset Song* traces the 'wrongness' of the break-up of the organic rural community accelerated by the men going away to the First World War, *Cloud Howe* (1933) the 'thinning' of social life encapsulated by the bitter defeat of the General Strike, and *Grey Granite* the 'recognition' by Chris that there is no place for her in the world of industrial capitalism and her final 'return' home. This structure suggests that, far from being a failure to represent revolutionary male subjectivity, *A Scots Quair* is actually a deliberate critique of what Deirdre Burton describes as the mobilised Left's lack of 'anything like an adequate vision with which to transform existing power relations' (p. 40). Instead, Burton argues that the trilogy is a feminist work that both deliberately exposes Ewan as a person of 'limited vision, limited growth – both personal and political' and more generally recognises how 'patriarchal attitudes have consistently excluded women, their experiences, their insights, their work from all radical movements and activities except their own' (p. 45). In this context, Alison Lumsden suggests that Chris's 'apparent death' at the end of *Grey Granite* might be seen as an escape from patriarchy into a Kristevan women's time offering the 'radically subversive possibility of textual "second birth"' (p. 51).

However, Chris's split subjectivity throughout the novels is not necessarily the deleterious consequence of patriarchy that Lumsden implies and might rather be thought of as a consequence of the paradoxical complexity of rural modernity. Consider, for example, the well-known and oft-quoted passage first outlining Chris's duality in *Sunset Song*:

> So that was Chris and her reading and schooling, two Chrisses there were that fought for her heart and tormented her. You hated the land and the coarse speak of the folk and learning was brave and fine one day and the next

> you'd waken with the peewits crying across the hills, deep and deep, crying in the heart of you and the smell of the earth in your face, almost you'd cry for that, the beauty of it and the sweetness of the Scottish land and skies. (p. 37)

While this tension is often identified in the text as being between 'English' Chris and 'Scottish' Chris, it is equally between what we might term 'alienated' Chris and 'organic' Chris. This rural duality can be considered in terms of what William Empson described as the double attitude of pastoral. Empson's *Some Versions of Pastoral* (1935) begins with a discussion of 'Proletarian Literature' in the aftermath of the 1934 Soviet Writers' Congress call for socialist realism, the context in which Gibbon's trilogy would be regarded a failure. Empson argued that socialist realism could not possibly function as an unmediated expression of proletarian subjectivity: 'To produce pure proletarian art the artist must be at one with the worker; this is impossible, not for political reasons, but because the artist never is at one with any public' (p. 19). Instead, he argued that one way in which such literature could work successfully would be if it functioned as a form of pastoral 'based on a double attitude of the artist to the worker, of the complex man to the simple one ("I am in one way better, in another not so good.")' (p. 19). Gibbon's own double attitude to the worker is represented in the text through Chris, whose circumstances resemble his own childhood. She spends her days at college thinking of farm life 'till she was sick to be home again' (p. 45), but when the men laugh at her going to college while she is preparing food at threshing time, she sees them as 'yokels and clowns everlasting, dull-brained and crude' (p. 74). Then, when Chae Strachan and Long Rob of the Mill speak up for her and the value of education, she feels ashamed of her thoughts of clowns and yokels, for they are the poorest folk in Kinraddie. In coming to understand herself as both better and worse than her rural neighbours, Chris develops a complex consciousness characteristic of modernity, one rooted in rural rather than a purely 'metropolitan form of perception'.[6] This third Chris, at ease with rural modernity, comes to rule over 'those other two selves of herself, content, unquestioning' in the years preceding the war (p. 153), fully conscious of her relationship with the men and the wet clay ground and the sky above. But then, when the war comes, Chae, Long Rob and her husband Ewan – already unrecognisable as the man she loved in his last period of leave with her – all die in France, and their rural way of life is ruined forever. The 'wrongness' of this destruction, however, is made most apparent in the damage wreaked upon the land itself. Chae is horror-struck when he comes home on leave to discover that the woods that shelter his own land and the other holdings in Kinraddie have been cut down for the high prices generated by wartime needs. He realises that, with the land now exposed to northeasterly winds, it is 'fair the end of a living here now' (p. 155). By the end of *Sunset Song*, Blawearie, where Chris had grown up and later farmed the land, has become fit only to be grazed by sheep:

> And that was the way things went in the end on the old bit place up there on the brae, sheep baaed and scrunched where once the parks flowed thick with corn, no corn would come at all, they said, since the woods went down. And the new minister when he preached his incoming sermon cried *They have made a desert and they call it peace*; and some had no liking of the creature for that, but God! there was truth in his speak. (p. 189)

At the beginning of the second volume of the trilogy, *Cloud Howe*, Chris has turned away from this picture of environmental exploitation. After marrying the minister, Robert Colquhoun, she moves from the land to the small town of Segget, an historical trajectory that will be completed by her eventual move to the industrial city of Duncairn (Aberdeen). This trajectory, reflected in the maps printed on the endpapers of the original editions of the novels, demonstrates a shift not just in focus but also of scale, so that we see more, not less, of the 'land' with each successive move (Figures 9.1, 9.2, 9.3). As a consequence, while the map in *Sunset*

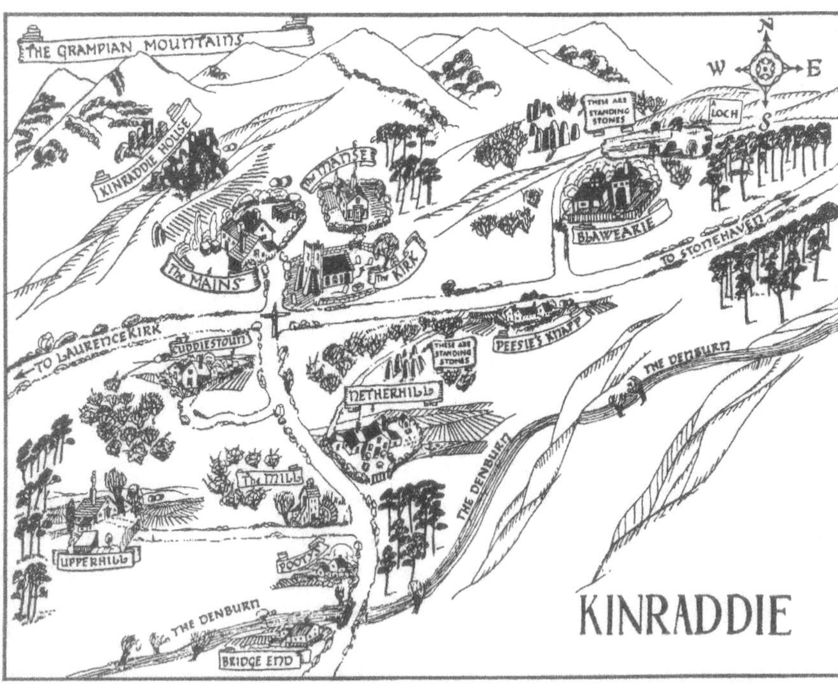

Figure 9.1 'Map of Kinraddie', endpapers in first Jarrolds of London edition of *Sunset Song*, 1932. The Mitchell Literary Estate and the Grassic Gibbon Centre.

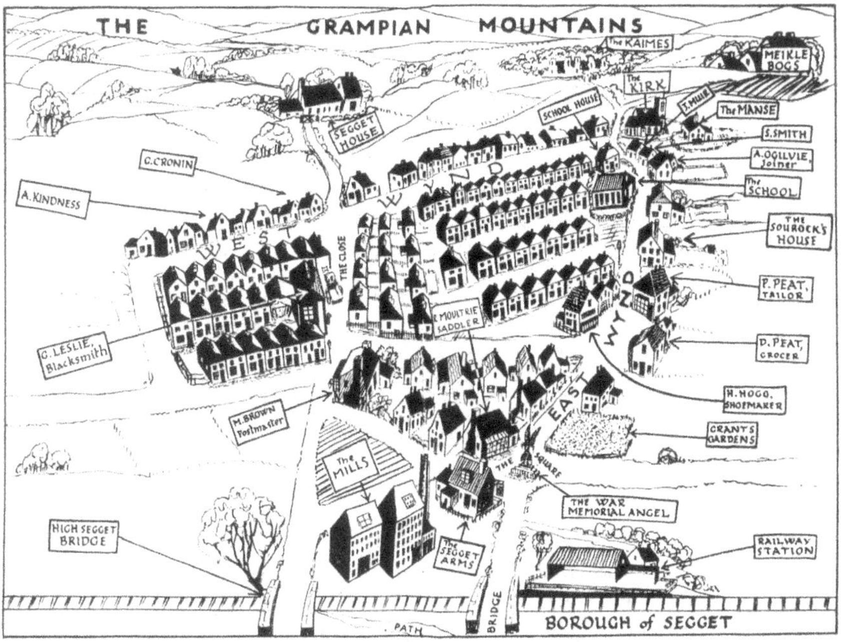

Figure 9.2 'Map of Segget', endpapers in first Jarrolds of London edition of *Cloud Howe*, 1933. The Mitchell Literary Estate and the Grassic Gibbon Centre.

Song depicts Kinraddie as coterminous with the land, the map in *Grey Granite* shows Duncairn to be no more than just one place among many, dwarfed by the vastness of the land.

Rural modernity and metropolitan perception

In her essay, 'Modernism and Marxism in *A Scots Quair*', Margery Palmer McCulloch notes that

> What is so significant about *A Scots Quair* itself is the way in which [Gibbon] has succeeded in marrying a modernist fictional form with a Marxist exploration of contemporary and historical force, an exploration more often conducted in fiction through socialist-realist methodology. (p. 29)

Gibbon discussed his own work in the third person in 'Literary Lights', which first appeared in *Scottish Scene* (1934), the book that he wrote with Hugh MacDiarmid:

> The technique of Lewis Grassic Gibbon in his trilogy *A Scots Quair* [. . .] is to mould the English language into the rhythms and cadences of Scots spoken speech, and to inject into the English vocabulary such minimum number of

> words from Braid Scots as that remodelling requires. His scene so far has been a comparatively uncrowded and simple one – the countryside and village of modern Scotland [. . .] whether his peculiar style may not become either intolerably mannered or degenerate, in the fashion of Joyce, into the unfortunate unintelligibilities of a literary second childhood, is [. . .] in question. (p. 135)

McCulloch discusses this allusion to Joyce, pondering whether it is being used ironically 'to forestall criticism of [Gibbon's] own experimentation' and noting that Gibbon is, elsewhere in the same essay, more positive about Joyce.[7] Gibbon is probably making a distinction between the instalments of 'Work in Progress', which appeared in journals such as *transition* and the *Transatlantic Review* throughout the 1920s and 1930s, and *Ulysses*, which is held out as only a future possibility due to what he perceives as a Scottish resistance to experimentation such as his own: 'one may guess that in another fifty years or so a Scots Virginia Woolf will astound the Scottish scene, a Scots James Joyce electrify it'.[8]

Gibbon's point is both that without embracing the experimental innovations of modernism it will be at least fifty years before Scottish literature will have a transformative societal impact (as arguably happened exactly according to his schedule with the work of James Kelman, Alasdair Gray and others in the 1980s), and that without including the longer history behind industrial class relations – including the rural relationship with the land – within its depiction of the sum of social reality, modernist innovation will degenerate into meaningless strings of words. The completion of *A Scots Quair* with *Grey Granite*, with its blurring of the distinction between the voices of narrator, characters and readers within a rhythmic Scottish free indirect discourse, was designed to evade the twin pitfalls of rejecting modernism or embracing it only as a metropolitan phenomenon. For McCulloch, this innovative blend works especially well for *Grey Granite* because it enables the trilogy's focus on women in general, and Chris in particular, to offer 'an alternative, even sceptical perspective on Ewan's ideological commitments' that renders 'the book's ending as an open one'.[9]

In *Scottish Modernism and Its Contexts 1918–1959* (2009), McCulloch relates this openness to a sense of 'history in the making' in *A Scots Quair* (p. 143), which is particularly acute because the history of social development from the land via small towns to the industrial city is effectively compressed into a period of a little less than a quarter of a century across the three books. One consequence of this compression is that it highlights Raymond Williams's conception of 'metropolitan perception' – the awareness of changed social relations, the mutability of conventions and a new sense of different social possibilities – as in part a product of the continued immigration into the city of people from rural or otherwise more traditional societies, drawing on their memory of precapitalist social relations or at least the vestiges of such.[10] The adaptation of Chris to the city in *Grey Granite* is both a process of converting her sense of rural modernity into metropolitan perception and a demonstration of how that metropolitan perception is, in any case, generated by folding the traces of pre-urban history into everyday life. Rather than providing an individualist (male) bourgeois subjectivity for the reader to identify with, Chris acts as a conduit to an ungendered, second-person Scots narrative voice made up of many personal and community perspectives, both rural and urban, weaved in together with no linguistic hierarchy.

This is because Chris enables readers to share the pastoral double attitude of both the simple and the complex; she does not have to abandon her specialised feelings to imagine those of the simple person because she can see from both perspectives anyway. As Empson explains in his discussion of John Gay's *The Beggar's Opera* (1728) in *Some Versions of Pastoral*, the double attitude of characters in pastoral can lead to 'Comic Primness, the double irony in the acceptance of a convention' (p. 72). This is a complex position in which the speaker simultaneously accepts and rejects the convention he or she is ironising and so is forced into a position of isolation and therefore independence. The following passage from *Grey Granite* provides a good example:

> [Ellen] and Ewan were indifferent, polite, Chris thought them too much alike to take heed of each other. But Miss Lyon couldn't abide [Ellen] at all, and would sniff as she watched her, Just a Vulgar Flirt, she didn't let me take Liberties with *her*. She told this to Chris after breakfast one day, didn't Mrs. Colquohoun think the Johns girl Common? And Chris smiled at her sweet. *I don't know, Miss Lyon. You see I'm awfully common myself.* (p. 392)

On one level, Chris's reply illustrates what Empson would describe as second-level comic primness. Chris is being critically ironic in that the implication of her retort is that both Miss Lyon and the social conventions of correct behaviour she upholds are wrong. Nevertheless, her reply does not actually contradict Miss Lyon so much as to confirm the arbitrariness of the convention, which she does not actually challenge, suggesting that she herself is still comfortable with complying with this convention that she does not actually believe in. Empson suggests that this would be the basis for a '"critical" comedy' (p. 171). However, the scene also demonstrates third-level comic primness, in that Chris is displaying what Empson describes as

> Ironical Humility, whose simplest gambit is to say, 'I am not clever, educated, well born', or what not (as if you had a low standard to judge by), and then to imply that your standards are so high in the matter that the person you are humbling yourself before is quite out of sight. (p. 171)

What makes this different to the second level is that Chris's statement that she is common carries with it a sense of precapitalist social relations for the reader, who is aware that she comes from the organic rural community depicted in *Sunset Song*. On another level completely, therefore, Chris is not accepting Miss Lyon's sense of social propriety at all but implicitly advancing an alternative set of social values that are not entirely rooted in class relations because they still contain the trace of an unalienated experience. In this respect, more generally, Chris is pushed into isolation and independence throughout the trilogy; she becomes increasingly ill at ease with urban social conventions because her consciousness of the alternative values she holds, rooted in rural modernity, becomes unbearable.

Early in *Grey Granite*, second-person narration is combined with Chris's free indirect discourse to communicate to the reader that her status has changed from being the minister's wife in a small town – as

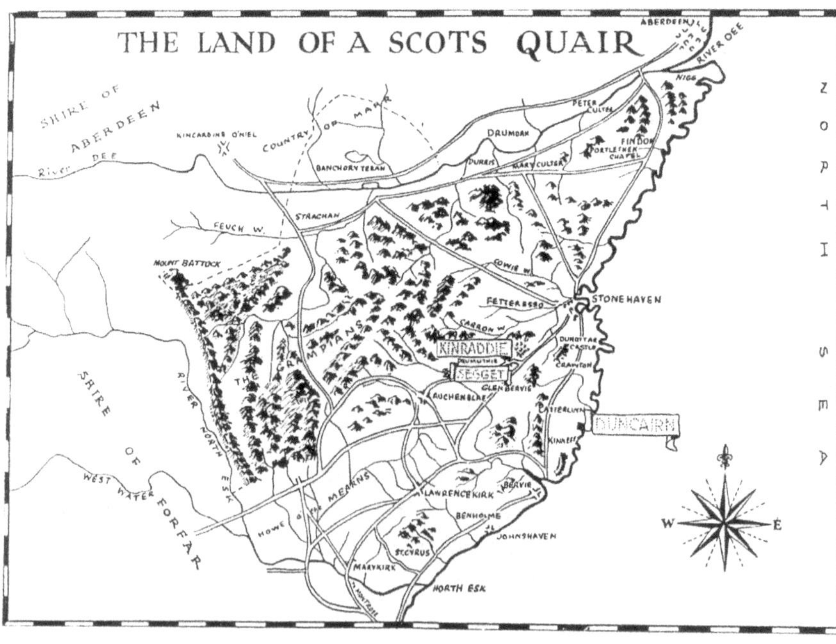

Figure 9.3 'Map of the Land of A Scots Quair', endpapers in first Jarrolds of London edition of *Grey Granite*, 1934. The Mitchell Literary Estate and the Grassic Gibbon Centre.

she was in *Cloud Howe*, which was itself a significant change from her life on a smallholding in *Sunset Song* – to having become the junior partner in running a boarding house in the industrial city of Duncairn: 'At half-past five the clock would go *birr!* in the narrow long room you had ta'en for yourself' (p. 362). And so starts a long description of a day of preparing meals, administering to boarders and cleaning bedrooms. However, the narrative then cuts to an unemployed worker:

> On the Broo since the War and five kids to keep, eating off you head – och, why did you live? – never a minute of quiet to yourself, nothing but the girnings of the wife for more silver, the kids half-barefoot, half-fed, oh hell. (p. 369)

And then the musings of his wife: 'Hardly believe it was him you had wed, that had been a gey bit spark in his time, hearty and bonny, liked you well: and had hit you, the bloody brute coming drunk from the pub' (p. 370). By including Chris and other women in this second-person narration, Gibbon prevents urban consciousness being reduced solely to that of a masculine proletarian viewpoint. However, a counter-narrative focused on Ewan emerges in the story of how he is at first treated as a toff by the other apprentices at the engineering works where he is now based until he gets involved in a fight with them. The section describing his return to work afterwards, when he becomes accepted and involved in union meetings, begins and ends with second-person narration from another apprentice. This starts off 'you couldn't but wonder what Tavendale would do' (p. 389) and ends up on first-name terms with the 'funny chap [. . .] but you'd like him to tea some Saturday night' (p. 391). Until this point, Ewan has been an enigmatic figure but now he is aligned, despite his difference, with both the workers and the general narrative voice of the novel. The same run of pages includes Chris's mealtime exchange with Miss Lyon discussed above, but also an earlier encounter with a working man in which she gets him reluctantly to return a sixpence to her:

> *There you are, mistress. Enjoy your money while you have it. There's a time coming when your class won't have it long.*
> Chris's temper quite went with her a minute, silly fool, the heat she supposed, she didn't care:
> *My class? It was digging its living in sweat while yours lay down with a whine in the dirt. Good-bye.* (p. 377)

Here, Chris's independence is asserted not against petty-bourgeois snobbishness but against a worker. It is a response triggered by a loss of temper, but it also indirectly makes the point that the labour of the industrial working class is not the only source of material value historically, nor the essential component of modernity. Chris does not accept that the labour of the industrial working class gives them an agency in history that outweighs her memories of an unalienated connection with the land. Henceforth, Chris and Ewan represent opposed forms of consciousness in *Grey Granite*.

The limits of revolutionary male subjectivity

This transfer of roles by which Ewan becomes one with the workers and Chris seems to become isolated is finalised by the march organised by the communist Jim Trease in protest against the means test. This begins with a return to the second-person stream of consciousness of the anonymous unemployed worker, describing how he gets involved in the march despite just going to watch and pretending not to hear the shouts from the communists to join up: 'And a man'd look shamefaced at another childe, and smoke his pipe and never let on till Big Jim himself came habbering along, crying you out by your Christian name, and you couldn't well do anything else but join' (p. 393). McCulloch analyses this passage to show how the man's perspective is also a group perspective, which furthermore incorporates the perspective of his wife and all the wives, before reflecting the change of mood by which he and the other men get swept up in the passion of the march as 'memories of his past army service come flooding into his present thoughts'.[11] This passion leads them to attack the police when they are prevented from reaching the town hall, and they are saved from the retaliatory mounted charge only when Ewan, who is just passing by and not even on the march, directs them to a brewery lorry full of empty bottles with which they can fight back.

While this is a vividly described dramatic scene that engages the reader directly in the action, it can also be read as a critique of the tactics of the communists and working-class movement at the time. Gibbon's account of the march is psychologically acute in the way it replicates the process by which mass participation in an event is generated. The men look at each other and see their experiences reflected in each other, a form of shared expression that reminds them of marching as a mass during the war. Participation in the march creates a collective identity, like that of the army, which is based not on everyday knowledge but on a temporary sense of being at one with each other and, therefore, of being in possession of an agency, which is in reality false because there has been no accompanying change in their material circumstances.

Gibbon's criticism is not just directed at communist tactics and aestheticised politics but also is a gendered criticism of the limits of revolutionary male subjectivity, as is made clear from the description of the men, in various bloodied states, reliving the fight through the night afterwards in the tenements, while the women look on in disbelief. When asked what the use of more fighting is, the anonymous second-person focaliser says you only have to die once, and it would be worth it with your fist in a policeman's guts. However, in this passage, the second-person narrative, which by definition is gender-neutral, can also be seen to challenge gender norms, as it arguably does throughout the trilogy. The women feel sick to see their particular man, face dripping with blood, whispering '*I'm fine, lass, fine*. Oh God you could greet if it wasn't that when you did that you would die' (p. 398). This creates a momentary confusion in the reader as to whose thoughts are being focalised. It comes immediately after the man speaking, and so there is a possibility that it might be his thoughts. In the context of the paragraph, however, it is probably the focalised thoughts of a woman, or, at least, that is the way that readers with gendered consciousnesses are likely to reconcile the passage with their worldview. On the other hand, the two mentions of death in quick succession suggest both that masculinity is something to be demonstrated primarily by being prepared to die for it and that the desire for such a death is itself a primary ingredient of that masculinity. Readers of *A Scots Quair* are already aware of this idea from the way that the men in *Sunset Song* were unable to resist the compulsive need to set off to die in the First World War. A similar compulsion is echoed later in *Grey Granite* in the account of an evening spent together by Ewan and Trease. The two become great comrades following the march and its aftermath in the unacknowledged but implicitly shared understanding that 'they *are* the workers', a feeling reinforced later when, with Mrs Trease out at the cinema, they can feel themselves men alone together. Then Mrs Trease comes back singing 'Ta-ra-ra, 'way down in Omaha':

> Trease twinkled at Ewan: That's what you get. Not revolutionary songs but Ta-ra-ra, 'way down in Omaha. Mrs Trease said Fegs, revolutionary songs gave her a pain in the stomach, they were nearly as dreich as hymns, the only difference being that they promised you hell on earth instead of in hell.
>
> And Ewan sat and looked on and spoke now and then, and liked them well enough, knowing that if it suited the party purpose Trease would betray him to the police tomorrow, use anything and everything that might happen to him as propaganda and publicity, without caring a fig for liking or aught else. So he'd deal with Mrs Trease, if it came to that . . . (p. 482)

While Gibbon never gives Ewan anything but his full imaginative conviction, this passage – perhaps more than any other in the novel

– exposes exactly how the revolutionary fantasy of mutual betrayal and death functions to underpin male homosocial relationships and maintain women as objects.

The land transformed

On the one hand, as McCulloch notes, the age difference between Gibbon, born in 1901, and other major modernists means that, unlike that of Joyce, Lawrence, Woolf or MacDiarmid, the decisive change in human relationships from his perspective occurred neither in 1910 nor as part of the direct experience of the First World War, but rather as a result of the Russian Revolution in 1917 and his subsequent involvement with the foundation of the Aberdeen Soviet in 1918 and in the political ferment of Red Clydeside in 1919.[12] As a consequence, he had a clear conception of the potential of revolutionary socialism to generate wholesale social change by overturning class society. On the other hand, Gibbon's feminist politics and his linked belief in diffusionist theories of a neolithic golden age – both of which feature in his two science fiction novels (written under his real name of James Leslie Mitchell), *Three Go Back* (1932) and *Gay Hunter* (1934) – gave him a perspective similar to that advanced by Walter Benjamin in 'Theses on the Philosophy of History' (1950). Benjamin describes history as an angel being blown backwards out of paradise by the storm of progress, so that when we look back on a chain of events, the angel 'sees one single chain of catastrophe which keeps piling wreckage upon wreckage and hurls it in front of his feet'.[13] In Gibbon's first book, *Hanno, or, The Future of Exploration* (1928), having invoked the myths of Avalon and Atlantis, he discusses exploration as the search for an equivalent post-scarcity utopia for humanity to return to, before concluding 'Looking up at the night upon the untrodden starfields, it needs no robust faith to believe that in the Future of Exploration lies the Future of Mankind' (p. 94). His concept of exploration was not, therefore, one of colonial expansion or the instrumental acquisition of wealth and raw materials, but of a utopian desire to find a location in which to revive the unalienated social relations of the past. This is reinforced by another work of non-fiction, *Nine Against the Unknown* (1934), published in the same month as *Grey Granite*, which seeks to distinguish between the ideals of the explorers themselves, such as Vasco da Gama and Mungo Park, and the exploitative motives of those who sent or funded them. As Ian Campbell notes, Mitchell repeatedly turns to the idea of 'the fortunate isles – the dream of an undiscovered, unexplored, "undeveloped" source of riches or beauty',[14] which could inaugurate a new golden age far away from the spoilage and ravening exploitation of civilisation. Both *Hanno* and *Nine Against the Unknown* are prefaced with part of Tennyson's Ulysses (1842), culminating in these four lines:

> To sail beyond the sunset and the baths
> Of all the western stars, until I die.
> It may be that the gulfs will wash us down:
> It may be we shall touch the happy isles.

Similar ideas underpin the ending of *Grey Granite*, in which, as described earlier, Chris sits alone at sunset on the hillside above Cairndhu until the lights in the little towns go out and she can no longer feel the touch of the rain or hear the sound of the lapwings going by. Rather than dying, this might be seen as indicating that somehow she has reached the utopian haven of the 'happy isles' just 'beyond the sunset'. The penultimate sentence of the novel – 'Time she went home herself' (p. 496) – would therefore be referring to home in the sense of a return to the golden age. We know from the earlier visit to Cairndhu by Chris, Ewan and Ellen that on the hill is an 'old Pict fort built by the men of antique time, a holy place before Christ was born' (p. 386). However, suggesting that home is really the neolithic past is not necessarily regressive because, as Ellen points out, '*If there was once a time without gods and classes couldn't there be that time again?*' (p. 387). The ending of the novel, therefore, is directly connected to one of the key political discussions in the trilogy: the relationship between socialism and feminism. It is in this earlier scene that Ewan first expresses socialist ideas in his complaint concerning civilisation as a calamity from the point of view of that ancient society. Rather than bringing him closer to Ellen, who is already a socialist, this triggers a disagreement between them that anticipates their irrevocable split later in the novel. While Ewan thinks the prospect of a golden age to come is of no concern to him because he will not live to see it and he has his own life to lead, Ellen castigates his complacency regarding the urgent need to transform society in the face of capitalist crisis and the rise of fascism. Ewan's rejoinder – '*They won't rule me. I'm myself*' (p. 387) – is a straightforward assertion of the nineteenth-century bourgeois male self-consciousness that underpins revolutionary male subjectivity. The conclusion of the trilogy, therefore, may be seen as Gibbon's endorsement of the need for a wider-ranging feminist–socialist transformation of society as a whole rather than a narrower socialist transformation of economic relations leaving other forms of oppression in place.

In textually working out both Chris's and Ewan's processes of self-realisation, Gibbon was working though his own double attitude to Scotland, gender and class politics. Feeling the weight of the arguments on all sides, as in Empson's account of comic primness, pushed him into a position of political isolation and independence of thought. During 'the last supper' of Chris and Ewan before both leave Duncairn, she for Cairndhu and he as leader of a hunger march, they talk of Segget, the small town in which they lived during the events of *Cloud Howe*. Ewan finally recognises that in his conversion to communism he has found the clear, sharp creed that his stepfather talked of in his final sermon. In other words, he is motivated by faith but this is a faith that Chris rejects: '*The world's sought faith for thousands of years and found only death or unease in them. Yours is just another dark cloud to me – or a great rock you're trying to push up a hill*' (p. 495). This is a judgement on Ewan's masochistic denial of the social life around him and an indictment of communism as a narrow creed. The effect of this on Ewan is to bring him out from behind the tenets of communism so that he speaks 'openly and honestly, kindly and wise' in the realisation that the opposition between Chris and himself is, in fact, that between 'FREEDOM and GOD' (p. 495). At this moment, therefore, Ewan is between the second and third sorts of comic primness because he is now – temporarily at least – fully aware that communism is simply a convention that is offering him a possibility for an otherwise unrealisable self-liberation from the intersubjective ties of society: indeed, a darkly comic critical irony. In this respect, Ewan's future remains ambiguous, as we do not know if he will slip back into sheltering behind the conventions of communism or if he will develop a broader independence of thought. This latter, of course, would not necessarily lead to him leaving the Communist Party but might entail him continuing to pursue social revolution with a more independent mind set – an opportunity that became possible historically because of the transition from the 'class against class' policy to the advocacy of a popular front. A variety of possible sequels featuring Ewan can be imagined.

Paradoxically, Chris's 'freedom', despite its connection to the idea of a classless golden age that may yet come again, seems more final – especially if it were to be read as a return to oneness with nature, which, after all, is just another way of thinking about death. However, it is difficult to see why Gibbon would choose to criticise the limitations of revolutionary male subjectivity in the name of an equally monolithic outlook. One way of resolving this paradox of the apparent simultaneous identification of Chris with 'FREEDOM' and a monolithic oneness is to consider whether she has literally, rather than metaphorically, returned home to the golden age. The last sentence of the novel insists that she is still sitting on the hill even as she no longer feels the touch of the rain. One alternative interpretation to her being dead would be that the universe around her has changed while she continues to sit on the hill. This transformation is in keeping with the tendency of mid-twentieth-century fantasy novels to turn away from the world following the destruction and horror of the First World War in order to recover what Cairns Craig describes in respect to the ending of *Grey Granite* as 'a universe of which the self need no longer be afraid' (p. 69). Such a universe would be free of the gendered and political constraints of the 1930s because it would enable imaginary identity with subject and object positions outside the symbolic order of patriarchy. In this respect, Burton reads the ending of *Grey Granite* as prefiguring the 'feminist personal–political experiential cosmology' emerging in the 1980s across disciplines from history to ecology and concludes that the trilogy offers us knowledge 'beyond the confines of both capitalism and patriarchy' (pp. 43, 46).

Glenda Norquay argues that the 'project to imagine a different world, a project with women at its centre, shapes all Gibbon's fiction' (p. 88). His twin critique of bourgeois society and male revolutionary society is not simply a product of the kind of total desire for liberation that Williams feared could never be 'achieved in a settled relationship or in a society'.[15] Instead, it is a call for an implicitly feminist recalibration of our conception of relationships and society so that these are no longer considered from an alienated urban (male) perspective but instead from a self-reflexive rural perspective conscious of how the relationship to nature is organic as well as alienated. Chris's return to the 'enduring, encompassing' land (p. 496) at the end of *A Scots Quair* is fiction's most passionate articulation of the possibility of radical change inherent in rural modernity.

In dialogue with: Chapter 5 'Windmills and Woodblocks' (II: Landscapes) [Scottish artists; feminist analysis]; Chapter 12 'Celebrating England' (IV: Heritage) [representations of women; nationalism and cultural identity].

Notes

1. Gibbon, 'From Lewis Grassic Gibbon', p. 179.
2. Gibbon, *Scots Quair*, p. 37.
3. 'Work', p. 186. See also Barke, 'Lewis Grassic Gibbon', and MacDiarmid, 'Lewis Grassic Gibbon: 1901–1935'.
4. 'Rural Modernity', p. 247.

5. Clute, 'Fantastika in the World Storm'.
6. Raymond Williams, *Politics*, p. 46.
7. 'Modernism and Marxism', p. 128.
8. Gibbon, 'Literary Lights', pp. 126–7.
9. 'Modernism and Marxism', p. 38.
10. Williams, *Politics*, pp. 39–47.
11. *Scottish Modernism*, p. 142.
12. *Scottish Modernism*, p. 132.
13. *Illuminations*, p. 257.
14. 'Introduction', p. xiii.
15. *Politics*, p. 57.

Part IV

Heritage

Chapter 10

Borderlands: Visual and Material Culture in the Interwar Anglo-Scottish Borders

Ysanne Holt

The development of visual and material culture practices across the interwar Anglo-Scottish border region provides a fertile field for rethinking assumptions inherent in that apparently contradictory term, 'rural modernity'. This region, much of it seemingly remote and elemental, was widely perceived in the interwar period to be steeped in the romantic legacy of Walter Scott and the turbulent histories of the construction of Hadrian's Wall and later generations of wild Border Reivers. As such, its tangible and intangible heritage appealed to many tourists and incomers who were yearning for a simple, unsophisticated life and felt jaded, at least for a while, by fashionable metropolitan modernity. Nonetheless, across a period characterised by severe economic depression – most particularly in the north – a culture of production emerged to which notable artists and designers were to contribute, but which was fundamentally dependent on increasingly modernising traditions and the skills of resident makers and designers from each side of the border. Rural modernity, then, as this chapter will demonstrate, is an especially apt characterisation of the experience of many of those who inhabited this geographical region in the decades between the two world wars.

This chapter considers diverse forms of art, craft and design, but focuses most particularly on textile production. These forms are understood not simply as products of a specific space in the 1920s and 1930s, but as embedded in a system of rural–modern networks that in effect 'produced' the place identified elsewhere more generally as the Anglo-Scottish 'borderlands'.[1] The concern overall is to underline the dynamic nature of the social and material interactions between interwar artists, designers and manufacturers, the materials with which they engaged, the training and experience of workforces, and connections across rural and urban contexts (particularly where, as here, a city is fundamentally a large market town and surrounding villages are substantial sites of manufacture). This investigation reveals a process of cross-bordering resulting from a cultural and creative production that merged city and country, and modernism and modernity, brought traditional skills into line with new technologies, and combined national and international sources with local histories and forms of tangible and intangible heritage. In this regard, we see the interwar Anglo-Scottish borders as an avowedly modern space, despite frequent attempts to imagine it otherwise.

Rethinking borders and boundaries

Consideration of the development of forms of cultural production within this time period and geographical space requires us to rethink several conventional assumptions. We need, for example, to cast aside still-recurrent, generalising distinctions between rural and urban spaces, between centres and peripheries, between north and south, as well as singular perceptions of modernism and modernity. We need to reject notions of space as somehow fixed and with stable characteristics, in favour of more processual or relational understandings in which space is always under construction, always the product of reactions and interrelations.[2] To try to understand the particularities of spatial interrelations as they were experienced, represented and understood within one historical moment is the task here. In this regard, the spaces and practices considered are perceived as being in states of continual flux and as being constituted by evolving relationships between actors and actants that are both human and non-human entities. Here writings of the sociologist of science Bruno Latour and the social anthropologist Tim Ingold are influential. In Latour's formulation of Actor Network Theory, inanimate objects and materials are understood to have as much agency in any specific set of relations as human actors and are of equal significance in any analysis. For Tim Ingold, however, the emphasis is less on the concept of a network as such, which, for him, implies a series of connections between points or entities, and more, borrowing from Henri Lefebvre, on the notion of a 'meshwork'. It is in the 'entanglement of lines, not in the connection of points that the mesh is constituted' and 'every relation is one line in a meshwork of interwoven trails'.[3]

These theories of interconnected agents are predicated on the necessary rethinking or dissolution of fixed conceptual borders and boundaries. In terms of geographical borders – here the stretch of terrain crossing England and Scotland – a similar rethinking is required. This involves disregarding insistent perceptions of a border as an impermeable line or a boundary irrevocably drawn between two societies, cultures, practices, ways of living and so on, for understandings of a border region as a site with common resources, ecologies, skills, patterns of existence, and tangible and intangible forms of heritage. It means thinking of a hybrid site of interconnections, of networks or meshworks involving both nested and mobile identities. What follows, then, is an effort to view the outputs of interwar artists and designers, products and processes as both acted upon and acting within a broader context, and to contribute to a further dismantling of still-persistent polarities and conceptualisations such as 'rural' and 'modern'. To do so means adopting a much wider lens on to the social, cultural and economic circumstances, the local (and national and international) conditions, that made up the experience of those who inhabited this particular space across those two decades.

The border region under discussion here is in the western half of the UK mainland. It incorporates the two Scottish counties of Dumfries and Galloway and the Scottish Borders with their small towns of Hawick, Jedburgh, Selkirk and Galashiels, all mill towns with long histories of textile production. It extends across the border into England and the county of Cumberland (now Cumbria) with the ancient, physically very compact 'Border city' of Carlisle, another long-established site of textile manufacture. Both sides of the border benefited from an extensive interconnection of both rivers and, at that time, small railway lines. Nearer to that border itself lies the small market town of Brampton, where, in the 1930s, textile designer Alastair Morton commissioned a house, Brackenfell, by London-based modernist architects, Leslie and Sadie Martin. Brampton is close by both Hadrian's Wall and Naworth Castle, seat of the landowning Earls of Carlisle, ancestors, in fact, of Morton's acquaintance, the modernist painter Winifred Nicholson (née Roberts). Amid extensive European travels and exhibitions, Winifred spent much of her long working life at Banks Head, her farmhouse in the village of Banks near Naworth, or at the nearby family home, Boothby, both before and long after her divorce from Ben Nicholson. This, then, with its surrounding agricultural land of primarily rough grazing for sheep, is the geographical context with which this chapter is concerned.

As outlined above, much at stake here relates to the consideration of networks and relationships. John Scott's references in *Social Network Analysis* to the work of the social anthropologist Alfred Radcliffe Brown (1881–1955) are especially apposite here, given the nature of the subject matter. Radcliffe Brown influenced research from the 1930s onwards, and in particular, research into kinship patterns in rural towns and villages. His focus was on the concept of social structures, or the social relations within a given social unit, pursuing, as Scott identifies, 'textile-based metaphors' aimed at understanding the density and 'texture' of social connections, the 'fabric' and 'web' of social life, the 'pattern' of relationships and the 'interweaving' and 'interlocking' relations, the close or loose ties through which social actions are organised.[4] Such a shuttling back and forth within social networks in a loosely bounded space creates the possibility of social capital – of advantages and opportunities for some – or, in all events, engenders an endlessly shifting set of interrelations between people, objects and nature. This leads productively back to Ingold's textile-based metaphor of the meshworld, that binding together of a 'tangled mesh of interwoven and complexly knotted strands'.[5] Ingold's conceptualisation frames the discussion that follows.

For the most part, historical accounts of modernism and modernity in the visual and material culture of interwar England are concentrated on the geographical south. When the north has been considered, it is largely through the lens of contemporary social documentarists such as the photographer Humphrey Spender, alert in the 1930s, in particular, to the visual evidence of the decline of industry – shipbuilding, coal mining and steel manufacture – and the resulting inner-city or small-town poverty and deprivation. Discussions of the contemporary Scottish cultural context focus for the most part on the centres of Edinburgh and Glasgow or on the significance to the national identity of the Highlands and Islands: locations that assume particular importance in the time period, given the rise of the Scottish nationalist movements from the 1920s. In 1934, the year J. B. Priestley published his condition of England survey, *English Journey*, key northern regions, including Tyneside, west Cumberland and southern Scotland, were designated by National Government's Special Areas Act as being in urgent need of support and reconstruction. Textile manufacturers were suffering from cheaper imports from overseas, and agriculture in the rural areas of the north in general was similarly depressed. Those rural workers who inhabited the largely tenant farms or smallholdings in the Borders were equally as affected by national and international economic forces, including competition from overseas food producers.

Cultural heritage and tradition across the borders

Despite the interwoven nature of rural and urban economies, signs of that persistent, largely urban desire to perceive the rural as site of escape, retreat and a peaceful existence in unsullied nature were clearly manifest in particular ways across this Borders region. The apparently 'marginal' and 'remote' character of this terrain with its rolling hills and moorland,

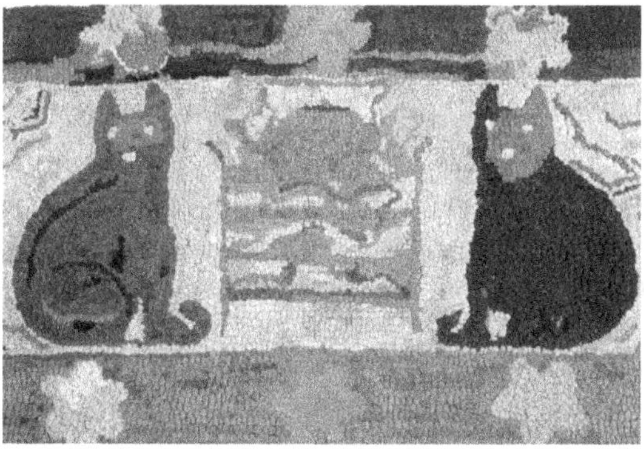

Figure 10.1 Margaret Warwick, *Two Cats by the Fire*, 1923. Tullie House Museum and Art Gallery, Carlisle.

and the simple, in some cases dilapidated, nature of the surrounding farmhouses and cottages rendered it yet more attractive to the London Group and Seven and Five Society exhibiting artists Christopher Wood and Ivon Hitchens, who, in the 1920s, painted for extended periods of time at Banks Head. Bare hills depicted through cottage windows and modest interiors all contributed to an apparent continuation of those 'simple life' ideals that had been disseminated amongst a largely cultural elite from the later nineteenth century.[6] In this context appears Winifred Nicholson's encouragement of local women such as Margaret Warwick and her own involvement in the tradition of making hooky and proggy rugs from saved-up scraps of household materials: a craft born out of necessity and limited means.[7] Jessie Mothersole, Slade-trained artist, author and illustrator of the popular 1922 travel book *Hadrian's Wall*, noted there the 'wadded quilts which one sees so often along the wall' and the 'stubbed matts' made from home-dyed rags, like 'bits of stained glass' (p. 136). Here remnants of local craft traditions, passed down through generations, reinforced – or, we could say, effectively 'produced' through acts of repetition – a particular sense of place and contributed to the making of a cultural landscape, one constituted through that continual over-layering and weaving together of history and heritage, forms of interaction, knowledge and skill. The emphasis was on values of continuity, simple means and a right-thinking approach to materials (Figure 10.1).

Another valuable contemporary voice belongs to Winifred's younger brother, Wilfrid Roberts. A Liberal Member of Parliament and also a farmer and owner of the *Carlisle Journal*, Roberts broadcast a series of radio talks for the BBC Home Service in 1934 on the subject of 'Living in Cumberland'. As reported in the newspaper, their focus was on the 'craftsmen of his moorland district, both those of today and yesterday'.

The reports signal the broadcasts' undertow of nostalgia for traditions lost, the uneasy recognition of change but alertness still for signs of connections between past and present:

> This is the first of a series of broadcasts which will give a picture of an English countryside which has so far escaped the ravages of speculative builders and the ugliness of filling stations. The denizens of this district, close to the Scottish border, go about their work, find their own amusements, and are one with nature. Here live those who can thatch ricks and tickle trout, who see more than a 'yellow primrose' in a primrose by a river's brim, and a warning in a red sky at morning. Wilfrid Roberts lives among these people and knows them as well as he knows the cattle and poultry of his farm. The hill shepherd with his lonely life; the housewife clattering in clogs out to the byre to milk the cows; the wood-man slicing the hazel and plaiting it into the hedge; the isolated miner keeping whippet or racing pigeon for sport and profit; the district nurse cycling in all weathers on her errand of mercy . . . .[8]

In this first broadcast, a series of 'rural types' appear in contexts that are reassuringly timeless:

> The blacksmith is still to be seen in his forge, but his sons are probably mechanics with an eye on the motor industry that is creeping in year by year. The younger generation ride their own motor cycles maybe, and prefer the smell of petrol to that of singeing hoof . . . Potters still exist. Like gypsies, they are a distinct class in Cumberland, but they are not gypsies. They all deal in everything from scrap iron to feathers; and in horses, too . . . But the fame of the villages for hand-loom-weaving is a thing of the past. Few people remember it, though many, curiously enough, indirectly suffer from it. For in the old days the ground floors of houses were sunk below ground level with the object of keeping the raw material for weaving moist. Today, though the atmosphere is no dryer, people insist on inhabiting these below-ground rooms, despite threats from rheumatism and medical officers. (12 February 1934)[9]

Here time has passed on, but the social and cultural traditions of the region persist through recollection and re-use, including the tuberculosis-inducing habitation of old, damp weaving parlours, and all with the final comforting reassurance that some rural types at least still 'haunt the moors'.

Those moors, much of them mires, peat bogs and heather scrub, extend without noticeable boundary across the borders of the English counties of Cumbria and Northumberland into Scotland. There are miles of largely uncultivated, sheep-grazed terrain (especially before the advent of World War II-era afforestation), with occasional small villages until the Scottish Border towns are reached. As with Wilfrid Roberts's account, this border region was subject to much attention in the interwar period in the form of illustrated travel guides, including

Jessie Mothersole's, and it became an increasingly popular tourist destination, particularly for those better-off tourists in possession of a motor car and likely to tune in to radio broadcasts such as Roberts's. For the benefit of these tourists – intent on ancient Border castles, ruined abbeys, monasteries and pele towers – numerous histories were published of the romance, myths and legends of the region, already embroidered in the early 1800s by Sir Walter Scott in his *Border Ballads*. Scott's tales included those of the marauding Border Reivers, whose raids across both sides wreaked havoc up until the Union of the Crowns in 1605. Wilfrid and Winifred Roberts's ancestor, Lord William Howard, then at Naworth ('Belted Will', as named in Scott's 1805 poem *Lay of the Last Minstrel*), was Commissioner for the Border in the early 1600s and tasked with retaining order across the region. The family therefore was long steeped in the region's history and heritage, and they themselves, artist and politician, played a significant role in the extent to which particular imagined geographies or identities of place were circulated.

The interwar years see much popular interest in the performance of place-making cultural heritage practices, and that popularity was encouraged through widely disseminated forms of visual culture. Contemporary photographs and Pathé newsreels provide evidence of a fascination with border customs and the unveiling of monuments, as well as the enacting of rituals and festivals, including the annual Galashiels Braw Lads Gathering, first held in 1930. Documented too was the Annan Riding of the Marches, one of the annual ancient Common Ridings in which local populations on horseback ride the boundaries of the common land.[10] In the period following the First World War, there was a particular reassurance to be gained from the continuation of these commemorative events. They acquired new signification with each restaging, and the newsreel documentation was circulated nationally and across the empire and colonies.

Another important place-making ritual was the 1928 historical pageant in Carlisle. As Jan Rupp has observed, the phenomenon of pageants in English towns and cities from the Edwardian era onward involving local populations in large scale re-enactments of their history and heritage were 'a powerful means of (re-)constructing collective self-images' (p. 189). They were intent not only on remembering the past but also, perhaps more importantly, on observing the present and marking communal aspirations for the future – often accompanied, as here, by industrial exhibitions. As Rupp notes, the interwar years saw a shift from grander national and imperial narratives towards a focus on collective identity (p. 191). Through its specific performances and narratives, the Carlisle pageant in particular signalled a move away from assertions of national identity and notions of 'Englishness' towards what, given its geographical location and its long history and heritage, we might perceive instead as an expression of a fluid and hybrid 'Anglo-Scottishness'. A Borders identity was conveyed earlier too: for example, in the artist Maurice Greiffenhagen's 1924 London, Midland and Scottish (LMS) travel poster depicting a medieval knight on horseback, pointing the way towards snow-capped Scottish hills above the title, 'Carlisle, the Gateway to Scotland' (Figure 10.2). Like Hadrian's Wall before it, the border, or gateway, here was in reality an open and permeable one, characterised by centuries of exchange and mobility.

The Carlisle pageant was an ambitious celebration of border history, a thickly woven tapestry of historical fact and local legends, and for nearly a week between 6 and 11 August it attracted 10,000 visitors, with tickets sold nationally via Thomas Cook. Some 4,000 community performers took part, wearing elaborate period costumes that many created themselves, clearly underlining the dress-making skills of the local population. Recent research has pointed to the pageant phenomenon of Weldon's Fancy Dress Patterns, purchasable paper patterns ranging from Celtic to Pict to eighteenth-century costumes drawing on the expertise of fashion and costume historian Herbert Norris.[11] Accurately clad and directed by numerous costume mistresses, performers for the nine episodes took part in six full-dress rehearsals, enacting scenes beginning with the arrival of Hadrian, with local railway workers playing the Romans and members of the Border Regiment taking the role of the invading Picts from the north. The Reivers history was marked through the reconstruction of the famous escape from medieval Carlisle Castle of one of the most infamous Reiver outlaws, Kinmont Willie, a figure immortalised in Scott's *Minstrelsy of the Scottish Border* (1802). The imprisonment of Mary, Queen of Scots, in that same castle in 1567 also featured, with the then Countess of Carlisle from Naworth Castle in the role. Despite the centuries of turbulent conflict, the pageant closed with the invented tale of an eloping couple helped by the legendary Cumbrian huntsman John Peel and members of the (Scottish) Dumfriesshire Hunt in their flight to be wed over the Scottish border at the old blacksmith's shop in Gretna Green, a final note of cross-border cooperation.[12] That so many of the 1928 pageant scenes focused on events that took place outside the actual city itself and in the rural and primarily border regions helped to construct these sites of memorialisation. As Tatiana Zhurzhenko observes, commenting on border regions more widely, local myths and narratives emphasise 'strong regional distinction from national homelands . . . Borderlands, [therefore] sites of cruel territorial conflict and wars in the past, become . . . attractive tourist destinations' (p. 70).

Figure 10.2 Maurice Greiffenhagen, *Carlisle, the Gateway to Scotland*, 1924. NRM Pictorial Collection/Science and Society Picture Library.

Modernity and the Borders

To emphasise an Anglo-Scottish borderland identity made up of long-standing cross-border affiliations and ceaselessly rehearsed through ritual and practices of visual and material culture is not to suggest a community trapped in the past in a uniquely bounded space. As noted, the Carlisle pageant was concerned to underline the present as well as the future importance of the city and its surrounding areas. And, as Wilfrid Roberts made clear, this predominantly rural region was as implicated in the experience of modernity as any other location. As the village graveyards and the memorials in small market towns reveal, many lives on both sides of the border were lost in the Great War, all with severe implications for interwar rural communities.[13] At the same time, mobility was and always had been a crucial aspect of border experience. Throughout wartime itself, in the region of 17,000 workers, the majority of whom were women, were drafted into H. M. Factory, the largest cordite (for ammunition) manufacturing works in the UK, occupying a vast site straddling the English/Scottish border outside Gretna, chosen in particular for its remoteness from densely populated areas. Many of those who moved to the site to take up work remained in the area with their families after the war. Persistent patterns of movement and continual national and international connections then constantly complicate any perceived, even idealised, sense of isolation from modern existence up (or down) the largely rural borderland between England and Scotland.

In this context of process and mobility and through the examples of three firms, I now turn to textile production, as well as textile metaphors. While some vernacular traditions such as domestic hand-weaving were perceived to be in decline, the interwar Borders saw important developments in modern methods of manufacture. Woven textiles associated with small, semi-rural mill towns such as Selkirk and Hawick had long been a cross-border trade and a vital source of employment. As noted, it was a trade dependent on shared resources – both human and non-human – all with international export dimensions. The first example here is Linton Tweeds, established from 1912 when Selkirk-born tweed designer William Linton moved across the border to Carlisle, where a skilled workforce and the junction of three rivers had already proved an ideal site for water-powered industry. Shifting from production of a rugged tweed of the type suitable for local farmers towards softer and more light-weight versions, Linton contributed to a contemporary technological modernity, producing 'jazz-age' yarns for the interwar public and even special clients including Coco Chanel, at that time reportedly keen on shooting holidays in Scotland.[14] The textiles trade itself therefore produces an interweaving of past and present and of local, regional, national and international markets, all assuming different values and signification at different stages in the process.

Alastair Morton, the second example, was especially skilled in the attribution of particular values with modern textile designs. Morton was the third generation in a family of textile designers. In 1931–2, he was involved in the transfer and then control of Edinburgh Weavers, the more experimental, contemporary and exclusive branch of his family firm, Morton Sundour, from Corstorphine to the west of Edinburgh, south across the border to Carlisle, where the larger firm itself was long established. As Lesley Jackson's detailed and authoritative account documents, the fortunes of the firm fluctuated throughout the Depression. Nevertheless, Morton secured significant success amongst fashionable contemporary national and international markets through his development of distinctively modernist woven and printed fabrics. The success was in good part achieved by his strategy of commissioning designs from, by this point, well-known modern artists including Paul Nash (another visitor to Banks Head in the mid-1920s), Winifred herself, her then husband Ben Nicholson and their son Jake. As illustrated in Jackson's text, their simple repeat patterns of abstract and geometric forms largely perpetuated that purist aesthetic developed in paintings and reliefs over the previous decade. Successfully displayed in London's fashionable Bond Street showrooms and at international exhibitions, certain of the Edinburgh Weavers' designs carried locally inspired names following the example of 'Solway blue' (the Solway Firth is the sea inlet that in itself forms a western border between Dumfries and Galloway and Cumbria) for one of the renowned, unfadeable fabric dyes Alastair's father James had developed after the outbreak of the war when access to German dye manufacturers was impossible. Other fabrics bore local place names, including 'Dundrennan', an ancient village with abbey in Dumfries and Galloway, and, most strikingly here, Naworth, home of the Earls of Carlisle, the latter a simple zigzag pattern in a cotton and rayon weave. Nature, tradition and modernity, the rural and the metropolitan, all coalesce here.

In a revealing discussion of the conditions of contemporary design, Morton made clear his own sense of a necessary unity, an interweaving of nature, of human and machine life, the city and the country, remarking that

> in this international, city-centred machine age the first great phase in contemporary decoration was cosmopolitan and urban . . . But we still grow

> from the earth . . . and so the next great step in architecture and decoration is the penetration of life and feeling.[15]

Such a statement resonates with the sentiment of the contemporary campaigning body, the Design and Industries Association (DIA). Formed in 1915 but most active in the interwar period, the DIA sought to instil the principles of 'good design' – a restrained or, in the Association's terms, a 'fit for purpose' aesthetic – into the manufacture of everyday objects from craft to industrial design. DIA ideals proposed something of a fusion of an Arts and Crafts, Morrisian sensibility – 'have nothing in your house you do not know to be useful or believe to be beautiful'[16] – with the modernist ethos of the German Deutscher Werkbund and the Bauhaus. Such an aesthetic has a particular resonance with the contexts described thus far: a simple, right-thinking and unpretentious quality that emphasised the importance of past traditions and craftsmanship, but with an understanding of modern materials and methods of manufacture, and all underpinned by the necessary elimination of excessive or inappropriate ornamentation in favour of fundamental forms. It was an aesthetic and a set of design principles of acute significance in the period of the interwar slump, when markets were at their most vulnerable. It therefore became a national and international campaign enrolling articulate advocates, as Morton proved to be.

Morton's voice resonates too with that of the influential contemporary national and international magazine, *The Studio* (where his firm, of course, advertised), itself transitioning in the interwar period from its advocacy of largely Arts and Crafts and Art Nouveau principles of the 1890s and 1900s, most associated with rurally oriented hand-crafted techniques, to those appropriate for methods of modern manufacture. In this period, significantly, *The Studio* diversified – like Morton Sundour – taking over additional titles, including, in 1927, *Decorative Art*. Across these publications the artist, along with the designer, was encouraged to adopt an ideal of adaptability and to understand the value of artistic training in practical affairs. The need to encourage the producer at a time of keen competition and acute economic crisis was clearly understood. Through its editorial pages and in its advertisements detailing commercial art courses and new art materials, it was the young artist–designer who was most consistently addressed. He or she was deemed most susceptible to these modern requirements.[17]

From the mid-1930s, Morton Sundour staff were provided with their own 'in-house' publication, *The Sundour Shuttle*, its cover design, commissioned from designer Ashley Havinden, depicting a full-petalled flower on a sofa (upholstered with unfadeable fabric)

Figure 10.3 *The Sundour Shuttle'*, 1937, cover design, Ashley Havinden. Courtesy of Carlisle Library and Archive,

(Figure 10.3). Amongst its regular features (information about staff social gatherings such as Burns Suppers, competitions, reports of annual excursions, accounts of the firm's subsidiaries Donegal Carpets in County Donegal and Scottish Folk Fabrics in Corstorphine), we find essays and reports of speeches on standards of modern design. One states 'we who are concerned with furnishing fabrics and interior decoration should think deeply on what the principles of contemporary decoration and design should be . . . a living, genuine modern movement'.[18] The local workforce, which in itself drew upon the surrounding rural areas as well as the city, were as much exposed to these modern, educational discourses as those in the metropolitan areas. They contributed to and read reports of both national and international exhibitions. For example, in 1937, the Earl of Carlisle presided over the Carlisle and District Textile Manufacturers exhibition (as part of the wider coronation celebrations that year), and six local firms showed at the Exposition Internationale des Arts et Techniques de la Vie Moderne in Paris that same year.

The third example of textile manufacture is not a 'cross-border' firm but nevertheless underlines the difficulties in assuming marked rural and urban distinctions. The Stead McAlpin works located in the village of Cummersdale, once a wooded valley on the River Caldew three miles outside Carlisle, was still in 1924 without a bus service, and workers walked or travelled there by train. In 1905, Edmund Stead had taken over the by then closed Dalton's cotton mills and disused dye works (as well as two rows of back-to-back houses) and transferred the trade from cotton spinning to block printing. By the time of the 1921 publication *Rambles in Borderland with the 'Clan'*, the Cummersdale print business was flourishing, its cotton prints had 'made the name of this village famous in every corner of the world', and the author could celebrate the fastness of the prints' colours, 'a quality which springs to some extent from the excellent water with which the works are supplied by the Caldew'.[19] Council housing and improved community facilities were developed in the village through the 1930s via the Carlisle Rural District Council and so a 'rural modernity' was well established here by the end of the interwar period. At the Cummersdale print works local skills, processes, accumulated experience and natural resources combined to connect regional, national and international markets. The rural versus the urban is a meaningless polarity here amidst a context of evolving relations and mutual dependencies.

Arts education and training for a borderland

In terms of the training of skilled local workforces, the strategies of *The Studio* magazine and of designer–manufacturers such as Alastair Morton understandably had an impact upon the education delivered in art schools and technical colleges through the interwar period and on into the 1940s. Morton, for example, was later to serve as an assessor for Scottish art schools; he played a role at the Scottish College of Textiles in Galashiels and was later commissioned to produce an enquiry into the state of the textile industry.[20]

In Carlisle, which traditionally trained students from the rural areas, including those from across the border too, interesting developments occurred that parallel these broader national, cultural and economic concerns and developments. Across the decades, a shift in emphasis is clear, even from the cover designs of its art school's annual prospectus, changing, for example, from a 1923 line illustration of Dixon's Chimney (belonging to one of the city's cotton mills) and a flowing Art Nouveau nymph to a starkly modernist, semi-abstract design of interlocking forms reminiscent of the Vorticist, Edward Wadsworth (Figures 10.4 and

Figure 10.4 *Carlisle Art School Prospectus*, 1923–24. Courtesy of Carlisle Library and Archive.

10.5). The prospectus lists embroidery, costume design, cabinet making, the provision of courses 'for craftsmen and others whose occupation requires knowledge of drawing, painting, modelling, architecture or design', and national preparation for the Royal College of Art entrance examination. Evening class courses were available too – appropriate, perhaps, for Morton's or Stead McAlpin's workers – on abstract design: 'Space-filling, designs for repeating pattern, proportions of borders in flat tints of colour, Growth of plant forms and the suggestions to be derived'. The 1935–6 prospectus references advanced courses including lithography, poster design, rug design, weaving and, notably at this point, mural design.

In the context of that broader interwar shift towards a public art informed by a national collective consciousness, mural design played an especially significant role. Here the now nationally and internationally celebrated figure of Frank Brangwyn was an important influence. Brangwyn himself epitomised *The Studio* magazine's ideal of the adaptable artist–designer appropriate for modern times and was

Figure 10.5 *Carlisle Art School Prospectus,* 1935–36. Courtesy of Carlisle Library and Archive.

frequently reviewed there. His diverse output ranged across landscape painting, scenes of masculine labour, parables of empire, and the design of travel posters and, latterly, of carpets, and he was frequently commissioned to produce murals for churches and civic buildings. He was exemplary to the extent that his own practice consistently defied borders and boundaries between genres, subject matter (rural or urban) and forms of production.

In 1927, Carlisle's Tullie House Museum, where the school of art was still housed at this point, held a Brangwyn exhibition, which was popularly received in the local press. His apparent inspiration of the art students, along with the spirit of the DIA, appeared five years later in 1932 in the mural designs they executed for the walls of the Tullie House Reference Library. Under the supervision of the Principal, Rudolf Pickles, the students, in a collective workshop practice of master and apprentice, adopted important local industries as their theme. Amongst their nine panels, which included printing, tin box and biscuit making, weaving and furnishing fabric manufacture, are scenes of agriculture and of livestock auctioneering, clearly registering the students' lived, everyday

Figure 10.6 Decorations for Tullie House Reference Library: *Weaving and Furnishing Fabrics*. Courtesy of Carlisle Library and Archive.

sense of the interpenetration of the city and countryside, the inextricability of rural and urban economies, and the circulation of resources, skills and knowledge (Figures 10.6 and 10.7). With a sense of their greater national significance, the small text produced to accompany the murals announced, 'It may be that through such things, when sympathetic co-operation with local craftsmanship is fostered with pride, a tradition of British mural painting may even yet emerge.'[21] A national example here was provided from a northern, primarily rural context.

Two years following the completion of the murals, members of the Tullie House Museum Committee took the initiative of contacting the then Principal of the Royal College of Art, Sir William Rothenstein, with an invitation to advise on acquisitions for an art collection, which included an annual sum to be at his disposal. Rothenstein, a northerner from Bradford and always a keen supporter of young, provincial students – obvious beneficiaries of such a collection – secured works by later nineteenth-century artists such as G. F. Watts and Burne-Jones, and, for the most part, landscapes and rural scenes by contemporaries such as Paul Nash and brothers Gilbert and Stanley Spencer. The latter's style in particular was equivalent to the flatly applied, decorative

Figure 10.7 Decorations for Tullie House Reference Library: *Livestock Sales*. Courtesy of Carlisle Library and Archive.

Post-Impressionist influence already clearly apparent in the students' Reference Library murals.

To return to the textile metaphors introduced at the start of this chapter, the visual and material cultural practices examined above contribute to our understanding of the multiple elements that come together in the 'tangled mesh', the inextricably interwoven and interlocking social and cultural networks current within the interwar period. In this period, discourses about art, craft, design, aesthetic ideals, and notions of taste circulated locally, nationally and internationally and, thus, undermine any sense of an inevitable dichotomy between north and south, centres and peripheries, tradition and modernism, the past and modernity, the rural and the urban. It is in large part the mobile nature of these networks – their accompanying skills and practices, and the shared history, heritage and resources upon which they were able to draw – that in effect produced the interwar Anglo-Scottish borderland. It is a cultural landscape fundamentally characterised by porous and permeable boundaries, by continuous and dynamic interweavings, and by the 'cross-bordering' processes inherent in 'borderland' textile manufacture itself.

In dialogue with: Chapter 2 'Change in the Village' (I: Networks) [visual culture; emerging technologies]; Chapter 13 'Altered Countrysides' (V: Wars) [regional art and archives].

Notes

1. See Holt, 'Performing the Anglo-Scottish Border'.
2. See, for example, Massey, Wylie and Crouch.
3. *Lines*, pp. 81, 90.
4. John Scott, p. 2. See Scott, Chapter 2, 'The History of Social Network Analysis'. Scott refers, for example, to post-1945 Manchester University research into rural and small-town Britain, which combined network analysis with sociological concepts.
5. *Being Alive*, pp. 69–70.
6. For discussion of artists' depictions of Banks Head in the 1920s, see Collins and also Holt, 'Landscapes of the 1920s'. Significant too is the fact that Winifred Nicholson's maternal grandfather, George Howard, the 9th Earl of Carlisle at Naworth and an artist himself, was a friend of the Pre-Raphaelite circle and associated with the Arts and Crafts movement. Howard arranged for Morris's associate, the architect Philip Webb, to build St Martin's church in Brampton in 1878 and for Edward Burne-Jones to design a set of stained glass windows that were executed in Morris's studio. Webb also designed two houses for the Naworth estate.
7. For reference to the atmosphere of simple domesticity at Banks Head, see Jake Nicholson's essay, pp. 10–11. Jake Nicholson also notes that his mother Winifred had earlier brought female students from the Byam Shaw Art School in London, where she herself trained, to work as Land Girls in the First World War.
8. Wilfrid Roberts, 'Living in Cumberland' [1 January 1934].
9. Listings for and summaries of Roberts's broadcasts can be found at the BBC's Genome: Radio Times project.
10. The Scottish Screen Archive possesses a 1932 film of the Galashiels festival, 'Crossing the Tweed', as well as two films of the Annan Ridings from 1935 and 1938. Footage too exists here of the unveiling of the memorial to the Border poet Robert Burns in Dumfries by Prime Minister Ramsay Macdonald in 1936.
11. See *The Redress of the Past: Historical Pageants in Britain, 1905–2016*, a website that is the result of an Arts and Humanities Research Council project of that name involving Kings College London, University College London, and the universities of Edinburgh and Glasgow. Tullie House Museum and Art Gallery in Carlisle contributed to the project with a display on the Carlisle pageant. The pageant drew ticket sales of £10,000 making a £7,000 profit, sums of which were distributed to local charities.
12. For a detailed description, see Angela Bartie and others, 'Carlisle Historical Pageant'.
13. The unveiling of these war memorials was also respectfully recorded on

newsreel. See, for example, film of the 1925 unveiling of the Galashiels memorial by Field Marshal Earl Haig in the Scottish Screen Archive

14. See Hitchon.
15. Jackson, p. 92.
16. Morris, 'Beauty of Life'.
17. See Holt, 'The Call of Commerce'.
18. *Sundour Shuttle*, 'We'll Tak' the High Road', p. 6.
19. Topping, pp. 36–7.
20. Agnes Linton, who managed the Carlisle firm following the death of her father William, had earlier travelled across the border to train at the Galashiels college in 1921. Reputedly she was the first woman to train there. The college was founded in 1883. The fact underlines the growing visibility of women in the field of design manufacture in the interwar period.
21. Text in the collection of Carlisle City Libraries.

Chapter 11

Beyond Portmeirion: The Architecture, Planning and Protests of Clough Williams-Ellis

Nigel Harrison and Iain Robertson

For much of his long and productive life, Clough Williams-Ellis was known as the second-rate architect who designed the bizarre Welsh holiday village of Portmeirion. Jonah Jones's 1996 biography of him may have perpetuated this view, its title including the phrase *The Architect of Portmeirion.* Williams-Ellis himself seemed, somewhat modestly, to endorse that diminished assessment by calling his (first) autobiography *Architect Errant* (1971), a decision that was consistent with a career spent 'enduring considerable scorn from his fellow professionals'.[1] In contrast to such characterisations, this chapter champions Clough Williams-Ellis as an important figure in modern and modernist architecture. It claims that his achievements can best be conceived through his articulation of rural modernity and that any study of rural modernisation is incomplete without consideration of Williams-Ellis's work.

In line with the late twentieth-century influence of postmodernism and the development of the heritage industry, both Portmeirion and Clough Williams-Ellis began to rise in stature and reputation. In 1996, the Council for the Preservation of Rural England (CPRE) even republished Williams-Ellis's book *England and the Octopus* (1928) to celebrate their seventieth anniversary. As David Matless notes in *Landscape and Englishness*, Williams-Ellis was one of the key English rural preservationists of the interwar period, especially in his role with the CPRE in its influential early years. Matless argues that the preservationist movement of the CPRE aimed to 'plan a landscape simultaneously modern and traditional'.[2] Particularly notable was the CPRE's attack on the government for failing to curb the *laissez-faire* of uncontrolled development. The organisation maintained that planning should be guided by a modernist doctrine of 'fitness for purpose', even though this might suggest a preference for tradition above modernity.[3] In his study of this period, Matless understandably concentrates discussion about

Williams-Ellis on landscape matters. Yet he does not fully recognise that Williams-Ellis was a busy architect and prolific writer on diverse topics throughout his long life. This chapter will argue that, although landscape was important to him, Williams-Ellis regarded himself primarily as an architect, and that it was the totality of his various interests (which include what he regarded as his 'sidelines') that set him apart from other architects and preservationists.[4]

Setting the stage for this recovery work are studies by Pyrs Gruffydd, who has emphasised Williams-Ellis's achievements in a Welsh rural context – especially at Portmeirion – and Alan Powers, who has stressed the connectedness of Williams-Ellis's many talents and interests, referring to the reappraisement of Portmeirion in the 1970s as 'an exemplar for picturesque planning and for the freedom to use architectural styles'.[5] Both scholars point to the primary claims of this chapter: that Williams-Ellis has been unfairly pigeon-holed as a cranky, even absurd preservationist with a simple politics firmly allied with conservative heritage movement; that he deserves instead to be recognised as a man of diverse interests and talents, with correspondingly complex ideological allegiances and political effects; that, of his many talents, it is his role as architect and designer, particularly of modern structures in rural places, that most deserves critical regard; and finally, that it is the diversity and scope of his various interests and activities that distinguish him as a key figure of rural modernity. Additional evidence for these claims comes from Williams-Ellis himself; his output in the form of buildings, architectural drawings, autobiographies and other writings, together with archives at the National Library of Wales, provide significant support, as do interviews with currently practising architects.

Clough Williams-Ellis engaged with rural modernity in his various separate, but connected, interests, the scope of which can be seen by the brief biographical summary contained in Table 11.1. This chapter will explore the range of Williams-Ellis's activities to show that he was an underrated and serious moderniser, though one with a rural bias; Williams-Ellis's modernity was one of newness combined with progress, and one of adaptation rather than creative destruction, with combinations of the modern and the traditional.[6]

Writing and campaigning: the progressive preservationist

Matless's rather harsh treatment of Williams-Ellis, although convincingly executed, has helped create the impression that the diversity of his life's work, particularly his books *England and the Octopus* (1928) and

Table 11.1: Life and Times of Clough Williams-Ellis

BACKGROUND EVENTS	ARCHITECTURE	PLANNING AND PRESERVATION	OTHER WRITING	PORTMEIRION
Born 1883				
From c.1905	Arts and Crafts			
Pre-World War II				
Living in London	Arts and Crafts	Campaign to Protect Rural England committee member 1928–39; Council for the Preservation of Rural Wales chair 1930–47	*The Pleasures of Architecture* 1924	Opens 1926
	Neo-classical	*England and the Octopus* (1928)		Vernacular development
	Modernist (1930–4)	*Britain and the Beast* (1937)	Journal articles	Neo-classicism
Post-World War II				
Living in North Wales	Neo-classical: private country houses	Town planning schemes: Bewdley 1944–5; Bilston 1946–7; Stevenage New Town 1946–7; Weston-super-Mare 1947	Journal articles	*The Prisoner* (1967) Neo-classical expansion
Rise of heritage			Autobiographies	Fallen buildings
Neo-classical Revival				
Died 1978				

Britain and the Beast (1937), and his work with the CPRE, amounts to little more than preservationist activities. While certainly important, these activities were but one aspect of a complex, modernising figure who engaged widely with the rural. Having been brought up in Snowdonia, inheriting a family home there in 1908 at the age of twenty-five, and starting on Portmeirion in 1926, he was always very much at home in rural settings, in ways that readily translated into his personal and working environments.[7] Initially, he was prepared to accept almost any architectural commission but later, when he could afford to choose, he clearly identified with, and excelled at, rural designs.

England and the Octopus is perhaps Williams-Ellis's most widely cited and most influential book. It is also his most notorious; the use of the octopus metaphor in the title of the book colourfully emphasised how uncontrolled development was eating up the English countryside (Figure 11.1). *England and the Octopus* was not, however, Williams-Ellis's first book. At the end of World War I, he negotiated his early release from active service by agreeing to write a history of the Tank Corps, followed in 1920 by another military book and the architectural book, *Cottage Building In Cob, Pisé, Chalk & Clay: A Renaissance*, then, in 1924, the more theoretical but populist *The Pleasures of Architecture*, jointly authored with his wife, Amabel.[8]

In the context of these other early writings on architecture, *England and the Octopus* announces Williams-Ellis's lifelong opposition to all things Victorian. Urban squalor is condemned, as is especially the impact on the countryside of ribbon development and unsightly bungalows, with the ten years since 1918 producing a 'spate of mean building all over the country that is shrivelling up the old England – mean and perky little houses that surely none but mean and perky little souls should inhabit with satisfaction' (p. 15). At times like this, Williams-Ellis's preservationist campaign took on distinctly patronising tones, as with his damning of house names such as 'Mon Abri', 'Loch Lomond' and 'Kia Ora'. He was even more offended by the cheap, cottage-like, almost temporary construction, known as the 'Cottabunga', which he felt constituted 'England's most disfiguring disease'.[9]

Nevertheless, even at his most outspoken, Williams-Ellis remained mindful of differing demographic needs and influences; thus, he emphasised both the right of all to enjoy the countryside's beauty and the need to protect it from unsightly development. For Williams-Ellis, this amounted to the concept that lay at the heart of the CPRE's modernising agenda: that of rural visual amenity. Williams-Ellis argued that a key demand in society was for 'an ordered, reasonable, humanistic setting for our lives', exemplified by our pre-Victorian ancestors.[10] There are, of

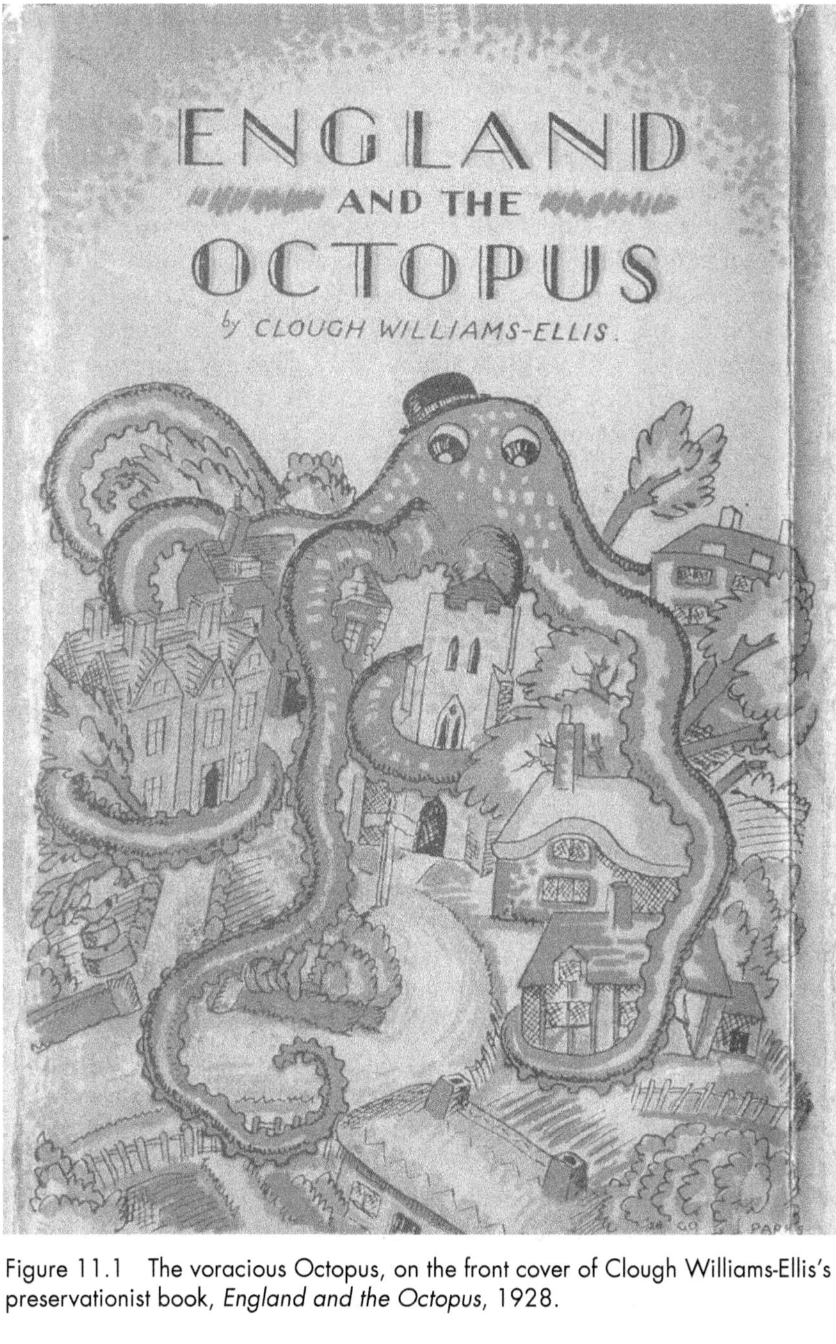

Figure 11.1 The voracious Octopus, on the front cover of Clough Williams-Ellis's preservationist book, *England and the Octopus*, 1928.

course, strong elements here of Williams-Ellis's somewhat authoritarian socialism. He was particularly vocal on the need for planning controls to curb the excesses of the *laissez-faire* culture, with its visually obnoxious results encouraged by the 'grotesquely inadequate' legislation of all post-1918 governments.[11] Williams-Ellis may have been lamenting the loss of traditional countryside, but he did so whilst advocating orderly, forward-looking development. This position, underscored by his promotion of national parks and new towns, cannot be reduced to a single influence, architectural style or ideological or political position.

That said, it is beyond question that the 1945 Labour government represents the point at which Williams-Ellis's ideas and campaigns, with the aid of many other people, were most clearly realised. In the interwar years, the CPRE became the driving force behind the movement to establish national parks. Williams-Ellis supported this movement with journal and newspaper articles, such as those for the *Journal of the Royal Society of Arts*, arguing that national parks were '*for* the people' and should be a key part of British democracy. This policy was adopted by the new Labour government, and Williams-Ellis was co-opted on to the committee, out of which was to emerge the National Parks and Access to the Countryside Act 1949.[12] In 1947, the Town and Country Planning Act was similarly celebrated.[13] For Williams-Ellis, this was a 'triumph' for his vision of rural modernity – that of progressive preservation.

The Labour government of 1945 also took up the plans for new towns, a cause epitomising mid-twentieth-century rural modernity, in that it aimed to protect the countryside from uncontrolled development. Once again, Williams-Ellis played a central role, being appointed the first chair of the first new town at Stevenage, although typically he did not last long in the post.[14] Nevertheless, his vision for new towns combined garden city principles with high qualities of architecture, thereby drawing together backward-looking aesthetics with forward-looking theories of place and space.[15] The emphasis on the latter was revealed by his writing on exclusively modernist matters, such as the text of the 1951 Official Record of the Royal Festival Hall and his review for the *Manchester Guardian* of Le Corbusier's book, *The Marseilles Block*.[16] Moreover, for the decade after 1956, Williams-Ellis was an active member of the government's Advisory Committee on the Landscaping Treatment of Trunk Roads. Particularly significant in this, and typifying his appeal to diverse constituencies and design projects, was his work for that ultimate symbol of modernity, the M1 motorway.[17] These postwar works were a logical extension of Williams-Ellis's interwar activities, in which he continued to be at the cutting edge of modern rural design.

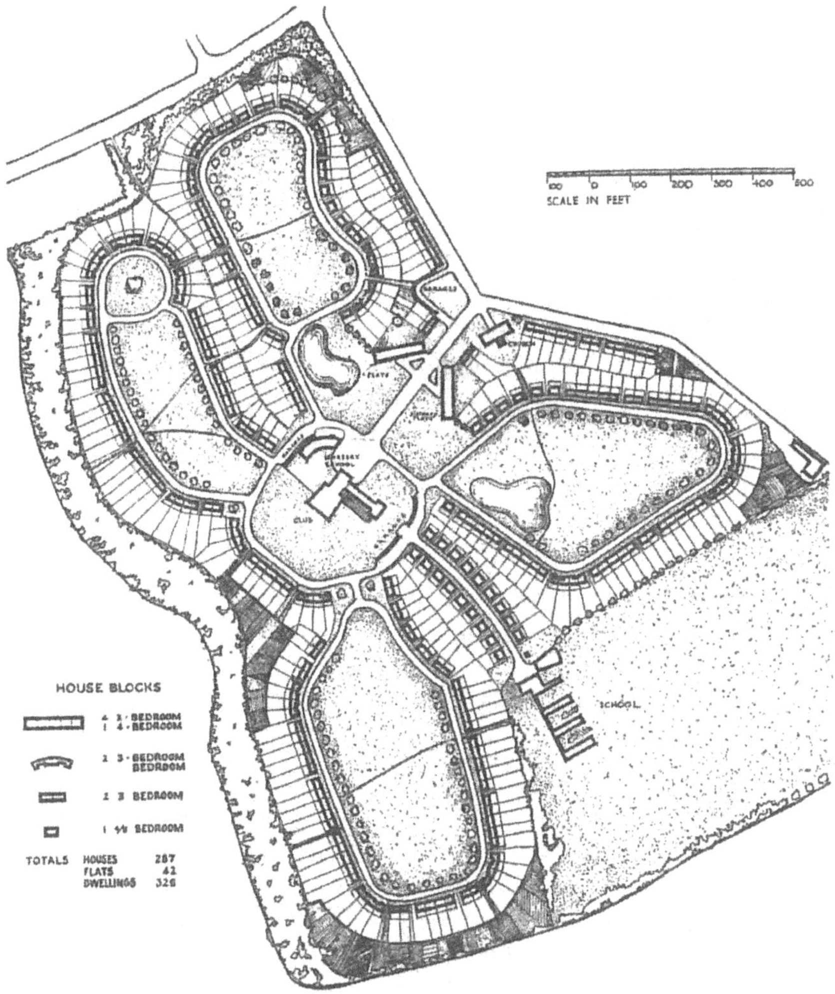

Figure 11.2 Plan for proposed 'Reilly Green' by Clough Williams-Ellis and Lionel Brett at Bilston, Staffordshire.

While falling outside the chronological limits of this present study of *Rural Modernity in Britain*, these activities have been included here to demonstrate the strong element of continuity within William-Ellis's work and his particular conception of the rural modern. This is further demonstrated by his design for one of Sir Charles Reilly's housing developments (Figure 11.2). For many conservatives sympathetic towards the aims of the CPRE, however, the social engineering proposed by schemes like this was a modernising step too far. It is also evidence of the tensions that underlay Williams-Ellis's vision of the modern world.[18]

A distinctly English geography shaped his modern world, albeit one that extended to Wales. Because of this, he attracted considerable criticism from Iorwerth Peate and others who found modernisation alien to a Welsh identity that should protect vernacular architecture and the Welsh language.[19] Clearly, the identity Williams-Ellis espoused was radically different. He insisted that the headquarters of the Council for the Preservation of Rural Wales (CPRW) should be in London, and he supported a proposed Royal Air Force training camp at Porth Neigwl on the Lleyn peninsula, which he saw as a symbol of modernity. Sufficiently well planned, he argued, it would aesthetically be less disfiguring than the bungalows of Abersoch and Aberdaron. Objectors interpreted the requisitioning of a site that was a vital part of the 'spiritual and cultural heritage' of Lleyn as English dictatorial interference. The aerodrome was duly built.[20] After the war, Williams-Ellis courted further controversy by supporting development of the Butlins holiday camp at Pwllheli, contrary to the wishes of the CPRW; for Williams-Ellis, this was unfinished interwar business, as the camp had been approved before 1939.[21]

Preservation and design

Clough Williams-Ellis was born in 1883 to a father who was a clergyman and Cambridge academic. After a private school education and less than a year at Cambridge University, he decided to become an architect. He was able to have some useful (building) work experience with a distant relation, A. H. Clough, before starting architectural training at the Architectural Association, where he stayed for only three months. On becoming an architect, he might well have been expected to have designed Victorian Gothic buildings. From the outset, however, he deplored that style, first designing small cottages in simple, vernacular Arts and Crafts style, influenced by William Morris and his followers. As an architect, Williams-Ellis became noted for designing buildings that were 'rooted in the landscape', a quality that aligned with the Arts and Crafts movement and at the same time equipped him to be a successful rural moderniser.[22] This early architectural phase further located him in discourses of both progressive social planning and the heritage industry, and seems, in retrospect, to predict his status as a progressive preservationist.

Portmeirion is perhaps the most characteristic model of his ideas about modern design. From its beginnings in 1926, it always included picturesque, traditional cottages, designed in conservative styles that owed more to the Cotswolds or the English West Country than to Wales. It was at Portmeirion that Williams-Ellis experimented with,

Figure 11.3 Government House, Portmeirion, 1928–29. Precursor of post-postmodern. © Portmeirion Limited.

and developed, many of his characteristic traits and progressive practices. In architectural terms, this often took the form of mixing and matching styles and scales, a practice often referred to as 'Cloughing up'.[23] Eventually, Williams-Ellis moved beyond his beginnings in Arts and Crafts-based architecture, following the lead of Sir Edwin Lutyens in converting to neo-classicism. This was a style and perspective that would become Williams-Ellis's favoured genre throughout his career, inventively adapted and utilised as one of several styles employed by him, and arguably a precursor of architectural modernism.[24] At Portmeirion, for example, what could have been simple neo-classical buildings, such as Government House (1928–9) (Figure 11.3), innovatively reflect the influence of 1920s Scandinavian buildings. An absence of string courses or mouldings allows the colour-washed walls to change subtly and seamlessly and be darker at the bottom than at the top, making a distinctive contribution to the Mediterranean look of the village.[25]

The setting of Portmeirion clearly points out the creator's affinity for the rural and was a key part of his stated aims for this creation: the distillation of his conceptualisation of rural modernity in built form. Designs for rural settings were produced by him in bungalows of pisé (rammed earth) construction and traditional thatched cottages, including one

Figure 11.4 Laughing Water Restaurant, Cobham, Kent, 1933. Modernist 'roadhouse' in natural surroundings with a nautical theme. © Architecture Club.

with a very modern, drive-through garage and a petrol station with a canopy in the style of a pagoda.[26] As in his writings and campaigns, Williams-Ellis aimed to show that a picturesque site could be developed without despoliation and that good architectural manners are also good for business.[27] Here, then, was an agenda-setting modern approach to twentieth-century architecture and development.

It was at Portmeirion in 1930, with Pilot House, that Williams-Ellis made his first venture into modernist architecture. This is a weather-boarded building, with nautical connotations, incorporating progressive metal-framed windows. It expresses the modernist ideal of 'form follows function'.[28] This was soon followed by modernist extensions to the hotel at Portmeirion. As architect of some of the earliest modernist buildings in Britain, Williams-Ellis was – for the moment and in a distinctly rural context – at the forefront of modern architecture.[29]

Portmeirion was only the beginning, with a number of other modernist buildings following in the next decade. Significantly, virtually all of these were of the same type: non-residential, in rural settings and – as was the case with most of his architecture – built for wealthy private clients. Particularly successful was the 1933 Laughing Water Restaurant at Cobham in Kent (Figure 11.4). Here, in one of his most celebrated and creative designs, was Clough, the arch-modernist. He had visited the Swedish architectural exhibitions at Gothenburg in 1923 and Stockholm in 1930, with Gunnar Asplund's exhibition building for the latter a clear and important influence at Cobham.

Figure 11.5 Williams-Ellis's modern, but ambivalent 'functional hut' at Maeshafn.

Adopting a boat-like design for the lakeside setting, the 'international' styling included ship-like railings and flat roofs, as advocated by Le Corbusier. It was favourably received in the architectural press, being described as appropriately modernist for its location and an excellent example of the new Americanising phenomenon: the 'roadhouse'.[30]

In Wales, Williams-Ellis also designed two wholeheartedly modernist, rural restaurant buildings, the first at the summit of Snowdon and the second at Conway Falls. The fact that neither was built to its original design does not detract from the uncompromising nature of the original proposals. In 1931, he designed the first purpose-built hostel for the Youth Hostels Association at Maeshafn (Figure 11.5). Evoking the spirit of the organisation, the design had strong modernising elements. In particular, Williams-Ellis incorporated an innovative system of movable partitioning, which allowed the numbers of male and female users to vary from day to day. Thus, in 'Williams-Ellis's functional hut', form unquestionably follows function, whilst the slightly later hostel at Holmbury St Mary followed Cubist principles.[31] Supporting this chapter's characterisation of Williams-Ellis as an architect always looking in multiple directions – to the past, to the future, to English traditional design, to European architecture, to the local geography – is the fact that even in his most intense modernist phase, he continued to design non-modernist buildings. Moreover, after World War II and a permanent move to rural North Wales, he was to build only one further modernist design: the seaside Morannedd Café at Criccieth. In moving forward beyond simple, orthodox modernism towards a light-hearted eclecticism that is unafraid of

Figure 11.6 Derivative classical/vernacular use of colour and texture at Poundbury, Dorset, c. 2005.

'getting things wrong', Williams-Ellis appears to Alan Powers as a 'proto postmodernist': his buildings resemble 'caricatures, that are deliberately flat, and that are not trying to convince you of their period authenticity'.[32] Thus Clough Williams-Ellis was more modern than the modernists.

Williams-Ellis returned after World War II to neo-classicism. This change may have upset purists, but it did prefigure the mood of a general public gradually becoming disillusioned with much modernist architecture, especially for domestic building in a rural environment. This was part of a shift accelerated by the 1968 Ronan Point disaster (the partial collapse of a new high-rise block of flats in East London) and the turn to a nostalgic and commercially driven version of heritage during the last four decades of the twentieth century.[33] In his own way, Williams-Ellis was always in tune with, if not a step ahead of, the cultural milieu. It is understandable, then, that Williams-Ellis's influence and legacy are openly acknowledged in the 'gentle architecture' of François Spoerry's 1960s seaside town of Port Grimaud on the French Riviera and the English equivalent of Poundbury (Figure 11.6).[34] As George Saumarez Smith claims, Poundbury is the 'closest modern equivalent' of

Portmeirion, notwithstanding the wider mix of building types, interests and uses, which means that it 'lacks the coherence of a single designer and the romance of Italian coastal towns'.[35]

Finally, in a further important prefiguring of much of post-1945 housing development, at Portmeirion Williams-Ellis adopted strong elements of the townscape design approach since favoured by modern developers in order to maximise densities and thus increase profits. Indeed, it is to a sense of the growing commodification of the past as signifier and trope of modernity that we now turn.

Prefiguring heritage: Portmeirion and beyond

From its roots in the Arts and Crafts movement and the foundation of the Society for the Protection of Ancient Buildings in the closing decades of the nineteenth century and across the twentieth century, concepts of preservationism have become interwoven with – and helped generate – the rise of the heritage industry. Although somewhat neglected, Clough Williams-Ellis is a key figure in the history of the networks out of which the heritage discourse emerged and, mirroring the multi-layered nature of heritage, his buildings have themselves gone on to become heritage icons. Further, given that heritage and modernity are coeval, to ignore Williams-Ellis's place in heritage tropes excludes a constituent element of his progressive preservationism that is as complex and nuanced as any other aspect of his activities.

In his approach to conservation and the deployment of the past in the present, Williams-Ellis sought to strike a balance between preserving what he deemed to be the historic and beautiful and enabling appropriate adaptation or other development. More telling was his ambivalent attitude towards the work of the National Trust, icon of the Authorised Heritage Discourse. On the one hand, Williams-Ellis applauded the saving of threatened buildings and landscapes, but he also saw the Trust as 'England's executor, the pious curator of rare little remnants of loveliness, ticketed specimens of what we have already largely lost or wantonly thrown away'.[36] There is no little irony, therefore, in the ultimate outcome of one of his key campaigns of the mid-1920s, that to save the Brownian landscaped garden at Stowe House in Buckinghamshire from intrusive development. Williams-Ellis purchased the Grand Avenue, subsequently passing it to Stowe School, an act indicative of a philosophy that combined preservation with modernity. In 1989, however, the gardens passed into the ownership of the National Trust, whose philosophy combines preservation and commodification.

Figure 11.7 Paganhill Anti-Slavery Arch, Stroud, Gloucestershire, saved from the Council's demolition order.

Revealed in his attitude to the Trust is Williams-Ellis's polysemic approach to the past. His intervention in the campaign to save the Paganhill Anti-Slavery Arch, built near Stroud in Gloucestershire in 1834 to celebrate the abolition of slavery, is a case in point (Figure 11.7). The arch fell into disrepair in the 1950s and the local council obtained approval for its demolition in 1959. On learning of the council's decision, Williams-Ellis arranged to see the arch, with publicity from the visit resulting in several promises of donations and the council reversing its decision. In attaching his name to the preservation of a memorial to counter-hegemonic beliefs, Williams-Ellis was here prefiguring the rise and recognition of a category of the deployment of the past in the present that can be encapsulated as heritage from below: expressions of a sense of inheritance of beliefs and actions that challenge the dominant.[37] And yet even here there is ambivalence. Heritage expressed from below and within is concerned with local distinctiveness. Williams-Ellis's involvement in the campaign to save the arch reveals that, despite his emphasis on beauty and amenity, he did not always share an emphasis on the maintenance of the distinctive patina of local places and spaces.

At Paganhill, Williams-Ellis suggested that the arch should be moved to a 'better' site (no doubt more grandiose or imbued with greater visual amenity), or as a last resort to Portmeirion. His principal aim was to save the arch from demolition: the proposed relocation was subsidiary.

Williams-Ellis's dualistic, progressive preservationist and social philosophy is, however, perhaps best seen in what he did at Portmeirion. As the village developed, it became a 'Home for Fallen Buildings', such as the seventeenth-century plaster ceiling and mullioned windows from Emral Hall in Flintshire and the colonnade from Arnos Grove in Bristol.[38] Incorporated in the town hall and prominently displayed, these elements convey, at first glance, the dead hand of heritage preservation: a nostalgic, romanticised backward-looking discourse that speaks only of the authorised and of commodification. A second, deeper glance reveals something more complex. First, whilst there was nothing new in the removal of historic artefacts, Portmeirion was a radical departure from the norm. Prior to Williams-Ellis's initiative, the aim of preservation by removal was only to enhance a collection with foreign antiquities; with Portmeirion, the aim was to protect British buildings threatened with demolition, an exemplar of forward-looking preservation that significantly predated St Fagans and the Weald and Downland Museum.[39] The rescued buildings at Portmeirion add to the illusion of authenticity and visual variety, but also comprise separate legacies in their own right.

A similar ambiguity and polyvocality underscore Williams-Ellis's decision to commodify Portmeirion through entrance fees, the hotel, shops and other catering facilities. But here too he was prefiguring important modern trends, including one of the defining characteristics of the late twentieth-century heritage industry: the commodification of the past. As practised by Williams-Ellis, such commodification of the past embraced the industry trend of appealing to diverse social and cultural groups. It was important to him that fine architecture and craftsmanship be accessible to 'an ever-widening audience', so that 'this wider public will come to consider these treasures as in some sort their own'.[40]

Finally, Portmeirion now exploits the fact of its setting for the 1960s cult television series *The Prisoner* through 'Prisoner' weekends and the 'music, arts and culture' of *Festival No 6*. Festival publicity claims the village as 'our main stage . . . a Mediterranean-inspired Grade II listed, fantasy village', which forms 'a unique series of surreal and inspiring venues'.[41] Beyond question, Williams-Ellis would not have recognised the designation as 'fantasy village', but equally beyond doubt is the fact that his actions laid the foundations for Portmeirion's emergence as the hyperreal postmodern simulacrum it has become.

The essence of this modernity (both at Portmeirion and in

Figure 11.8 Flamboyant 'forced perspective' of the Belltower (or Campanile), Portmeirion. © Portmeirion Limited.

Williams-Ellis's life and work) is captured in the idea of Clough Williams-Ellis as *homo ludens*. He rarely appears to have taken himself fully seriously or settled on any project or direction for long. As such, there are strong elements of the *flâneur* about him: that inhabitant and archetype of the modern city, always observing, always spectating, never still. For Zygmunt Bauman there are important links between the *flâneur* and *homo ludens* in which play and playfulness are central to culture and 'the joy of strolling is the joy of playing'.[42] All this is evident at Portmeirion in at least two distinct ways. First, in its design, the village must be understood as a performance, which began with the 'dramatic gesture' of the Belltower (or Campanile): part of a *coup de théâtre* that evokes Portofino and towns on the Amalfi coast (Figure 11.8).[43] Here, in order to make it look higher, the upper windows are half the size that they appear to be from the ground, 'a virtuoso display of forced perspective'.[44] Similar playfulness is found in his use of colour and fallen buildings.

An additional layering of the connections between the twin notions

Figure 11.9 Strube's 'Little Man' in the Daily Express in the 1930s.

of the *homo ludens* and *flâneur* is to be found in the circulation pattern at Portmeirion, a narrative typology crucial to any heritage display. In his design, Williams-Ellis included 'perambulations', a conscious echo of the 'stage sets' of great landscape designers such as William Kent, which offered not just picturesque vistas and private strolling for the designer, but also the 'careful canalizing of day visitors on certain routes'. Portmeirion was designed to interweave playful surface qualities with philosophically driven statements encompassing forward-looking modernity and the view that development of a physically beautiful site could enhance it.[45]

Perhaps the ultimate example of Williams-Ellis as *homo ludens* is to be found beyond Portmeirion on the front cover of his book, *England and the Octopus* (Figure 11.1). This bizarre jacket image pointed out the impact of ribbon and other uncontrolled development on the English countryside with 'The Octopus' depicted as an ordinary middle-class man with bowler hat set at a similarly jaunty angle to that of the popular *Daily Express* cartoon character, Strube's 'Little Man' (Figure 11.9). In the 1920s, the notion of the 'Little Man', combining the character of the modern gentleman and suburban office worker, seems to have replaced John Bull as a kindlier and 'more domesticated' national English archetype. By alluding to this discourse and identity on the cover of his most significant work, Williams-Ellis reveals once more his claims to and on behalf of modernity. And whilst there are clear issues around class and gender in this and his other works, what is revealed here is something far from the one-dimensional picture painted by Matless. It is to a consideration of this essential polyvocality that we now turn by way of conclusion.

'A man of our own age': a very [post]modern man

This chapter has demonstrated how Clough Williams-Ellis was a lifelong rural moderniser. He regarded himself first and foremost as a practising architect. From the outset, he rejected Victorian Gothic styles; as an admirer of William Morris, he initially designed Arts and Crafts, vernacular buildings. After taking up neo-classical designs, he experimented with the modernist 'international' style, always avoiding brutalist modernism. His active interest in architectural history and a continuing penchant for the traditional meant that he would not commit himself entirely to modernist architecture; he was particularly adept at identifying with restricted or sensitive rural sites. These multiple sympathies, tastes and ideological commitments inevitably resulted in disorienting, and sometimes contradictory, tensions in designing buildings in the countryside. An important actant in Williams-Ellis's network was the magazine *Country Life*, a key arbiter and architect of the rural imaginary. Notwithstanding a brief flirtation with rural modernism in the early 1930s, in its pages the rural, stable, stratified and romanticised came to signify a particular vision of England and Englishness. By 1934, the editor of *Country Life*, Christopher Hussey, had become disenchanted with the 'false functionalism' of rural modernist architecture, believing it disruptive of and antithetical to dominant tropes of classical Palladianism.[46] Williams-Ellis obviously needed to retain the magazine's approval but, as this chapter has shown, his was a polyvocal perspective that permitted the abandonment of pure modernism in his architecture but the maintenance of a progressive preservationism in his writings and sidelines.

It is this progressive preservationism, moreover, that permits the appreciation of the relationship between landscape and Englishness (and Welshness) that Williams-Ellis epitomised as something more than a one-dimensional, somewhat authoritarian, moderniser. His sidelines were a key part of the man and his philosophy, which, as the American architectural historian Henry-Russell Hitchcock noted in his 1929 book, *Modern Architecture*, set him apart from his peers (p. 199). This singular polyvocality emerges ever the stronger in the simultaneously traditionalist and modernist *England and the Octopus*, in which Lewis Mumford's 'man of our own age', 'a very modern man', emerged fully realised.[47] In keeping with the notion of Williams-Ellis as a proto-postmodernist is the fact that he deliberately adopted a writing style and cultivated a personal appearance that masked his essential seriousness. The threads, however, that bind much of this polyvocality together are practicality and a certain pragmatism. Wherever possible, Williams-Ellis would opt for an adaptive form of rural modernisation, with, for instance, his vision for new towns drawing heavily on garden-city principles. This was also an ideal he strove to maintain in his own architectural designs and buildings.

In sum, *England and the Octopus*, and perhaps Williams-Ellis's whole multi-faceted life, career and œuvre, has the seemingly (and fittingly) contradictory impact of a small pebble causing an avalanche. In attempting to capture the nature of his rural modernity, we can do no better by way of a conclusion than to agree with Mumford that this 'singular moment . . . brought on the avalanche of ecological diagnoses and proposals that hopefully characterizes our age'.[48]

In dialogue with: Chapter 3 'Electricity Comes to the Countryside' (I: Networks) [rural design; planning]; Chapter 15 'Rural Modernity in a Time of Crisis' (V: Wars) [rural preservation].

Notes

1. Haslam, *Clough Williams-Ellis*, p. 9.
2. *Landscape and Englishness*, p. 25.
3. *Landscape and Englishness*, pp. 25, 31, 51.
4. Preservationist campaigning and writings, and even his development of Portmeirion, were 'sidelines'. See Williams-Ellis, *The Architect*, pp. 151–9 and 173–84.
5. Powers, 'One Man's Fight', p. 54; Powers, *Britain*, p. 164.
6. See Ogborn, 'Modernity and Modernization', pp. 339–49; Giddens, *The Consequences of Modernity*, pp. 36–7.
7. *Architect Errant*, pp. 24–55, 92–3 and 205–7.
8. Williams-Ellis, *Tank Corps*; Clough and Amabel Williams-Ellis, *The Pleasures of Architecture;* Williams-Ellis (under pseudonym Graphite), *Reconography.*
9. *Octopus*, pp. 27 and 141, and endpapers.
10. *Octopus*, p. 12.
11. *Octopus*, p. 108.
12. Williams-Ellis, 'National Parks', pp. 429–36; *Architect Errant*, p. 95.
13. Howkins, p. 189.
14. *Architect Errant*, pp. 246–8; Jones, *Clough Williams-Ellis*, pp. 158–60.
15. Eleanor Smith Morris, p. 97; Powers, *Britain*, pp. 86–7.
16. Williams-Ellis, 'Idea and Realisation'; Williams-Ellis, 'Architecture'.
17. Williams-Ellis, *Roads in the Landscape*; Williams-Ellis, *Around the World in Ninety Years*, pp. 18–20; Merriman, 'A Power for Good or Evil', pp. 116–20.

18. For example, by E. M. Forster and his tenants at Rooks Nest. *Architect Errant*, pp. 246–8; Matless, *Landscape and Englishness*, pp. 205–8.
19. Gruffudd, *Land*, pp. 7–12.
20. Gruffudd, *Land*, pp. 7–12; Gruffudd, 'Landscape and Nationhood', pp. 211–21; CPRE Executive Committee Meeting minutes; Gruffudd, *Land*, pp. 7–12.
21. *Architect Errant*, pp. 243–6.
22. Haslam, pp. 12, 101; Jones, pp. 77–8.
23. Jones, pp. 74, 77.
24. *Architect Errant*, pp. 66–7 and 73; Jones, pp. 31–3.
25. Originally, Williams-Ellis personally mixed these colour washes. Alan Powers, Interview, p. 12.
26. See *Cottage Building in Cob, Pisé, Chalk and Clay*, pp. 91–5; and the Architectural Press's 1924 book, *The Smaller House*, pp. 14–19.
27. Gruffudd, 'Building Sites', pp. 242–3; Gruffudd, '"Propaganda for Seemliness"'.
28. Hitchcock and Johnson, *The International Style*, pp. 81–9.
29. Gold, *The Experience of Modernism*, p. 84; Powers, *Modern*, p. 100; William J. R. Curtis, *Modern Architecture*, p. 338; Powers, *Modern*, pp. 22–3, 34.
30. Featured in Architecture Club, *Recent English Architecture*, illustration number 28, and his own jointly authored book, Williams-Ellis and Summerson, *Architecture Here and Now*, p. 73.
31. Matless, *Landscape and Englishness*, p. 73.
32. Powers, Interview, p. 34.
33. Gold, *Practice*, pp. 276–80.
34. Williams-Ellis, *Around the World*, pp. 88–94.
35. Saumarez Smith, Interview, pp. 1–2.
36. *Britain and the Beast*, pp. xvi–xvii; *Octopus*, p. 108.
37. Stroud Urban District Council, Minutes; Williams-Ellis, letter to *The Times*; *News Chronicle* Report.
38. Llywelyn, pp. 232, 228; Haslam, Orbach and Voelcker, pp. 688, 695.
39. Respectively dating from 1946 and 1967.
40. Howard, p. 187; Hewison, pp. 51–80; Williams-Ellis, 'I- Prospects of the Post-War Countryside', pp. 530–2.
41. 'A Festival Unlike Any Other'.
42. 'Desert Spectacular', p. 142.
43. Williams-Ellis, *Portmeirion*, p. 36.
44. Alwyn W. Turner, pp. 55–6.
45. Lewis Mumford, 'Epilogue: Crotchet Castle to Arthur's Seat', pp. 91, 93; Gruffudd, '"Propaganda for Seemliness"', pp. 404–8.
46. See Hussey, 'Oare House' and 'Cotswold Village'.
47. *Octopus*, new edition, pp. xi–xii.
48. Mumford, *England and the Octopus*, Introduction to 1975 edition, pp. xiii–xiv. Similar views were expressed by the modernist town planner, Robert Gardner-Medwin, when he reviewed the 1975 edition of *England and the Octopus*. See Gardner-Medwin.

Chapter 12

Celebrating England: 'Heritage' Writing and the Rural Novelist

Dominic Head

This chapter is concerned with the non-fictional writing about England undertaken by a series of novelists, prominent in the interwar years, who take their inspiration from rural life. As novelists, Doreen Wallace, H. E. Bates, Adrian Bell, Leo Walmsley and Francis Brett Young all manage to resist generic convention, enlarging our understanding of the persisting relevance of the rural to the literary imagination and to social history. But in their 'heritage' writing commissions – extending into the 1940s, with implications beyond the interwar era – they have to confront the social conservatism implicit in the concept of heritage, 'the condition or state transmitted from ancestors' (*Oxford English Dictionary*). One of the more interesting elements of the rural novelists' heritage pieces is the extent to which they resist the straitjacket of convention and the easy equation between the celebration of the rural and an unchanging verdant England. The heritage works considered here are written (at least partly) against the grain of the stability implied or assumed in generic convention, so that the rural illuminates the social changes ushered in by modernity.

The perception of rural conservatism is rooted in ideas about the *reception* of literary treatments of the countryside, with commentators writing from the 1980s onwards detecting a fixed idea about English identity; coloured by the equation between place and nationalism, heritage titles have been seen to underscore a static projection of Englishness that is merely implicit in fiction and other forms of nature writing, especially where the attributes of southern England are perceived to have fashioned the national character. Krishan Kumar, for example – effectively summarising the critical view of the 1980s and 1990s – argues that popular appropriations of rural literature from Hardy onwards were part of a process by which 'the "south country" . . . imposed itself on the national consciousness, to the point where it was endlessly reproduced as an image of "timeless" England' (p. 210). In this view, the tendency of the English to wax lyrical about the countryside is a sign of apoliticism, a national characteristic in which social division and political strife are transcended by 'the idea of a land and people living together softly and naturally', in the words of Robert Colls (p. 204). This ideological nexus has been presumed to dictate the orientation of heritage titles, such as the Collins 'Britain in Pictures' series, with its 'emphasis on a common heritage', as Alexandra Harris puts it (p. 140). 'Britain in Pictures' is chiefly a wartime project, its celebration of British cultural (and institutional) life driven by patriotism, but it is interesting to see how this project compares to other guidebooks and how it taps in to pre-existing interwar intellectualism, where the nationalistic obligations were less restricting. The relationship between the rural, the literary imagination and English heritage needs to be reconsidered in the work of those writers who take their primary inspiration from the rural. In their work, the straightforward ideological interconnections between rural writing and nationalism detected in later twentieth-century commentaries are often subtly undermined.

Doreen Wallace

This chapter begins with a novelist who is not much read today – Doreen Wallace – and, to give an impression of her sensibility, starts with an account of one of her novels. The idea here is to establish the ways in which Wallace, in common with the better rural novelists of the 1920s and 1930s, is capable of extending generic conventions. This will establish a principle of subtle subversion that can then be traced in her prominent heritage titles, where the subversion is sometimes harder to descry. In this respect, the fiction illuminates the non-fiction, but also helps identify the distinctiveness of Wallace's enrichment of heritage writing.

Wallace was 'one of the Somerville writers, a grouping that included Vera Brittain and Dorothy L. Sayers'.[1] In her fiction, she is capable of inventive moments within an unremarkable middlebrow formula, finding ways of reinvigorating the rural tradition that highlight the limitations of its conventions, thus signalling a progression beyond those limitations for the attentive reader through an access of self-consciousness. Her novel *Barnham Rectory* (1934) is, in many ways, a distillation of provincial English novelistic convention; it uses the role of the clergyman, and the site of the rectory, as the focus for its exploration of rural–provincial social mores. Set in 1930–1, the novel is also typical of the interwar rural novel in its explicit treatment of the agricultural depression.

By the end of the novel, however, the treatment of social mores has been overtaken by tragedy, and Wallace's protagonist, Audrey Mapperley, facing penury, has agreed to marry her persistent suitor (and so become a clergy wife rather than a teacher), in the process 'surrendering unconditionally the Intellectual Woman' (p. 282). The dramatic shift in tone does not obscure Wallace's more urgent themes, however. The issue of class change, for example, is underscored when Audrey quotes from an essay by Virginia Woolf (without naming her, simply calling her 'a great woman') on 'the confines of the middle classes', and the barriers to genuine social interaction that can exist in English society (p. 135).[2] Wallace is here importing avant-garde debates about gender and class from mainstream literary culture into genre fiction and allowing the conventions of her chosen mode to wither in the face of the pressing questions of social change. If she loses interest in her feminist heroine, that is because the English village, as a fictional setting, cannot accommodate her vision – but that is also a central point of her novel.

Barnham Rectory recognises the inevitability of social change and the disruption of rural society, and registers this by pushing generic convention to breaking point. It might seem too great an expectation to look for similar effects or challenges to English conventions in Wallace's two contributions to 'The Face of Britain' series, *East Anglia* (1939) and *English Lakeland* (1940). Guidebooks of this era often catch the tone of works like *England and the Octopus* (1928) by Clough Williams-Ellis, or C. E. M. Joad's *The Horrors of the Countryside* (1931), published by Leonard and Virginia Woolf at the Hogarth Press, where there is a palpable class connotation to the account of despoliation. In her volume *East Anglia*, with reference to the Norfolk Broads, Wallace makes complaints in a similar vein – for example, when she observes how 'catering for holiday-makers always seems to mean ugliness and squalor'. She continues: 'I suppose it's very convenient for the holiday-maker to have the choice of three or four sticky wooden sheds at which to buy his packet of fags, his bottle of lemonade and his ice-cream' (p. 88). Referring to the coast east of Cromer, Wallace writes 'soon we are in the land of bungalows; which I'm sure are delightful for their owners in the holiday months, but are a blight on the landscape for anyone else' (p. 102). Yet her tone shifts as she acknowledges that the insides of these homes may suggest a different conclusion: 'for all I know, they are one and all perfect little homes from home'. She then goes on to identify the real nub of the objection: 'the outsides are so distressing, the little plots of bare grass, the wire fences. And as they are only summer dwellings, they will never be anything else – they will never grow to look bowery, like cottages, like the real thing' (p. 102). Wallace objects to the failure of inhabitation. Empty holiday homes are not proper dwellings; they are not inhabited and cherished by permanent members of a community and so bear the signs of absenteeism and neglect.

In *English Lakeland*, Wallace's snobbishness mellows, and is even acknowledged, so that the social significance of rural experience – the bedrock of *Barnham Rectory* – comes into view in ways that the guidebook genre does not easily facilitate. Enticing her readers to visit Dungeon Ghyll at Great Langdale, she writes:

> Personally, I have a contrariness in me which suggests continually that too many trippers spoil the beauty-spot. But this snobbishness in the realm of the aesthetic must not be pandered to. A more strict regard for reason would suggest that what the multitude finds beautiful, probably *is* beautiful. (p. 16)

It is true that the contradiction persists – 'one way of forgetting hikers and their litter in the sublimity of Nature is to go right up the chasm of the Ghyll' – but the cat is out of the bag: elitist perceptions of the natural sublime are bankrupt because the appreciation of place is a democratic leveller. *English Lakeland* ends with a surprising intervention in national economic policy, which is also arresting in its plea for greater equality:

> The great mistake which was made by the industrialists of the last century was in amassing money for themselves while keeping their workers at starvation level. (And not industrialists only: farm wages were starvation wages, and many a worker lived on bread, onions, and turnips, never seeing meat save on high days and holidays.) (p. 115)

The analysis may be over-simplified but Wallace succeeds in using the platform of a rural tourist guide to offer a wartime commentary on economic policy in an egalitarian spirit.

A related political concern is evident in Wallace's *How to Grow Food* (1940), published in the Batsford 'Home Front Handbooks' series as a practical guide aimed at 'those who have never grown food before' (p. 1). The pragmatism is softened by the conceit of Wallace using the character of a 'weather-beaten lady' to offer advice to a suburban couple, 'Mr. and Mrs. B'. The conceit allows her some moments of self-deprecation (for she is the lady) but the emphasis is on productivity without sentiment, which means (for example) being prepared to shoot birds and sabotage their nests: 'one has to effect a compromise with conscience, and adore the song of the darkling thrush while planning to put a stop to his depredations' (p. 46). Literary heritage is evoked in the allusion to Hardy but is sidelined by the national need. Some historians now tend to see the 'Dig for Victory' campaign as less successful in practical terms than it is often still deemed to have been. By 1944, home production of fruit and vegetables had not had a huge impact: 'with the exception of potatoes, cabbages and rhubarb, there was no very great difference in the amount that gardeners and non-gardeners bought in the shops', Ursula Buchan records.[3] Lizzie Collingham sees the statistics differently, celebrating the fact that 'more than half the manual workers in Britain kept a garden or allotment, and every class increased its vegetable and thus its vitamin consumption'.[4] Yet Collingham also acknowledges the monotony of a diet based on root vegetables, especially potatoes, even if the effect of wartime policies was to produce a new social levelling in nutritional terms (pp. 392, 394). *How to Grow Food* encourages variety (there is advice on asparagus growing, for example (p. 29)), yet its intended contribution to the national life may have been more ideological than practical. At the same time, this book transcends its moment and makes rural experience the *site* of social change, the very dynamic heritage writing is presumed to resist.

H. E. Bates

The ambivalence of Doreen Wallace's heritage writing, comparable to the paradoxical effects of her novel *Barnham Rectory*, sometimes implies the need to preserve a traditional England while acknowledging the social change that must transform it. Such ambivalence is a recurring feature in the heritage writing of rural novelists, frequently gesturing beyond the limits imposed upon them by their commissions. A good example of this is H. E. Bates's *Down the River* (1937), which has the air of a timeless classic of English nature writing – it is reissued periodically – and which can certainly be read in generic terms as a conventional celebration of a more rural era, in which simple nostalgia bestows a vague and ahistorical mood. Bates evokes 'a quieter age' and 'a wilder century' when he filters his account through the nineteenth-century lore passed on to him by his grandfather, a very influential figure in his life.[5] Yet, in a manner that is typical of Bates's more complex nostalgia (ostensibly straightforward, ultimately challenging), he overturns the very generic expectations with which he also lures his readers. Here a village scene from boyhood memory brings him up short:

> I could see there two of the things which most delight me in village life: a stream crossing the village street and on it an endless patrolling and procession of ducks. There, at that point, stone walls and houses and grass and duck and water and woodland fused to make a scene that was almost too idyllic. (p. 23)

With adult understanding, Bates reveals the clichéd convention: 'it was that scene with which, in the eighteenth century, and still more in the nineteenth, third-rate engravers embellished the title pages of third-rate poets. It was pastoral, lyrical, a scene observed and drawn with half-closed eyes' (pp. 23–4). Re-envisioning the scene ('I see it still, but not quite like that'), Bates makes us see 'the greenish duck-turds on the water's edge, the curled floating duck feathers, the print of ducks' feet in the washed-up mud' to stress that 'it is the ducks and the memory also of snake-lines of golden ducklings fluffed by spring winds that give the scene its life' (p. 24). From this fastidious point – that pastoral convention sanitises the scene, missing the actual life to be viewed close up – much more follows. With this capacity for detailed observation and readiness to flout the conventions of rural representation, Bates is attuned to social factors that are historically specific and the kind of revelation that his complex nostalgia is apt to produce.

The clearest example of this is when Bates considers the 'Ouse folk' inhabiting 'a long chain of charming towns and villages' such as Pavenham, Turvey, Olney, Stevington, Harrold, Odell and so on: place names which 'are exactly appropriate to such a soft-spoken and in a way soft-thinking people' (pp. 75–6). The easy appeal of soft causal–environmental anthropology is suddenly disrupted by the caustic phrase, 'soft-thinking people'. Bates's thesis is that the Ouse folk are 'not only half-asleep, but still in servitude' to a feudal past because the industrial revolution has not (on the surface of things) changed life much in such rural backwaters. A very damning critique of 1930s provincial life emerges from this, an observed sham gentility in people adopting a 'pseudo-cultured accent', surrounded as they are by 'gentility in the shape of retired captains, seedy lords, real shabby gentry clinging to their absurd mansions . . . by hunting people, by doubtful Honourables' (pp. 76–7). Outwardly, the Ouse villages are hard to match for 'beauty of shape and scene', as defined by 'setting and form and architecture'; but, again, the long lens of conventional depiction fails to reveal 'the thatch which leaks, the sweet cottage with no drainage and a wooden privy . . . The idyll begins to crack when you bear too hard upon it' (pp. 84–5).[6] In a rhetorical move to complete the chapter, Bates reverts to the external view, the angle from which he best knows the villages of the Ouse: 'serene little bunches of stone and thatch and coloured plaster on the river's edge' (p. 85). The pastoral scene retains its appeal in a charged nostalgia shaken by a consciousness of historical change and social impoverishment.

Adrian Bell and Leo Walmsley

One of the recognised classics of English rural non-fiction, penned by a novelist, is Adrian Bell's *Men and the Fields* (1939), a book that in some ways epitomises the facility of this kind of writing to achieve complex effects against the apparent transparency of its intent and style. The book is structured as a series of encounters with rural people, and many of these episodes convey a sense of bemusement about the changing social and economic world. In the foreword to the republished Little Toller edition of *Men and the Fields*, Adrian's son, Martin Bell, describes it as 'a work of practical mysticism and a celebration of things as they were and would never be again' (p. 6). The intriguing oxymoron 'practical mysticism' pinpoints Bell's tendency to discover life-affirming consequences in the muck and sweat of everyday farming activities. This implies that the mechanised world of modernity consigns the possibility of such rewards to the past, so that the mystical celebration of the rural becomes an instance of simple nostalgia, without nuance. Ronald Blythe adds another dimension to this analysis. Seeing the work as a 'shared creation' between Bell and the book's original illustrator, the artist John Nash, Blythe argues that both Bell and Nash were confined by their historical moment, since neither one 'knew any farming world other than that in slump'.[7] The Second World War brought 'subsidies and unprecedented recovery and wealth', but 'would also destroy the apparently timeless universe' Bell evokes. Consequently, Blythe concludes, *Men and the Fields* 'can be seen as an unconscious threnody to a scene which was about to disappear for ever, for neither writer nor artist looked ahead, or indeed looked back' (p. 8). The compelling mood peculiar to the book, in this reading, is consequent upon its steady and unselfconscious 'commentary . . . of the present', which makes the reader feel 'present at those final sowings and reapings, those pea-pickings, those naked plungings in the summer river, and in those social divisions', a keenly felt response to modernity's impact on the rural (p. 8).

An arresting moment of implied social responsibility in a traditional farming community occurs in Chapter 4, when Bell visits an elderly farming couple, old friends on the verge of retirement. But their farm has another incumbent, 'a little old woman who lives in a room at one end of the house'. The daughter of previous owners, long dead, she comes with the farm when it is sold on, and has 'outstayed three owners of the farm' (p. 48). Unpaid but 'with a little money from a parent's will', she takes it upon herself to look after the livestock, moving about the farm 'like an animated sack with a hat on top' (p. 49). Asking her about her simple life, Bell discovers she is entirely devoted to the animals, up and tending to them at a quarter to five in the morning, after just three hours asleep. Bell wonders what she finds to think about: '"I find plenty to think about . . . I think about these." She nodded her hat towards the bullocks and pigs' (p. 50). Bell draws his reader in to the speculation about the significance of this encounter:

> What had left me with such an impression of ruddy light about that glimpse of her face? Had it been caught at that moment by a gleam of sun, as she turned, smiling to herself, and went into the dim bullock yard? (p. 51)

The rhetorical question invites us to think about the 'practical mysticism' that Martin Bell identifies as his father's chief effect in writing this book. But this is not a straightforward evocation of simpler living that can be replicated. Bell also registers the distinct oddity of the situation, which suggests that the radiance of fulfilment ascribed to the existence of the old lady, fully absorbed in the care of animals, is arresting because of its uniqueness. In this elegiac moment, we realise that what is now astonishing was once representative, merely.

Bell encounters a traditional figure in rural writing: an old man gathering firewood. In this case, it is a pensioner given permission to take the tops of trees being felled in a wood half a mile from his cottage, but far enough to make the transportation of the fuel a challenge, carried 'a piece at a time on his back'. The fact that a form of charity encourages these 'ant-like labours' – and the 'large heap of fuel' that accumulates as a consequence (p. 30) – connects the episode to a significant strand in rural literary history: the treatment of the vagrant in need of support. Bell's wood gatherer seems to represent a further stage in the presentation of this rural figure, going beyond Wordsworth's old Cumberland beggar, for example, and the defence he embodied (in Raymond Williams's reading) against 'the selfish ease of ordinary society'.[8] There is a further erosion of community in the person of Bell's wood gatherer because Bell sees the careless felling of the wood as a symptom of 'the great machine of the economic system smashing down a host of trees and leaving the greater part of them in chaos' (p. 31); the 'charity' enjoyed by the old man is thus an accidental by-product of destructive modernity. Bell wants to present the old man as representative of gentler times: he is 'a little Crusoe, making repeated journeys to the wreck: his home was an island in an alien world'. Yet his consciousness is infiltrated by modernity, animated only by thoughts of an impending boxing match, news of which must reach him by radio broadcast: his 'great interest in life was boxing' despite the fact that 'he had never been to a match in his life, nor seen the heroes of his dreams' (p. 31).

Leo Walmsley's *Fishermen at War* (1941) adds another dimension to this ambivalent use of generic form, in the quiet resistance of nationalism. It bears the hallmarks of a hastily written wartime book, a contribution to the ideological battle against Nazism. Yet this is not a piece of propaganda. It is true that Walmsley draws a stark contrast between the stoicism of English fishermen and the ruthless tactics of the Germans, attacking fishing and merchant vessels in defiance of international rules of engagement. But this is very much the sentiment of the time and a view shared by the people interviewed for the book. Walmsley records a lengthy and harrowing first-hand account of Dunkirk told to him by a member of 'one of the oldest seafaring families in the port of Whitby', to whom he gives the alias 'Curly' (p. 219). Enlisted as a private in the army, Curly has a knowledge of boats that serves him well when he finally makes it aboard a sea-worthy vessel. But his account of several near-death experiences, of the repeated attacks on the retreating forces and their civilian rescuers, of the corpse-strewn beach at Dunkirk is a horrifying contemporaneous account (pp. 222–54). Appearing as a significant chunk at the book's end, this eye-witness testimony, in Walmsley's rendering, is a *tour de force* that seems intended to contribute to the broader national interest of demonising Nazism; but there is no apparent attempt to sanitise the account, to unhook the heroism from horror, or to excise anything that might adversely influence the civilian effort. A good example of this is the discovery of a small flotilla of abandoned vessels at the water's edge, including small yachts, barges and rowing boats – some intact, some wrecked. The meaning of this discovery is revealed by the 'scores' of 'bodies lying on the beach' nearby (p. 233).

If the idealistic worldview Walmsley ultimately calls for in *Fishermen at War* is partly born of a willed wartime optimism, it also reveals something genuine about his evolving regionalism. The concluding pages put this optimism in the service of a global rallying call. Here Walmsley reminds us of the shared treasures of the human race – artistic and cultural achievements, as well as geographical wonders – as an indicator of what will be destroyed if the war with Nazism is lost. His account of the 'bravery and fortitude and self-sacrifice and kindness' of 'the British fishermen' is then claimed to 'symbolise the good in mankind, which in this fight must inevitably triumph' (p. 256). It is important to empathise with the situation in which this is written, shortly after, if not during, the Battle of Britain in 1940. Yet we can also see something interesting evolving about Walmsley's identity, beyond the immediate pressures of this context:

> I am English, but more than that I am of this earth, and of the human race. I love the moors, the cliffs and scaurs, the red-roofed villages and the fisherfolk

> of the Yorkshire coast, but to me they belong to the earth rather than to one small section of it that is called England. (p. 255)

More than a wartime appeal for solidarity, this global orientation finds a place in Walmsley's ongoing attempt to interpret his rural–regional origins in relation to his international experiences and intellectual development. The immediate resonance of this outward look is to register the signs of self-contained regionalism on the wane. Listening to the 'minesweeper lads', Walmsley is struck by the variety of accents, but also by how regional accents are already overlapping:

> there was very broad Scotch and even pure Gaelic, and Tyneside, which has something of Scotch in it and something of Yorkshire, just as the Norfolk and Suffolk speech is mingled with Yorkshire and Lincolnshire phrases and sounds and those of the south coast. (p. 219)

We are left to conclude how the effects of World War II are serving to accelerate regional cultural exchange and cross-influence. But the larger force registered that impacts upon regional difference, and the insularity of the rural, is popular culture: of the 'men from the sweepers' Walmsley recalls in the passage just quoted, 'at least one in every six we passed was whistling "South of the Border"' (p. 119). This 'universally popular ballad' has already been established as a motif of a new cultural experience (p. 95). It is popular cinema, however, that emerges as the major agent of this new experience, as in Walmsley's other books, registered here as a form that shrinks the world (p. 125).

The village and Englishness

The global perspective emerges in surprising places, as this concluding section of the chapter reveals, where writers reappraise the treatment of the English village. We see above how H. E. Bates in *Down the River* successfully writes back to 'generations of writers' who 'have painted the English village as a golden thing' (p. 84), and to a long pastoral tradition in which the idealised English village lies at the heart of a romanticised rural community. In insisting on the social contradictions and impoverishment that may inhere in village existence, he is also sounding a warning note to his readers, especially those looking for a celebration of English heritage and also, perhaps, those looking for tips on places to visit. Bates is here contesting the publishing trend that he is also perpetuating, in which the celebration of the rural encourages tourism, implicitly or explicitly. With acute perception, Bates understood in 1937 the point made this century by Trevor Wild, that the 'process of opening up rural and village England was imposed upon a predominantly depressed and decaying countryside'. This meant that, in the 1920s and 1930s, 'there was a clear contrast between the poverty and sleepy backwardness of the old village life, and, with its motor cars, bustle and insensitivity to traditional rural values, the energy and modernity of the new'.[9] The poor infrastructure observed by Bates continued into the Second World War. In 1942, it was estimated that 'one out of every three villages in England was still without any piped water'. Change was abroad, and much decried by preservationists, yet significant alterations to the architectural composition of many villages did not begin until after the Housing Act of 1936, which produced a surge in council-house building. In some areas, of course, the suburbanisation of villages 'within reach of the largest cities' was well under way.[10]

The village is the ideological battleground of this discussion. It is at the heart of conservative ideas about English heritage, yet it is also a barometer of social change. Edmund Blunden's *English Villages* (1941), in the 'Britain in Pictures' series, was a wartime publication that perpetuated a myth, perhaps partly in the propagandist spirit of the times.[11] It may well be that the series was conceived, as Michael Carney suggests, as 'the best sort of propaganda' (p. 28), yet there is also a sociological impetus behind Blunden's book, over and above the celebration of village England. His exemplar is the village of his childhood, at Twyford Bridge near Yalding in Kent (he calls it simply 'Twyford'), which is made to embody the resistance of the village to social change: 'a few great houses in our parish are still regarded with a degree of veneration', he claims. He acknowledges that 'wealth is reduced and the social order modified', yet insists that these great houses 'even now . . . are relied upon for various kinds of leadership', a false-sounding attempt to defend the status quo against the social flux of modernity.[12]

Francis Brett Young is close to Bates in his understanding of the village. He is a fascinating figure for anyone interested in the complexities underlying the many depictions of rural life in the inter-war era.[13] *Portrait of a Village* (1937) is exemplary; not a novel, but neither strictly non-fiction, its subject is the imaginary village of 'Monk's Norton'. However, Brett Young drew on his own experiences living on his Craycombe estate in Worcestershire for the account of rural life in the *Portrait*, which depicts a recognisable landscape of the Severn basin, with views of the Malvern Hills and (more distant) the Clee Hills, in a handsomely produced snapshot of English village life, in all its attributes.[14] This landscape – associated with A. E. Housman, Edward Elgar and a persisting twentieth-century celebration of the rural – becomes the setting for an unexpectedly unsettling treatment of contemporary rural society.

This is surprising because the book is presented as a plush, celebratory artefact printed on heavy paper and illustrated with a fine series of wood engravings by Joan Hassall. Indeed, the book was conceived 'partly as a vehicle' for the engravings, already commissioned by Heinemann. Delayed by Hassall, Brett Young sold the serial rights to *Good Housekeeping*, which, as Hall explains, 'published the story, illustrated by Rowland Hilder, before the appearance of Heinemann's edition' (p. 127). *Portrait of a Village* thus appeared in different versions, each one illustrated by an artist associated with the celebration of the English landscape; and, superficially, its defining characteristics seem to corroborate that understanding of Englishness that Peter Mandler has anatomised, characterised by 'the squirearchical village of Southern or "Deep" England as the template to which the national character had been formed and thus the ideal towards which it must inevitably return':

> Purveyed by the 'dominant classes' to the wider culture by means of a potent array of educational and political instruments – ranging from the magazine *Country Life* to the folk-song fad to the national trust to Stanley Baldwin's radio broadcasts – 'Englishness' reversed the modernizing thrust of the Industrial Revolution and has condemned late twentieth-century Britain to economic decline, cultural stagnation and social division.[15]

Mandler's purpose is to contest this simplistic analysis, in which traditional Englishness is the opponent of modernity; and, in the spirit of Mandler's more nuanced understanding, it is interesting to see how *Portrait of a Village*, the work of Baldwin's 'preferred author', distances itself from the ideological construction of a timeless England that it seems to court.

The account of the imaginary village, contained 'on the East by a cressy watersplash, impassable in seasons of flood' and on the West by a canal, is initially presented as a surviving remnant of 'un-industrialized England', preserved 'as a fly in amber': it is 'a self-sufficient, self-centred and (almost) a self-supporting community' (pp. 12–13). That 'almost' is revealing and hints at the subtle ways in which Brett Young unravels that sense of self-containment. His method is to present portraits of his imaginary villagers as 'types', in the process quietly uncovering the unstoppable elements of technological and class change and also revealing the aspects of rural life that were seemingly too distasteful to appear in contemporary accounts of rural society. Farmer Collins, for example, becomes emblematic of necessary agricultural evolution: although he takes pride in being 'an old-fashioned farmer' and 'makes a show of laughing at his sons' scientific modernity', he is still 'shrewd enough to listen to all they have to say and . . . to give their ideas a trial' (p. 115).

Not all change in Monk's Norton is beneficial for all inhabitants: the 'petrol age', which has elevated George Mason from mere bicycle mechanic to garage proprietor, has also reduced Mr Webber, owner of the saddler's shop, to 'a retailer of dog-leads and muzzles and purses and such leathery trifles' (pp. 23–4). Neither is farming routinely rewarding. Harry Hawley has set himself up as a successful country butcher after selling the family farm, recognising that 'the retailer of meat takes less risk and makes more profit than the producer' (p. 26). And the various unsuccessful schemes of Mr Rudge to make his smallholding a success see him finally surviving on plums (p. 106).

Like Bates in *Down the River*, Brett Young challenges the stereotype of the picturesque village, effectively probing beneath the surface of Joan Hassall's beautiful depiction of the thatched cottages at the end of his imaginary village main street (p. 37). To spring and summer visitors, 'adventurous strangers exploring the countryside', these dwellings seem part of an 'idyllic' life: 'where could one's days be more placidly spent, the stranger asks himself, than in these humble dwellings where life demands so little?' (pp. 41–2). However, their poor 'sanitation and comfort' are the abiding effects for their inhabitants and for the book's narrator (whose voice we assume to be Brett Young's), who pronounces them 'a social disgrace' by twentieth-century standards of living, despite their 'romantic picturesqueness' (pp. 40–1).

Perhaps the most striking way in which Brett Young undermines squirearchical village England is through its contrasting politics. On the one hand, there is the popular scoutmaster, Captain Grafton, who feels 'more "like himself" on the rare occasions when he dons a black shirt . . . to parade with the North Bromwich Fascists' (pp. 97–8). On the other, there is his socialist 'schoolmistress', Miss Martin, an object of class scorn and suspect morals on account of her failure to betray 'any partiality to men' (p. 21). Miss Martin transcends the villagers' prejudice and is 'probably more completely alive than anyone else in Monk's Norton' (p. 22). Significantly, Miss Martin is made to conjoin progressive politics with a profound sympathy for nature; she is 'an earnest field-naturalist, enjoying the fresh air that seems her appropriate element' (p. 23).

This association between political change and the response to nature is a startling aspect of Brett Young's book and obliges us to recalibrate its celebratory dimension. This handsome volume, ostensibly about the values of an invented generic 'un-industrialized' English village, preserved 'in amber', reveals itself to be lauding the capacity for social reinvention. The book's frame contributes gently to this effect: the introduction to Monk's Norton is given in a 'Prelude', a cuckoo's-eye view of the terrain in the spring. Three cuckoos migrating from 'mid-Africa' alight on the village, disrupting our sense of enclosed Englishness before it is described (pp. 3–8). This is the perspective that frames the book, as these cuckoos prepare to catch 'the southward current' in the 'Postlude' (p. 180). A perennial and insufficiently recognised feature of heritage writing about England has been its propensity to unite reflections on nature with a repudiation of nationalistic sentiment, and in this respect Brett Young is anticipating effects that are more overt in the 'new' nature writing of the twenty-first century. Indeed, the cuckoo's-eye perspective on the English village, with the geopolitical reflection it invites, is a milder instance of the message contained on the cover of the literary nature magazine *Archipelago*, an 'inverted' image of the British Isles where the 'Celtic fringe . . . suddenly begins to occupy foreground and centre stage . . . as London and the south east fade away over the curvature of the Earth and behind a gannet's head'.[16] In the hands of novelists, the treatment of the 'local' in non-fictional rural heritage writing sometimes inspires a defence of nationalist sentiment, but the larger understanding of the rural continually unsettles that perspective, producing the oscillating effects illustrated throughout this chapter.

In dialogue with: Chapter 8 'The Spinster in Eden' (III: Communities) [rural fiction; women writers]; Chapter 15 'Rural Modernity in a Time of Crisis' (V: Wars) [Batsford publishers; war culture].

Notes

1. Alistair and Gina Wisker, 'Introduction', p. xvii.
2. The essay in question is Woolf's 'Memories of a Working Women's Guild', which was reworked as the introduction to *Life As We Have Known it*, ed. Margaret Llewelyn Davies.
3. Buchan, *Green and Pleasant*, p. 79.
4. Collingham, *Taste of War*, p. 391.
5. Bates, *Down the River*, pp. 37, 22.
6. The depiction of the rural slum is not commonly associated with heritage writing of this kind but rather with impassioned urban descriptions, such as those found in George Orwell's *The Road to Wigan Pier*, also published in 1937.
7. Blythe, 'Introduction', p. 8.
8. Raymond Williams, *The Country and the City*, p. 130.
9. Wild, *Village England*, pp. 114–15.

10. Wild, pp. 123, 126–8, 129.
11. Michael Carney supplies the publication date of Blunden's *English Villages* in *Britain in Pictures*, p. 78.
12. Blunden, *Villages*, p. 16.
13. On Brett Young's literary reputation, see Michael Hall, *Francis Brett Young*, p. 8.
14. Young, *Portrait*, p. 36; Hall, *Francis Brett Young*, p. 127.
15. Mandler, p. 155.
16. See Jos Smith, 'An Archipelagic Literature', p 10.

Part V

Wars

Chapter 13

Altered Countrysides: Paul Nash, David Jones and Eric Ravilious in Wartime

Eluned Summers-Bremner

Reviewing Erich Maria Remarque's *All Quiet on the Western Front* in 1929, Herbert Read quoted a passage from the novel indicating that the men who fought in World War I would be 'rootless' after the war compared to the generation that preceded them, and irrelevant to the next generation to come. Although a sense of loss is central to the story Read wants to tell, a phrase from Remarque reveals another condition that is not quite the same as being bereft of home or purpose. 'We shall be superfluous even to ourselves,' Remarque writes, 'we shall grow older, a few will adapt themselves . . . most will be bewildered . . . and in the end we shall fall into ruin.'[1] This chapter examines the condition of being superfluous to oneself as it appears in rural English landscapes created in the wartime, interwar and, more briefly, early post-Second World War periods, a condition that landscape itself demonstrates on behalf of soldiers and civilians as a wartime legacy.

Not all of the works considered here were produced in wartime, as wartime can be a condition of body and mind that outlasts conflict, perhaps especially so in the aftermath of World War I. Freud, encountering the symptoms of World War I combatants, discovered that a surplus in the form of an affective charge arises in humans when we yield to a larger cause and when we fulfil an impulse beyond the point of need repeatedly in a way that does not necessarily bring pleasure. This surplus seems to confirm our survival, as though mere existence is not enough for us.[2] But it can also threaten survival, making human life superfluous to a collective or individual drive to experience further satisfaction and meaning. This surplus is first created as the result of interaction with the worlds in which we find ourselves and for this reason is always partly alien to us, for while lands and their historical conditions give rise to humans, we typically wish not to be reduced to them.

Both actions, that of yielding to a cause and that of repeated acts of fighting, are involved in wartime. For English combatants, the fact that

World War I was fought on foreign soil further complicated matters that were already complicated by the nature of the conflict. In World War I specifically, combatants and some civilians used the concept of an English Arcadia, 'a green and pleasant land', as an object of imagined nostalgic comfort – the opposite of alienation – and as a cause for which to fight.[3] This focus on an Arcadian fore-time and after-time was arguably necessary because World War I in particular was experienced by combatants at the Western Front as an extreme form of the mechanisation processes that had been adopted on an industrial scale in recent peacetime. The irony was that the machinery of the Front brought into being men who lived to fight and die, a reversal of the increase in productivity envisaged and enacted in peacetime factories.[4]

In wartime, land gained means the risk of lives lost, and in this sense combatants embody and symbolise their home countries. When wartime is experienced as a monstrous inversion of largely urban, modern, industrialised factory culture, then combatants' relations to the countryside are bound to be overdetermined. This is the case with regard to both the rural landscape one is fighting *in*, in the case of World War I, and the landscape one is fighting *for*, often imagined as beatifically rural. For we should not forget that while the World War I Front was experienced and recalled by many combatants as a gigantic factory for death, it was mostly based and produced its material effects in *countrysides*. The production of death and the imagining of an idealised landscape that does not necessarily exist are instances of a superfluity of meaning that was created not only in human beings but also in the landscapes combatants inhabited during and following World War I.

In England in the interwar years, the countryside was often superfluous to itself in a literal sense as well. Between 1921 and 1929, over half a million acres of mostly arable land in which cereals were grown went out of cultivation as landowners sold land off or cut workers to survive, switched to dairying or financed other ventures.[5] And while it produced spatial incoherence in the event and after, World War I also changed the relation combatants and many civilians had to time and thus to history. The Arcadian England Patricia Rae has identified as part of the imagined experience of many frontline soldiers and officers was often, after the war, regarded not only as pre-existent but also as the *result* of lives lost in combat. In this understanding, a new Eden would be restored only if the British remembered those who had died for their country in its first incarnation.[6] When it appeared that a second world war was likely, however, English Arcadianism itself became a casualty. As the coming war was arguably rooted in the severe terms of the Treaty of Versailles and as insufficient time had passed for the earlier combatant generation to have been replaced by carefree youth, it became clear that the 1920s and 1930s had not yielded the kind of peace (nor the landed work) on which people could rely a second time for imaginative succour. The natural order of the countryside was to be fractured and the genre Rae terms 'proleptic elegy' or advance mourning in poetry and other literary and narrative forms resulted: 'The recurrence of war . . . made a mockery of familiar consolations, destroying the very resources for which it . . . also produced a need.'[7]

Rural landscape drawings and paintings by Paul Nash, David Jones and Eric Ravilious from the wartime, interwar and early postwar periods supply renditions of this kind of temporal and spatial overdetermination, in which landscape is not consoling in the idealised sense but nor is it presented as a place of total confusion. It becomes, rather, a site of the transmission of wartime's disorientations. Both Nash and Ravilious were war artists – Nash in both wars and Ravilious in the second – while Nash and Jones both fought in World War I (Nash albeit briefly) as officer and soldier, respectively. The superfluity that Read, following Remarque, feared his generation would embody – too much of oneself to bear or put to useful purpose – took other symbolic forms in the English and European countrysides recorded by these artists. It chiefly appears as an uncanniness of the kind familiar to combatants at the Front, as signalled, for instance, by the way in which a tea tray has a 'voice' that fills the horizon when it crashes during a blast in Ford Madox Ford's *No More Parades* (1925), while flames become 'the settled condition of the night'.[8] Here the inversion whereby a tea tray is active and flames form a familiar background is accompanied by a further strangeness: the tea tray's 'voice' occludes or replaces the human, even while it is humans who have brought such situations about. In the paintings, similarly, the countryside is no longer available to serve as background in expected ways but shows what humans make it into when they fight for it: something strange and estranging. Once relied upon as a wartime cause, the countryside reveals the uncertainties it did not help people escape in combat.

Paul Nash: disquieting things

Nash joined the 28th Battalion London Regiment (Artists' Rifles) in 1914 for home service before registering for overseas service, which began in 1917. He was invalided home with an injury due to a fall that May and later learned that most of his fellow officers had died in an attack that would probably have also killed him. He became an Official War Artist in October 1917.[9] Almost all of Nash's landscapes from the World War I period on create a sense of something 'unfamiliar', as Christopher Neve has noted. Neve regards Nash's true subject as 'something unpaintable, indefinable' (p. 6), the place of which could be subtly marked in a landscape painting such that the viewer cannot reduce the landscape to the painted place or the place to the landscape but must look anew without being able to grasp the full meaning of all the elements. In *The Menin Road* (1919) (Plate 6), most famously, Nash expresses what Reginald Farrer, visiting the Western Front in 1916, called a domain 'full of emptiness . . . an emptiness that is not really empty at all'.[10] Calling this 'the Void of War', Nash created in *The Menin Road* a scene full of material menace. The barrages that have produced the destruction we can see remain present, to the extent that there is no space in the painting that has not been altered beyond recognition as a natural form. As Paul Gough observes, here Nash

> d[oes] away with the normal hierarchies of motif and background, presenting both negative and positive forms as equal, implying that objects in a landscape are not standing free but are locked in place by overwhelming invisible forces – sound waves, noxious gases, pervasive dangers, and, overhead, reconnaissance planes and sausage balloons. (p. 155)

The forms of soldiers near the centre of the painting are mimicked by – or mimic – the slanting trees, and the upright trees themselves recall soldiers because their tops are uniformly blasted, producing peeling fronds that suggest men's broken internal organs, including brains. The fractured foreground and the leaden, light-striated sky make the middle ground of the painting look both strangely inescapable and flat, indicating the relentless press of combat's transformed countryside. As Gough notes, the ditches that do not progress and the horizon made largely invisible by smoke combine to make this and other wartime works by Nash somehow 'stilled and muted', despite their turbulence.[11] They are silent witnesses to an unbearably noisy dislocation of the aural, visual and kinetic fields.

Both Nash and Jones suffered from wartime trauma,[12] which, by definition, cannot be foreseen and so breaks from the future into the present with such unexpected force that it often becomes retrospectively unlocatable. 'The historical power of [a] trauma', writes Cathy Caruth, 'is not just that [an] experience is repeated after its forgetting, but that it is only in and through its inherent forgetting' or 'the collapse of understanding' that 'it is first experienced at all' (pp. 7–8). This helps to explain what is otherwise a seeming irony in the work of the three artists here considered. While wars present, past and yet to come – occasions on which modernity disrupted or would disrupt rural continuity, real and imagined – could not but inform their images of countrysides, these artists were all also interested in ancient landscape forms, the origins of which were often, like traumatic events for traumatised combatants, lost to history. Yet the forms, like combatants, had also enigmatically survived.

Standing stones, chalk figures, tree crosses and other land formations from earlier times appear in their images, as they do when modern viewers see them in the landscape, necessarily without the contexts that gave rise to them. But wartime causes the trees and pools in a painting like *The Menin Road*, in which there is only a discontinuous road and a denaturalisation of all once-natural objects, to appear overwhelmed by wartime context. The strangely claustrophobic, crowding flatness of the scene in this image conveys a sense of the feelings to which landscapes at the Front must have given rise remarkably acutely. What we are not shown as such in the image, and are thus moved to supply imaginatively ourselves, is the oppressive three-dimensionality of such a landscape, which, if experienced, would annul the constructed stasis of the painted scene. It is the two-dimensionality, the built-in foreshortening, of the image's three planes (foreground, middle ground and background) that show the viewer that she or he cannot see the full picture of the Front from the painting and that nor could any officer or soldier.

Yet while what is missing from such a landscape is a symbolic form such as a standing stone or chalk figure that provides for modern viewers of the landscapes in which those forms are found a point of historical difference from the present and an implied import, this landscape also works similarly to those that hold such forms. It shows us that the countryside, in wartime, can no longer be found. The standing stone missing its purpose and the paintings that show that war could never be as planar as *The Menin Road* suggests – instead, multi-directionally assaulting – are visual forms that testify to their now unlocatable historical contexts: rural Europe before the war came to it and the worldview that gave rise to standing stones.

The interest in ancient symbolic land forms coincided, in the 1930s, with an emphasis on abstract and constructivist forms in the sculptural and other work of a significant number of English artists, Nash included. When the sculptor Barbara Hepworth held a solo exhibition in London in 1937, crystallographer Desmond Bernal wrote a foreword to the catalogue that likened Hepworth's art to neolithic forms.[13] Nash himself wrote about his encounters with the standing stones at Avebury, which he represented at times as 'personages',[14] and which, in works such as *Landscape of the Megaliths* (1934), become temporally dislocating,

Surrealist-type objects. Nash's explanation of his work *Equivalents for the Megaliths* (1935) (Plate 7) indicates that he

> wished to avoid the very powerful influence of the antiquarian suggestion, and to insist only upon the dramatic qualities of a composition . . . of shapes equivalent to the prone or upright stones, simply as upright or prone, or leaning masses grouped together in a scene of open fields and hills.[15]

Yet the clearly skewed perspective of one of the two rectangular shapes in *Equivalents* makes most of the hilly landforms behind them appear somewhat two-dimensional as well, as do the two non-cylindrical forms. Of the two central forms, the first an upright cylinder and the second a leaning rectangular block of wood or stone, the end of which is scored with vertical lines, the second is the most improbable. It appears to be shorn off at a 45-degree angle at the top to lean against the rectangular gridded plane behind it. This would make the plane fall if we did not posit something invisibly behind that form, the one nearest to the hill fort that forms part of the background of the painting. The two forms might support each other to a point of median balance, were the central rectangular block set at a 45-degree angle to match that of the gridded rectangular board.

The impossible physics of the arrangement as it stands do, in part, convey the sense of another world in which such arrangements might exist, although it is not this one. There are surrealist images, by contrast, in which none of the spatial arrangements depicted could exist, except in the world of dream or nightmare; the 1934 version of *Landscape of the Megaliths* is closer than *Equivalents* to this kind of painting, combining aerial with standing views of Wittenham Clumps,[16] a favourite Nash subject. The 'trick' the objects play in *Equivalents* is to get the viewer to see the unpicturable or impossible along with what would make it picturable, the physical basis for equivalents: a different angle for the central rectangle, a boulder behind the gridded plane. In this way, we are brought quite close to experiencing equivalents for the megaliths because ancient megaliths are both stones and something else that is more mysterious, given that they were placed in the landscape by earlier humans for now indiscernible reasons. We see here that we have lost the framework with which to interpret those earlier megaliths since the crafted forms in this painting are monuments that could likewise exist only in a world the physical and symbolic laws of which remain incompletely known.

In the 1937 version of *Landscape of the Megaliths* (Figure 13.1) Nash presents some of the Avebury stones in a compressed landscape, in which Silbury Hill, a round pyramidal form, and the hill-fort at Oldbury Castle,

Figure 13.1 Paul Nash, *Landscape of the Megaliths*, 1937, watercolour on paper. Albright-Knox Gallery / Art Resource, NY.

a similar, stepped form also shown in *Equivalents*, appear in the same image, with the largest of the stones in the foreground between them. The snake, symbolising rebirth and the Druids' doctrine of 'the migration of souls' and that seemingly touches the sun in the foreground,[17] makes the sun appear simultaneously as though it were a flowered form on a snake-like stem as well as a star, the complement to the convolvulus below it. Its two-dimensionality contrasts with the stones, which appear, like persons, to be advancing across the landscape, an effect partly created by the foremost stone's face-like upper markings, as well as by the angle, lower diagonal right, from which we see them as a series. This, emphasised by the foremost stone's angled front, which suggests stepping, creates the effect of a pageant passing before us across the landscape.

Such an inversion of the dynamic (the sun) with the static (the stones) helps create a sense of the missing context in which the stones once served as embodiments of, or statements addressed to, supernatural forces, such as those that were thought to control the actions of the stars and planets. The sun's part-reduction to a more transient form in this painting is, arguably, connected to Nash's earlier attempts to capture the denaturalising work performed in rural environments by wartime. Although this image is benign and, unlike *The Menin Road*, has a lengthening horizon, it pictures a world in which one enduring natural form, the sun, can be exchanged for another transient form, a flower, so that both are kept in view and the landscape itself remains somewhat mysterious. Nash used this method in more extreme form to depict the Front, where trees are neither trees nor soldiers, and the question of what they are instead is uncomfortably unavailable from within the field of vision.

David Jones: enchantment

Roger Cardinal describes Nash's method in the 1920s and 1930s as poetic, to the extent that an object 'shows itself available to imaginative development, ceding to the artist a kind of magician's power to visualise it as *something else again*' (p. 47). The work of Anglo-Welsh artist and poet David Jones also shows this tendency. Jones served on the Western Front from late 1915 to mid-1916 and from October 1916 to January 1918 with the 15th Battalion (London Welsh) of the 113th Brigade of the Royal Welch Fusiliers. His service included the capture of Mametz village in the Somme, on 1 July, later described as 'the bloodiest day in British military history'.[18] Jones said he would 'relive in memory' his experience of the Somme for the rest of his life, remarking in 1971, 'my mind can't be rid of it'.[19] There were a number of shell-shocked men at Ditchling, a rural artists' community in Sussex, where Jones worked with Eric Gill soon after the war. These artists may have found continuity in the bleak conditions there, while finding it useful to be set to work at physical tasks, such as fixing windows and making forks and spoons, which had immediate use and relatively short-term meaning.[20]

In literary circles, Jones is often regarded as a poet of high modernism because he bemoaned the loss of a recognisable context for art and poetry in the early to middle years of the twentieth century. Yet Jones's impugning of the interwar and postwar periods in England for their technocratic disregard for the conditions necessary to the work of aesthetic symbol can also be read as a wartime symptom. Jones's description of the England he saw around him in 1947, a place of 'extreme stress, oblique approach, acute experimentation, rareness of complete integration, specialness of effort, [and] extreme contradiction',[21] is also a rendition of life at the Front. He wrote these words after his second breakdown in 1947, which occurred when the Second World War reawakened memories of the first.[22] While Jones envisaged, by contrast, a kind of living, natural medium running from past through present, which he believed England had lost and which we might now call fantasy, this imagined continuity is not so far from the Edwardian worldview that was tested and found wanting in the trenches. Yearning for a missing wholeness might well be a symptom of wartime trauma, since shell-shocked soldiers like Jones embodied the loss of the myth of easy generational continuity, a myth that Vincent Sherry points out had been used to encourage them to enlist.

Jones's long poem of 1937, *In Parenthesis*, follows the men of 'B company', part of an Anglo-Welsh battalion, from December 1915 to the Battle of the Somme in 1916, in their course through 'wholesale slaughter'. Jones's training as an artist and his attempt, like Nash's, to include in his work a sense of war's uncapturable chaos by means of the controlled chaos of art are clear in his description of the work's poetic method: 'I have . . . tried to make a shape in words, using as data the complex of sights, sounds, fears, hopes, apprehensions, smells, things exterior and interior, the landscape and paraphernalia of that singular time and those particular men' who experienced it with him.[23]

In rural tree images Jones painted in the late 1940s while recovering from his breakdown, a strange atemporality occurs. In *Vexilla Regis* (1948) (Plate 9), the title of which refers to a sixth-century hymn by Venantius Fortunatus, written to accompany the translation of a piece of the True Cross to Sainte-Croix in Poitiers, Jones works the motif of the Cross at Calvary along with the Cross as world-tree to show the collapse of the Roman Empire.[24] He was also influenced by the Anglo-Saxon dream vision poem *The Dream of the Rood* (before 1100), in which the Cross becomes a co-participant in the Crucifixion, remaining alive after the death of its lord.[25] What Jonathan Miles and Derek Shiel describe as 'curiously stylised scrolling' at the top of the central tree is uncomfortably reminiscent of Nash's war-blasted curling tree fronds – the opposite of fresh growth – and Jones has added History in the form of Roman soldiers, frightened horses and a grotto–pavilion to a reworked drawing from nature. The scene is troubled with historical repetitions that neither meet nor explain the present: this we can see from the visible layering in the image that – again, not unlike Nash's *Menin Road* – makes for a foreshortened horizon and a sense of pressurised menace. The only place to go in the image is upwards, but what we find there is relatively inconsequential, given the overloading of the rest of the drawing.

While we might readily see Jones's troubled state of mind in this crowded scene, in which the rural is saturated with temporally overlapping uses, a less troubling instance is found in *In Parenthesis*, Part 3, 'Starlight Order', where:

> silver beams search the interstices, play for breech-blocks
> underneath the counterfeiting bower-sway; make-believe a
> silver scar with drenched tree-wound; silver-trace a fes-

tooned slack; faery-bright a filigree with gooseberries and
picket-irons – grace this mauled earth –
transfigure our infirmity –
shine on us. (pp. 34–5)

The notes indicate that 'festooned slack' refers to '[h]anging telephone wire', a 'frequent impediment in trench or on roads by night', where they 'ran in unexpected fashion at any height'; 'gooseberries' to 'barbed-wire hoops', fastened together with barbs thrust outwards, which could also be thrown; and 'picket-irons' to '[t]wisted iron stakes used in the construction of wire defences'.[26] While in *Vexilla Regis* past conflicts crowd out the present, these lines and their accompanying notes provide two wartimes: the painfully tedious zone one makes one's way through repeatedly and the imaginatively rich place war's alteration of the rural makes available in reflective moments. The alliteration joins up components of the Front's impressions so they attain a kind of coherence that was more often absent in reality.

In the poem, stars are regularly barbed-wire stars as well as the distant, sky-lighting kind, with the ground 'mauled' not only physically in memory but also symbolically. In equating the earlier, Dark Age human time in which trees bore wounds with conditions at the Front, Jones draws on the Anglo-Saxon riddle tradition in which a picture of an object is sketched in words, enigmatically. To 'see' the solution to the riddle is to perform a double task, not so different from that involved in Nash's equivalents for megaliths. Following the clues provided by the description, the riddle-solver must simultaneously forget these clues and work laterally to place a variety of objects in the imaginative frame because the clues, like barbed-wire stars, are deliberately misleading as well as descriptive. The detemporalising effect of a rural landscape simultaneously 'faery-bright' – enchanted – and 'mauled', needing a call for eternal 'grace', shows that it does not exist in the kind of present that becomes the past but in a strangely unchanging place in which each once-natural event, like dew and starlight, keeps a traumatic memory alive forever.

Eric Ravilious: estranging the rural

If in Nash natural landforms become historical agents whose interpretative contexts are signalled in their absence, and in Jones into detemporalised signs of wartime's overloading of the rural, Eric Ravilious's interwar and early wartime landscapes enact the estrangement

Figure 13.2 Eric Ravilious, *Downs in Winter*, 1935. Watercolour and pencil on paper. Towner Art Gallery, Eastbourne.

of the rural by modernity in a less overtly confrontational manner. A member of the generation of 'Bright Young Things', who were briefly able to envisage a postwar world relatively free of social strictures,[27] Ravilious worked, like Jones, in wood engraving and created murals for public buildings in the 1920s before turning to ceramics design in the 1930s. He painted landscapes throughout his career, which ended when the plane he was in was lost near Iceland in 1942, but it is the English rural scenes he painted in the 1930s and early 1940s that demonstrate the characteristic melancholy as well as the playfulness of his work.[28] In these scenes, landscape has been subtly altered so that the viewer is almost tricked into taking carefully underplayed stylisation for a naturalistic view.

Downs in Winter (1935) and *Windmill* (1934) are examples of this method. In *Downs*, the foregrounding of an object of land modification, a land roller, provides an anchoring in verisimilitude that the rest of the scene mimics: furrows, probably made by a larger implement, appear in the far distant fields in the painting (Figure 13.2). In *Windmill*, at least four segments of rolling hillside echo the waterwheel's shape if it were to be laid on its side, forming a subtle cross effect also present in the 'x'-shaped metal lengths supporting the legs of the structure. To see these echoes we need to turn our gaze to occupy more than one angle. The grey and white sky is sectioned into rhomboid shapes not unlike the paddle-shaped components of the wheel itself, and this pattern can also be seen on the longest, central section of hillside. The naturalistic rendering of implements for modifying or interacting with the land or other element against a representationally modified rural scene makes for an ingenious reversal, given that we are inclined to associate the rural with the natural, and naturalistic and modificatory elements with modernity.

In *Downs in Winter*, the upright handles of the roller are echoed by the angles of the trees in the painting's middle ground, and in *Windmill* it is strange to see the sky and the grass in the middle ground bearing a pattern akin to that of the entirely human-made component. It is not an effect of natural light; it is an echoing the artist has introduced, such that, given the prominent verisimilitude of the windmill, the landscape appears more stylised, so that the rural elements follow an introduced pattern. Both images create a sense of relative emptiness in the landscape, leaving viewers tantalised by the surrounding landscapes' serving as the artificially altered components of the scenes, while the built elements are less visibly altered. The emptiness of the vistas takes the viewer just to the point where we might desire to see the unreconstructed scenes that were the basis for the paintings. The whimsical containment provided by selective harmonising amidst relatively open space is pleasing to look at because we know, on some level, that it is an effect of artistic reconstruction. Such stylised containment, in reality, is not always available for seeing.

A semi-rural image, finally, *Ship's Screw on a Railway Truck* (1940) (Plate 8), has the marks made by vehicles in a roadway adjacent to a railway siding mimic the spiralling shape of the ship's screw wings on its platform, while a ship to the left is improbably flush with the adjacent, curving harbourside. It is impossible not to see the ship's screw as a kind of art object on its 'plinth'; even the footsteps in the snow around it echo its shape, and the track marks in the roadway and the branches in the foreground of the image suggest the unseen swirling of the snowflakes, which are shown diagonally falling instead. In this way, Ravilious makes presciently clear that the industrial components of the war machine will shape how the world is seen in the postwar period, given that the seeing modern industry enables is more often presented without a formal indication that a landscape is being altered. By painting countrysides as places altered by artistic selection as much as by human endeavours *in* the rural landscape, Ravilious shows that deeper, less clearly visible changes to it are yet to come.

In 'Art in Relation to War' (1942–3, 1946), Jones wrote that art has 'outflanked "the fall"' of humankind (p. 164), which makes it 'analogous not to faith but to charity'.[29] In other words, art is something that is always being made, and it may protect us from some of our most potentially devastating blindnesses – those that result from and operate in wartime, as well as those that accompany our work in peacetime. Art in this sense is a useful excess, something added to the world, whether or not we believe in it, as a kind of disinterested offering to humanity. In depictions of the rural by these three artists we see landscapes rendered superfluous to themselves, unavoidably changed and made subject to ongoing change by modernity. And while we seem largely powerless to halt the continual world alteration that is war, work by combatant and documentary artists makes it clear that wartime does not author the sum total of our relations to the worlds it alters. There always remains a bit of the rural in its earlier form, prehuman nature, which we never see and which our actions, thoughts and feelings cannot subdue entirely. We are indebted to artists who show us that this remainder is a source of promise we can support, paradoxically, by attesting to its invisible presence within our landscapes.

In dialogue with: Chapter 4 'Weighing Down the Landscape' (II: Landscapes) [landscape painting]; Chapter 9 'Transformative Pastoral' (III: Communities) [rural surreal and rural fantastic; World War I].

Notes

1. Remarque, pp. 317–18. Quoted in Read, p. 116, quoted in Hynes, p. 440. As Hynes points out, Read's quotation is 'slightly inaccurate', although not in its substantial terms (p. 505n).
2. Freud, 'Beyond', pp. 1–65.
3. Rae, p. 216; Howkins, p. 41.
4. Fussell, *Great War*, pp. 40–3.
5. Howkins, p. 64.
6. Rae, p. 220.
7. Rae, pp. 221, 226.
8. Ford, pp. 293, 291.
9. Gough, pp. 133–4, 147, 150.
10. Quoted in Gough, p. 154.
11. Gough, p. 161.
12. Miles and Shiel, pp. 243, 252, 259, 262; Dilworth, pp. 186–7.
13. 'Foreword' to *Catalogue of Sculpture*. Quoted in Smiles, 'Equivalents', p. 199.
14. Nash, 'Stones', p. 76.
15. Letter from Nash to Lance Sieveking, quoted in Smiles, 'Equivalents', p. 211.

16. Russell, p. 15.
17. Smiles, 'Ancient Country', p. 34; Causey, 'Paul Nash and Englishness', pp. 110–12.
18. Dilworth, p. 104. There were 57,470 British casualties in the Battle of the Somme, of which 21,000 were 'killed or mortally wounded'. Dilworth points out, however, that 'this was not, as is often claimed, the greatest loss of life in battle on a single day: the French had lost 27,000 on 14 August 1914' (p. 104).
19. Letter to Tom Burns, 2 July 1971. Quoted in Dilworth, p. 118.
20. Miles and Shiel, pp. 46–7.
21. Notes for his doctors at Bowden House, 1947. Quoted in Miles and Shiel, p. 262.
22. Letter to Dr Charles Burns, 29 May 1940. Quoted in Miles and Shiel, p. 260.
23. Jones, 'Preface', p. x.
24. Edsall, pp. 21–2. Jones, Letter to Mrs Ede, 28 August 1949. Quoted in Miles and Shiel, p. 196. See also Murphy.
25. Johnson, p. 90.
26. *In Parenthesis*, pp. 194–5n.
27. Powers, *Eric Ravilious*, p. 8.
28. Constable and Simon, p. 13.
29. McInerney, p. 72.

Chapter 14

Eden in Sussex: Atheist Moderns and the Berwick Church Murals

Hana Leaper and Polly Mills

In 1916, towards the end of what has been celebrated as their high modernist period, Bloomsbury artists Duncan Grant and Vanessa Bell moved to Charleston, an isolated eighteenth-century farmhouse in East Sussex with no modern amenities. Facing 'east with its shoulder to the South Downs' and with a northerly view over the Weald, the house is a sunlit painters' paradise in the summer but weathers harsh winters.[1] They arrived in autumn just as the weather broke, seeking farm work as conscientious objectors. Despite initial privations, they revelled in the enormous creative potential and social liberation afforded by this isolated Sussex farmhouse and maintained this rural home for the rest of their lives. Together with their extensive cast of family and friends, the artists wove a domestic fabric that drew on local landscapes and traditions, combined with cosmopolitan philosophies and artefacts from their life in London and travel abroad. Charleston is now open to the public as a house museum, testifying to the idiosyncratic, resourceful and provocative living it harboured. A scenic hike from the house over the layers of human and natural history embedded in the chalk Downs brings visitors to the church in nearby Berwick, whose murals were painted by Bell and Grant in the 1940s. This chapter argues that these rural church murals are not a betrayal of Bell and Grant's earlier metropolitan, high modernist radicalism but rather boundary-pushing and meaningful contributions to modernity and late modernism that adjust our gaze from the urban and universal, to the rural and particular.

Key to realisation of the radical potential of the rural to facilitate meaningful artistic encounters is the seemingly contradictory nature of the Berwick Church murals project. The rural and religious have been positioned as the conservative opposition of modernism, modernity and liberal subcultures. Yet what the mural project and others like it clearly show is that communal rural practice, staged away from galleries and the art market, has the capacity to produce significant work resistant to conventional high modernist narratives of the new and of the solo genius. These murals offer fresh and personal yet historically situated ways to engage with enduring human aspirations to cultivate and commemorate belonging within communities rooted in time and place. Their atheist creators recognised the capacity of religion (or religious edifices and stories) to meet these needs. Engaging with the longstanding institutions of church patronage and churches as centres of worship, the Berwick Church murals serve as a riposte to the modernist *tabula rasa* and its call for the erasure of the past, of faith and of traditional frameworks for the production of art. Not recognisably modernist, the Berwick wartime project did not work in contretemps to modernity but foregrounds an enduring spirit of place, inflected by new modes of transport, leisure, consciousness and models of community.

During a period in which the landscape intensified as a national concern, a sacred significance became attached to the sense of continuity and community that historical sites represented. Nowhere was this more acutely focused than the countryside. As attested by the diverse chapters of this book, by the interwar period rural locations had become a totem of national identity, a focus of Englishness, an emblem of rootedness that must be preserved. Yet heritage cannot flourish without custodians to perpetuate and appreciate it. The Charleston artists became part of a generation of cultural custodians using new means of expression to celebrate and add to their heritage.

Suggesting that these atheist moderns imposed their metropolitan values on the denizens and buildings of Sussex implies that rural communities could only be insular, reactionary and inherently conservative: that they were static and unchanging. This chapter gives instead an example of how, responding to the stimulus of place and people, Vanessa Bell and Duncan Grant created works that reflected the capacity of the *genius loci* for elasticity and the potential for a creative union of the traditional and modern. Their participation in a rural church mural-painting scheme undermines notions of the village church as a time warp, an immutable monument unaffected by the pressures and pleasures of twentieth-century existence. Rather, this project and the themes it incorporates are representative of a cultural landscape changing rapidly and heterogeneously with the impetus of modernisation.

The Berwick Church murals commission

In 1940, Dr George Bell, Anglican Bishop of Chichester between 1929 and 1958, commissioned the Charleston artists to design murals for Berwick

Church. This commission was consistent with his belief that engaging with the creators of contemporary culture was key to both revitalising the church and promoting humanist values in wider society.[2] In his enthronement address at Chichester Cathedral in 1929, Bishop Bell (no relation to Vanessa) had pledged to 'seek ways and means of a re-association of the Artist and the Church' in order to set in motion 'a spiritual awakening of our country'.[3] In 1938, he commissioned Hans Feibusch's nativity cycle at St Wilfrid's in Brighton and early in November 1940 met Grant to discuss possible decorations for Berwick. Grant suggested that the practising artists living at Charleston at this time, including Vanessa Bell, Quentin Bell and Angelica Bell, could collaborate on drawing up a design.

Grant and Bell already had an established reputation for painting murals in a secular context. Their illustrations for Lady Wellesley's dining room at Penns in the Rocks (another artistic and non-heteronormative East Sussex outpost) and art critic Raymond Mortimer's library were shown in 'Mural Paintings in Great Britain 1919–1939', a major exhibition at the Tate Gallery in 1939. Grant had also been a founder member of the Society of British Mural Painters, which supported the Tate show. However, taking on a mural commission under church patronage was an incongruous and unprecedented undertaking for the atheist artists and this, along with the initial purpose for commissioning the works, sets the scene for the aesthetic, social, religious and cultural issues at stake – issues that would play out during the murals' genesis and become embedded in the materiality of the works.

Bell reflected on the peculiarity of their religious affiliation in a 1941 letter to fellow artist and longstanding family friend Janie Bussy:

> you'll never guess what we are up to . . . It starts by the curious fact that Duncan is in touch with a bishop, the Bishop of Chichester. So friendly have they become that it seems extremely likely that we shall all, Duncan, Quentin, Angelica and I, be turned into the neighbouring church [Berwick] and allowed to cover the walls with large works. What a war time occupation![4]

Apart from their lack of belief, the vision of Charleston 'all a-dither with Christianity' is all the more remarkable in the light of their shared aversion to narrative painting and privileging of form over content.[5] Yet this seeming discrepancy between their beliefs and the parameters of the project is ameliorated when considered in the light of their lifelong study of church art. Spring 1904 found Bell 'hard at work seeing pictures and churches',[6] whilst Grant copied from Piero della Francesca and Masaccio in Florence during winter 1904–5. During their many holidays together, they explored the mosaics at Ravenna in 1913, and in 1952 visited 'a church beautifully empty and light with about eight works by Siennese masters' in Perugia. Bell also kept abreast of more contemporary developments with a visit to Matisse's decorations at the Chapel of the Rosary (1949–51), Vence, in 1953.[7]

Another context that helps us make sense of the Charleston artists' acceptance of the Berwick church murals commission is the presence of other artists working in Sussex. The countryside, it transpired, was a particularly fruitful location for modern sacred art. The Roman Catholic Guild of St Joseph and St Dominic at Ditchling considered their relocation from London to the village of Ditchling as a creative and religious 'Exodus' from the bondage of capitalism to new imaginative and formal freedoms.[8] Elsewhere, in (predominantly) Anglican towns and villages away from the scrutiny of the metropolis, Hans Feibusch, John Piper and Graham Sutherland created works that both embraced the traditional role of the church artist and transformed conventional religious depictions through visceral Expressionistic translations of biblical stories and liturgical apparatuses.[9]

Although certainly rural and relatively remote, Sussex was by no means sequestered from the events and anxieties of the world. Travel to London and Dieppe was quick and easy, and most of the artists living in Sussex had spent formative time in the capital and on the continent. Their proximity to Europe meant that, during the war, residents had to make contingency plans in case of invasion. Rather than incubating an insular nationalistic attitude, the coastal location 'became a place from which to think about links to the continent', as Hope Wolf demonstrates in her catalogue to her 2017 exhibition 'Sussex Modernism'.[10] Despite ideologies of a threatened timeless landscape perpetrated by concerned lobbies like the Council for the Preservation of Rural England, Sussex did not operate in isolation, and the art produced there was not based in escapist fantasy, but rather on the realities of modern experience.[11] By attesting to dynamic and meaningful dialectics of rural modernism, the Charleston artists' decoration of Berwick underscored the evolving nature of a living heritage.

'England was itself sacred'

The Berwick Church (officially titled St Michael and All Angels) is located less than four miles from Charleston. Dating back to the twelfth century, it had undergone numerous transformations since its original construction, and by 1940 it was a small, unadorned church with plain white walls. The church restoration project advisor, Frederick Etchells, a former Omega artist, asserted that, as few of the church's original features remained, the proposed murals would not interfere with the its sacred, historic structure. The commission was sensitive not only to the sanctity of the church's authentic structure, but also to the local tradition of ecclesiastical painting in Sussex, where medieval artists had decorated the walls of churches in Hardham, Clayton and Keymer with biblical narrative. Whilst Berwick was a modern project, undertaken by atheist artists, its foundations were rooted in a sacred tradition.

The resulting works were executed in oil on plasterboard, fitted together with battens affixed to the church between 1941 and 1944. They include Bell's *Annunciation* and *Nativity* on the north and south walls, Grant's *Christ in Glory* above the chancel arch and *Victory of Calvary* on the west wall of the nave, and Quentin Bell's *The Wise and Foolish Virgins* on the side of the chancel arch facing the chancel and *The Supper at Emmaus* on the east wall of the north aisle. Created by three different artists, they are disparate in size and style, and speak to each painter's particular interests. Grant's etiolated crucified Christ of *The Victory of Calvary* (Plate 10) calls to mind the distortion that the English Post-Impressionists admired in pre-Renaissance artists. Unlike traditional depictions of the Crucifixion, Grant's painting does not emphasise brutality and suffering, but draws attention to the sensuality of the male body. In a time of violence, Grant's Christ encourages the viewer not to meditate on Christ's physical pain, but on his similarity to themselves. Presenting the homosexual body of fellow artist Edward Le Bas as unthreatening, sacred and benevolent problematises the church's persecution of homosexual love for the male body and speaks to Christ's tenderness for all of humanity.

Bell's Anglicised *Nativity* plays on the English Christmas tradition of the staging of the story of Jesus's birth with local children and people playing the roles, rather than recreating the original scene in a Bethlehem stable (Plate 11). Her inclusion of her own children and home states her conviction of the value of family life. The lack of uniformity; the replacement of the dark, rich colours more common in continental ecclesiastical paintings in favour of bold (the orange escutcheon-like background of *The Victory of Calvary*) or pastel tones (the Virgin's pale blue veil and light pink dress in *The Nativity*); self-conscious use of decorative effect, such as the dappled grey marbling and architectural features highlighted in yellow and pink throughout the building; and the multiple references to the many church interiors they had explored throughout their travels create a bright and breezy collaged, and attractively impulsive effect, continuous with the artists' Post-Impressionistic aesthetic and the synthesis of abstraction and representation that characterises their late work. One of the most compelling things about this complex and astonishing project is its inclusion of a cast of local people and sights within the works. Whilst the depiction of living individuals in church mural painting was common in medieval art, there are fewer contemporary examples, with the notable exception of Stanley Spencer's Sandham Memorial Chapel.

Though taking on a mural commission under church patronage may seem to us an incongruous undertaking for the atheist artists, Bell and Grant had previously advertised precisely these services on a 1922 business card announcing 'decorations, domestic, ecclesiastical, theatrical'.[12] The specificities of the Berwick project provided a testing ground for the artists' beliefs in the capacity and responsibility of art and its makers to reflect and investigate the human condition during a period of catastrophic disturbance. Their commitment to cite the 'local and particular' within the murals aligns them with an ancient tradition of church painting.[13] Their works may not be sacred in the traditional Christian sense, but they are sensitive to the inherent expression of human spirituality and respect for spirit of place found in much ecclesiastical art. Both the rural location and church patronage placed the work beyond the dictates of official war work and demands of the art market. As this was not a government-sponsored commission, the artists were not required to find a language to depict fractured and disorienting scenes of bombings or to produce cheering propaganda. Their specific rural location in the village of Berwick required them to respond appropriately to the immediate environment and wartime context there. The results weave together the long histories of the area, telling a story of new faces in old places.

Painting the native landscape as the setting of biblical scenes, the artists put into imagery an idea that Stephen Spender expresses in his book *The Thirties and After*: that 'England was itself sacred' (p. 96). Housed in an ancient church, nestled deep in the Sussex countryside with a graveyard boasting magnificent views of the South Downs, the Berwick Church murals were created at a pivotal point in British history and art history. Established imperialist national identities based on Britain's role at the centre of a vast empire and as a key player in global industry were disintegrating, and new ones celebrating the sensations and routines of everyday life 'on this island' were being forged.[14] Changing social conventions were forcing a revaluation of the role of the church as a central element in national life, whilst conservationist movements attempted to preserve the familiar. Various artistic schemes played out both of these positions, problematising the notion of the countryside as removed from the vicissitudes of the modern-day world.

The countryside that Bell and Grant depict in the Berwick Church murals serves as a reminder of the human activity shaping the natural environment of the parish from both the modern moment and ancient times. Firle Beacon, the site of a neolithic long barrow and several round barrows, and Mount Caburn, an Iron Age hill fort, are visible in the radiant depiction of the landscape that expands away behind Vanessa Bell's *Nativity* and Grant's *Christ in Glory*, and through the window in the *Supper at Emmaus*, respectively.[15] The histories of these ancient human settlements gently assert the existence of human intervention in the landscape over a 6,000-year period, belying ideas about the stasis and naturalisation of the rural landscape, and insisting on its enduring power for creative inspiration. Paradoxically, the distinct moment that Alexandra Harris describes as 'the imaginative claiming of England' in response to the menace of the war occurred largely in relation to the countryside because evidence of modernisation was less visible and the material of the landscape was perceived to be more vulnerable to destruction and destabilisation than the cityscape.[16] By placing contemporary lives into dialogue with older scenes, our muralists invested the past, present and future of the rural landscape and their family's role within it with sacred power, rather than privileging stasis or nostalgia, proving the pliability and endurance of the rooted and regional.

In the face of the chaos of the Second World War, the murals celebrate the simple routines and natural cycles that structure human lifespans. Quentin Bell's *The Sacraments* roundels on the rear of the chancel screen depict the rites and rituals of the St Michael and All Angels community, and Grant's *The Seasons* roundels depict seasonal rural labour. The pastoral setting is not only identifiably English, but also specific to the artists' East Sussex location. Drawing on their immediate landscape and populace for material, the murals provide a record of the artists' household and the agricultural activities that constituted local wartime existence. Grant shows the September harvest, and winter skaters crossing a frozen pond that looks very like the one at Charleston; Quentin Bell includes a baptism party outside of Berwick Church. Vanessa Bell's *Nativity* and *Annunciation* scenes actively illustrate T. S. Eliot's idea of the local parish's attachment 'to the soil' by using a cast of local people, armed with locally grown and manufactured props as models.[17] Locally grown produce, including carrots, cabbages and turnips, is presented in a Sussex trug (a traditional, hand-made basket) in *The Nativity*, rather than the more traditional luxury gifts of gold, frankincense and myrrh. The Charleston garden's horticultural yields clearly influenced Bell's work during this period, and a similar arrangement of vegetables, probably nurtured by Walter Higgins to supplement the family's war rations, can be found in Bell's private practice, in her painting of longstanding housekeeper Grace Higgins working in *The Kitchen* (1943).

Annunciation pictures Bell and Grant's daughter as the Virgin, with her friend Chattie Salaman as Gabriel, viewed just inside the doors of the artist's ground floor bedroom, the symbolic *hortus conclusus* of the walled

Figure 14.1 Preparatory study for *The Annunciation*, Vanessa Bell, c. 1942, graphite on paper. Angelica Garnett Gift, Charleston, © The Estate of Vanessa Bell. Courtesy of Henrietta Garnett.

garden behind them (Plate 12). A preparatory study of Salaman posing as the angel can be seen in the collection of several thousand works on paper and canvas held at Charleston and known as the Angelica Garnett Gift, giving an insight into Bell's working process (Figure 14.1). Bell's mother, Julia Duckworth Stephen, who was also an atheist, had posed as the Virgin Mary in 1879 for Burne-Jones's *Annunciation* (1876–9) while pregnant with Bell. This intergenerational mirroring suggests that Bell is purposefully depicting her own family as the Holy Family, making her case for their sacred import. Investing this scene with symbols of the things most sacred to her, Bell's transformative reimagining is no less radical and disturbing than Salvador Dalí's *Atavisms at Twilight* (1933–4), a reworking of Millet's *The Angelus* (1857–9), or Alberto Savinio's Surrealist *Annunciation*, in which the artist transforms the Virgin's head into that of a pelican to symbolise maternal self-sacrifice.

Other elements in the murals that insist on the integration of the modern and local in scenes of the ancient and sacred are the children in *Nativity* worshipping at the crib, who current rector Peter Blee identifies as 'Ray

Figure 14.2 Duncan Grant, *Christ in Glory*, Berwick Church, 1943, oil on board. Berwick Church, © The Estate of Duncan Grant.

and Bill West' and 'John Higgins', the sons of the Charleston gardener and housekeeper, dressed in the uniform of the local village school (p. 75). Blee recognises the lamb as an example of 'the South Downs breed developed by John Ellman, grandfather of the nineteenth-century rector of Berwick Church', pointing to a deliberate highlighting of continuities (p. 80). The Holy Family, the Virgin Mary again modelled on Angelica Garnett, the Christ child on Quentin Bell as a baby, are surrounded by local shepherds carrying Pyecombe crooks, a regional variety made in the village of Pyecombe, fifteen miles from Charleston. The numerous preliminary sketches for the murals in the Angelica Garnett Gift demonstrate the intensity of the artists' focus on this commission. Many are annotated, revealing the accuracy of the working process and the importance placed on obtaining details like measurements of the height of the crook and commentary on the colour scheme. As spiritual leader of the congregation, Reverend George Mitchell (Rector of Berwick during the period the paintings were created) also carries a Pyecombe crook in Grant's *Christ in Glory* (Figure

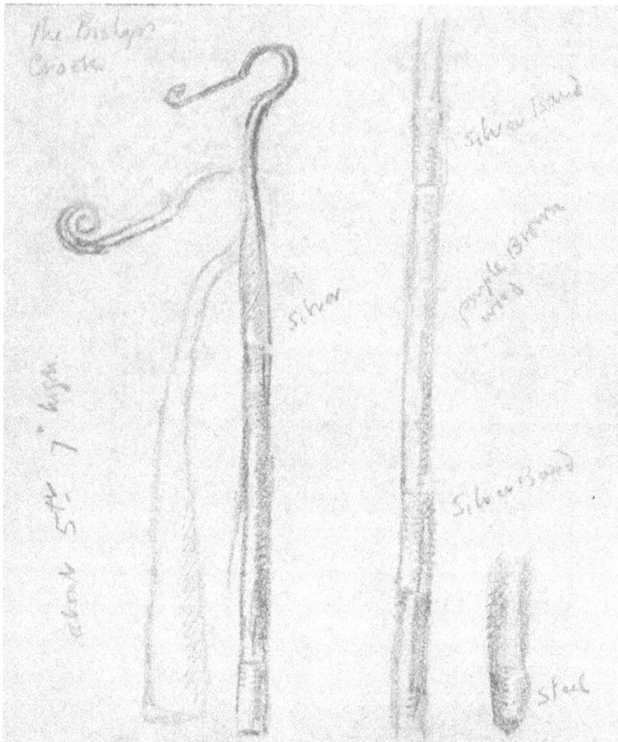

Figure 14.3 Duncan Grant, 'The Bishop's Crook' study, c.1943. Angelica Garnett Gift, Charleston, © The Estate of Duncan Grant.

14.2), depicting a regional shepherd for a local flock – a concept with real meaning in this location. A sketch labelled 'The Bishop's Crook' shows the level of attention Grant bestowed on this small detail, and the fact that the crook held by Mitchell was originally intended to be held by Bishop Bell (Figure 14.3). Other drawings in the Angelica Garnett Gift evincing Bishop Bell's involvement as a model for the paintings and suggesting that he offered his possessions for the artists to study for the project include a preliminary sketch of him kneeling as he appears at the right-hand side of the arch in the completed mural *Christ in Glory*, in which the hook of the crook appears to be looped around his right hand (Figure 14.4), and a detailed study of his mitre, an item that does not appear in the final work.

The Church in conflict

The Berwick Church murals were part of a broader trend for figures ranging from bishops to petroleum company marketing directors to

Figure 14.4 Duncan Grant, 'Dr Bell Kneeling' study, c.1943, graphite on paper. Angelica Garnett Gift, Charleston, © The Estate of Duncan Grant.

artists of many stripes to address the topographical, organisational and spiritual roles the Church played in contemporary English life. Some sought to forge fresh and dynamic relationships between the Church and contemporary culture, particularly in rural areas, others to reinstate reactionary norms. For example, the 'Recording Britain' scheme was inaugurated by Sir Kenneth Clark at the outbreak of the Second World War to create a watercolour archive of beauty spots, including ancient churches threatened by war and development. Its four categories were: 'A: Fine Tracts of Landscape'; 'B: Towns and Villages'; 'C: Parish Churches' and 'D: Country Houses and their Parks', and Clark emphasised that subjects ought to be selected as 'characteristic' of a sense of [the] historical continuity', rather than for 'outstanding architectural merit'.[18] The approved scenes were recognised as particularly significant heritage sites due to their stasis. Concurrently, this acknowledgement of their material and psychosocial vulnerability revealed that they were, in fact, contested sites of modernity. A similar contradiction animates posters of the 1920s and 1930s commissioned by Shell Petroleum's publicity director, Jack Beddington. Intended to advance the very modern interests of the petroleum industry through advertising motor tourism, these posters focused on supposedly quintessential, unchanging rural scenes; several, like Vanessa Bell's *Alfriston*, prominently feature a village church.

Some Berwick parishioners saw the murals project as detrimental to the sanctity of the church. One resident, 'a well-known churchwoman, the Hon. Mrs Sandilands', objected so strongly to the project that she entered an Act of Petition, which meant that the case had to be tried before a Consistory Court.[19] Mrs Sandilands and her supporters' grounds were not merely aesthetic. They objected to both the decorations and the decorators – as the Tate website records, specifically, to 'modern' artists creating the murals.[20]

The correspondence from the trial between the various parties involved gives an insight not only into the plans for the artworks but also into the values and position of the protestors. Mrs Sandilands was not the only member of the community who disapproved of the work being carried out during wartime. She wrote to the Bishop:

> Mr Grant must be a strong and very clever man to be able to do this strenuous job of mural painting; let him turn his talents in other directions for the time being to help his country as so many others are doing.[21]

The artists were pacifists and had been conscientious objectors during the First World War, when, instead of performing military service, Grant had undertaken farm labour. There was a great degree of social stigma attached to being a conscientious objector and the plaintiffs attempted to use this as part of their case against the project. A document from 17 September 1941 notes that Mrs Turner, a member of the jam-making centre run by Mrs Sandilands, claimed: 'it is said that one of the artists is a conscientious objector' at the trial as evidence against the artists.[22] The criticism was ostensibly levelled against Quentin Bell but Grant defended them all with his response:

> I myself am, at present, above the age for military service, and have to make my living painting, which is my profession. Mrs Clive Bell is also a professional artist, Mr Quentin Bell who by profession is also an artist, has not been accepted for Military Service for reasons of health, having been in the first instance persecuted from joining the territorials on these grounds. He is now driving a tractor on a farm.[23]

Mrs Sandilands inadvertently raised pertinent questions about the value of culture and the purpose of the war. Grant was, in fact, also employed as an official war artist, and his *Christ in Glory* chronicling Berwick complements this body of wartime art.

Resistance to the murals seems also to have arisen from the artists' estrangement from members of Berwick village. The inhabitants of Charleston had had limited involvement with Berwick village beyond the commission, and writing in *Charleston Past and Present* (1987), Angelica Garnett confirmed their private existence, stating that they made no effort to intermingle with the locals and that 'we owed nothing to our neighbours with whom we had little contact; locally we played no social role, and it was largely this that gave us our sense of freedom'.[24] Yet the war intervened within this structure of social separation between outsiders and interlopers. The famously taciturn Vanessa Bell began to participate more in the local community, joining the pig club, teaching art at Millers Gallery and Art Centre in Lewes, and temporarily taking in refugees and relations. The consequences of modern history eroded previous divisions and caused new interactions to take place within the parish.

The triumphant outcome of the trial suggests the innovation and adaptation inherent in local examples of rural modernity. Just as Paul Nash had argued that it was possible to be both British and Modern in the early 1930s and exercised his modernism in a body of work consisting mainly of rural landscapes, the legal action surrounding the mural made a strong case that the countryside could, without losing its sense of identity, foster international connections and serve as a fertile ground for modern art.[25] Whilst the support of influential patrons from outside the area may ostensibly seem to be a case of trespassers imposing metropolitan values on to a rural community, this view would misrepresent the existing creative and 'subcultural' aspects of country living and imply that the values of Mrs Sandilands and her supporters were hegemonic.

Memorialisation, commemoration, community

By July 1940, places within ten miles of the south coast, including the Sussex villages around Berwick and Charleston, were under threat of invasion and declared a 'restricted area', with roadblocks set up and incomers checked. Less than ten miles from Charleston at Rodmell, Virginia Woolf recorded hearing air battles taking place overhead and, writing in her diary, noted:

> Yesterday, 18th, Sunday, there was a roar. Right on top of us they came. I looked at the plane, like a minnow at a roaring shark. Over they flashed – 3, I think. Olive green. Then pop pop pop – German? Again pop pop pop, over Kingston. Said to be 5 Bombers hedge hopping on their way to London. The closest shave so far.[26]

Bell and Grant were sharing the same Sussex sky, and Bell's private letters disclose her feelings of agitation and futility caused by the war. She wrote to friend and fellow artist Janie Bussy on 6 June 1940, asking 'Are you and your father able to work? I hope so. Sometimes it seems to me very difficult but then again one gets so miserable if one doesn't that one has to make an effort and at least keep oneself sane.'[27] Bell remained at Charleston throughout the Second World War. There she would have heard local accounts of soldiers returning home that resonated with the recent loss of her eldest son Julian in the Spanish Civil War in 1937.

As a result of the context of war in which they were created, the Berwick Church murals have sacred resonances in their function as memorials recording how deeply scarred by loss the English countryside became. After the finishing touches had been put to the murals in 1943, Douglas Hemming, the soldier Grant depicted in *Christ in Glory*, was killed near Caen at the age of 26 (Figure 14.2). By sensitively and individualistically showing the three uniformed men – sailor Mr Weller, airman Mr Humphrey and Hemming, 'son of the local station master' – not as proud warriors but peacefully worshipping amid their community, *Christ in Glory* situates them within a localised rural context and refers to their national duty.[28] The death of one of the men is memorialised by the mural but so too are the lives of everyday citizens who also faced war, making the murals an important piece of social history as well as Second World War art.

Amid their work on the project, the artists experienced their own personal losses. In 1941, Virginia Woolf committed suicide in the River Ouse. Kenneth Clark commented that the suffering caused by her death was representative of the period of adversity they were living through: 'To lose Virginia Woolf just now seems symbolic of the general loss of all fairness.'[29] Like Clark, Angelica Garnett saw the loss of her aunt as part of the wider collapse of the world they knew and cherished. Writing in her autobiography, *Deceived with Kindness* (1984), she notes that 'Virginia's death merely confirmed the general sense of pessimism and sense of futility which surrounded us.'[30] Yet the murals do not convey a sense of grieving and pessimism; rather, through their improbable creation against a backdrop of opposition, atheism and war, and in their depiction of scenes of family life with both ancient and modern precedents, they achieve a sense of overarching faith in the value of ordinary human life, beauty and art. Richard Shone recorded that Kenneth Clark was 'delighted with the two panels by Mrs Bell. They seem to me to be amongst the best things she has ever done.'[31] While religion provided no comfort to the artists during their bereavements, the visual and verbal record suggests that painting an ordinary community and landscape at an ancient site of human continuity and connection offered the artists a means of facing their wartime frustrations and constructing local community amid the chaos of war.

The early function of public sacred art was to allow illiterate believers to comprehend biblical stories visually. Many modern viewers became alienated from religious works, regarding them as full of arcane symbolism. The Berwick murals, in concert with ecclesiastical works like Hans Feibusch's murals, rendered the stories, emotions and essential humanity of these subjects comprehensible once more. While the cathedrals of Rome demanded formal grandeur, the community centres of rural and semi-rural Sussex enabled a more sensitive and emotive art, an art that represented the ancient and modern, the biblical and local.

Although it is possible on a glorious summer's day to construe Charleston as an 'Eden', it is by no means a time capsule immune from war or indeed from other intrusions of modernity such as the railway, telephone and tourism. The Berwick Church murals address the ongoing human cultivation and commemoration of community in an epoch of world war and globalisation. The Charleston artists became part of a generation of cultural custodians consciously and carefully developing a living heritage.

In dialogue with: Chapter 4 'Weighing Down the Landscape' (II: Landscapes) [painting; regional art and archives]; Chapter 11 'Beyond Portmeirion' (IV: Heritage) [built environment; rural dissent].

Notes

1. Clarke, p. 145.
2. The clergyman was no relation to Vanessa Bell or her wider family, and for clarity, only the artist will be referred to as 'Bell' throughout. Bishop Bell was a leading figure in mid-century church reform, playing vital roles in the Ecumenical movement, the Christian Council for Refugees, the formation of Christian Aid, and the Campaign for Nuclear Disarmament.
3. Bishop Bell, 'Enthronement address', quoted by Blee, 'Bishop Bell of Chichester'.
4. Marler, p. 472.
5. Vanessa Bell to Angelica Bell, 24 November 1941. Quoted in Spalding, *Duncan Grant*, p. 382.
6. Vanessa Bell to Margery Snowden, 6 April 1904; Marler, p. 13.
7. Vanessa Bell to Quentin Bell, 9 June 1952; Marler, p. 153.
8. The January 1922 front cover of the Guild's monthly magazine bears the quotation 'I am the Lord thy God who brought thee out of the land of Egypt and out of the house of bondage' (Exodus 20:2); *The Game: A*

Monthly Magazine, 1922. See Hope Wolf, *Sussex Modernism, Retreat and Rebellion* for an account of the Guild at Ditchling within the context of Sussex modernism.

9. This was not confined exclusively to rural locations, and Feibusch and Piper both also created works for urban churches, of a range of denominations. Feibusch's first commission was for the Methodist Chapel in Colliers Wood, London, in 1939; Piper designed stained-glass windows for many sacred spaces, including Liverpool's Catholic Cathedral, though this was largely after 1950.
10. Wolf, p. 9.
11. See Abercrombie, *Preservation*, and Williams-Ellis, *England and the Octopus*.
12. Reproduced in Spalding, *Virginia Woolf*, p. 116.
13. Roger Fry used this phrase in his sustained formal analysis of church mural painting in 'Giotto', p. 97.
14. W. H. Auden, 'On This Island'.
15. See Wainwright, p. 231, and also Drewett and Hamilton.
16. Harris, *Romantic Moderns*, p. 10.
17. Eliot, *Idea*, p. 27.
18. Clark, 'A Scheme', p. 12. The MS is in the Pilgrim Trust Archives LMA/4450/C/01/0042 RB (1939–53).
19. Shone, p. 5.
20. 'Berwick Church decorations: Grant and Bell'.
21. Shone, p. 6.
22. 19 August 1941. Berwick Papers, West Sussex Archive.
23. 28 September 1941. Berwick Papers, West Sussex Archive.
24. Bell, Garnett, Garnett and Shone, p. 117.
25. See Nash, '"Going Modern" and "Being British"', p. 323.
26. *The Diary of Virginia Woolf, Volume Five*, 19 August 1940, p. 330.
27. Marler, p. 470.
28. Blee, *The Bloomsbury Group in Berwick Church*, p. 101
29. Kenneth Clark to Vanessa Bell, 1941. SxMs56: The Charleston Papers, The Keep.
30. Garnett, p. 191.
31. Shone, *The Berwick Church Paintings*, p. 16.

Chapter 15

Rural Modernity in a Time of Crisis: Preservation and Reform in the Books of B. T. Batsford

Peter Lowe

Writing in 1943, Charles Fry looked back with satisfaction on the decision taken in the 1930s by the publishing firm of B. T. Batsford to switch production from the lavish books on culture and landscape that had made its late-Victorian reputation to a new range of inexpensive volumes aimed at widening public awareness of the natural and man-made environment of Britain. 'I think we can honestly say', he reflected, 'that in presenting these cheap books to the public we performed an important service in revealing the immense wealth of its heritage and in stimulating appreciation which, in time, leads to preservation and respect.'[1] At a time when, as David Matless notes, domestic tourism was rising in popularity and it was feared that motorists in search of unspoilt rural idylls would destroy those very idylls even as they sought them out, Fry remained convinced that Batsford's two series of books – British Heritage and The Face of Britain – offered a 1930s readership not only the opportunity to learn more about the country and the inspiration to go and see its riches for themselves, but also an underlying reminder of the need, through enjoyment of Britain's heritage, to assume responsibility for its preservation too.[2]

Heritage in peacetime

Rather than target the upper reaches of the book-buying market, the volumes in British Heritage and The Face of Britain sold for 7s 6d each, giving readers a richly illustrated series of guides to British life at a relatively cheap price. Indeed, Fry recalled that others in the publishing trade had concluded that, with the number of photographs in each volume, the low price would prove as unsustainable a business model as the country villages they celebrated, but he noted with satisfaction how wrong those assumptions were. Having risked a 10,000-book initial print run for each title, he could report in 1943 that almost all volumes had sold their initial printings and that several were already in fourth or fifth editions.

Looking at these books today, it is easy to see why they were successful. Catherine Brace argues that Batsford's output 'naturalised a version of rural England in which timelessness and continuity were powerful recurring motifs' (p. 367). Each volume deals with a specific region of the country (in the case of the Face of Britain series) or a facet of national culture (in the British Heritage series) in which the words 'The English' precede 'Castle', 'Abbey', Village Church', 'Country House', 'Garden' or some similar topic. The prose is clear and accessible, and line drawings and photographs help the reader appreciate the development of the building or feature under discussion. To complete the package, each book came with a brightly coloured dust jacket featuring a design by Brian Cook (nephew of the company chair, Harry Batsford), printed using Art Deco colours that rendered the 'traditional' scene in a strikingly modern way. A shelf full of such books would, the company's publicity suggested, make a fine addition to any room, and judging from the prices that copies of many volumes fetch today (particularly if the dust jacket is intact and not too faded), the books have lost none of their collectable appeal.

In focus and content, the British Heritage series of books was arguably more about 'England' than any concept of a 'British' identity. Of the twenty-seven volumes in the series, twenty-two featured 'England' or 'English' in their titles, with a twenty-third being devoted solely to *The Spirit of London*. Two volumes were allocated to Scotland, and Ireland and Wales received one volume each. The Face of Britain series was slightly more egalitarian, although of the twenty-three volumes sixteen were focused on English regions, with Scotland receiving two, Ireland one and Wales one. A further two were dedicated to *Scottish Border Country* and *Welsh Border Country* (thereby blending English content with that of the country on the other side of the border), while T. G. Miller's *Geology and Scenery in Britain* at least provided an overview of the country as a geological entity.[3]

Although they represent a particularly successful story, in the interwar period the Batsford books were by no means unique in their focus on those elements of British life – embodied either in the buildings and landscapes of the country or in the patterns of life found within them – that informed a sense of national 'uniqueness' in a rapidly changing world. The rhetoric of national defence had been strong in the First World War, even though Britain itself was not (naval bombardments and the odd Zeppelin raid excepted) materially threatened in the way that other nations certainly were. In the 1920s and 1930s, as the trauma of the war was processed by a shocked nation, images of stability and ordered tranquillity were welcome, and recognition of the longevity of rural life was woven into nostalgia for an age when technology was not seen to have been so pervasive. This nostalgia was itself problematic, of course. The photographs in Batsford guides of country villages, churches or public houses were often carefully manipulated so that overhead cables and motor vehicles were not visible – the latter an ironic touch when much of the books' content inspired readers to visit, by car usually, the sites that had been introduced to them in their armchair travels.

Much of the rhetoric in interwar travel writing sounds a warning note when it comes to the risk of the rural idyll being overrun by modernity in its various forms. The dust jacket of Clough Williams-Ellis's *England and the Octopus* (1928) used a cartoon to depict the 'octopus' of ribbon development (by which towns spread their 'tentacles' of roads into the countryside, thereby claiming ever more land for building) as a giant pink creature, with a very English bowler hat, sitting atop the buildings of an idyllic village, the church, country house and thatched cottages obscured by its spread (Figure 11.1). Williams-Ellis, himself an architect, went on to edit a collection of essays, *Britain and the Beast* (1937), in which a host of commentators call for urgent action to defend and safeguard the fragile beauty of a land aware of its riches but aware too of the ease with which they could be lost. In his own contribution to the volume, S. P. B. Mais (later to become a Batsford author) challenged his readers to consider what had already come to pass in England, and what they intended to do to arrest this dreadful process. Suggesting that his readers would 'shudder at the thought of Salisbury Cathedral being converted into a cinema', Mais provocatively assures them that 'in your own lifetime you have seen changes as dreadful . . . village after village being torn asunder to permit of an arterial road running through it . . . wanton destruction proceeding without a murmur of dissent in the name of "progress"'.[4]

Rather than hymn the beauties of the village or hamlet as though they could never be lost, the Batsford books reminded readers of the need for responsible tourism and, where necessary, for a willingness to raise one's voice in protest at decisions made that disturbed the delicate balance upon which the nation's beauty rested. In *Cotswold Country* (1937), H. J. Massingham considers the broad sweep of limestone-rich geology that runs across the country from Dorset in the west to Lincolnshire in the east, noting that the Cotswold belt possesses an essential harmony in terms of landscape and architectural fabric that makes it clearly identifiable amongst other areas of England. He then laments that, in recent years, this regïonal 'character' has come under threat from an 'invader, a barbarian impervious to the values and harmonies in instinctive loyalty to which man has from age to age translated the manuscript of the earth into the terms of his own thought and use'. This menace is, in short, the building industry, which wilfully ignores 'the varieties in expression of the *genius loci* . . . between the raw material below and the finished structure above the ground'. To study, as the informed Batsford reader should, this 'rhythmic interplay between beginnings and ends, element and product, is to become conscious of a violation of the essential order of things in the act of breaking this cardinal law' (p. 3).

An oppositional relationship between the rural and the modern is very much in evidence here, and it may indeed be said that the Batsford books published before 1939 explicitly voice their anxiety over the modern erosion of the traditional ways of life and the spaces within which they were framed. The ribbon development, the litter-dropping tourist, the new houses built with the wrong stone, the new entertainment media that draw young people away from the village and into the town for leisure, the increasingly busy road widened to accommodate more traffic: all of these threatened the rural idyll that was so crucial a part of what the nation had always been. To buy and read a Batsford book was not only to be enlisted in a community of people celebrating the riches of one's national heritage, but also to recognise one's own share in that heritage and, correspondingly, one's responsibility for its preservation in a hostile age.

Wartime

Having been encouraged for much of the 1930s to regard the heritage of their country as 'threatened' by the forces of modernity, the British public were, in many respects, perfectly conditioned to respond when that same country was threatened with invasion in the summer of 1940. Villages like those praised in a Batsford volume were reproduced in the pages of *Picture Post* in its 6 July 1940 issue, where a feature entitled 'The Land We Are Fighting For' included views of the villages of Kersey (Suffolk), Wilmcote (Warwickshire) and Broadhembury (Devon). The difference now was that the danger facing these idylls was even more urgent than that of ribbon development or increased road traffic. The following week, the magazine was published under the title 'What We Are Fighting For' and, unsurprisingly, the village, as a location and a symbol, featured heavily. One view of an English village, which would not look at all out of place in a Batsford guide, showed a shepherd driving his sheep through an empty street past the church, reproduced with the title 'Sunday Afternoon in England: All is Peace'. On the opposite page, the caption 'Sunday Afternoon in Germany: All is Peace' shows massed ranks of Sturmabteilung (SA) men marching through the flag-lined streets as bystanders look on.[5] Presented as they are on opposite pages, it is easy – for the reader looking back and forth between the images – to place the marching men mentally in the English village and, in doing so, imagine a situation in which the German reality could swiftly become an English one.

There was more to England (or, indeed, Britain) than the village green and the medieval church, of course, but, in trying to articulate a sense of what was simultaneously most vulnerable and most valuable about the country, it was easy to conflate the semi-pastoral locations and the sense of older, 'traditional' ways of life persisting within them, to give a vision of an 'unchanging' land in need of defence. Batsford's publications had put the nation's heritage on the 'frontline' before the war started: it was just that the enemy had assumed a more direct and more threatening form as the *Wehrmacht* waited on the Channel coasts for the signal that Operation Sealion (the codename for the German invasion of Britain) was to begin. In 1942, with the war still very much in the balance, the artist Frank Newbould was commissioned by the Army Bureau of Current Affairs to supply images for a series of propaganda posters, each with the slogan 'Your Britain: Fight for it Now'. The images he produced were guaranteed to invoke the sense of attachment to 'Britain' that would turn civilians into soldiers. In one, an oak tree spreads across a village green, around which are clumped traditional cottages, a pub and the entrance to a churchyard. In another, young and old enjoy a funfair on the village green at Alfriston in East Sussex – a world of swing boats and carousels utterly at odds with images of the regimented 'leisure' that the Third Reich afforded its subjects. In another, Salisbury Cathedral is seen framed by trees in a view not dissimilar to the famous paintings by John Constable that were stored for safekeeping in a slate mine in Wales with the rest of the National Gallery's collection. Finally, in the image entitled 'South Downs', the viewer is in Sussex again, as a shepherd and his flock make their way homeward to a farm set in a valley. Aside from the funfair rides, no indication of modernity is visible in these images. Fight to keep Britain materially intact, the posters urge the viewer, and fight to preserve the patterns of life that have carried on unchanged within it. With echoes of Cook's dust jacket designs clearly visible, Newbould's art made sure that the 'Batsford country' was fully engaged in the war effort.

As physical objects, the Batsford books themselves were actually playing a vital wartime role simply by being available when others were not. As nearly all the titles in the Heritage and Face of Britain series sold their initial 10,000 copy print runs in the years before the war, Harry Batsford's decision to order reprints of all of them at the very start of the conflict was an inspired piece of thinking. The business had been relocated to Malvern in Worcestershire after the Munich Crisis of 1938, enabling employees to feel closely connected to the England that its books promoted so avidly, working 'with the country coming generously right up to our doorstep', as he wrote in 1943.[6] While other publishers were trying to replace bomb-damaged stock or to cope with paper rationing, Batsford had thousands of works ready to satisfy the demands of a reading public grateful for any new material, releasing books on to the market in the second half of the war in a business decision that also proved to have enormous significance for the ongoing debate over the fate of England's social and cultural fabric. Aside from the commercial benefits of Batsford's wartime publishing policy, their books served to keep the theme and the *idea* of England's heritage at the forefront of peoples' minds while the struggle to defend that heritage was most intense.

Given that the majority of pages in each volume were printed before the war, there was often little opportunity to incorporate wartime alterations into the text, and this increased the risk of the books referring to locations that no longer quite matched their prewar condition. The 1942 reprint of *The Cathedrals of England* still featured a photograph and description of Coventry Cathedral, with a single sentence appended to the entry noting the destruction of the building in a bombing raid of November 1940. In a sense, though, this slippage between the reality of the book and that of the country reinforced the idea of England as a fundamentally regenerative entity. The dust jacket blurb of F. H. Crossley's 1941 volume, *English Church Craftsmanship*, for example, expressed the hope that 'the wanton destruction lately of some of the heritage of English Church Craftsmanship at London, Bristol, Coventry and elsewhere will perhaps direct attention to the riches which still remain to us in our churches, often unregarded, misunderstood, and neglected'. The destruction of cultural sites in bombing raids is, subtly, equated with their already having been 'lost' to people through a general lack of interest or understanding. As the book seeks, on the one hand, to *preserve* in its content places that are at risk of destruction, it also seeks to *reclaim* this heritage for the enjoyment of all, making church craftsmanship part of a wider 'England' standing against the Nazi threat and enduring, even when it appears most threatened.

While the British Heritage books celebrated continuity, they also carried a clear message of reform for unsatisfactory aspects of the prewar world. It often proved to be the case that those guides that, in their prewar editions, held up the past as a measure of the shortcomings of the present became, when reissued in wartime, still more vocal in their criticisms of those failings of planning or construction that had left

1930s England feeling so at odds with itself. This may be seen in Clive Rouse's *The Old Towns of England*, first published in 1936 and reissued in 1944. In the first edition, Rouse provides a spirited defence of the town, representing, as it does, 'a heritage we cannot prize too highly or protect too strenuously', adding that if familiarity has led us to take for granted the church, the market square, the town hall, or the river with its elegant houses, it requires only imagination to roll back the years and connect such places with the flow of life that they have seen (p. 1). 'Traditions and institutions die hard in this country', Rouse observes, and 'when one has the ancient setting for them, as we have in so many of our old towns, it is a combination of which to be justly proud' (p. 3).

Even before the war, Rouse acknowledges that towns were changing as old buildings were demolished and roads widened to accommodate increased traffic. The process of demolition – already well advanced in peacetime – had, however, been greatly exacerbated by the war, as whole districts had been lost to enemy bombs, bringing to a crisis issues evident long before its own beginning. 'It is unfortunately the fact that many of our local councils are responsible for almost as much destruction as the Luftwaffe,' Rouse argues, reminding the reader that the combination of speculative building and minimal co-ordination on the part of local authorities and planners is a destructive mix (p. 5).

In his preface to the second edition, Rouse tells his reader that, since the book's first appearance, 'some slight modifications in the text' have been necessitated by the outbreak of the war – an understatement, perhaps, when he adds that, in some cases, a book that was, on its first appearance, a celebration of town life is now perhaps one that 'must therefore be regarded as mainly historical in character' (p. v). The fact that Rouse thanks his publishers for undertaking on his behalf so many of the changes to the work assumes added poignancy when we see that his Preface is dated 'Officers' Mess, R.A.F Medmenham, Autumn 1943', thus showing the author to be very much a part of the defence of those towns that he praises. Even at this point, however, his thoughts are as much in the future as in the past, noting that whilst neither prewar mistakes nor wartime destruction can be undone, the cause of urban preservation may yet prosper in the postwar years.

In the same way that B. T. Batsford had anticipated the urgency of 'national defence' before the war and kept the issue at the forefront of the reader's mind during it, the firm's authors anticipated the reformist agenda that would sweep Britain in 1945. Surveying what had been spared from destruction, they were also looking at what had been altered by the war and what, more importantly, would need reform in the future. Rather than lapse into nostalgia, its books were fully engaged in advocating a better version of British life, in which the phrase 'Your Britain, Fight for it Now' was both a rallying cry for tradition and a manifesto for reform. Both the town and the countryside had been blighted by wartime destruction. Could a new, more balanced relationship be forged through their combined reconstruction and renewal?

Planning for peacetime again

The Batsford books had hymned the 'traditions' of English life, but they had never wholly ignored the fact that traditions develop organically and that simply resisting all forms of change was both impossible and – in the final analysis – self-defeating. To ensure that postwar Britain emerged in the best condition, it was necessary to see the conflict as an agent for change not only in its capacity to redefine people's sense of 'town' and 'country' as they were displaced or evacuated, but also in fostering a sense of national cohesion in which people thought more about common values than differences. Batsford volumes had kept alive a sense of the idyll when it was impossible to see it in any form beyond the printed page, and it was important that such a country should be felt to be still in existence. At the same time, though, when the tide of war seemed to have turned in the Allies' favour, and thoughts turned with it away from the survival of the prewar order towards the (re)construction of a postwar one, the company's products would, once again, help to shape the debate by advocating thoughtful planning for a postwar society.

Traces of this position were evident in those publications that were actually composed *during* the war rather than updated from prewar text, such as S. P. B. Mais's 1943 volume *The Home Counties* in the Face of Britain series. Before the reader is allowed into the text of his survey of Essex, Surrey, Hertfordshire, Kent and Middlesex, Mais provides a 'Prefatory Note', pondering the nature of 'home' within a wartime frame, blending nostalgia for what is unavailable (either briefly or indefinitely on account of service overseas or domestic evacuation) with hints of a renewed sense of purpose for the postwar world in which there will be 'a tremendous home-coming [with] rich compensations for our present deprivations'.[7] England, Mais reminds his reader, is essentially still *there*, whether one has been fighting abroad or evacuated from one's home in a large town or city. On the dust jacket design for the volume (painted by Brian Cook in 1941), a red bus winds its way through a quiet country landscape, replete with a church, cottages and signs of farming in the fields (Figure 15.1). In the foreground, a milepost reads 'London XX miles', and in the distance, rows of houses with grey roofs

Figure 15.1 Brian Cook, dust jacket design for *The Home Counties*, by S. P. B. Mais, Batsford, 1943. Reproduced with kind permission of B. T. Batsford, part of Pavilion Books Company Limited.

(as opposed to the rustic brown of the countryside) can be seen receding from the viewer. The red bus, significantly, is travelling *towards* London, no longer ferrying evacuated people away from the city but taking them back, re-establishing the commuter lifestyle of Home Counties suburbia.

Rather than lament the rise of ribbon development, though, evacuation and relocation due to the necessities of war work became things that could support Batsford's policy of national self-awareness and, where necessary, self-improvement. At the same time as the Heritage series of Batsford guides was appearing in the midst of the war, the publishers also launched another, smaller, project: a series of Home Front Handbooks. These were less expensive (retailing for 3s 6d) but they were still produced to Batsford's high standards, with Brian Cook supplying the dust jacket artwork. The four volumes in the series: Edmund Vale's *How to Look at Old Buildings*, Frances Pitt's *How to See Nature*, Doreen Wallace's *How to Grow Food* and Harry Batsford's *How to See the Country*, were all examples of a desire to introduce the countryside and its contents to those who were, as the publisher's blurb attests, 'living in the country for the first time, that they may use their leisure constructively for their own benefit and for the benefit of the nation in general'.

As in other Batsford publications, the process of coming to understand how a street, town or city has developed as an architectural and social entity leads to understanding something of the life of the community it houses. Leading on from that, though, as Edmund Vale told his readers, is the equally important issue of what the *future* of such a place may resemble, a pressing issue indeed in the Britain of 1940:

> It is a fact that through ignorance and lack of resources a lot of unnecessary damage has been done to beautiful and instructive relics of the past. But a lot of good has been done as well. Vandals must be let loose sometimes or our rubbish dumps would never be cleared. And now the vandals have had a good innings and a new war has interrupted both building and demolition it is high time that the local inhabitant took stock of things before electing new fathers to influence the destinies of his native place. (p. 88)

The war, halting as it is has both building *and* demolition, thus affords time to think, to reflect on the current state of things, and to consider what will be required in the future – a future in which Batsford readers are encouraged to feel they have a role to play.

Batsford authors were quick to point out that not all the dilapidation in postwar England could, or should, be ascribed to the Luftwaffe. In 1949, when W. G. Hoskins wrote his survey of *Midland England* and considered the swathe of England from Leicestershire in the west to Huntingdonshire in the east, he found a region where the old ways had long been in decline and the newer suburban world had failed to offer a viable substitute. Visiting the Leicestershire village of Stoke Golding, seeing both 'the beautiful medieval parish church and the tumble-down village houses', he pondered whether

> from the gaping holes in the roofs and the fallen walls [that] it had been hit by a casual bomb intended for a Coventry factory: but it was not an enemy bomb that had done this – it was the impact of modern civilisation. (p. 113)

The country's problems were inherent before the conflict, and Hoskins believes that the war has provided a chance to redress *peacetime* neglect – a chance that he is saddened to see being overlooked:

> When I hear of the difficulties of getting slate from the North Wales quarries so that the housing of homeless millions is held up yet again, I think of . . . the wealth of building stone still in the Midland soil . . . waiting to be used. And yet they are carrying prefabricated (the word is as ugly as the thing it describes) houses, made in distant factories, to plant on top of some of the most beautiful building stone in Oxfordshire and among decent old houses built of it two and three hundred years ago. (p. 113)

Rather than present his reader with a comforting conclusion, Hoskins demands to know whether, with so much to rebuild, Britain should revert to the policies that contributed to its prewar malaise or whether a better country was indeed possible. In *North Midland Country* (first published in late 1948), J. H. Ingram similarly argues that the war was an event that brought to a head issues that had been at work for a long time, pointing out that whilst the current housing shortage is acute, it was through hasty, unplanned development before the war that 'the big industrial centres dumped their surplus populations on the neighbouring countrysides . . . to the detriment of agriculture and natural amenities' (p. xi). This process, under way before the war, was halted by it and, for a moment at least, there is the possibility of a different course, charted with a greater sense of regional/national identity and purpose. It is not just the countryside that has a part to play in this national transformation, however. The postwar nation will also need to address 'the England we are not so proud of':

> The England that has been spoiled by slums (rural as well as urban), by ribbon development and jerry-built housing estates, by the destruction of its woodlands and the pollution of its rivers, by slag-heaps, by surface iron-mining which makes square miles of the countryside look as though a major war had been fought there: so much of England to-day is a sad memorial to years of ruthless exploitation in the sacred name of profit. (p. 19)

It is fascinating that Ingram describes areas of this ruined England in terms suggestive of a battlefield, the ground churned up not by the invasion that never came but polluted and mined by industrial greed. Responding, on one level, to Newbould's pastoral idyll, he suggests that much of rural England was lost *before* the war, broken not by fascism but by the drive for profit that allowed industrialists and speculators 'the power of destroying England for their private gain' (p. 18). If such a situation were allowed to recur in the postwar world, then the struggle to 'fight for' Britain will have been in vain. The opportunity to realign the country must be seized, making sure that the public interest supplants the individual one in the nation's relationship to its land and resources, a coherent scheme in which 'town and regional planning, the decentralisation of government and of industry, future agricultural policy, afforestation, compulsory labour service for youth, these things as well as the question of National Parks and access to the countryside are all linked together' (p. 19). This has the cadence of a manifesto, blending as it does central government schemes and, no less importantly, a devolution of decision making to the local level, as Ingram calls for a revival of the *public* life, for a process of re-engagement with the land and a sense of shared purpose akin to that found in wartime. The 'fight' for the country did not end in 1945; rather, in the postwar world, it was entering its most important phase, and the readers of the Batsford guide to *North Midland Country* are right in the thick of it.

Postwar homes, towns and countryside

If one volume encapsulated Batsford's approach to 'the land of Britain' and its hopes for the future, it was a collection of short essays edited by Gilbert and Elizabeth McAllister and published in the summer of 1945. *Homes, Towns and Countryside* was divided into four sections, each one drawing upon the theme of 'Planning', whether for 'Town and Country', for Industry, for 'the Family and the Community' or with regard to the administration that planning itself would require. Contributors ranged from Professor Sir Patrick Abercrombie, whose plan for London's rebuilding had recently been published, to the Archbishop of York, whose essay, 'Planning for Human Needs', was a call to respect those elements of human nature that could not readily be absorbed into a governmental scheme. In its own words, the book 'presents an outline of a practical plan for Britain', bringing together town and country, industry and agriculture, and pursuing in all areas 'the healthiest environment for men, women, and children' (p. iv).

An indication of what this new Britain might look like can be found on the dust jacket, which is *not* by Brian Cook, marking this study as distinct from Batsford's earlier output, even as its subject matter remains so indebted to such volumes. In Sydney Jones's design we see a semi-rural landscape, where an estate of red-roofed, semi-detached houses sits comfortably next to an angular glass and concrete complex, which may be a school or factory (Plate 13). All of these buildings are framed by trees and hedges, and there are only a few vehicles to be seen on the roads that wind gently through the landscape of green fields. In the middle distance, a more typical Batsford-style hamlet can be seen, its church tower rising above the cottages like a symbol of continuity, while in the far distance we see, as a grey haze, the skyline of London, with the dome of St Paul's, Tower Bridge and the Palace of Westminster readily recognisable as the vanishing point towards which these bucolic country roads are ultimately headed. Rather like the design for Mais's *The Home Counties* volume, we are in a semi-suburban idyll here, both organic and planned, where modernity is never out of proportion. When, in the course of Abercrombie's chapter on 'Towns in the National Pattern', the reader sees photographs of the New Town at Welwyn Garden City in Hertfordshire, the architectural similarities between its building mix and Jones's jacket art are clear.

Gilbert McAllister's introduction leaves the reader in no doubt as to the importance of 'positive planning' in the postwar world. The process of reconstructing the nation is nothing less than the necessary fulfilment of the war effort – a process to be undertaken with all the vigour of the war years, for 'it offers the possibility not of a sterile peace, but a peace in which all the instincts of self-sacrifice and devotion, displayed in the war, may find equal scope in the great constructive task of rebuilding a nation' (p. xiii). Prewar Britain, seen from this vantage point, offers multiple examples of what should *not* be permitted. Whether looking at the depression of its industries, the decline of its rural life, the blight of ribbon development or the lack of a coherent transport policy, the country that entered the war had many faults. Even its cultural life was diminished and 'divorced from everyday life', either by class or by economic barriers that left many feeling alienated (p. xiv). To avoid these mistakes being repeated, the country needed to be rebuilt from the ground up, a process that required clear and decisive action.

Homes, Towns and Countryside offered readers 'a picture . . . of a new and fairer Britain' and guidance for the task ahead:

> It is for us to decide. The crowded city or the pleasant town. The city in decay or the city revitalised. A blighted agriculture or a prosperous and unspoiled countryside. Distressed areas or . . . towns planned and constructed by the best architects and builders. Both are possibilities. We can have which we choose. (p. xxx)

In all the essays that make up the volume, the need for planning is held to be paramount, and with this comes a near-unshakeable faith in the role of the state as a force for good in Britain's rebuilding process.

William Robson's contribution to the volume, for example, reminds the reader that postwar planning is not restricted to the built or natural environment; it extends, through the fabric of the country, into the lives of its people. He argues the need not for more planning staff but for better *trained* planners, more alert to the needs of those they serve, more responsive to the challenges of designing lives as well as buildings. If postwar Britain is to be rebuilt anew, reconstruction must take place on many levels. It is perhaps fitting, then, that the volume closes with the thoughts of the Archbishop of York, making the case for planning in so far as 'only through it can there be met satisfactorily some of the deepest and most persistent of human needs' (p. 160). These needs are found in the home, where space and a degree of comfort combine to create feelings of security and stability. They are found in the workplace, where a sense of purpose and relative security are important. They are found, too, in the desire for a *communal* life, knitted together either by the Church or the institutions of public office. Whilst not denying that much was wrong with the medieval town or village, the Archbishop finds in them a cohesive sense of community absent in the modern age. Today, 'our great towns absorb the individual, and his next-door neighbours ignore him unless he is a nuisance to them. He is uninterested in local politics . . . frequently he is as unaware of the existence of the parish church' (p. 161).

Right at the last, then, *Homes, Towns and Countryside* returns to a familiar Batsford theme: the value of the nation's man-made and natural heritage as a measure of centuries of tradition, spiritual life and human endeavour. In the postwar world, better planning and more coherent policies would be required from government, but these are not the steps towards a fully planned, futuristic utopia so much as the essential reaffirmation of the values that had always underpinned the nation's life. Even in its postwar visions, the reader is urged to appreciate that a 'new' Britain will be happiest if it remains at heart a Batsford country – a land where the rural and the modern could blend harmoniously for the good of all.

In dialogue with: Chapter 3 'Electricity Comes to the Countryside' (I: Networks) [print media; popular visual culture]; Chapter 8 'The Spinster in Eden' (III: Communities) [literary Englands].

Notes

1. Bolitho, p. 66.
2. Matless, pp. 62–70.
3. For a complete list of volumes in both series, see Brian Cook Batsford's *The Britain of Brian Cook*, pp. 140–2.
4. Mais, 'The Plain Man', p. 220.
5. Anon., 'What We Are Fighting For', pp. 10–11.
6. Bolitho, p. 97.
7. Mais, *Home Counties*, p. iii.

Notes on Contributors

Edward Allen is a Lecturer in the Faculty of English, University of Cambridge, and a Fellow of Christ's College. His research spans the nineteenth and twentieth centuries, and is broadly transatlantic in scope. He has a particular interest in the changing forms, institutions and effects of sound culture.

Kristin Bluemel is Professor of English and Wayne D. McMurray Endowed Chair in the Humanities at Monmouth University. Her work in progress is 'Enchanted Wood: Four Women Wood Engravers and the Twentieth-Century Illustrated Book Trade'. She is editor of *Intermodernism: Literary Culture in Mid-Twentieth-Century Britain* (Edinburgh University Press, 2009) and author of *George Orwell and the Radical Eccentrics: Intermodernism in Literary London* (Palgrave, 2004).

Stella Deen is Associate Professor of English and World Literature at the State University of New York at New Paltz. She has published on interwar British women writers Enid Bagnold, Clemence Dane and E. H. Young. She is the editor of *Challenging Modernism: New Readings in Literature and Culture, 1914–45* (Ashgate, 2002). She is currently writing on Dane's guidance for middlebrow readers in *Good Housekeeping*.

Nigel Harrison is an independent scholar currently working on the cultural history of early twentieth-century English architecture. He followed a legal background with heritage management studies at the University of Gloucestershire, where in 2014 he completed his PhD on the life and legacy of Clough Williams-Ellis. He has a monograph on the topic currently in preparation.

Dominic Head is Professor of Modern English Literature at the University of Nottingham, where he served as Head of School from 2007 to 2010. He is the author of eight books, including: *Modernity and the English Rural Novel* (Cambridge University Press, 2017), *Ian McEwan* (Manchester University Press, 2007), *The Cambridge Introduction to Modern British Fiction, 1950–2000* (Cambridge University Press, 2002) and *The Modernist Short Story* (Cambridge University Press, 1992). He is also editor of *The Cambridge Guide to Literature in English*, third edition (Cambridge University Press, 2006), and *The Cambridge History of the English Short Story* (Cambridge University Press, 2016).

Ysanne Holt is Professor of Art History and Visual Culture at Northumbria University. Her research engages with early twentieth-century visual culture in Britain, and her publications include the monograph *British Artists and the Modernist Landscape* (Ashgate, 2003). She is currently preoccupied with cultural landscapes in the rural north, and is co-editor of *Visual Culture in the Northern British Archipelago: Imagining Islands* (Routledge, 2018).

Chris Hopkins is Professor of English at Sheffield Hallam University. He has published *Thinking about Texts – An Introduction to English Studies* (Palgrave, 2001, 2009) and *English Fiction of the 1930s: Language, Genre and History* (Continuum, 2006). His book on Walter Greenwood's *Love on the Dole: Novel, Play, Film* was published by Liverpool University Press in 2018.

Nick Hubble is Reader in English at Brunel University London and the author of *Mass-Observation and Everyday Life: Culture, History, Theory* (Palgrave Macmillan, 2006) and *The Proletarian Answer to the Modernist Question* (Edinburgh University Press, 2017). Co-edited collections include *The Science Fiction Handbook* (Bloomsbury Academic, 2013), *The 1970s* (Bloomsbury Academic, 2014), *The 1990s* (Bloomsbury Academic, 2015), *The 2000s* (Bloomsbury Academic, 2015), *London in Contemporary British Fiction* (Bloomsbury Academic, 2016) and *The 1950s* (Bloomsbury Academic, forthcoming, 2018).

Hana Leaper is the John Moores Painting Prize (JMPP) Senior Lecturer and Development Manager. Based at Liverpool John Moores University (LJMU), she works closely with colleagues at LJMU, the Walker Art Gallery and Shanghai University to lead the development of the JMPP competition, exhibition and archive. She and Polly Mills were the first pair of curatorial fellows to work in Vanessa Bell's studio at Charleston on the Angelica Garnett Gift of over 8,000 works.

Peter Lowe is a Senior Lecturer in English at the Bader International Study Centre (Queen's University Canada), Herstmonceux Castle, East Sussex. His research interest is in the poetry and prose of the Modernist period. He is the author of *English Journeys* (Cambria, 2012), a study of cultural and national identity in Britain in the 1930s and 1940s.

Michael McCluskey is Lecturer in English and Film Studies at the University of York. He is currently working on a monograph on 1930s British documentary and an edited collection on aviation and interwar Britain.

Polly Mills is Project Assistant for the international touring exhibitions at the British Museum. She has also held positions at the National Gallery, Royal Academy and the Peggy Guggenheim Collection, Venice. She and Hana Leaper were the first pair of curatorial fellows to work in Vanessa Bell's studio at Charleston on the Angelica Garnett Gift of over 8,000 works.

Iain Robertson is a historical geographer and Reader in History at the University of the Highlands and Islands. His research interests include the relationship between rural modernities and the deployment of the past in the present as manifest in a sense of heritage from below. In 2012, he published *Heritage From Below* (Ashgate, 2012), a collection of essays that explored global manifestations of the concept.

Samuel Shaw is an art historian, artist and writer. Recent publications include the co-edited collection *Edwardian Culture: Beyond the Garden Party* (Routledge, 2018) and the co-authored *Zebra* (Reaktion, 2018). He currently teaches at the University of Birmingham.

Rosemary Shirley is Senior Lecturer in Art Theory and Practice at Manchester School of Art, Manchester Metropolitan University. Her research looks at everyday life and visual cultures in rural contexts. She is the author of *Rural Modernity, Everyday Life and Visual Culture* (Routledge, 2015) and co-editor of *Creating the Countryside: The Rural Idyll Past and Present* (Paul Holberton, 2017).

Eluned Summers-Bremner is Senior Lecturer in English at the University of Auckland. The author of *Insomnia: A Cultural History* (Reaktion,

2008) and *A History of Wandering* (Reaktion, forthcoming), she is currently working on a history of the sea and human emotions for Reaktion, and on the literature of the Second World War.

Andrew Walker is Assistant Professor of English at Liberty University, Lynchburg, Virginia, where he teaches courses in twentieth-century poetics and drama. He is currently at work on a book-length study of verse drama and its relation to the lyric, treating poets like T. S. Eliot, Gertrude Stein and Derek Walcott, among others.

Bibliography

Primary sources

Abercrombie, Patrick, *The Preservation of Rural England* (London: Hodder & Stoughton, 1926).

[Anon.], 'Mr. Thomas Hardy "Listens In"', *Dorset Daily Echo*, 29 November 1923, p. 1.

[Anon.], 'What We Are Fighting For', *Picture Post*, 13 July 1940, pp. 10–11.

Architectural Press, *The Smaller House: Being Selected Examples of the Latest Practice in Modern English Domestic Architecture* (London: Architectural Press, 1924).

Architecture Club, *Recent English Architecture: 1920–1940, selected by the Architecture Club* (London: Country Life, 1947)

Around the Village Green, dir. by Marion Grierson and Evelyn Spice (TIDA, 1937), British Film Institute Archive.

Auden, W. H., 'On This Island', in *Look, Stranger!* (London: Faber, 1926).

Baldwin, Stanley, 'England', in *On England and Other Addresses* (London: Philip Allan & Co., 1926), pp. 1–16.

Barke, James, 'Lewis Grassic Gibbon', *Left Review*, 2 (1936), 220–5.

Bates, H. E., *Down the River*, with 83 engravings on wood by Agnes Miller Parker (London: Gollancz; New York: H. Holt & Co., 1937; repr. London: Victor Gollancz, 1987).

—, *The Fallow Land* (London: Jonathan Cape, 1932; repr. 1936).

—, *The House with the Apricot and Two Other Tales* (London: Golden Cockerel, 1933).

—, *Through the Woods: The English Woodland – April to April*, with 73 engravings on wood by Agnes Miller Parker (London: Gollancz; New York: Macmillan, 1936; repr. London: Frances Lincoln, 1995).

—, *The Poacher* (London: Jonathan Cape, 1935; repr. London: Breslich & Foss, 1984).

Batsford, Brian Cook, *The Britain of Brian Cook* (London: B. T. Batsford, 1987).

Batsford, Harry, *How to See the Country* (London: Batsford, 1945).

Baudelaire, Charles, 'The Painter of Modern Life', in *The Painter of Modern Life and Other Essays*, trans. by Jonathan Mayne (New York: Phaidon, 1970), pp. 1–40.

Bell, Adrian, *Men and the Fields* (1939; Wimborne Minster: Little Toller Books, 2009).

—, *Corduroy. Silver Ley. The Cherry Tree* (London: John Lane the Bodley Head, 1936).

Bell, Clive, 'The Aesthetic Hypothesis', *Art*, 1914, 1–13, <http://web.mnstate.edu/gracyk/courses/phil%20of%20art/printer-friendly/Clive%20Bell%20Art%20TWO%20COLUMNS.pdf > [accessed 30 March 2017].

Bell, Martin, 'Foreword', in Adrian Bell, *Men and the Fields* (1939; Wimborne Minster: Little Toller Books, 2009), pp. 5–6.

Benjamin, Walter, 'The Storyteller: Reflections on the Works of Nikolai Leskov', in *Illuminations*, ed. by Hannah Arendt, trans. by Harry Zohn (1955; New York: Schocken, 1968).

—, 'Theses on the Philosophy of History', in *Illuminations*, ed. by Hannah Arendt, trans. by Harry Zohn (1955; New York: Schocken, 1968), pp. 253–64.

Bentley, Phyllis, *The English Regional Novel* (London: George Allen and Unwin, 1941).

Berwick Papers, West Sussex Archive.

Blunden, Edmund, *English Villages* (London: Collins, n.d. [1941]).

—, *The Face of England* (London: Longmans, Green, 1932).

Bolitho, Hector, *A Batsford Century* (London: B. T. Batsford, 1943).

Bourne, George, *Change in the Village* (1912; London: Penguin, 1984).

Chair Bodging and Chair Making in the Chiltern Hills, Eustace A. Alliott (1934–5), East Anglia Film Archive.

The Charleston Papers, The Keep, SxMs56.

Chilham: A Kentish Village, John and William Barnes (1934), Screen Archive South East.

Clark, Kenneth, Letter to Vanessa Bell on the loss of Virginia Woolf in 1941, Undated, The Charleston Letters, Container, No 0021158, The Keep, Item Chichester, Bishop of, See Bell, George Kennedy.

—, 'A Scheme for Artists to Record Changing or Vanishing Aspects of Britain', in *Recording Britain*, ed. by Gill Saunders, exhibition catalogue (London: V&A Publishing, 2011).

'Concrete Bridges and Transmission Poles', *Architectural Review*, May 1929, p. 248.

Cooper, Lettice, *National Provincial* (1938; London: Victor Gollancz, 1988).

The Corn Is Green, dir. by Irving Rapper (Warner Brothers, 1945).

Council for the Preservation of Rural England (CPRE), Executive Committee Meeting minutes, 1926–1939, CPRE Archives, SR CPRE A/1–A/4, held at the Museum of English Rural Life, Reading.

Country Magazine, F. P. Barnitt (1930s), Screen Archive South East.

Courtney, Janet, *Countrywomen in Council: The English and Scottish Women's Institutes with Chapters on the Movement in the Dominions and on Townsman's Guilds* (London: Oxford University Press, 1933).

Davies, Margaret Llewelyn, ed., *Life as We Have Known it* (London: Hogarth Press, 1931).

Davies, Rhys, *Daisy Matthews, and Three Other Tales*, with wood engravings by Agnes Miller Parker (Waltham St Lawrence: Golden Cockerel Press, 1932).

Deanston Mill, Perthshire, unknown (c.1923), National Library of Scotland Moving Image Archive.

'A Diagrammatic Representation of the Distribution of Electricity in Rural Areas', *Electricity in the Countryside* (London: BEDA, 1939).

Edwards, Hugh, *Helen between Cupids*, intro. by James Agate, decorated by Agnes Miller Parker (London: Jonathan Cape, 1935).

'Electrical Development', *Architectural Review*, 1 November 1933, p. li.

Electricity in the Countryside (London: BEDA, 1939).

Electricity on the Farm (London: BEDA, 1935).

Eliot, T. S., *The Idea of a Christian Society* (New York: Harcourt, Brace, 1940).

Elsted Manor Farms, Eric Shaxson (1932–48), Screen Archive South East.

Empson, William, *Some Versions of Pastoral* (1935; Harmondsworth: Penguin, 1995).

Evans, Caradoc, *My People*, intro. by John Harris (London: Andrew Melrose, 1915; Bridgend: Seren, 1987).

Evans, Mair, 'Tradition and The Faber Stories', *Wales*, 4 (March 1938), 150.

[Faber & Faber advertisement], *Times Literary Supplement*, 7 June 1934, p. 405.

The Fables of Esope, Translated out of the Frensshe in to Englysshe by William Caxton, with engravings on wood by Agnes Miller Parker (Newtown, Montgomeryshire: Gregynog Press, 1931).

Face of Britain, dir. by Paul Rotha (Gaumont – British Instructional Films, 1935).

Farr, William, 'Documentaries', *Sight and Sound* (Winter 1937), p. 201.

Farrer, Reginald, *The Void of War: Letters from Three Fronts* (London: Constable, 1918).

Fenwick Events of 1931, Rev. George Allan (1931), National Library of Scotland Moving Image Archive.

Fenwick Events of 1933, Rev. George Allan (1933), National Library of Scotland Moving Image Archive.

Fenwick Events of 1934, Rev. George Allan (1934), National Library of Scotland Moving Image Archive.

Fernhurst Village Bus, C. L. Rickett (c.1936), Screen Archive South East.

Ford, Ford Madox, *No More Parades* (1925; Manchester: Carcanet, 2011).

Freud, Sigmund, 'Beyond the Pleasure Principle', in *The Standard Edition of the Complete Psychological Works of Sigmund Freud*, Vol. 18, ed. and trans. by James Strachey, Anna Freud, Alix Strachey and Alan Tyson (1920; London: Hogarth Press, 1955), pp. 1–65.

Fry, Roger, 'Giotto', in *Vision and Design*, 8th edn (1920; London: Penguin, 1961), pp. 87–116.

Gibbon, Lewis Grassic [as James Leslie Mitchell], *Hanno, or, The Future of Exploration* (London: Kegan Paul, Trench, Trubner, 1928).

—, 'From Lewis Grassic Gibbon', *Left Review*, 1 (1935), 179–80.

—, 'Literary Lights', in *Smeddum: A Lewis Grassic Anthology*, ed. by Valentina Bold (1934; Edinburgh: Canongate, 2001), pp. 123–37.

—, *Nine Against the Unknown* (1934; Edinburgh: Polygon, 2000).

—, *A Scots Quair* (*Sunset Song* [1932], *Cloud Howe* [1933], *Grey Granite* [1934]) (Harmondsworth: Penguin, 1986).

Glenboig Clayworks, Alexander McKendrik (1935), National Library of Scotland Moving Image Archive.

Hardy, Emma, *Some Recollections, Together with Some Relevant Poems by*

Thomas Hardy, ed. by Evelyn Hardy and Robert Gittings (London: Oxford University Press, 1961).

Hardy, Florence, 'Florence Hardy to John Drinkwater', 12 March [1924], Box 3 Letters, Letters from Florence Hardy, MS 684 02/03, Library of Eton College.

Hardy, Thomas, *Desperate Remedies*, ed. by Mary Rimmer (1871; London: Penguin, 1998).

—, *Far from the Madding Crowd*, ed. by Shannon Russell (1874; London: Penguin, 2000).

—, *A Laodicean*, ed. by John Schad (1880–1; London: Penguin, 1997).

—, *The Mayor of Casterbridge*, ed. by Martin Seymour-Smith (1886; London: Penguin, 1978).

—, 'Memories of Church Restoration', in *Thomas Hardy's Personal Writings*, ed. by Harold Orel (Macmillan: London, 1967), pp. 203–18.

—, 'No Bell-Ringing: A Ballad of Durnover', in *The Complete Poems*, ed. by James Gibson (Basingstoke: Palgrave Macmillan, 2001), pp. 911–12.

—, *The Personal Notebooks of Thomas Hardy*, ed. by Richard H. Taylor (Basingstoke: Macmillan, 1978).

—, *The Pursuit of the Well-Beloved* and *The Well-Beloved*, ed. by Patricia Ingham (London: Penguin, 1997).

—, 'Real Conversations', *Pall Mall Magazine* (April 1901), repr. in *Thomas Hardy Remembered*, ed. by Martin Ray (Aldershot: Ashgate, 2007), pp. 51–64.

—, *The Return of the Native*, ed. by Tony Slade (1878; London: Penguin, 1999).

—, *Tess of the D'Urbervilles* (1891), ed. by Tim Dolin (1891; London: Penguin, 2003).

—, 'Thomas Hardy to Emma Lavinia Hardy', [16 July 1908], *The Collected Letters of Thomas Hardy: Volume 3: 1902–1908*, ed. by Richard Little Purdy and Michael Millgate (Oxford: Clarendon Press, 1982).

—, 'Thomas Hardy to George Macmillan', 8 March 1924, *The Collected Letters of Thomas Hardy: Volume 6: 1920–1925*, ed. by Richard Little Purdy and Michael Millgate (Oxford: Clarendon Press, 1987.

—, 'Thomas Hardy to J. C. Squire', 3 June 1924, *The Collected Letters of Thomas Hardy: Volume 6: 1920–1925*, ed. by Richard Little Purdy and Michael Millgate (Oxford: Clarendon Press, 1987).

—, *Two on a Tower: A Romance*, ed. by Sally Shuttleworth (1882; London: Penguin, 1999).

Henderson, Charles, 'Preface', in *The Pageant of Bradstone 970–1820* (No known publisher, 1929).

Hitchcock, Henry-Russell, Jr, *Modern Architecture: Romanticism and Reintegration* (New York: Payson & Clarke, 1929).

Hitchcock, Henry-Russell, and Philip Johnson, *The International Style: Architecture since 1922* (1932; New York: W. W. Norton & Company, 1995).

Holtby, Winifred, 'Bring Up Your Rears', *Time and Tide*, 15 October 1926, in *Testament of a Generation: The Journalism of Vera Brittain and Winifred Holtby*, ed. by Paul Berry and Alan Bishop (London: Virago, 1985), pp. 199–201.

—, 'Is Family Life a Handicap?', *Evening Standard*, 2 November 1929, in *Testament of a Generation: The Journalism of Vera Brittain and Winifred Holtby*, ed. by Paul Berry and Alan Bishop (London: Virago, 1985), pp. 282–5.

—, *South Riding*, Virago Modern Classics 273 (1936; London: Virago–Little Brown, 1988).

—, *Women and a Changing Civilization* (1935; Chicago: Cassandra Editions Academy Press, 1978).

Hoskins, W. G., *Midland England* (London: B. T. Batsford, 1949).

Hovingham Compilation, Col. Sir William Worsley (1930–48), Yorkshire Film Archive.

How Green was My Valley, dir. by John Ford (20th Century Fox, 1941).

Hussey, Christopher, 'Oare House, Wiltshire, The Property of Mr. Geoffrey Fry', in the series 'Country Homes and Gardens Old and New', *Country Life* (March 1928), 334–41.

—, 'A Cotswold Village Reconditioned: Cornwell Manor, Oxfordshire-I', *Country Life* (May 1941), 432–6.

Ingram, J. H., *North Midland Country* (London: B. T. Batsford, 1948).

Isherwood, Christopher, and Edward Upward, 'The Garage in Drover's Hollow', in *The Mortmere Stories* (London: Enitharmon Press, 1994), pp. 76–85.

Joad, C. E. M., *The Horrors of the Countryside* (London: Hogarth Press, 1931).

—, 'The People's Claim', in *Britain and the Beast*, ed. by Clough Williams-Ellis (London: J. M. Dent, 1937), pp. 64–85.

Jones, David, 'Art in Relation to War' [1942–3, 1946], in *The Dying Gaul and Other Writings*, ed. by Harman Grisewood (London: Faber and Faber, 1978), pp. 123–66.

—, *In Parenthesis: Seinnyessit e gledyf ym penn mameu* (London: Faber and Faber, 1937).

—, 'Preface', in *In Parenthesis: Seinnyessit e gledyf ym penn mameu* (London: Faber and Faber, 1937), pp. ix–xv.

Jones, Glyn, review of Rhys Davies, *A Time to Laugh* (1937), *Wales*, 1 (1937), 30–1.

Jones, Jack, *Rhondda Roundabout* (London: Hamish Hamilton, 1934; repr. 1949).

Jones, Sydney, *English Village Homes* (London: B. T. Batsford, 1936).

Kaye-Smith, Sheila, *The Village Doctor* (London: Cassell, 1929).

Kelly, Mary, *How to Make a Pageant* (London: Sir Isaac Pitman & Sons, 1936).

—, *Village Theatre* (London: Thomas Nelson & Sons, 1939).

Leavis, F. R., and Denys Thompson, *Culture and Environment: A Training in Critical Awareness* (London: Chatto & Windus, 1933).

Le Corbeau, Adrien, *The Forest Giant*, trans. by J. H. Ross, with wood engravings by Agnes Miller Parker (London: Jonathan Cape, 1935).

Leighton, Clare, *Four Hedges: A Gardener's Chronicle*, with wood engravings by Clare Leighton (London: Gollancz; New York: Macmillan, 1935).

Lenham: A Kentish Village, John and William Barnes (1936), Screen Archive South East.

Linthwaite, Lucy Fairbank (1938), Yorkshire Film Archive.

Llewellyn, Richard, *How Green was My Valley* (1939; Harmondsworth: Penguin, 2001).

McAllister, Gilbert and Elizabeth, eds, *Homes, Towns and Countryside* (London: B. T. Batsford, 1945).

MacDiarmid, Hugh, 'Lewis Grassic Gibbon: 1901–1935', *Our Time*, 7 (1948), 307–8.

Mais, S. P. B., *The Home Counties* (London: B. T. Batsford, 1943).
—, 'The Plain Man Looks at England', in *Britain and the Beast*, ed. by Clough Williams-Ellis (London: J. M. Dent, 1937), pp. 212–24.
Martin, John Leslie, 'The State of Transition', in *Circle: International Survey of Constructive Art*, ed. by John Leslie Martin, Ben Nicolson and Naum Gabo (London: Faber, 1937), pp. 215–19.
Massingham, H. J., *Cotswold Country* (London: B. T. Batsford, 1937).
—, *Country Relics* (Cambridge: Cambridge University Press, 1939).
Mitchell, James Leslie, *Gay Hunter* (London: Heinemann, 1934; Edinburgh: Polygon, 1989).
—, *Three Go Back* (London: Jarrolds, 1932; Edinburgh: Polygon, 1995).
Morris, William, 'The Beauty of Life', in *Hopes and Fears for Art: Five Lectures Delivered in Birmingham, London and Nottingham, 1878–1881* (London: Ellis and White, 1882).
—, *News from Nowhere: Or, An Epoch of Rest, Being Some Chapters from a Utopian Romance* (1890; London: Routledge & Kegan Paul, 1970).
Mothersole, Jessie, *Hadrian's Wall* (London: John Lane, 1922).
Mumford, Lewis, 'Epilogue: Crotchet Castle to Arthur's Seat', from *The New Yorker*, January 1962, in Clough Williams-Ellis, *Portmeirion: The Place and its Meaning* (London: Faber, 1963), pp. 90–4.
Mumford, Lewis, 'Introduction', in Clough Williams-Ellis, *England and the Octopus*, new edition (Portmeirion: Golden Dragon, 1975), pp. xi–xii.
Nairn, Ian, *Outrage* (London: Architectural Press, 1955).
Nash, Paul, '"Going Modern" and "Being British"', *Week-end Review*, 12 March 1932, p. 323.
—, 'Stones', Unpublished MS, c.1944, Tate Archive, quoted in *Paul Nash: Modern Artist, Ancient Landscapes*, ed. by Jemima Montagu (London: Tate, 2003), p. 76.
National Art Library (NAL), London, Victoria and Albert Museum, Agnes Miller Parker: Correspondence with Philip Gibbons Concerning Her Work as a Wood Engraver, 1933–1976', Manuscript, MSL/1983/26 (formerly catalogued as MS.L.26–1983).
National Library of Scotland, Edinburgh, Agnes Miller Parker Collection, Manuscripts Division, Inventory Acc. 11238.
National Portrait Gallery, 'remainder' collection: NPG x135567 – NPG x135569.
The New Farming Age: Electricity Comes to the Countryside (London: BEDA, c.1933).
News Chronicle, 19 August 1959, Report entitled 'Want an Arch?', p. 7.
Orwell, George, *The Road to Wigan Pier* (1937; London: Penguin, 2001).
Our Village, E. R. Wood (1935), Screen Archive South East.
Personalities in Hovingham Village, Col. Sir William Worsley (1930s compilation), Yorkshire Film Archive.
Pitt, Frances, *How to See Nature* (London: B. T. Batsford, 1940).
Priestley, J. B., *English Journey* (1934; Harmondsworth: Penguin, 1977).
Purdon, James, 'Landscapes of Power', *Apollo*, January 2013, pp. 42–9.
Read, Herbert, 'A Lost Generation', *Nation and Athenaeum,* 27 April 1929, p. 116.
Remarque, Erich Maria, *All Quiet on the Western Front*, trans. by A. W. Wheen (London: G. P. Putnam's Sons, 1929).

Rhys, Keidrych, 'Notes for a New Editor', *Wales*, 8/9 (August 1939), 246–50.

—, ed., *Wales*, 11 vols, facsimile No. 7 in the English Little Magazines Series (London: Frank Cass, 1969).

Rothenstein, William, *Goya* (London: Sign of the Unicorn, 1900).

—, *Men and Memories, Vols I and II* (London: Faber & Faber, 1931–32).

—, *Since Fifty* (London: Faber & Faber, 1939).

Rouse, Clive, *The Old Towns of England* (1936; London: B. T. Batsford, 1944).

—, 'South Country', in *The Beauty of Britain*, ed. Charles Bradley Ford (London: B. T. Batsford, 1935), pp. 71–91.

'Rural Awakening', *The Times*, 5 October 1933, p. 15.

Rural Electrification (London: BEDA, 1928).

Scholes, Peroy A., 'Pylons and Wires', *The Times*, 11 October 1929, Letters to the Editor, p. 10.

Scott, Walter, *Minstrelsy of the Scottish Border: Consisting of Historical and Romantic Ballads, Collected in the Southern Counties of Scotland; with a Few of Modern Date, Founded upon Local Tradition* (Kelso: printed by J. Ballantyne, for T. Cadell, jun., and W. Davies, London, 1802).

Shakespeare, William, *Hamlet*, ed. by Ann Thompson and Neil Taylor (London: Arden Shakespeare, 2006).

Simmel, Georg 'The Metropolis and Mental Life', in *Simmel on Culture*, ed. by David Frisby and Mike Featherstone (London: Sage, 1994).

Spenoe, Kenneth, 'Electricity in Lakeland', *The Times*, 2 November 1929, Letters to the Editor, p. 8.

Stillington, York, and Easingwold, G. F. Baker (1931–42), Yorkshire Film Archive.

Stroud Urban District Council, Minutes of the Meeting of the Finance and General Purposes Committee on 27 May 1959, Gloucestershire County Council Archives, Reference 100/33.

Stucley, E. F., *The Village Organizer* (London: Methuen, 1935).

Sundour Shuttle: Magazine of Morton Sundour Fabrics Ltd and Associated Companies, December 1937, 'We'll Tak' the High Road: The Trend in Interior Decoration', pp. 5–6.

Symons, Arthur, *Studies on Modern Painters* (New York: W. E. Rudge, 1925).

Thatchers Old World Tea House, Kenneth D. Chown (1934), Screen Archive South East.

Thomas, F. G., *The Changing Village* (London: Thomas Nelson and Sons, 1939).

—, 'The New Learning', in *The New Learning: An Experiment with Educational Films in the County of Devon* (London: Workers' Educational Association, 1932).

Thomas, W. Beach, *The Happy Village* (London: Ernest Benn, 1928).

To-Day We Live, dir. by Ruby Grierson and Ralph Bond (Strand Film Company, 1937), British Film Institute Archive.

Topping, George (The Scribe), *Rambles in Borderland with the 'Clan'* (Carlisle: Charles Thurnam & Sons, 1921).

The Triumph of Electricity at the Royal Show (London: BEDA, 1936).

Vale, Edmund, *How to Look at Old Buildings* (London: B. T. Batsford, 1945).

Wales, vols 1–11, ed. by Keidrych Rhys, facsimile 7, English Little Magazines Series (London: Frank Cass, 1969).

Wallace, Doreen, *Barnham Rectory* (London: Collins, 1934).
—, *East Anglia* (London: Batsford, 1939).
—, *English Lakeland* (1940; rev. 2nd edn, London: Batsford, 1942).
—, *How to Grow Food* (London: Batsford, 1940).
Walmsley, Leo, *Fishermen at War* (London: Collins, 1941).
Walter, Meurig, 'Rhondda Poems', *Wales*, 4 (March 1938), 150.
Warner, Sylvia Townsend, *Lolly Willowes, or the Loving Huntsman* (1926; Chicago: Academy Chicago, 1979).
Watkins, Vernon, 'The Collier', *Wales*, 6/7 (March 1939), 205–6.
West, Geoffrey, review of Jack Jones, *Rhondda Roundabout* (1934), *Times Literary Supplement*, 7 June 1934, p. 406.
Williams, Emlyn, *The Corn is Green* (London: Heinemann, 1938).
Williams-Ellis, Clough, *The Architect*, in 'The Life and Work Series' (London: Geoffrey Bles, 1929).
—, *Architect Errant* (Portmeirion: Golden Dragon, 1971).
—, 'Architecture', under heading 'Books of the Day', review of Le Corbusier, 'The Marseilles Block', *Manchester Guardian*, 7 August 1953, p. 15.
—, *Around the World in Ninety Years* (Portmeirion: Golden Dragon, 1978).
—, ed., *Britain and the Beast* (London: J. M. Dent, 1937).
—, *Cottage Building in Cob, Pisé, Chalk and Clay: A Renaissance*, 2nd edn (London: Country Life, 1920; rept Milton Keynes: Lightning Source UK, 2007).
—, *England and the Octopus* (London: Geoffrey Bles, 1928).
—, 'Idea and Realisation', in *Royal Festival Hall*, ed. by London County Council (London: Max Parrish, 1951), pp. 5–57.
—, letter to *The Times*, re: Paganhill Anti-Slavery Arch, 29 August 1959, p. 10.
—, 'National Parks', *Journal of the Royal Society of Arts*, 94 (June 1946), 429–36.
—, *Portmeirion: The Place and its Meaning* (London: Faber, 1963).
—, 'I- Prospects of the Post-War Countryside', in the series 'Green and Pleasant Land: Aims and Needs in Replanning Rural England', *Country Life* (September 1941), 530–2.
—, (under pseudonym Graphite), *Reconography: Simplified Reconnaissance Sketching* (London: Pelman, 1920).
—, *Roads in the Landscape* (London: HMSO, 1967).
—, *The Tank Corps*, in the Country Life series of military histories (London: Country Life, 1919).
Williams-Ellis, Clough, and John Summerson, *Architecture Here And Now* (London: Nelson, 1934).
Williams-Ellis, Clough, and Amabel Williams-Ellis, *The Pleasures of Architecture* (1924; London: Jonathan Cape, 1924).
Woolf, Virginia, *Between the Acts* (1941; San Diego: Harvest–Harcourt, 1969).
—, *The Diary of Virginia Woolf, Volume Five: 1936–1941*, ed. by Anne Olivier Bell (New York and London: Harcourt Brace Jovanovich, 1979).
—, 'Introductory Letter', in *Life As We Have Known It*, ed. by Margaret Llewelyn Davies (London: Hogarth Press, 1931), pp. xv–xxxix.
Young, E. H., *Miss Mole* (1930; Garden City, NY: Dial–Doubleday, 1985).
—, *Portrait of a Village* (London: Heinemann, 1937).

Secondary sources

Alexander, Neal and James Moran, eds, *Regional Modernisms* (Edinburgh: Edinburgh University Press, 2013).

Andrews, Margaret, *The Acceptable Face of Feminism: The Women's Institute as a Social Movement* (London: Lawrence and Wishart, 1997).

Arkley, Sarah, Mike Browne and Ewan Hyslop, *Craigleith Quarry: A Geological Trail* (Edinburgh: Lothian and Borders RIGS, 2005).

Art UK, <www.artuk.org> [accessed 11 August 2017].

Bailey, Christopher, 'Making and Meaning in the English Countryside', in *Technologies of Landscape: From Reaping to Recycling*, ed. by David E. Nye (Amherst: University of Massachusetts Press, 1999), pp. 136–58.

—, 'Rural Industries and the Image of the Countryside', in *The English Countryside Between the Wars: Regeneration or Decline?*, ed. by Paul Brassley, Jeremy Burchardt and Lynne Thompson (Woodbridge: Boydell Press, 2006), pp. 132–49.

Baldwin, Dean, 'H. E. Bates: *The Poacher*', in *Recharting the Thirties*, ed. by Patrick J. Quinn (Selinsgrove: Susquehanna University Press, 1996), pp. 124–33.

Bartie, Angela, Linda Fleming Mark Freeman, Alexander Hutton, Paul Readman and Tom Hulme, 'Carlisle Historical Pageant', *The Redress of the Past: Historical Pageants in Britain, 1905–2016*, <http://www.historicalpageants.ac.uk/pageants/1341/> [accessed 10 July 2017].

Bauman, Zygmunt, 'Desert Spectacular', in *The Flaneur*, ed. by Keith Tester (London: Routledge, 1994), pp. 131–55.

Beauchamp, Ken, *History of Telegraphy* (London: Institution of Engineering and Technology, 2001).

Bell, Ian A., '"Work as If you Live in the Early Days of a Better Nation": Scottish Fiction and the Experience of Industry', in *British Industrial Fictions*, ed. by H. Gustav Klaus and Stephen Knight (Cardiff: University of Wales Press, 2000), pp. 181–92.

Bell, Quentin, Angelica Garnett, Henrietta Garnett and Richard Shone, *Charleston: Past and Present*, rev. edn (London: Hogarth Press, 1993).

Benson, Richard, *The Printed Picture* (New York: Museum of Modern Art, 2008).

Berman, Jessica Schiff, *Modernist Fiction, Cosmopolitanism and the Politics of Community* (New York: Cambridge University Press, 2001).

Berman, Marshall, *All That Is Solid Melts into Air: The Experience of Modernity* (New York: Penguin, 1982).

Berry, Paul, and Alan Bishop, eds, *Testament of a Generation: The Journalism of Vera Brittain and Winifred Holtby* (London: Virago, 1985).

'Berwick Church decorations: Grant and Bell', *Tate*, <http://www.tate.org.uk/learn/online-resources/bloomsbury-group/art-collaboration/berwick-church-decorations> [accessed July 2017].

Bishop, Anne, 'Cartwright Memorial Hall and the Great Bradford Exhibition of 1904', *The Bradford Antiquary*, 4 (1989), 26–38.

Black, Jonathan, '"Constructing a Chinese-Puzzle Universe": Industry, National Identity and Edward Wadsworth's Vorticist Woodcuts of West Yorkshire,

1914–1916', in *Vorticism: New Perspectives*, ed. by Mark Antliff and Scott W. Klein (Oxford: Oxford University Press, 2013), pp. 89–101.

Blee, Peter, 'Bishop Bell of Chichester', <http://www.berwickchurch.org.uk/bishop%20bell.html> [accessed 14 March 2017].

—, *The Bloomsbury Group in Berwick Church: The Decorative Scheme by Duncan Grant, Vanessa Bell & Quentin Bell* (Berwick: St Michaels and All Angels, 2017).

Bluemel, Kristin, 'Rural Modernity and the Wood Engraving Revival in Interwar England', *Modernist Cultures*, 9.2 (2014), 233–59.

—, 'The Saltire Chapbooks, Twentieth-Century Wood Engraving and "A Vast New Public of Readers"', *Journal of the Edinburgh Bibliographical Society*, 10 (2015), 159–82.

Blythe, Ronald, 'Introduction', in Adrian Bell, *Men and the Fields* (Wimborne Minster: Little Toller Books, 2009), pp. 7–11.

Boyes, Georgina, *The Imagined Village: Culture, Ideology and the English Folk Revival* (Manchester: Manchester University Press, 1993).

Brace, Catherine, 'Envisioning England: The Visual in Countryside Writing in the 1930s and 1940s', *Landscape Research*, 28.4 (2003), 365–82.

Bradbury, Malcolm, and James McFarlane, *Modernism* (New York: Penguin, 1976).

Bradshaw, David, and Kevin J. H. Dettmar, eds, *A Companion to Modernist Literature and Culture* (Malden, MA: Blackwell, 2006).

Brassley, Paul, 'The Wheelwright, the Carpenter, Two Ladies from Oxford, and the Construction of Socio-Economic Change in the Countryside between the Wars', in *The English Countryside Between the Wars: Regeneration or Decline?*, ed. by Paul Brassley, Jeremy Burchardt and Lynne Thompson (Woodbridge: Boydell Press, 2006), pp. 212–34.

—, Jeremy Burchardt and Karen Sayer, 'Introduction', *Transforming the Countryside: The Electrification of Rural Britain* (London: Routledge, 2017), pp. 1–11.

—, Jeremy Burchardt and Karen Sayer, eds, *Transforming the Countryside: The Electrification of Rural Britain* (London: Routledge, 2017).

—, Jeremy Burchardt and Lynne Thompson, 'Introduction', in *The English Countryside Between the Wars: Regeneration or Decline?*, ed. by Paul Brassley, Jeremy Burchardt and Lynne Thompson (Woodbridge: Boydell Press, 2006), pp. 1–9.

—, Jeremy Burchardt and Lynn Thompson, eds, *The English Countryside between the Wars: Regeneration or Decline?* (Woodbridge: Boydell Press, 2006).

Briggs, Asa, *The History of Broadcasting in the United Kingdom: Volume I – The Birth of Broadcasting: 1896–1927* (London: Oxford University Press, 1961).

Brooker, Peter, and Andrew Thacker, eds, *Geographies of Modernism: Literatures, Cultures, Spaces* (London: Routledge, 2005).

Brown, Erica, and Mary Grover, eds, *Middlebrow Literary Cultures: The Battle of the Brows, 1920–1960* (Basingstoke: Palgrave Macmillan, 2012).

Buchan, Ursula, *A Green and Pleasant Land* (London: Hutchinson, 2013).

Burchardt, Jeremy, '"A New Rural Civilization": Village Halls, Community and Citizenship in the 1920s', in *The English Countryside Between the Wars:*

Regeneration or Decline?, ed. by Paul Brassley, Jeremy Burchardt and Lynne Thompson (Woodbridge: Boydell Press, 2006), pp. 26–35.

—, *Paradise Lost: Rural Idyll and Social Change since 1800* (London: I. B. Tauris, 2002).

Burt, Roger, 'The Extractive Industries', in *The Cambridge Economic History of Modern Britain, Vol. I: Industrialisation*, ed. by Roderick Floud and Paul Johnson (Cambridge: Cambridge University Press, 2004), pp. 417–50.

Burton, Deirdre, 'A Feminist Reading of *A Scots Quair*', in *The British Working-Class Novel in the Twentieth Century*, ed. by Jeremy Hawthorn (London: Edward Arnold, 1984), pp. 35–46.

Campbell, Ian, 'Introduction', in Lewis Grassic Gibbon, *Nine Against the Unknown* (Edinburgh: Polygon, 2000), pp. xi–xvi.

Cardinal, Roger, *The Landscape Vision of Paul Nash* (London: Reaktion, 1989).

Carney, Michael, *Britain in Pictures: A History and Bibliography* (London: Werner Shaw, 1995).

Caruth, Cathy, 'Introduction', in *Trauma: Explorations in Memory*, ed. by Cathy Caruth (Baltimore: Johns Hopkins University Press, 1995), pp. 3–12.

Casey, Janet G., *A New Heartland: Women, Modernity, and the Agrarian Ideal in America* (New York: Oxford University Press, 2009).

Causey, Andrew, 'Paul Nash and Englishness', in *Paul Nash: Modern Artist, Ancient Landscapes*, ed. by Jemima Montagu (London: Tate, 2003), pp. 23–9.

Cavaliero, Glen, *The Rural Tradition in the English Novel 1900–1939* (Totowa, NJ: Rowman and Littlefield, 1977).

Cave, Roderick, *The Private Press*, 2nd edn (New York: R. R. Bowker, 1983).

Chase, Malcolm, 'This Is No Claptrap; This is Our Heritage', in *The Imagined Past: History and Nostalgia*, ed. by Christopher Shaw and Malcolm Chase (Manchester: Manchester University Press, 1989), pp. 128–46.

Child, Benjamin S., *Uneven Ground: Figurations of the Rural Modern in the U.S. South, 1890–1940* (Athens: University of Georgia Press, forthcoming, 2019).

Ching, Barbara, and Gerald Creed, 'Recognizing Rusticity: Identity and the Power of Place', in *Knowing Your Place: Rural Identity and Cultural Hierarchy*, ed. by Barbara Ching and Gerald Creed (New York: Routledge, 1997), pp. 2–38.

—, and Gerald W. Creed, eds, *Knowing Your Place: Rural Identity and Cultural Hierarchy* (New York: Routledge, 1997).

Chinitz, David, *T. S. Eliot and the Cultural Divide* (Chicago: University of Chicago Press, 2003).

Clarke, Darren, 'The First Winter', *Vanessa Bell*, ed. by Ian Dejardin and Sarah Milroy (London: Philip Wilson, 2017), pp. 145–50.

Clewell, Tammy, ed., *Modernism and Nostalgia: Bodies, Locations, Aesthetics* (Basingstoke: Palgrave Macmillan, 2013).

Clute, John, 'Fantastika in the World Storm' (2007), <http://www.johnclute.co.uk/word/?p=15> [accessed 6 July 2017].

Collingham, Lizzie, *The Taste of War: World War II and the Battle for Food* (London: Allen Lane, 2011).

Collins, Judith, ed., *A Painter's Place: Banks Head, Cumberland, 1924–1931* (Kendal: Abbot Hall Art Gallery with Redcliffe Press, 1991).

Colls, Robert, *Identity of England* (Oxford: Oxford University Press, 2002).

—, and Philip Dodd, eds, *Englishness: Politics and Culture 1880–1920* (London: Croom Helm, 1986).

Constable, Freda, and Sue Simon, *The England of Eric Ravilious* (London: Scolar Press, 1982).

Contensou, Martine, *La Fée Électricité* (Paris: Petites Capitales, 2007).

Corbett, David Peters, Ysanne Holt and Fiona Russell, eds, *The Geographies of Englishness: Landscape and the National Past, 1880–1940* (New Haven, CT: Yale University Press, 2002).

Corbin, Alain, *Village Bells: Sound and Meaning in the Nineteenth-Century French Countryside*, trans. by Martin Thom (London: Papermac, 1999).

Craig, Cairns, *The Modern Scottish Novel* (Edinburgh: Edinburgh University Press, 1999).

Crouch, David, 'Flirting with Space: Thinking Landscape Relationally', *Cultural Geographies*, 17 (2010), 5–8.

Cunningham, Valentine, 'Somewhere the Good Place?', in *British Writers of the Thirties* (Oxford: Oxford University Press, 1988), pp. 377–418.

Curtis, William J. R., *Modern Architecture since 1900*, 3rd edn (London: Phaidon Press, 1996).

Dilworth, Thomas, *David Jones in the Great War* (London: Enitharmon Press, 2012).

Ditt, Karl, 'The Electrification of the Countryside: The Interests of Electrical Enterprises and the Rural Population of England 1888–1934', in *Transforming the Countryside*, ed. by Paul Brassley, Jeremy Burchardt and Karen Sayer (Abingdon: Routledge, 2017), pp. 15–37.

Drewett, Peter, and Sue Hamilton, 'Marking Time and Making Space: Excavations and Landscape Studies at the Caburn Hillfort, East Sussex, 1996–98', *Sussex Archaeological Collections: Relating to the History and Antiquities of the Counties of East and West Sussex*, 137 (1999), 7–37, <http://archaeologydataservice.ac.uk/archiveDS/archiveDownload?t=arch-285-1/dissemination/pdf/vol_137/01_drew_and_ham.pdf> [accessed 3 July 2017].

Drucker, Johanna, *Theorizing Modernism: Visual Art and the Critical Tradition* (New York: Columbia University Press, 1994).

Durey, Judith, 'Translating *Hiraeth*, Performing Adoption: Art as Mediation and Form of Cultural Production' (unpublished doctoral thesis, Murdoch University, 2010), Murdoch University Research Repository, <http://researchrepository.murdoch.edu.au/5815/2/02Whole.pdf> [accessed 10 September 2017>.

Edsall, Mary Agnes, 'The *Arma Christi* before the *Arma Christi*: Rhetorics of the Passion in Late Antiquity and the Early Middle Ages', in *The Arma Christi in Medieval and Early Modern Material Culture*, with a Critical Edition of 'O Vernicle', ed. by Lisa H. Cooper and Andrea Denny-Brown (Aldershot: Ashgate, 2014), pp. 21–51.

Esty, Jed, *A Shrinking Island: Modernism and National Culture in England* (Princeton: Princeton University Press, 2004).

Eysteinsson, Astradur, *The Concept of Modernism* (Ithaca, NY: Cornell University Press, 1990).

Farland, Maria, 'Modernist Versions of Pastoral: Poetic Inspiration, Scientific Expertise, and the "Degenerate" Farmer', *American Literary History*, 19.4 (2007), 905–36.

'A Festival Unlike Any Other', available at <http://festivalnumber6.com> [accessed 19 July 2017].

Ford, Mark, *Thomas Hardy: Half a Londoner* (Cambridge, MA: Belknap Press of Harvard University Press, 2016).

Forty, Adrian, *Objects of Desire: Design and Society Since 1750* (London: Thames and Hudson, 1986).

Frawley, Oona, *Irish Pastoral: Nostalgia and Twentieth-Century Irish Literature* (Dublin and Portland, OR: Irish Academic Press, 2005).

Friend, Andy, *Ravilious & Co: The Pattern of Friendship* (London: Thames & Hudson, 2017).

Fussell, Paul, *The Great War and Modern Memory* (New York: Oxford University Press, 1975).

—, 'On the Persistence of Pastoral', in *Thank God for the Atom Bomb and Other Essays* (New York: Summit, 1988), pp. 177–204.

Gale, Maggie B., 'Errant Nymphs: Women and the Inter-War Theatre', in *British Theatre Between the Wars 1918–1939*, ed. by Clive Barker and Maggie B. Gale (Cambridge: Cambridge University Press, 2000), pp. 113–34.

—, 'Introduction', in *British Theatre Between the Wars 1918–1939*, ed. by Clive Barker and Maggie B. Gale (Cambridge: Cambridge University Press, 2000), pp. 1–3.

Gan, Wendy, 'A Return to Romance: Winifred Holtby's Spinster Novels Between the Wars', *Orbis Litterarum*, 58 (2003), 202–18.

Gaonkar, Dilip Parameshwar, ed., *Alternative Modernities* (Durham, NC: Duke University Press, 2001).

Gardner-Medwin, Robert, review of 1975 edition of *England and the Octopus*, *Town Planning Review*, 47 (1976), 82.

Garnett, Angelica, *Deceived with Kindness: A Bloomsbury Childhood* (London: Chatto and Windus, 1984).

Giddens, Anthony, *The Consequences of Modernity* (Cambridge: Polity Press, 1990), pp. 36–7.

Giles, Judy, and Tim Middleton, eds, *Writing Englishness 1900–1950* (London: Routledge, 1995).

Gold, John R., *The Experience of Modernism: Modern Architects and the Future City, 1928–1953* (London: E & F. N. Spon, 1997).

—, *The Practice of Modernism: Modern Architects and Urban Transformation, 1954–1972* (London: Routledge, 2007).

Goodman, Gemma, and Charlotte Mathieson, eds, *Gender and Space in Rural Britain, 1840*–1920 (London: Pickering and Chatto, 2014).

Gough, Paul, *A Terrible Beauty: British Artists in the First World War* (Bristol: Sansom, 2010).

Grover, Mary, *The Ordeal of Warwick Deeping: Middlebrow Authorship and Cultural Embarrassment* (Madison, NJ: Fairleigh Dickinson University Press, 2009).

Gruffudd, Pyrs, 'Building Sites: Cultural Geographies of Architecture and Place Making', in *Cultural Geography in Practice*, ed. by Alison Blunt, Pyrs

Gruffudd, John May, Miles Ogborn and David Pinder (London: Arnold, 2003), pp. 238–50.
—, *Land of my Fathers? The Council for the Preservation of Rural Wales and Contested Conservation*, Discussion Paper Series No. 2 (Reading: Rural History Centre, University of Reading, 1996).
—, '"Propaganda for Seemliness": Clough Williams Ellis and Portmeirion, 1918–1950', *Ecumene*, 2 (1995), 399–422.
Gruffudd, Rolant Pyrs, 'Landscape and Nationhood: Tradition and Modernity in Rural Wales, 1900–1950' (unpublished doctoral thesis, Loughborough University of Technology, 1989).
Hall, Michael, *Francis Brett Young* (Bridgend: Seren, 1997).
Hannah, Leslie, *Electricity before Nationalisation: A Study of the Development of the Electricity Supply Industry in Britain to 1948* (London: Macmillan, 1979).
Harding, James, *Emlyn Williams: A Life* (London: Weidenfeld & Nicholson, 1993).
Harker, Ben, '"On Different Levels Ourselves Went Forward": Pageantry, Class Politics and Narrative Form in Virginia Woolf's Late Writing', *ELH*, 78 (2011), 433–56.
Harris, Alexandra, *Romantic Moderns: English Writers, Artists and the Imagination from Virginia Woolf to John Piper* (London: Thames and Hudson, 2010).
Harris, John, 'Introduction', in *My People* (Bridgend: Seren, 1987), pp. 7–48.
Haslam, Richard, *Clough Williams-Ellis: RIBA Drawings Monographs No 2* (London: Academy Editions, 1996).
—, Julian Orbach and Adam Voelcker, *Gwynedd*, in the Pevsner Buildings of Wales series (New Haven, CT: Yale University Press, 2009).
Head, Dominic, *Modernity and the English Rural Novel* (Cambridge: Cambridge University Press, 2017).
Hewison, Robert, *The Heritage Industry: Britain in a Climate of Decline* (London: Methuen, 1987).
Hirshler, Erica E., and Teresa A. Carbone, *John Singer Sargent: Watercolors* (Boston: Museum of Fine Arts, 2013).
Hitchon, Juliette M., *Chanel and the Tweedmaker – Weavers of Dreams* (Carlisle: P3, 2012).
Hodnett, Edward, *Five Centuries of English Book Illustration* (Aldershot: Scolar Press, 1988).
Holt, Ysanne, 'The Call of Commerce: The Studio Magazine in the 1920s', in *The Rise of the Modern Art Market in London, 1850–*1939, ed. by Pamela Fletcher and Anne Helmreich (Manchester: Manchester University Press, 2011), pp. 151–73.
—, 'Landscapes of the 1920s', in *A Continuous Line: Ben Nicholson in England*, ed. by Chris Stephens (London: Tate, 2008), pp. 21–41.
—, 'Performing the Anglo-Scottish Border: Cultural Landscapes, Heritage, and Borderland Identities', *Journal of Borderland Studies*, April 2017, pp. 1–16, available at <http://www.tandfonline.com/doi/full/10.1080/08865655.2016.1267586> (last accessed 4 August 2017).
Hopkins, Chris, 'Depressed Pastorals? Documenting Wales in the Nineteen Thirties', in *English Fiction in the 1930s: Language, Genre, History* (London: Continuum, 2006), pp. 61–74.

—, '*Wales* (1937–9) and *Welsh Review* (1939–40)', in *The Oxford Critical and Cultural History of Modernist Magazines, Vol. 1: Britain and Ireland, 1880–1955*, ed. by Peter Brooker and Andrew Thacker (Oxford: Oxford University Press, 2009), pp. 714–34.

Howard, Peter, *Heritage: Management, Interpretation, Identity* (London: Continuum, 2003).

Howkins, Alun, *The Death of Rural England: A Social History of the Countryside Since 1900* (London: Routledge, 2003).

Hynes, Samuel, *A War Imagined: The First World War and English Culture* (London: Pimlico, 1990).

Ingold, Tim, *Being Alive: Essays on Movement, Knowledge and Description* (London: Taylor and Francis, 2011).

—, *Lines: A Brief History* (London: Routledge, 2008).

Jackson, Lesley, *Alistair Morton and Edinburgh Weavers: Visionary Textiles and Modern Art* (New York: Harry N. Abrams, 2012).

Johnson, Anna, 'Wounded Men and Wounded Trees: David Jones and the Anglo-Saxon Culture Tangle', in *Anglo-Saxon Culture and the Modern Imagination*, ed. by David Clark and Nicholas Perkins (Cambridge: D. S. Brewer, 2010), pp. 89–109.

Jones, Jonah, *Clough Williams-Ellis: The Architect of Portmeirion: A Memoir by Jonah Jones* (Bridgend: Seren, 1996).

Katz, Tamar, *Impressionist Subjects: Gender, Interiority, and Modernist Fiction in England* (Urbana: University of Illinois Press, 2000).

Koehler, Karin, *Thomas Hardy and Victorian Communication: Letters, Telegrams and Postal Systems* (Basingstoke: Palgrave Macmillan, 2016).

Kumar, Krishan, *The Making of English National Identity* (Cambridge: Cambridge University Press, 2003).

Latour, Bruno, *Reassembling the Social: An Introduction to Actor-Network-Theory* (London: Oxford: Oxford University Press, 2007).

Leaper, Hana, '"Old-fashioned modern": Claude Flight's *Lino-Cuts* and Public Taste in the Interwar Period', *Modernist Cultures*, 11.3 (2016), 389–408.

Lefebvre, Henri, *La Révolution urbaine* (Paris: Gallimard, 1970).

Lefebvre Lowenthal, David, 'European Landscapes as National Symbols', in *Geography and National Identity*, ed. by David Hooson (Oxford: Blackwell, 1994), pp. 15–38.

Llywelyn, Robin, 'The Buildings of Portmeirion', in *Portmeirion*, ed. by Jan Morris, Alwyn Turner, Mark Eastment and Stephen Lacey (Woodbridge: Antique Collectors' Club, 2006), pp. 220–36.

Lowerson, John, 'Battles for the Countryside', in *Class, Culture, and Social Change: A New View of the 1930s*, ed. by Frank Gloversmith (Atlantic Highlands, NJ: Humanities Press, 1980), pp. 258–80.

Lowry, Glenn D., and Peter Galassi, 'Foreword', in Richard Benson, *The Printed Picture* (New York: Museum of Modern Art, 2008), p. 1.

Luckin, Bill, *Questions of Power: Electricity and Environment in Inter-war Britain* (Manchester: Manchester University Press, 1990).

Lumsden, Alison, '"Women's Time": Reading the *Quair* as a Feminist Text', in *A Flame in the Mearns: Lewis Grassic Gibbon, A Centenary Celebration*, ed. by Margery Palmer McCulloch and Sarah M. Dunnigan (Glasgow: Association of Scottish Literary Studies, 2003), pp. 41–53.

MacColl, D. S., 'Trimming the Ship', *The Burlington Magazine for Connoisseurs*, 61 (August 1932), 75–7.

McCulloch, Margery Palmer, 'Modernism and Marxism in *A Scots Quair*', in *A Flame in the Mearns: Lewis Grassic Gibbon, A Centenary Celebration*, ed. by Margery Palmer McCulloch and Sarah M. Dunnigan (Glasgow: Association of Scottish Literary Studies, 2003), pp. 27–40.

—, *Scottish Modernism and Its Contexts 1918–1959: Literature, National Identity and Cultural Exchange* (Edinburgh: Edinburgh University Press, 2009).

Macdonald, Kate, ed., *The Masculine Middlebrow, 1880–1950: What Mr Miniver Read* (Basingstoke: Palgrave Macmillan, 2011).

McInerney, Stephen, 'David Jones's Blessed Rage for Order: The "Will Toward Shape"', *Logos: A Journal of Catholic Thought and Culture*, 14.2 (2011), 59–81.

Mandler, Peter, 'Against "Englishness": English Culture and the Limits to Rural Nostalgia, 1850–1940', *Transactions of the Royal Historical Society*, 7 (1997), 155–75.

Marcus, Jane, '"A Wilderness of One's Own": Feminist Fantasy Novels of the Twenties: Rebecca West and Sylvia Townsend Warner', in *Women Writers and the City: Essays in Feminist Literary Criticism*, ed. by Susan Squier (Knoxville: University of Tennessee Press, 1984), pp. 134–60.

Marler, Regina, ed., *Selected Letters of Vanessa Bell* (London: Bloomsbury, 1993).

Massey, Doreen, *For Space* (London: Sage, 2005).

Matless, David, *Landscape and Englishness* (London: Reaktion, 1998).

Merriman, Peter, 'A Power for Good or Evil: Geographies of the M1 in Late Fifties Britain', in *Geographies of British Modernity: Space and Society in the Twentieth Century*, ed. by David Gilbert, David Matless and Brian Short (Oxford: Blackwell, 2003), pp. 116–20.

Middleton, G. A. T., *Building Materials: Their Nature, Properties and Manufacture* (London: B. T. Batsford, 1905).

Miles, Jonathan, and Derek Shiel, *David Jones: The Maker Unmade* (1995; Bridgend: Seren, 2003).

Miller, J. Hillis, *Thomas Hardy: Distance and Desire* (Cambridge, MA: Harvard University Press, 1970).

Miller, T. G., *Geology and Scenery in Britain* (London: B.T. Batsford, 1953).

Millgate, Michael, *Thomas Hardy: A Biography Revisited* (Oxford: Oxford University Press, 2004).

Moran, Joe, *On Roads: A Hidden History* (London: Profile, 2010).

Morris, Eleanor Smith, *British Town Planning and Urban Design* (Harlow: Longman, 1997).

Murphy, G. Ronald, *Tree of Salvation: Yggdrasil and the Cross in the North* (Oxford: Oxford University Press, 2013).

Neve, Christopher, *Unquiet Landscape: Places and Ideas in Twentieth-Century English Painting* (London: Faber and Faber, 1990).

Newby, Howard, *Country Life: A Social History of Rural England* (London: Weidenfeld and Nicolson, 1987).

Nicholson, Jake, 'What Does an Artist Look For in a Painting Place?', in *A Painter's Place: Banks Head, Cumberland, 1924–1931*, ed. by Judith

Collins (Kendal: Abbot Hall Art Gallery with Redcliffe Press, 1991) pp. 10–11.

Nicoll, Allardyce, *English Drama 1900–1930: The Beginnings of the Modern Period* (Cambridge: Cambridge University Press, 1973).

Norquay, Glenda, 'Lewis Grassic Gibbon and Women', in *The International Companion to Lewis Grassic Gibbon*, ed. by Scott Lyall (Glasgow: Scottish Literature International, 2015), pp. 76–88.

Ogborn, Miles, 'Modernity and Modernization', in *Introducing Human Geographies*, ed. by Paul Cloke, Philip Crang and Mark Goodwin, 2nd edn (London: Hodder Arnold, 2005), pp. 339–42.

Outka, Elizabeth, *Consuming Traditions: Modernity, Modernism, and the Commodified Authentic* (Oxford: Oxford University Press, 2009).

'Paintings – Lot 203' [Edward Wadsworth A.R.A. (1889–1949)], *Wooley and Wallis*, <https://www.woolleyandwallis.co.uk/Lot/?sale=PW190912&lot=213&id=228948> [accessed 11 August 2017].

Perriton, Linda, 'The Education of Women for Citizenship: The National Federation of Women's Institutes and the British Federation of Business and Professional Women, 1930–1959', *Gender and Education*, 21 (2009), 81–95.

Peters, John Durham, *The Marvelous Clouds: Toward a Philosophy of Elemental Media* (Chicago: University of Chicago Press, 2015).

Poggioli, Renato, *The Oaten Flute: Essays on Pastoral Poetry and the Pastoral Ideal* (Cambridge, MA: Harvard University Press, 1975).

Potts, Alex, '"Constable Country" Between the Wars', in *Patriotism: The Making and Unmaking of British National Identity*, ed. by Raphael Samuel (London: Routledge, 1989), pp. 160–88.

Powers, Alan, *Britain*, in the 'Modern Architecture in History' series (London: Reaktion, 2007).

—, *Eric Ravilious: Imagined Realities* (London: Imperial War Museum/Philip Wilson, 2003).

—, Interview, 14 January 2014.

—, *Modern: The Modern Movement in Britain* (London: Merrell, 2005),

—, 'One Man's Fight against the Octopus', *Country Life*, 191 (March 1997), 54–5.

Rae, Patricia, 'Double Sorrow: Proleptic Elegy and the End of Arcadianism in 1930s Britain', in *Modernism and Mourning*, ed. by Patricia Rae (Lewisburg, PA: Bucknell University Press, 2007), pp. 213–38.

Ravenhill-Johnson, Annie, 'Depicting the Worker', *The Art and Ideology of the Trade Union Emblem, 1850–1925*, ed. by Paula James (London: Anthem, 2013), pp. 35–45.

The Redress of the Past: Historical Pageants in Britain, 1905–2016, <http://www.historicalpageants.ac.uk/> [accessed 10 July 2017].

Regan, Lisa, *Winifred Holtby's Social Vision: 'Members One of Another'* (London: Pickering and Chatto, 2012).

Roberts, Gwyneth, *The Language of the Blue Books: Wales and Colonial Prejudice* (Cardiff: University of Wales Press, 2011).

Roberts, Wilfrid, 'Living in Cumberland' [1 January 1934], *BBC Genome: Radio Times 1923–2009*, <http://genome.ch.bbc.co.uk/b158818f36254b19bd4c79c0484d5c8d> [accessed 10 July 2017].

Rogerson, Ian, *The Wood Engravings of Agnes Miller Parker* (London: British Library, 2005).

Rothenstein, John, *Brave Day, Hideous Night* (London: Hamish Hamilton, 1966).

—, *Modern English Painters, Volume I* (London: MacDonald, 1976).

Rupp, Jan, 'English Pageant Fictions of the Interwar Years', in *Ritual and Narrative: Theoretical Explorations and Historical Case Studies*, ed. by Vera Nünning, Jan Rupp and Gregor Ahn [Transcript]: Cultural and Media Studies (Bielefeld: Transcript, 2013), pp. 189–217.

'Rural', in *Online Etymological Dictionary*, created by Douglas Harper, 2001–17, <http://www.etymonline.com/index.php?term=rural> (last accessed 16 March 2018).

'Rural', in *Oxford English Dictionary*, 3rd edn, March 2011, <http://bluehawk.monmouth.edu:2166/view/Entry/168989?redirectedFrom=rural#eid> [accessed 14 March 2017].

Russell, James, 'Brought to Book: Eric Ravilious's White Horses', *British Archaeology*, 129 (2013), 14–19.

Said, Edward, *The World, The Text and the Critic* (Cambridge, MA: Harvard University Press, 1983).

Sayer, Karen, 'Electrification and its Alternatives in the Farmer's and Labourer's Home', in *Transforming the Countryside*, ed. by Paul Brassley, Jeremy Burchardt and Karen Sayer (Abingdon: Routledge, 2017), pp. 117–34.

Schivelbusch, Wolfgang, *Disenchanted Night: The Industrialisation of Light in the Nineteenth Century* (Berkeley: University of California Press, 1998).

Scott, John, *Social Network Analysis* (1991; London: Sage, 2013).

Selborne, Joanna, *British Wood-Engraved Book Illustration, 1904–1940* (Oxford: Clarendon Press, 1998; repr. London: British Library, 2001).

Seymour, John, *The Forgotten Arts* (London: Dorling Kindersley, 1985).

Shepherd, June, *Doreen Wallace: Writer and Social Campaigner* (Lampeter: Edwin Mellen, 2000).

Sherry, Vincent, 'The Great War and Literary Modernism in England', in *The Cambridge Companion to the Literature of the First World War*, ed. by Vincent Sherry (Cambridge: Cambridge University Press, 2005), pp. 113–37.

Shirley, Rosemary, 'Pylons and Frozen Peas: The Women's Institute Goes Electric', in *Transforming the Countryside*, ed. by Paul Brassley, Jeremy Burchardt and Karen Sayer (Abingdon: Routledge, 2017), pp. 135–53.

—, *Rural Modernity, Everyday Life and Visual Culture* (Farnham: Ashgate, 2015).

Shone, Richard, *The Berwick Church Paintings*, rev. edn (Eastbourne: Towner Art Gallery, 1969).

Smiles, Sam, 'Ancient Country: Nash and Prehistory', in *Paul Nash: Modern Artist, Ancient Landscape*, ed. by Jemima Montagu (London: Tate, 2003), pp. 31–7.

—, 'Equivalents for the Megaliths: Prehistory and English Culture, 1920–50', in *The Geographies of Englishness: Landscape and the National Past 1880–1940*, ed. by David Peters Corbett, Ysanne Bolt and Fiona Russell (New Haven, CT: Paul Mellon Centre for Studies in British Art, Yale University Press, 2002), pp. 199–223.

Smith, George Saumarez, Interview, 20 May 2013.

Smith, Jos, 'An Archipelagic Literature: Re-Framing "The New Nature Writing"', *Green Letters: Studies in Ecocriticism*, 17 (2013), 5–15.

Spalding, Frances, *Duncan Grant: A Biography* (1997; London: Pimlico, 1998).

—, *Roger Fry: Art and Life* (Berkeley: University of California Press, 1980; Norwich: Black Dog Books, 1999).

—, *Virginia Woolf: Art, Life and Vision* (London: National Portrait Gallery, 2014).

Spector, Nancy, 'Paul Cézanne, Bibémus', *Guggenheim Collection Online* <https://www.guggenheim.org/artwork/785> [accessed 11 August 17].

Spender, Stephen, *The Thirties and After: Poetry, Politics, People* (London: Macmillan, 1978).

Spires, Thomas Bennett, *An Historical Geography of the British Quarrying Industry, c.1850–1950* (unpublished doctoral thesis, University of Manchester, 2002).

Steel, Carolyn, *Hungry City* (London: Vintage, 2011).

Sterne, Jonathan, 'Communication as Techné', in *Communication as ... Perspectives on Theory*, ed. by Gregory J. Shepherd, Jeffrey St John and Ted Striphas (Thousand Oaks: Sage, 2006), pp. 91–8.

Sturt, George, *The Wheelwright's Shop* (Cambridge: Cambridge University Press, 1923).

Thomas, Kate, *Postal Pleasures: Sex, Scandal, and Victorian Letters* (New York: Oxford University Press, 2012).

Tomalin, Claire, *Thomas Hardy: The Time-Torn Man* (London: Penguin, 2007).

Trotter, David, review of Mark Ford, *Thomas Hardy: Half a Londoner* (2016), *Critical Quarterly*, 59 (2017), 126–30.

Turner, Alwyn W., 'Portmeirion and Its Creator', in *Portmeirion*, ed. by Jan Morris, Alwyn Turner, Mark Eastment and Stephen Lacey (Woodbridge: Antique Collectors' Club, 2006), pp. 26–129.

Turner, Paul, *The Life of Thomas Hardy: A Critical Biography* (Oxford: Blackwell, 1998).

Uglow, Jenny, *Nature's Engraver: A Life of Thomas Bewick* (London: Faber and Faber, 2006).

Wainwright, Richard, *A Guide to the Prehistoric Remains in Britain. Volume 1: South and East* (London: Constable, 1978).

Walkowitz, Rebecca, and Douglas Mao, 'Introduction: Modernisms Bad and New', in *Bad Modernisms*, ed. by Rebecca Walkowitz and Douglas Mao (Durham, NC: Duke University Press, 2006), pp. 1–17.

Wallace, Diana, *Sisters and Rivals in British Women's Fiction 1914–39* (London: Palgrave, 2000).

Wallis, Mick, 'Delving the Levels of Memory and Dressing Up in the Past', in *British Theatre Between the Wars 1918–1939*, ed. by Clive Barker and Maggie B. Gale (Cambridge: Cambridge University Press, 2000), pp. 190–214.

—, 'Drama in the Villages: Three Pioneers', *The English Countryside Between the Wars: Regeneration or Decline?*, ed. by Paul Brassley, Jeremy Burchardt and Lynne Thompson (Woodbridge: Boydell Press, 2006), pp. 102–15.

—, 'Unlocking the Secret Soul: Mary Kelly, Pioneer of Village Theatre', *New Theatre Quarterly*, 16 (2000), 347–58.

Weightman, Gavin, *Children of the Light: How Electrification Changed Britain Forever* (London: Atlantic, 2011).

Wenzlhuemer, Roland, *Connecting the Nineteenth-Century World: The Telegraph and Globalization* (Cambridge: Cambridge University Press, 2013).

Wiener, Martin, *English Culture and the Decline of the Industrial Spirit 1850–1950* (Cambridge: Cambridge University Press, 1981).

Wild, Trevor, *Village England: A Social History of the Countryside* (London: I. B. Tauris, 2004).

Wilkes, James, *A Fractured Landscape of Modernity: Culture and Conflict in the Isle of Purbeck* (London: Palgrave MacMillan 2014).

Williams, Gwyn A., *When Was Wales?* (Harmondsworth: Penguin, 1985).

Williams, Raymond, *The Country and the City* (London: Chatto and Windus, 1973; London: Vintage, 2016).

—, *Keywords: A Vocabulary of Culture and Society*, rev. edn (New York: Oxford University Press, 1976).

—, *The Politics of Modernism* (London: Verso, 1996).

Wilson, Keith, *Thomas Hardy on Stage* (Basingstoke and London: Macmillan, 1995).

Wiseman, Sam, *The Reimagining of Place in English Modernism* (Clemson, SC: Clemson University Press, 2015).

Wisker, Alistair, and Gina, 'Introduction: A Literary Appreciation', in June Shepherd, *Doreen Wallace: Writer and Social Campaigner* (Lampeter: Edwin Mellen, 2000), pp. xvii–xxi.

Wolf, Hope, *Sussex Modernism, Retreat and Rebellion*, exhibition catalogue (London: Two Temple Place, 2017).

Wolfreys, Julian, *Dickens to Hardy: 1837–1884* (Basingstoke: Palgrave Macmillan, 2007).

—, *Thomas Hardy* (Basingstoke: Palgrave Macmillan, 2009).

Wylie, John, *Landscape* (London: Routledge, 2007).

Zhurzhenko, Tatiana, 'Borders and Memory', in *Ashgate Research Companion to Border Studies*, ed. by Doris Wastl-Walter (Burlington, VT: Ashgate, 2011), pp. 63–83.

Zimmermann, Patricia, *Reel Families: A Social History of Amateur Film* (Bloomington: Indiana University Press, 1995).

Index

Abercrombie, Patrick, 266–7
advertising, 57, 178
agriculture, 23–4, 34, 39, 122, 170, 208, 245, 265, 266, 267
  farms, 57, 58–9, 61, 138–9, 151, 152, 169, 170, 172, 182, 210–11, 213–14, 218, 219, 250, 259, 262
  see also workers
Alexander, Neal, 9
Allen, Edward, 11, 81, 133
Angelica Garnett Gift, 246, 248
Angus, Peggy, 75
Archer, William, 21
architecture, 64, 169, 187–205, 217, 243, 257, 264
archives, 48, 87, 94, 100, 188
art
  ancient, 229–30, 245
  modern, 5–6, 69, 70, 72, 73, 76, 84, 98–9, 100, 167, 169, 184, 239, 251
  regional, 11, 122, 124
atheism, 14, 239, 240, 243, 244, 246, 252

Bailey, Christopher, 34
Baldwin, Stanley, 3, 218
Barke, James, 149
Bates, H. E., 13, 84, 94–6, 99, 207, 211–12, 217
  Down the River, 211, 216, 219
  The Fallow Land, 94
  The Poacher, 94
  see also Parker, Agnes Miller
Batsford, Harry, 256, 259, 264
Batsford Books, 14, 255–68
  British Heritage, 255–6, 259, 260–2, 264
  Face of Britain, 209, 255–6, 259, 262–3
  Home Front Handbooks, 210, 264
Bauman, Zygmunt, 202
BBC (British Broadcasting Corporation), 22–3, 89, 110, 171, 185n
BEDA (British Electrical Development Agency), 11, 57–63, Plate 1
Beddington, Jack, 250
Beilby, Ralph, 92
Bell, Adrian, 13, 36, 39, 207, 213–14
Bell, Angelica *see* Garnett, Angelica
Bell, Clive, 5–6
Bell, George, 240–1, 248, 249, 250, 253n
Bell, Ian A., 149
Bell, John, 78–9
Bell, Martin, 213, 214
Bell, Quentin, 241, 243, 245, 247, 250
Bell, Vanessa, 13–14, 239–40, 241, 243–8, 250, 251–2
  The Annunciation, 243, 246, Plate 12
  The Nativity, 243, 245, 247, Plate 11
Bell, Walter, 77
Benjamin, Walter, 53, 142, 160
Benson, Richard, 91, 93
Bentley, Phyllis, 12
Berger, John, 115–16
Berman, Jessica, 148n5
Berman, Marshall, 4
Bernal, Desmond, 229
Berwick Church *see* churches, Anglican
Bewick, Thomas, 92–3
Binyon, Helen, 24
Blake, William, 143
Blee, Peter, 247
Bluemel, Kristin, 11, 48, 149–50, 163
Blunden, Edmund, 217

Blythe, Ronald, 213
Bourne, George *see* Sturt, George
Boyes, Georgina, 16n24
Brace, Catherine, 256
Bradford, 80, 82, 82n, 183
Bradshaw, David, 16n9
Brangwyn, Frank, 181–2
Braque, Georges, 70, 71
Brassley, Paul, 46
Bray, Horace Walter, 88
Brett Young, Francis, 13, 36, 39, 42, 44, 207, 217–20
Bristol, 138, 201, 260
Britain, 1, 2, 9, 13, 14, 33–4, 37, 42, 60, 72, 73, 75, 80, 84, 88, 90, 103, 112, 123, 241, 244, 249, 255–6, 259, 261–2, 264, 265, 266–8
  rural, 2, 8, 9, 10, 11, 12, 13, 14, 15, 33, 35, 39, 41, 46, 48, 60, 61, 75–6, 84, 85, 91, 100, 259, 268
  see also cities; England; Northern Ireland; Scotland; suburbs; Wales
'Britain in Pictures', 208, 217
British *see* identity; nationalism
British Drama League, 125
broadbrow *see* middlebrow
Brooker, Peter, 15n3
Brown, Alfred Radcliffe, 169
Buchan, Ursula, 211
Buckinghamshire, 90, 94, 199
Burchardt, Jeremy, 8, 15n2, 16n24, 46
Burne-Jones, Edward, 246
Burns, Robert, 185n10
Bussy, Janie, 241, 252

Campbell, Ian, 160
Cape, Jonathan, 94
Cardinal, Roger, 232
Carlisle, 169, 171, 173–5, 176, 177, 179, 180, 181, 182, 185n11, 185n20
Carney, Michael, 217
cars *see* transportation
Cartwright, Edmund, 80
Caruth, Cathy, 228
cathedrals *see* churches, Anglican
Cavaliero, Glen, 8–9
Cave, Roderick, 88
Cézanne, Paul, 69, 70–1, 73, 74, 75, 82n2
Chanel, Coco, 177
chapels, 107, 113, 114
Chase, Malcolm, 15n2
Child, Ben, 15
Ching, Barbara, 4–5, 7
Chinitz, David, 7
churches, Anglican, 14, 27–31, 36, 37, 44, 59, 114, 142, 239–54, 257, 258, 260, 261, 262, 267, 268; *see also* religion
cinema *see* film
cities, 2, 3, 4, 7, 8, 27, 46, 52–3, 56–7, 60, 78, 80, 88, 90, 107, 121, 132, 136, 137, 149, 152, 154–5, 157, 167, 177, 202, 267; *see also* Bristol; Carlisle; Coventry; Edinburgh; Glasgow; Liverpool; London
Clarke, Kenneth, 249, 252
class, 1, 2, 10, 12, 13, 57, 104, 123–4, 136, 137, 154, 156, 160–1, 162, 209, 267
  middle, 2, 139, 203, 209
  working, 116, 121, 122, 149, 154, 157–8
  see also politics; proletarian; workers
Clute, John, 150
Collingham, Lizzie, 211
Colls, Robert, 16n24, 208
community, 3, 135–8, 140, 142, 143–5, 155, 174, 240, 251–3, 264, 268
conscientious objectors, 239, 250
conservatism, 3, 12, 48, 88, 137, 146, 188, 193, 194, 207, 217, 240; *see also* nostalgia; politics; preservation
Cook, Brian, 256, 159, 262, 263, 264, 266
Cooper, Lettice, 147
Corbin, Alain, 28
country, defined, 3–4
country houses, 21, 36, 59, 64n13, 189, 249, 257; *see also* Gregynog
Country Life, 94, 218
countryside, 2, 4, 5, 8, 9, 10, 11, 13, 14, 16n5, 34, 40, 46, 50–65, 74, 84, 90–1, 92, 94, 100, 107, 123, 154, 190, 192, 207–8, 217, 225–7, 228, 229, 236, 240, 242–5, 251, 252, 257, 262, 264–8
  as idyll, 2, 4, 5, 8, 10, 53, 172, 225–6
  see also landscape; rural
Coventry, 260, 265
CPRE (Campaign to Protect Rural England), 13, 55, 61, 187–90, 192–4, 242
Craig, Cairns, 163
Creed, Gerald W., 4–5, 7

Crossley, F. H., 260
Croxall, Samuel, 92
Cubism, 70–2, 82, 87
Cumberland, 171–2, 214
Cumbria, 172
Cunningham, Valentine, 15n2

Dacre, Winifred (née Roberts) *see* Nicholson, Winifred
Dalí, Salvador, 246
Davies, Rhys, 91, 106
Deen, Stella, 12, 220, 268
Depression, 1, 8, 99, 167, 170, 177, 178, 208, 213, 217, 267
Derbyshire, 77
design, 13, 15, 54, 55, 56, 69, 70, 71, 79, 80, 82n18, 167, 169, 178–9, 184, 186n20, 235
  architecture, 64n15, 181, 185n6, 187–8, 190, 192, 193, 202–3, 204–5, 268
  print, 51, 58, 59, 61, 89, 91, 93, 101n1, 178, 179, 180, 181, 182, 256, 259, 262, 263, 267
  textile, 169, 176–7, 180, 181
Dettmar, Kevin, 16n9
development, 4, 7, 11, 13, 25, 41, 51, 52–3, 55, 56, 57, 62, 63, 64n3, 192, 199, 257–8, 261, 264, 265, 267
  social, 48, 52
  see also housing; industries; modernisation; urbanisation
Devon, 47, 122, 258
DIA (Design and Industries Association), 13, 178, 182
documentary, 34, 35, 39, 112
Dodd, Philip, 16n24
Dorset, 19, 21, 27, 73, 81, 198, 257
drama, 12, 22, 104, 113–14, 115–16, 124, 125, 243
  pageants, 121–34, 129–32, 173–4, 185n11
Drucker, Johanna, 6
Dufy, Raoul, 52

Edinburgh, 78, 170, 177, 185n11
education, 3, 37, 44, 47, 48, 86, 108–9, 112, 114–16, 121, 122, 124, 136, 143–4, 146, 151, 178–9, 180–4, 185n, 219
Edwards, Hugh, 94
electricity, 1, 2, 11, 16n, 35, 46–7, 50–65, Plate 1, Plate 2
  grid, 34, 51, 54, 56, 57, 58, 59, 60, 64n1
Electricity Supply Act, 51, 53
Elgar, Edward, 217
Eliot, T. S., 7, 127, 245
Empson, William, *Some Versions of Pastoral*, 5, 151, 155–6, 162
England, 2, 12, 13, 16n5, 23, 25, 31, 103–4, 105–6, 111, 114, 115, 116, 121–3, 126, 129, 135, 138, 141, 142, 170, 187, 189, 190–4, 196, 198–200, 226, 232, 242–53, 256, 257, 260, 261–2, 264, 265–6
  borderlands, 13, 167–85
  idealised, 2, 3, 7, 8, 13, 39, 41, 45, 226, 232, 242–5, 256, 258, 259
  writing of, 22–31, 135–47, 207–20, 255–62, 264–8
  see also Buckinghamshire; Cumberland; Cumbria; Derbyshire; Devon; Dorset, Essex; Gloucestershire; Hertfordshire; Huntingdonshire; Leicestershire; Lincolnshire; Middlesex; Midlands; Norfolk; Northamptonshire; Northumberland; Oxfordshire; Shropshire; Somerset; Staffordshire; Suffolk; Surrey; Sussex; Warwickshire; Worcestershire; Yorkshire
Englishness *see* identity: English
Essex, 262
Esty, Jed, 9, 129
Etchells, Frederick, 242
Evans, Caradoc, 105–6, 112
Evans, Mair, 106–7
everyday life, 5, 6, 9, 10, 14, 35, 36, 43, 53, 84, 125, 155, 158, 178, 182–3, 213, 244, 252, 267

factories, 40, 52, 61, 139, 176, 226, 265, 267
fantasy, 150, 163
farming *see* agriculture
Farrer, Reginald, 228
fascism, 219, 266
Feibusch, Hans, 241, 242, 253, 254n
feminism *see* politics: feminist
Fergusson, J. D., *Craigleith Quarry*, 78–9, 81, Plate 5
film, 11, 57, 60, 61, 104, 110, 116, 159, 186n, 216
  documentary, 33–49

newsreels, 173
technologies of, 33, 34, 42–8
Ford, Ford Madox, 227
Ford, John, 104
Ford, Mark, 26
Forster, E. M., 122
Forty, Adrian, 51, 64n3
Frawley, Oona, 16n4
Freud, Sigmund, 225
Friend, Andy, 75
Fry, Charles, 255
Fry, Roger, 69, 72, 74, 75, 82n, 254n
Quarry, Bo Peep Farm, 74, 75, Plate 4
Fussell, Paul, 6, 85, 86, 93

Gabo, Naum, 55
Gale, Maggie B., 133n8
Gan, Wendy, 148n14
Gaonkar, Dilip Parameshwar, 15n3
Gardner-Medwin, Robert, 206n48
Garnett, Angelica (née Bell), 241, 247, 251, 252
gender, 10, 12, 16n9, 124, 133n17, 136, 137, 142, 155, 158, 159, 162, 163
General Strike (1926), 150
George, Lloyd, 111
Gibbings, Robert, 91, 94
Gibbon, Lewis Grassic, 12, 149–64
Cloude Howe, 152, 153, 156, 162
Grey Granite, 149, 150, 153, 154–8, 159, 160, 161–3
Sunset Song, 150–3, 156, 157, 159
Gibbons, Philip, 88, 94, 95, 96, 99
Giles, Judy, 16n24
Gill, Eric, 232
Glasgow, 85, 86, 99, 100, 170
Gloucestershire, 200
Gollancz, Victor, 90, 94–6, 99, 100
Goodman, Gemma, 10
Gough, Paul, 228
Goya, 71
GPO (General Post Office), 32n20, 39, 64n3
Grant, Duncan, 13–14, 239–40, 241, 243–8, 250, 252
Christ in Glory, 243, 245, 248, 250
The Victory of Calvary, 243, Plate 10
Gray, Alasdair, 154
Gregynog, 86, 88, 91, 94, 98, 100
Greiffenhagen, Maurice, 174–5
Grierson, John, 39
Gruffydd, Pyrs, 188
guidebooks, 8, 172, 208, 209–11, 255–68

Hardy, Emma, 29, 32n32
Hardy, Florence, 21, 31n5
Hardy, Thomas, 11, 19–32, 207
Desperate Remedies, 26, 29
Far from the Madding Crowd, 29
A Laodicean, 24–5, 32n16
The Mayor of Casterbridge, 23–4
The Return of the Native, 28, 30
Tess of the D'Urbervilles, 27–8
Harker, Ben, 129
Harris, Alexandra, 9, 208, 245
Harris, John, 105
Harrison, Nigel, 13, 81, 253
Hassall, Joan, 91, 218, 219
Hawkins, Henry, 76
Head, Dominic, 10, 13, 163
Henderson, Charles, 129
Hepworth, Barbara, 229
heritage, 12, 13, 37, 39, 60, 126, 135, 147, 148n7, 168, 170–1, 173, 187, 194, 198, 199–201, 207–20, 240, 249, 253, 255–66
Hermes, Gertrude, 88, 91
Hertfordshire, 262, 267
Hilder, Rowland, 218
hiraeth, 12, 103–4, 106, 111
defined, 103, 115
Hitchcock, Henry-Russell, 204
Hitchens, Ivon, 171
Hodnett, Edward, 86, 92, 94
Holt, Ysanne, 13, 101
Holtby, Winifred, 138
South Riding, 12, 135, 136, 137, 139, 143–7
Hopkins, Chris, 11–12, 31
Hoskins, W. G., 264–5
housing, 56, 58, 193, 209, 217; *see also* development
Housman, A. E., 217
Howkins, Alun, 15n2
Hubble, Nick, 12, 116, 237
Hughes-Stanton, Blair, 88, 91
Huntingdonshire, 264
Hussey, Christopher, 204

identity, 5, 7, 13, 48, 109, 116, 142
borderland, 174, 176
British, 2, 6, 7, 8, 14, 33, 38, 63, 76, 116, 240, 244, 256, 265
English, 1, 8, 12, 14, 16n24, 24, 64, 104, 204, 207, 215–20, 240, 245

identity (*cont.*)
  regional, 36, 265
  rural, 4, 34, 48, 251
  Scottish, 151
  Welsh, 104–17, 151, 174, 232
  see also nationalism; rural
illustration, 84, 87–9, 91–9, 213, 218, 255–60, 262–4, 266–7
Impressionism, 71, 75, 77, 90
industrialism, 7, 51, 81, 103, 104, 112, 115, 116, 127, 128, 149, 170, 182, 225, 236, 258, 265, 266–7
industries, 7, 13, 6n24, 34, 38–42, 54, 56, 57, 59, 70, 72, 73, 75, 79, 104, 105, 107, 109, 112, 113, 258, 265, 266–7
  growth of, 7, 34, 51, 60, 76, 78, 81, 103, 104, 112, 115, 116, 127, 128, 149, 170, 182, 225, 226, 236, 265
  rural, 2, 11, 13, 16, 24, 34, 60, 61, 74, 75, 77, 105, 106, 115
  traditional, 2, 38–42
  see also development; film; housing; quarries; textiles
Ingold, Tim, 168, 170
Ingram, J. H., 265–6
Innes, James Dickson, 79
interdisciplinarity, 4, 10, 14
Ireland, 105, 256; *see also* Northern Ireland
Isherwood, Christopher, 36, 46
Ivins, William, 93

Jackson, Lesley, 177
Joad, C. E. M., 45, 209
Jones, David, 13, 14, 225, 228, 232–4, 237
  In Parenthesis, 233–4
  Vexilla Regis, 233–4, Plate 9
Jones, Glyn, 103, 106
Jones, Jack, *Rhondda Roundabout*, 103–4, 111–13
Jones, Jonah, 187
Jones, Sydney, 34, 267, Plate 13
Joyce, James, 154, 160

Kaye-Smith, Sheila, 45
Kelly, Mary, 12, 121–32
  How to Make a Pageant, 12, 121, 122, 129
  Village Theatre, 12, 123–4, 126–8, 132
Kelman, James, 154
Kent, 36, 37–8, 42, 43, 196, 217, 262
Kirkall, Elisha, 92
Kumar, Krishan, 207

landscape, 11, 12, 13, 14, 15, 40, 46, 51, 53–6, 59, 60, 61, 63, 69, 71–2, 73, 74, 75, 76, 77, 78–9, 80, 81, 84, 91, 106, 128, 131, 135, 140, 144, 171, 182, 183, 187–8, 194, 203, 217, 225–6, 227–37, 239–40, 242, 244–5, 249, 251, 252, 253, 255–7, 262, 267; *see also* countryside; pastoral
Latour, Bruno, 168
Lawrence, D. H., 116, 160
Le Bas, Edward, 243
Le Corbeau, Adrian, 94
Le Corbusier, Charles-Edouard, 197
Leaper, Hana, 13, 31, 133
Leavis, F. R. 33–4, 40
Lefebvre, Henri, 168
Leicestershire, 264, 265
Leighton, Clare, 94
Lewis, Saunders, 111
Lewis, Wyndham, 73
Lincolnshire, 50, 216, 257
Linton, Agnes, 186n20
Linton, William, 176
Liverpool, 254n9
Llewellyn, Richard, 104, 113–16
London, 4, 19, 26, 27, 30–1, 56, 84, 87, 88, 90–1, 99, 111, 112, 140, 141, 144, 149, 169, 189, 194, 198, 220, 229, 239, 242, 251, 254n9, 256, 260, 262–4, 267
Lowe, Peter, 14, 205, 220
Lowenthal, David Lefebvre, 53, 60
Lowerson, John, 8, 15n2, 41
Lumsden, Alison, 150
Lutyens, Edwin, 195

McAllister, Elizabeth, 266
McAllister, Gilbert, 266–7
McCance, William, 86, 88, 89, 94, 95, 99
McCluskey, Michael, 11, 185
MacColl, D. S., 69, 70–1, 72, 75
McCulloch, Margery Palmer, 153–4, 158, 160
MacDiarmid, Hugh, 149, 153–4, 160
Macdonald, Ramsay, 185n10
Macmillan, George, 22
Mais, S. P. B., 257, 262–3, 267

Mandler, Peter, 16n24, 218
Mao, Douglas, 16n19
Marconi, Guglielmo, 19, 20–1
Marcus, Jane, 148n10
Martin, John Lesley, 55
Massignham, H. J., 40, 41, 257–8
Mathieson, Charlotte, 10
Matisse, Henri, 242
Matless, David, 8, 16n24, 60, 187–8, 203, 255
Maynard, Robert Ashwin, 88
megaliths *see* art: ancient
Meynell, Francis, 89
middlebrow, 99, 113, 116, 208
Middlesex, 262
Middleton, G. A. T., 80
Middleton, Tim, 16n24
Midlands, 73, 76
Miles, Jonathan, 233
Miller, J. Hillis, 25
Millet, Jean-François, 246
Mills, Polly, 13, 31, 133
Mitchell, James Leslie, 160–1; *see also* Gibbon, Lewis Grassic
modernisation, 1, 2, 4, 6, 10, 11, 13, 15, 21, 23, 35, 38, 41, 63, 70, 76, 122, 124, 129, 187, 240, 245
modernism, 3, 6, 7, 9, 15n3, 16n9, 25, 26, 55, 73, 79, 85–6, 88, 107, 110, 116, 150, 154, 168, 170, 177, 178, 181, 184, 187, 192, 195–7, 204, 232, 239–40, 242
  British, 1, 2, 5, 7, 9, 13, 26, 79
  late, 9, 129, 239
  regional, 9, 12
  see also art; design
modernity
  defined, 3–7
  studies of, 7, 9–10, 51, 53, 60, 64n4
Moran, James, 9
Morris, Margaret, 82n20
Morris, William, 61, 185n6, 194, 204
Morton, Alastair, 169, 177–9, 180, 181
Mothersole, Jessie, 171, 173
Müller, William James, 77
Mumford, Lewis, 204–5
museums, 39, 69, 71, 91, 182–3, 185n11, 239
mythology *see* religion

Nairn, Ian, 56, 60
  Outrage, 56
Nash, John, 213
Nash, Paul, 13, 14, 72, 73, 82n18, 91, 225, 227–32, 177, 183, 251
  Equivalents for the Megaliths, 230–1, Plate 7
  Landscape of the Megaliths, 229–31
  Menin Road, 228–9, 231, 233, Plate 6
National Trust, 199
nationalism, 3, 170, 207, 215, 220, 242
Nazism, 131, 215, 260
Neve, Christopher, 228
new modernist studies, 3, 7
Newbould, Frank, 259, 266
Newby, Howard, 7, 15n2
Newdigate, Bernard, 89
Nicholson, Ben, 12, 55, 169, 177
Nicholson, Jake, 177, 185n7
Nicholson, Winifred, 13, 169, 171, 173, 177, 185n6, 185n7
Nicoll, Allardyce, 133n5, 134n25
non-fiction, 84–7, 90, 92, 94–9, 207–8, 209–20, 255–68
Norfolk, 209, 216
Norquay, Glenda, 163
Norris, Herbert, 174
Northamptonshire, 94
Northern Ireland, 16n4
Northumberland, 92, 172
nostalgia, 2, 3, 13, 70, 100, 103, 115, 122, 129, 131, 172, 198, 201, 211–13, 226, 245, 257, 261, 262
novels, 8, 9, 23–30, 103–6, 111–16, 135–48, 149–63, 208–10, 217

Outka, Elizabeth, 41, 133
Oxfordshire, 265

painting, 5, 69–81, 171, 183, 227–37, 262
  murals, 181–3, 235, 239–53
Palmer, Alfred, 72–3
Parker, Agnes Miller, 11, 84–100
  Down the River, 84, 95, 96, 97, 98, 99
  Fables of Esope, 86, 88, 89–90, 91, 93, 94, 98
  Through the Woods, 84, 94–5, 97, 99
Parker, Louis Napoleon, 129–30
pastoral, 3, 5–6, 11, 12, 15n2, 23, 85–6, 93, 100, 103–4, 112, 131, 141, 149, 150, 151, 155, 212, 216, 245, 259, 266
Paterson, James, 78–9, 81

Peate, Iorwerth, 194
Peters, John Durham, 29–30
petrol, 45–6, 54, 172, 196, 219
photographs, 20–1, 173, 255, 260, 267
Picasso, Pablo, 70–1, 82n7, 82n8
Piper, John, 242, 254n9
Pitt, Frances, 264
place, 4–5, 7, 9, 10, 26, 51, 56, 63, 81, 86, 121, 127, 134n40, 135, 147, 167–8, 171, 173, 192, 207, 210, 240
poetry, 8, 21, 106–9, 114, 232–4
Poggioli, Renato, 5–6, 85
politics, 113, 219
  Communist, 108, 112, 113, 149, 158, 162
  feminist, 6, 12, 99–100, 135, 138, 142–3, 145–6, 148n10, 148n14, 150, 158, 160, 161, 163, 209
  Labour, 113
  reactionary, 129
  revolutionary, 149–50, 158, 159, 160, 161–3
  socialist, 160, 161, 162, 192
  working-class, 162
  see also conservatism; fascism; Nazism
Portmeirion, 13, 187–8, 194–6, 198–9, 201–3
Post-Impressionism, 69, 71, 79, 184, 243
Potts, Alex, 8
Powers, Alan, 188, 196
preservation, 13, 14, 51, 53, 56, 61, 187, 188–92, 194, 199–201, 204, 205, 255, 258, 261
Priestley, J. B., 110, 170
print culture, 11, 14, 57–63, 84–5, 86–99, 103–16, 121, 167, 172, 175, 178–82, 207–20, 255–68
proletarian, 5, 151, 157
propaganda, 52, 58, 159, 215, 217, 244, 259
Purdon, James, 59
pylons, 51, 53–6, 60–1, 63, 64n15

quarries
  history of, 75–6, 82–4
  representations of, 11, 69–81

radio, 2, 21–3, 25, 34, 35, 42, 89, 132, 171–2, 173, 214, 218
Rae, Patricia, 226
Ravenhill-Johnson, Annie, 76
Raverat, Gwen, 91
Ravilious, Eric, 13, 14, 75, 83, 91, 225, 234–7
  Downs in Winter, 235–6
  Ship's Screw on a Railway Truck, 236, Plate 8
  Windmill, 235–6
Read, Herbert, 225, 227
Regan, Lisa, 144, 148n5, 148n13, 148n14
regional
  culture, 9, 11, 15, 70, 73, 79–80, 174, 177, 180, 185, 257
  literature, 9, 12
regions *see* Britain; England; rural
religion, 12, 127, 128, 152, 156, 233, 239, 240–1, 244–9, 252–3
  nonconformist, 105, 106, 110, 112, 139
  see also atheism; chapels; churches
Remarque, Erich Maria, 225, 227
Rhys, Keidrych, 106, 110
Roberts, Gwyneth, 115
Roberts, Wilfrid, 171–2, 173, 176
Roberts, William, 87
Roberts, Winifred *see* Nicholson, Winifred
Robertson, Iain, 13, 81, 253
Robson, William, 268
Rogerson, Ian, 87, 89, 91
romanticism *see* rural
Rotha, Paul, 60
Rothenstein, John, 71, 82n8
Rothenstein, William, 69–70, 73, 75, 79, 80, 81, 82n11, 82n16, 183
  The Deserted Quarry, 69–71, 80, 81, Plate 3
Rouse, Clive, 261
Rupp, Jan, 173
rural
  community, 3, 12, 14, 24, 34, 53, 63, 86, 150, 156, 176, 180, 210, 213, 214, 218, 240, 250–1, 252–3
  as concept, 3–4
  identities, 5, 48, 251
  people, 1, 2, 3, 4, 6, 9–10, 15, 58, 59, 60, 63, 123, 213
  as retreat, 2, 7–9, 15, 54, 60, 85–93, 100–1, 170, 218, 242, 244
  romanticism, 8, 10, 11, 13, 34, 35, 72, 81, 100, 128, 167, 207, 211–12, 216, 218, 219, 255, 257–8, 262, 266, 267

traditions, 33, 35, 36, 38, 39–41, 48, 239, 245
see also agriculture; countryside; England; identity; landscape; villages
rural modernity, defined, 1–10, 15
Russian Revolution, 160
rustic, 4

Sackville-West, Vita, 122
Said, Edward, 148n8
Sargent, John Singer, 72, 74
Savinio, Alberto, 246
Sayer, Karen, 46, 58
Schivelbusch, Wolfgang, 51–2
schools *see* education
Scotland, 2, 12, 16n4, 39, 80, 87, 100, 101, 154, 162, 170, 172, 177, 256
borderlands, 13, 167–85
writing of, 12, 149–63
see also Carlisle; Edinburgh; Glasgow
Scott, John, 169, 185n4
Scott, Walter, 167, 173, 174
sculpture, 72, 229
Second World War *see* World War II
Selborne, Joanna, 88, 91, 98
sex, 12, 124, 136, 138, 139, 243
Seymour, John, 40
Shakespeare, 29, 125
Shaw, Samuel, 11, 237, 253
Sherry, Vincent, 233
Shiel, Derek, 253
Shirley, Rosemary, 10, 11, 205, 268
Shone, Richard, 252
Shropshire, 94
Simmel, George, 53
slump *see* Depression
Smith, George Saumarez, 198
Society for the Protection of Ancient Buildings, 199
Somerset, 138–9
soundscape, 27
space, theories of, 168–9, 192
Space Between: Literature and Culture, 1914–1945, 15
Spanish Civil War, 252
Spencer, Gilbert, 183
Spencer, Stanley, 183, 244
Spender, Humphrey, 170
Spender, Stephen, 54, 244
Spoerry, François, 198
Squire, J. C., 31n5
Staffordshire, 193
Stead, Edmund, 180, 181
Steer, Philip Wilson, 72
Stein, Gertrude, 71, 82n8
Stephen, Julia Duckworth, 246
Sterne, Jonathan, 23
Stone, John Benjamin, 31n2
Stucley, Elizabeth, 45
Sturt, George, 1, 15, 33
suburbs, 2, 10, 56, 77, 78, 79, 121, 203, 210, 217, 264, 265, 267
Suffolk, 216, 258
Summer-Bremner, Eluned, 13, 101, 185
Surrealism, 77, 230, 246
Surrey, 262
Sussex, 14, 39, 40, 74, 75, 80, 232, 239–53, 59
Sutherland, Graham, 242

Tate Gallery, 241, 250
technology *see* industries
telegraph, 2, 19, 21, 25–6, 30
Telegraph Acts of 1868–9, 32n20
telephone, 2, 21, 34, 42, 253
television, 47
Tennyson, Alfred, 161
textiles, production of, 13, 39, 80, 167, 169, 170, 176–80, 184
Thacker, Andrew, 15n3
theatre *see* drama
Thomas, F. G., 35, 43, 44, 47, 48
Thomas, William Beach, 36, 47
Thompson, Denys, 33–4, 40
Times, 54, 63
Tolkien, J. R. R., 150
Tomalin, Claire, 21
tourism, 39, 41, 53, 167, 173–4, 209–10, 216, 250, 253, 255, 257–8
tradition *see* rural
transportation, 1, 35, 43, 51, 55, 112, 132, 217, 240, 255, 257–8, 261, 264, 267
Trotter, David, 27
turbines, 50–1, 53
Turner, Paul, 31n4

Uglow, Jenny, 92
unemployment, 8, 111, 158
Upward, Edward, 36, 46
urbanisation, 4, 7, 8, 10, 111

Vale, Edmund, 264
Van Gogh, Vincent, 70, 82n7
'village biography', 36–8
Village Drama Society, 122, 124, 125

village halls, 35, 47, 133n9
villages, 1, 2, 8, 11, 13, 33–49, 59, 112, 114, 121, 124, 125, 136, 137–8, 140, 142, 147, 154, 167, 172, 176, 180, 202, 209, 211–12, 216–19, 240, 242, 244, 247, 249–51, 255, 257, 258, 265, 266–7
visual culture, 5–6, 8, 11, 13–14, 34–48, 50–63, 69–81, 84–5, 86–99, 167–84, 227–37, 239–53, 255–6, 258–60, 262–4, 266–7

Wadsworth, Edward, 73–4, 75, 76–7, 180
Wales, 2, 16, 64n13, 80, 86, 88, 103–17, 187–9, 190, 194, 197, 256, 259, 265
  writing of, 11–12, 76, 103–17
Wales, 103, 105–10, 111, 112, 113
Walker, Andrew, 12, 48, 116
Walkowitz, Rebecca, 16n19
Wallace, Diana, 148n14
Wallace, Doreen, 13, 207, 208–11, 264
Wallis, Mick, 133n13
Walmsley, Leo, 13, 207, 215–16
Walter, Meurig, 107, 111
warfare, 13, 77; *see also* Russian Revolution; Spanish Civil War; World War I; World War II
Warner, Sylvia Townsend, 138
  Lolly Willowes, 12, 135, 136, 137, 138, 139, 140–3
wartime, defined, 225–7
Warwick, Margaret, 171
Warwickshire, 258
Watkins, Vernon, 108–9
Whitworth, Geoffrey, 125
Wiener, Martin, 16n24, 133n6
Wild, Trevor, 7, 15n2, 217
Wilkes, James, 81
Williams, Emlyn, 104, 111, 113–14, 115–16
Williams, Gwyn, 104
Williams, Raymond, 148n12
  The Country and the City, 7–8, 26, 52, 60, 214
  Keywords, 3
  The Politics of Modernism, 154, 163
Williams-Ellis, Clough, 13, 54–5, 56, 187–205
  Britain and the Beast, 190, 257
  England and the Octopus, 13, 54–5, 56, 61–2, 66n13, 187, 188–91, 203, 204–5, 209, 257
wireless *see* radio
Wiseman, Sam, 9
Wolf, Hope, 242, 254n8
women, 61, 150, 154, 157, 159, 160, 176, 177, 186n20, 219
  artists, 82n20, 83n24, 84–100, 169, 171, 239–47, 250–2
  writers, 12, 106–7, 121–32, 135–47, 208–11, 264, 266
Women's Institutes, 61, 122, 123–4, 128, 132, 133n13
Wood, Christopher, 171
wood engraving, 11, 84–102, 212, 218, 219, 235
Woolf, Virginia, 12, 75, 116, 122, 147, 154, 160, 209, 251, 252
Worcestershire, 217, 260
Wordsworth, William, 214
workers, 40, 41, 60, 72–3, 83n24, 83n31, 106, 112, 122, 126, 131, 132, 136, 151, 157, 158, 159, 170, 176, 180, 181, 210, 214, 245, 250; *see also* proletarian
Workers' Educational Association, 47
World War I, 8, 13, 132, 135, 136, 141, 150, 151, 158, 159, 160, 163, 176, 190, 225–8, 238n18, 250, 256
World War II, 14, 121, 127, 131, 172, 208, 210, 213, 215–16, 217, 226, 232, 240–1, 242, 245, 249, 250, 251–2, 258–62

Yeats, W. B., 134n25
Yorkshire, 36–7, 46, 70, 73, 79, 80, 81, 143, 144, 147, 215–16
Young, E. H., 138
  Miss Mole, 12, 135, 136

Zhurzhenko, Tatiana, 174
Zimmerman, Patricia, 34

CPSIA information can be obtained
at www.ICGtesting.com
Printed in the USA
JSHW020453280920
8208JS00001B/7

9 781474 473187